Mental Health
Counseling
(VOL. 144)

Titles of Related Interest

Cartledge/Milburn TEACHING SOCIAL SKILLS TO CHILDREN:
Innovative Approaches, Second Edition
Bornstein/Bornstein MARITAL THERAPY:
A Behavioral-Communications Approach
Brenner THE EFFECTIVE PSYCHOTHERAPIST:
Conclusions from Practice to Research
Hersen/Kazdin/Bellack CLINICAL PSYCHOLOGY HANDBOOK
Kanfer/Goldstein HELPING PEOPLE CHANGE, Third Edition
Nietzel/Dillehay PSYCHOLOGICAL CONSULTATION IN
THE COURTROOM
Pinkston/Linsk CARE OF THE ELDERLY: A Family Approach

Related Journals

CLINICAL PSYCHOLOGY REVIEW
CHILDREN AND YOUTH SERVICES REVIEW

GENERAL PSYCHOLOGY SERIES

EDITORS
Arnold P. Goldstein, Syracuse University
Leonard Krasner, Stanford University and SUNY at Stony Brook

Mental Health Counseling
Theory and Practice

David B. Hershenson
Paul W. Power
University of Maryland

With contributions by
MARITA M. DANEK and **MICHAEL WALDO**

ALLYN AND BACON
Boston London Toronto Sydney Tokyo Singapore

10 9 8 7 6 5 4 3   96 95 94 93

ISBN 0-205-14363-6

Library of Congress Cataloging in Publication Data

Hershenson, David B., 1933–
    Mental health counseling.

    Includes index.
    1. Mental health counseling. 2. Mental health
counseling—Practice. I. Power, Paul W. II. Title.
III. Series. [DNLM: 1. Community Mental Health Services.
2. Counseling. WM 30 H572m]
RCA66.H47   1987   616.89   86-18647

TO MARIAN AND BARBARA

Contents

Part VI. Epilogue

Preface

The profession of mental health counseling has developed rapidly over the last decade. An indication of this is provided by the fact that the American Mental Health Counselors Association, established in 1976 with a membership of 50, now numbers over 10,000 members. A professional credentialing process has been implemented by the National Academy of Certified Clinical Mental Health Counselors (NACCMHC), and a number of states now license mental health counselors. Bills are currently before Congress to amend the Social Security Act so that mental health counselors are recognized as "core providers" of mental health services, entitled to third party payment. As the field has been undergoing this growth spurt, it has relied on the textbooks of related mental health or counseling fields in the education of its practitioners. While many of the concepts and techniques presented in these textbooks are applicable to mental health counseling, these books do not provide any indication of the integrated, coherent framework that distinguishes mental health counseling both from other mental health professions and from other counseling specialties. Thus, although these books explain very adequately many of the "tools of the trade" used by most mental health professionals, they do not indicate when, where, how, or for what purpose these tools should be used by a mental health counselor. Just as a surgeon and a carpenter may both use a saw, they each use it quite differently in the pursuit of their respective professions.

As mental health counseling has grown, so have the number of graduate education programs preparing persons to enter the profession. Recent surveys of the field indicate over 100 universities offer master's degree programs in mental health counseling (albeit some of these programs are called by somewhat different titles, such as "agency counseling" or "community counseling"). Clearly, the field has reached a point where it no longer needs to rely on the texts of its neighbors, adapting or selectively reading them because there were too few potential readers within mental health counseling programs to justify their own textbooks.

HMHC—A•

In the opinion of the authors, the greatest immediate need was for an introductory textbook, for those persons beginning or contemplating graduate study in mental health counseling. As such, this book focuses on the principles and practices of mental health counseling. It does not, however, offer specific training in many of the skills commonly used by mental health counselors and other mental health professionals, because, as has been noted, many excellent books exist that perform this function for particular skills, and the development of each of these skills requires at least a full course of its own. These skills include client and environmental assessment; individual, family, and group counseling techniques; mental health rehabilitation; consultation methods; community intervention; and evaluation methods. References to textbooks on developing these skills will be provided where appropriate throughout this book.

The first chapter of this book presents an overview both of the principles of mental health counseling and of the social and historical context in which these principles evolved. The unique contributions of this profession to the mental health field are: (a) its orientation toward promoting healthy growth, rather than toward excising pathology; (b) its recognition of the importance of the environment in determining behavior; and (c) its focus on helping the client to cope by using or developing personal assets and skills and environmental resources. Essentially, the rest of the book spells out how these principles are applied in the professional practice of mental health counseling.

In constructing this book, chapters 3, 4, 7, and 14 through 16 were written by David Hershenson. Chapters 6, 8, and 10 through 13 were written by Paul Power. Because of his particular expertise in the area of group counseling, Michael Waldo was asked to write chapter 9. Marita Danek was involved in the initial formulation of this project and, along with Hershenson and Power, contributed to chapter 1. She also wrote chapters 2 and 5. Editing was done by Power and Hershenson.

The authors are deeply indebted to Bernadette Romeo, Barbara Power, and Mindy Vu for typing the manuscript.

We are indebted to our professional colleagues and to our students for providing us with the inspiration to undertake this project. Last but not least, we are indebted to our families for their support and help as we have engaged in the task of bringing this project to fruition.

I THE MENTAL
HEALTH COUNSELOR

1 Introduction and Overview*

It is estimated that there are 40 million people in the United States who are experiencing mental health difficulties at any given time. A recent comprehensive study by the National Institute of Mental Health ("Mental Disorders," 1984) indicated that 19% of adults over age 18 suffer from one or more mental health problems during a given 6-month period. This study further found that between 28% and 38% of those surveyed reported having a serious mental health problem at some time in their lives. These problems are on a continuum ranging from merely annoying feelings of anxiety to severe, incapacitating emotional disorders. Mental health problems have in common their capacity to disrupt lives and to interfere with optimal human functioning; however, they represent tremendous diversity in terms of etiology, severity, duration, prognosis, and appropriate treatment or intervention (Leighton, 1982).

It is easy to see why a number of health and helping professions have developed specializations to assist people who are experiencing these problems, given their prevalence. Principal among these fields are psychiatry, clinical psychology, psychiatric social work, psychiatric nursing, and mental health counseling. Although all these fields work toward the same ultimate purpose, they differ on a number of dimensions, including basic professional identification, length and content of professional and specialty education, practitioner's entry level graduate degree (MD for psychiatrists, PhD or PsyD for most psychologists, and master's degree for the other three fields), basic academic discipline, conceptualization of mental health problems, and approach to treatment.

---

*Marita Danek contributed to this chapter.

3

THE MENTAL HEALTH COUNSELING APPROACH

Basic Tenets

This book will present an introduction to the concepts and treatment approach employed by mental health counseling. This field is a specialization within the broader, more general field of counseling. Therefore, mental health counseling is based on certain general tenets of counseling, including the following:

1. Human behavior is a function of the interaction between an individual and that individual's environment at a particular point in time (that is, within the individual's personal development and the conditions prevailing in the environment). Hence, mental health counseling considers behavior in the context in which it occurs.

2. Human development naturally tends toward healthy growth. Counseling, including mental health counseling, derives its approach from the study of normal human development. Mental health difficulties are conceptualized as "problems of living." This premise differs markedly from the "medical model" espoused by psychiatry, in which mental health problems are conceived of as a form of illness.

3. The helping process consists of a relationship between a counselor and a client (help seeker) in which both work to assist the client to cope with the problem(s) of living for which help is sought by: (a) identifying and mobilizing relevant *client assets*; (b) identifying or developing needed *client skills*; and (c) utilizing *resources in the environment* that can reduce the client's problems of living and/or facilitate the client's ability to cope with these problems.

Assets may be defined as those personal qualities (traits, habits, behavior patterns, defenses, ways of thinking, "strong suits") that a client may apply to solving a given problem of living. It should be noted that a quality that may be an asset in relation to one problem may act as a liability in relation to a different problem. For example, aggressiveness may be an asset in some work settings (e.g., salesmen, boxers) but may be a liability in a family situation (when directed toward one's spouse or children).

Skills may be defined as physical, intellectual, and/or emotional techniques for achieving a specified objective.

Both assets and skills can be put in operational terms, can be measured, and can be systematically developed in a person. Skills are generally more specific in their application, less central to the person's personality, more concrete, and easier to teach.

4. In trying to help the client, the counselor uses empirically evaluated skills and techniques, that is, those methods of treatment that have demonstrated effectiveness through research.

Role Definition of Mental Health Counseling

The specialty of mental health counseling applies these tenets in:

1. Assisting clients (individuals, groups, organizations, or communities) to determine (through appraisal) and to attain (through direct intervention and/or consultation) *their optimal level of psychosocial functioning.* "Psychosocial functioning" refers to the domains of intellectual, emotional, interpersonal, and career behavior. "Their optimal level" implies that there is no absolute standard, but there is a standard set by the particular client that is optimal for that client, given that client's circumstances.
2. Assisting *individuals, groups, organizations,* and *communities* in a number of ways. Their aim, depending on the client's needs, may be:
   (a) preventive, that is, preventing a difficulty from arising.
   (b) facilitative, that is, assisting healthy growth to occur in an unimpeded manner.
   (c) remedial, that is, redirecting a maladaptive pattern of development to a healthy course.
   (d) rehabilitative, that is, assisting the client to compensate for existing limitations in ability to cope by promoting the use of other strengths that the client possesses.
   (e) enhancement, that is, improving the quality of life for the client.

The Distinctiveness of Mental Health Counseling

As its name implies, mental health counseling does not seek to cure illness (implicit in the terms *psychiatric* and *clinical* in the names of the most of the other mental health fields), but rather seeks to promote healthy development and coping. It works with both the client and the environment, building on existing strengths wherever possible and using scientifically evaluated methods.

Table 1.1 (see top of p. 6) illustrates how mental health counseling, the newest of the mental health fields, differs from the psychiatric medical model, the oldest, in its approach to treatment. These differences follow directly from the differences between the academic and professional premises of the parent disciplines from which these fields stem (mental health counseling from counseling, which in turn has its roots in education, and psychiatry from medicine).

SOCIETAL TRENDS AND MENTAL HEALTH COUNSELING

Mental health counseling has developed in a particular social context. Consequently, its development has been influenced by society's changing conception of what constitutes appropriate, healthy behavior and of the role of society in working with individuals who experience problems in living.

TABLE I.I. Comparison of Mental Health Counseling and Medical Model

ITEM FOR COMPARISON	MENTAL HEALTH COUNSELING	MEDICAL MODEL
Parent discipline	Counseling	Medicine
Basic science	Normal human development	Psychopathology
Characterization of mental health difficulties	Problems of living	Mental illness
Term used for help-seeker	Client	Patient
Desired outcome of treatment	Client develops ability to cope	Patient is cured
Treatment strategy	Utilize/develop assets and skills	Eliminate pathology
Diagnostic labeling	Largely irrelevant to treatment method	Central to choice of treatment method
Emphasis on environmental modification	Equal to client change	Secondary to patient change
Use of empirically evaluated techniques	Important	Important

Contemporary Social Pressures

Major societal changes have occurred within the past few decades. Most of these changes have been well documented in the media: the shift from an industrial production to an information processing society, less reliance on institutional sources of help, and an increased range of personal options (Naisbitt, 1982). These changes permeate every area of our lives: work, family life, and leisure activities.

The changing work place can be noted in such phenomena as rapid job obsolescence, increased numbers of women in the labor market, expanded occupational roles for women and minorities, the rise of entrepreneurship, a greater emphasis on financial incentives than on the intrinsic satisfactions of work in the choice of occupations, and the acceptance of career changes in mid-life and beyond.

Changes in family life include the increased isolation of nuclear families, a decreased birthrate, divorce, blended families, single-parent families, two-parent wage earners and the concomitant blurring of traditional parental roles, and the increased responsibility for aged parents resulting from greater longevity.

Personal options encompass a complex array of decisions which include, but go beyond, those mentioned under work and family life. The freedom to choose among an exceptionally broad range of lifestyles is now a reality.

This freedom of choice of personal lifestyles, however, has exacted a toll: Individuals must display an incredible array of adaptive skills in order to respond flexibly and creatively to life's options. These adaptive demands tax the resources of all of us, and not everyone is capable of such sustained adaptive performance. Populations considered most "at risk" for emotional and other health disorders are frequently minorities and economically disadvantaged individuals who often have not had the opportunity to develop the personal coping skills expected by the dominant society and who lack the environmental resources to respond adequately to the demands of contemporary life.

Even the hypothetical "average person" in today's society is susceptible to mental health problems. Striving for (but not always achieving) personal, economic, and occupational success invites a variety of exogenous stressors. The more society promotes the concept of each of us as controller of his or her destiny, the more unattainable and mythical a perfect existence becomes. The price paid by the average person when life's demands exceed personal coping skills is reflected in such contemporary catchwords as "stress" and "burnout" (Farber, 1983) or in our attempts to cope by attaining "self-management" or "high level wellness" (Dunn, 1977).

Definitions of Health and Mental Health

Mental health draws its definition from the broader, general definition of health. Our perceptions of what constitutes health have changed greatly over the past century. A longer average life span, the advent of antibiotics that provides freedom from many life-threatening diseases, and scientific and technical advances in diagnosis and treatment have resulted in a current concept of health that embodies not only the absence of illness, but also the potential of attaining a heightened state of wellness. This concept requires a balance among all dimensions of a person's life: physical, mental, social, vocational, and spiritual. These dimensions interact continuously, each influencing and being influenced by the others and by the environment. The term *holistic* is used to describe the combination of these many elements influencing an individual's level of functioning.

As the public has become increasingly aware of the impact that lifestyle and behavioral habits have on one's overall health status, wellness has become recognized as something controlled by the individual as much as by the environment (Eberst, 1984). The maintenance of a healthy lifestyle goes beyond illness prevention and incorporates active, personal responsibility for wellness. This philosophy is in marked contrast to a former dependence on a cure through the intervention of professionals. Rather, the healthy individual takes responsibility for prevention of illness by actively pursuing a balanced and wellness-promoting lifestyle. This trend is obvious in the current emphasis on physical fitness, avoidance of self-destructive behaviors (smoking, chemical abuse, overeating, etc.), and control or avoidance of environmental contaminants.

In similar fashion, mental health assumes not only the absence of mental illness, but a level of functioning in which we are comfortable with ourselves and our lifestyle. In essence, we are perceived to have control over our lives and, therefore, have the power to change those portions of ourselves or our lives that are not comfortable. The responsibility for mental health is centered primarily in the individual, and is no longer seen as the exclusive purview of mental health service providers or even as the responsibility of society as a whole. This approach entails a competency, rather than a deficit orientation. The individual is to be empowered with the resources to cope with and change maladaptive responses. Mental health problems, which represent a breakdown in the individual's coping abilities, may involve maladaptive responses in any of four broad areas of human functioning, including:

1. Social behavior, such as inadequate social or relationship skills, problems with aggression or in dealing with societal institutions and expectations;
2. Emotional behavior, including depression, anxiety, phobias, and emotionally based sexual disorders;
3. Health-related issues: insomnia, pain control, weight control and self-destructive behaviors, such as smoking, alcoholism, and drug abuse; and
4. Work-related issues: occupational "burnout," boredom, absenteeism, alienation, work disincentives, vocational indecision, underemployment, restricted occupational mobility, "workaholism," and similar issues.

The treatment of such problems has evolved in response to society's changing perception of their causes and nature.

Conversely, it may be noted that particularly during the 1950s, a number of professionals attempted to draw up lists of the criteria for positive mental health (as opposed to the more prevalent, negativistic approach of listing the problem areas that represented lack of mental health). Thus, Jahoda (1959) proposed the following list of categories of positive mental health: (a) positive attitudes toward oneself; (b) degree of growth, development, or self-actualization; (c) a central synthesizing or integrating psychological function; (d) personal autonomy or independence; (e) adequate perception of reality; and (f) environmental mastery.

Other lists were compiled by Allport (1955), Maslow and Mittelman (1951), Rogers (1959), and numerous other clinicians and personality theorists. Eventually, a reaction set in, and Smith (1961) pointed out the futility of generating these lists by demonstrating that they all really included the same basic concepts, under different names. He proposed, instead, that dimensions of mental health should be selected on the basis of their: (a) representing positive human values, (b) capability to be specified and measured, (c) articulation with personality theory, and (d) relevance to the social context for which they are being defined. Thus, subsequent writers, such as Offer and Sabshin (1966) or Hudson (1975), assiduously avoided making lists, but instead focused on global concepts such as *normality* or *sanity*. Currently, the concept of *coping* as the criterion of positive mental health has pervaded the literature of the various mental health professions (for example, Hamburg & Adams, 1967, in psychiatry; Brickman et al., 1982, in psychology). Ironically, this has led, in turn, to the generation of new lists, seeking to define the areas in which a mentally healthy person should be able to cope competently. These include Adler's (1982) list of: (a) performing major social roles, (b) self-concept, (c) interactions with others, (d) managing affect, (e) navigating developmental transitions, (f) handling stressful events, (g) accessing available resources, and (h) cognitive functioning.

Alternatively, Lewis and Lewis (1984) proposed the following list: (a) building satisfying relationships with others, (b) developing effective cognitive problem-solving skills; (c) managing personal stress; (d) gaining access to available resources for help when needed; (e) becoming involved in productive activities; (f) taking responsibility for one's own behavior; and (g) maintaining a self-concept that is positive but realistic.

It is the view of the authors of this book that the criticisms Smith (1961) leveled against the lists of criteria of positive mental health will prove equally true of lists of areas of coping. Therefore, in this book, coping will be defined as one's ability to achieve appropriate purposes effectively and efficiently within the specific context in which one is functioning. Thus, coping:

1. Is situation-specific, but involves the application of strategies that one learned in prior situations;
2. Involves using one's assets and resources, is largely a matter of "what you do with what you've got";
3. Can be helped or prevented by environmental factors, so that failure to cope need not necessarily reflect inadequate mental health.

THE EVOLUTION OF MENTAL HEALTH SERVICES

Having briefly reviewed contemporary ideas of mental health and mental health care, it is of interest to examine how those ideas evolved. The history of mental health services has been closely linked with changing client needs, cyclic government interest and funding, and the social concerns in a given historical period. As social conditions change, so do our views about mental health care. Zilboorg (1941) suggested that the development of mental health services consists of a series of revolutions. The first revolution took place in the period immediately following the French Revolution, around 1800. In this period, treatment came to replace confinement and punishment as the basis for dealing with the mentally disturbed. "The second revolution centered on the work of Sigmund Freud and occurred in the culture emerging from the Victorian era" (Hollander, 1980, p. 561), that is, a century later. There is no general agreement on the time and place of the third revolution, though Hollander

(1980) believed that a change has been taking place in the mental health field since 1950. This change is characterized by a rejection of professional domination in the mental health sphere, accompanied by a more equal relationship between professional and consumer.

Because the current practice of mental health care is the product of so many historical trends, varied federal and state laws and policies, and diverse social problems, the authors believe that it would be helpful to divide the modern history of mental health care into five periods: 1875–1940: The Beginnings; 1941–1950: The Awakening Period; 1951–1965: Growth Period; 1966–1979: Consolidation and Reassessment; and 1980—: Current and Emerging Issues.

1875–1940: The Beginnings

The modern practice of mental health counseling can trace its origins to the late 19th and early 20th centuries. Prior to this time, there was the widespread belief that heredity had irrevocably stamped each individual. It was assumed that there was little to be gained in attempting to improve those who were mentally disturbed. The professions of social work, clinical psychology, and psychiatry working in the community were almost unknown until the 1900s (Musto, 1975). Rarely were new approaches developed to deal with emotional disability or to explore the functional or social causes of abnormal behavior.

At the turn of the 20th century, the social milieu came to be viewed as an important factor in maladjustment (Musto, 1975). Effective treatment evolved, then, from a fundamental change in the environment. Beginning efforts were made to change "disorders" in society, such as slums. Also, as the person with a mental problem was viewed holistically, it became recognized that to understand the individual, one must be familiar with the whole social context in which the person lives. Paradoxically, however, during this period the practice of therapy was mainly aimed at the individual and directed to individual adjustment.

Such a holistic belief generated new professions, such as social psychologists and psychiatric social workers (Ewalt, 1975; Musto, 1975). Outpatient clinics were developed that, in turn, promoted the rise of the treatment team in mental health. Each member of the team would utilize a distinct professional perspective to meet the needs of the individual. Resources were to be quickly available through this team approach. Moreover, with the development of this community orientation and outpatient resources, there was a focus on the prevention and treatment of juvenile delinquency. In the late 1930s, child guidance clinics and the child guidance movement emerged. The movement stressed the early detection of emotional disorders, and treatment was directed both to the child and to the immediate environment.

Even though the role of the environment was emphasized in mental health care, psychoanalysis entered the treatment scene in the 1900s. It claimed its usefulness as an approach to change individual personalities (Musto, 1975; Saccuzzo, 1977). Leading Americans who followed the practice of psychoanalysis were A. A. Brill, Ernest Jones, Adolph Meyer, and Harry Stack Sullivan. Sullivan was among those who sought to integrate psychoanalytic theory with the social sciences.

Of added interest during this beginning period is that even with the new directions of treatment, massive sums of federal monies were not available. Mental health leadership was with the states and with many voluntary agencies and private foundations, such as Russell Sage, Carnegie, and Rockefeller. They were the funding resources for many years. The small federal role began to change as the Depression of the 1930s prompted the initiation and then support by government of social welfare programs. Though direct federal aid to health services (including mental health services) was limited, federal support for research on mental health was being increased (Ewalt, 1975).

1941–1950: The Awakening Period

The Second World War brought a new awakening to the mental health field. Many believe that mental health policy as we know it today is largely a post-World War II development. The rejection of over 1 million men during World War II for psychiatric reasons and the development of psychiatric evaluation and mental hygiene clinics at recruitment and training centers alerted America to the extent and seriousness of mental health problems. Also, by utilizing intensive treatment techniques, psychiatric workers were able to return to active duty a large number of servicemen who suffered sudden emotional breakdowns. Both the techniques and recovery rates impressed many clinicians who were more traditional in their mental health treatment approaches. During this war, legislation was developed to establish the National Institute of Mental Health.

From these war experiences, both government and informed laypersons became aware of the necessity to learn more about the causes of mental health problems and the means for preventing them. In 1946, the National Mental Health Act was adopted. This legislation authorized funds for research, demonstration, training, and assistance to states in the use of the most effective methods of prevention, diagnosis, and treatment of mental health disorders. In the late 1940s, state budgets began to show their largest financial obligation for mental health concerns; but considering the mental health needs, these budgets were still quite low.

Another effect of mental health practices during World War II was the stimulus the war provided to devise new treatment techniques that were feasible in dealing with relatively large groups of patients (Mechanic, 1980). Group techniques were seriously studied. Drug therapies began to be developed. Unfortunately, however, these advances had very little impact on practices in mental hospitals. Most states still lacked the facilities, personnel, and financial resources to implement the many new ideas spawned in the mental health field (Mechanic, 1980).

1951-1965: Growth Period

This was a time of optimism, a period that saw an increase in expenditures for training mental health professionals, mental health services, the construction and staffing of new community mental health centers, and a broad increase in the boundaries of mental health concepts. It was the beginning of a postwar generation that became the catalyst for an extraordinary period both of ferment and of searching for new ways to understand a broad range of issues (Hollander, 1980). In the early 1950s, continued research and developing theories concerning the possible link between environment and individual mental health prompted the renewed or enhanced development of outpatient clinics that could postpone or prevent hospitalization. Early detection of emotional problems was again emphasized by mental health practitioners. The concept of *crisis intervention* was introduced, which implied that "in emotional crisis an individual's behavior patterns were much more easily directed to new and ideally healthier forms than in periods of better adjustment" (Musto, 1975, p. 8). Also, new estimates of the number of citizens needing evaluation and treatment were made known, stimulating a perceived need for many more mental health workers to work at all levels in each community.

Many of these advances were the result of a report that was a product of the Joint Commission on Mental Illness and Health. In the late 1950s, the Mental Health Study Act authorized an appropriation to the Joint Commission to study and make recommendations concerning various aspects of mental health policy. In 1961, the commission published its well-known report (Mechanic, 1980). Though basically an ideological document, it strongly emphasized the necessity of an increased program of services and of more funds for basic, long-term mental health research. It also recommended that expenditures in the mental health field be doubled in the next 5 years and tripled in 10 years. The report argued for new and better recruitment and training programs for mental health workers, and it suggested the expansion of treatment programs for acutely ill patients in all facilities, including community mental health clinics, general hospitals, and mental hospitals (Mechanic, 1980).

This report generated a vigorous battle at the federal level between those mental health workers who wanted to develop new approaches for patient care and those workers who believed that, within the traditional medical model, more federal assistance should be invested in improving the quality of mental hospitals. After all the arguments, pro and con, the final decision was to give the greatest impetus to community mental health centers (Mechanic, 1980).

The National Institute of Mental Health budget also expanded during the late 1950s, and the Kennedy administration gave special attention to mental retardation and dramatically increased support for the delivery of mental health services. Such funding was facilitated by the Community Mental Health Centers Act of 1963, which also encouraged a national network of mental health centers (Musto, 1975; Ewalt, 1975).

The federal budget, which provided for growth and development of new approaches and additional manpower in mental health, resulted not only from the commission's report, but also because abundant funds were available in the American economy for meeting domestic needs. President Kennedy was very much committed to programs in mental health and mental retardation. Also, the development and widespread use of psychiatric drugs has changed the climate of mental health care as well as administrative attitudes (Mechanic, 1980).

As the number of mental health professionals grew, these same practitioners were seeking greater recognition and were pressing for more and better training in clinical practice (Caddy, 1981). The 1965 Chicago Conference brought the issues of professional training in psychology into greater prominence, and various models of doctoral training were discussed. The conference finally reaffirmed the scientist-professional educational approach that utilizes the traditional academic-university setting for training.

1966-1979: Consolidation and Reassessment

During the beginning years of this period and even until the onset of the Vietnam War, the number of both care settings and mental health care specialists increased. For example, there was considerable expansion in the numbers of psychologists, psychiatric social workers, psychiatric nurses, counselors, and individuals in other fields (such as the ministry) who work part- or full-time in mental health service delivery. Between 1955 and 1977, moreover, outpatient care episodes rose 282% (Beigel & Sharfstein, 1984).

A shift away from public mental hospitals was taking place, with more acute psychiatric illnesses being treated in general hospitals and outpatient clinics. Behavioral techniques for treating many types of mental health problems were commonly adopted, and treatment of disorders became more focused and diversified (Mechanic, 1980). The institutional setting was no longer depended upon as a vehicle for change, and many patients in need were recognized and treated more quickly in the community. An understanding of new psychoactive drugs and their adverse effects increased. Private and nonprofit insurance companies providing medical coverage substantially increased outpatient coverage for mental health services.

Hollander (1980) believed that the third revolution in the history of mental health care, mentioned earlier in this account, began taking place from the early 1960s. This revolution has resulted in some of the most important contemporary trends in mental health. Community mental health centers, for example, began to move in the direction of a real sharing of power between the consumer and the agency. Implications of this involvement were that consumers or citizens can push for services that they identify as relevant to their needs. No longer are they passive recipients of services, but consumers now have a responsible share in the decision-making process of a particular agency. Another implication of this "third revolution" was the therapeutic community concept. It implies that both patients and paraprofessionals become genuine partners in the helping process. Consequently, more attention was given to increasing social interaction, group involvement, informal patient status and living arrangements, and creating expectations for "normal" responsible living (Sprafkin, 1977).

Interesting contributors to the growth of mental health care systems during this period were the so-called "boom areas." These are areas of rapidly shifting population, with communities experiencing above-average growth. This is particularly true in the southwestern rim of the United States (Moffic, Adams, Rosenburg, Blattstein, & Chacko, 1983). What occurred and continues to occur is an increase in certain populations at particular risk for mental problems. Minority groups, migrants and refugees, people in communities with inadequate health services or who are subject to rapid urbanization, and people at sensitive periods in the life cycle all are included as "at risk" for mental problems. Boom areas produce crowding, people who have been uprooted and who lack the accustomed extended family and communal support systems, and people who suffer from depression and substance abuse. Such problems generate an urgency for mental health services.

The Vietnam War and the years immediately following brought a curtailment of the funds for mental health programs. During the Nixon years, the administration phased down or out or allowed only minimal funds for such existing programs as mental health centers, research, training, and professional manpower development. Massive deinstitutionalization revealed the poor planning for release of patients into the community and the inadequacy of continuing supervision and treatment (Mechanic, 1980). Deinstitutionalization began in the 1950s in response to several converging factors. The cost of keeping individuals in institutions began to exceed acceptable levels. At the same time, legal decisions that individuals must be maintained and treated in the "least restrictive environment" required that individuals with emotional problems remain in or return to society. Finally, advances in medication made noninstitutional care not only permissible, but possible.

In the early 1970s, moreover, Congress became increasingly concerned about alcoholism and drug abuse. With the limitation of funds, traditional mental health monies were used to develop new national efforts in these areas. The Alcohol, Drug Abuse, and Mental Health Administration was formed by merger to oversee a variety of service programs, research efforts, and professional training programs.

During this consolidation period, previously little-known treatment methods such as Gestalt, Transactional Analysis, and Reality therapies began to grow at a rapid pace. Mental health workers were also taking a broader view of their helping role in the context of social responsibility. There was a willingness to train new professionals and to extend service to low-income persons. There appeared to be a renewed movement away from the one-to-one model of treatment to exploring and implementing again varied methods of group treatment of mental problems. Family techniques also grew.

Of importance for the growth of the profession of mental health counseling was the formation in 1978 of the American Mental Health Counselors Association (AMHCA). This organization has focused on such issues as defining the parameters of professional practice; assuring appropriate curriculum in graduate training; overseeing certification and licensure of practitioners, and accreditation of training programs; assessing the job outlook for master's and doctoral level mental health counselors; and providing advocacy for third-party payment. These issues are interrelated: For example, credentialing through certification or licensure is necessary before third party payments are made. The AMHCA initiated a national certification program for mental health counselors at the master's degree level in 1979, a first step in credentialing in this field.

In reviewing this period, it becomes apparent that the issues of core concern were deinstitutionalization, the development of community service programs, the prevention and treatment of alcohol and drug problems, and how to survive with reduced funding. Many of these issues received a new, more encouraging focus when in February 1977, President Carter established a Commission on Mental Health to review the mental health needs of the nation and to make recommendations. The commission looked at such issues as the organization of community services, community supports, financing, personnel, legal rights, research, prevention, and public understanding. The report recommended a greater investment in mental health services. Though mental health problems are one of the largest in terms of number of persons involved (Mechanic, 1980; "Mental Disorders," 1984), it receives only 12% of general health expenditures. The report cited the need to develop community-based services; to make them financially, geographically, and socially accessible; and to make them flexible so as to serve the needs of varying social and racial groups. All in all, the recommendations of the commission provided a new stimulus for the delivery of mental health services.

1980 - Present: Current and Emerging Issues

Since 1980, inflation in the American economy has been a prime concern, and health care costs have been increasing much more rapidly than the economy as a whole. Government expenditures on health care are high and even uncontrollable, in part due to the structure of the Medicare and Medicaid programs (Mechanic, 1980). Policymakers appear reluctant to make large new investments in health care initiatives. Unemployment has been rising the past few years, and the percentage of those out of work is higher in certain geographic areas, in specific occupations, and within specific population groups (Dumas, 1983).

There have been recent decreases in the availability of categorical federal funding for mental health care, and progress has been limited with regard to reimbursement practices (Beigel & Sharfstein, 1984). Despite intensive efforts, the mental health professions have been unsuccessful in getting congress to expand mental health benefits under either Medicare or Medicaid (Beigel & Sharfstein, 1984). With fewer opportunities for employment in the public sector as a result of reduced categorical funding, more mental health professionals are entering private practice. More practitioners are becoming involved with emerging health care settings, such as health maintenance organizations, and seeking full recognition within these environments.

There are other related legislative, social, and economic trends that have received sharper identification since 1980. One trend is related to the broadened consumer movement and its concomitant reliance on self-help and distrust of professional help. This movement has spawned self-help groups seeking personal assets and, accordingly, rejecting the unequal doctor-patient relationship in every area of health care (Gottlieb, 1979).

Avoidance of professionals has led to a demystification of the helping process. No longer is what occurs in therapy attributable to inscrutable unconscious or preconscious forces. No longer are unobservable, subjective phenomena acceptable benchmarks for progress in therapy. The counseling process must rely on skills that are observable, clearly understood, empirically based, and amenable to evaluation (Anderson, 1975).

As the helping process has become demystified, the stigma attached to seeking help has been reduced. As client and counselor are seen as active, equal partners in the change process, a greater acceptance of services has occurred. As services become specific and time-limited, clients can obtain help at savings of both time and money.

Another trend is the wider range of professionals to provide services. As treatment moved into the community and as individuals became more sophisticated in the understanding of how change occurs, mental health specializations appeared within a number of established disciplines. Mental health counseling, for example, has its roots in the counseling profession, which, in turn, is based on a developmental/educational model of human growth.

Mental health counseling focuses on social-emotional competency but is also concerned with vocational-educational competency. Whereas this latter area of functioning has traditionally been the primary concern of other counseling specializations, all areas within the counseling profession have to come to recognize the interrelatedness of these aspects of life. Thus, it has become recognized that social and emotional problems affect one's performance at school or work (absenteeism, inattention to tasks, etc.) and that, conversely, problems at school or work affect one's social and emotional functioning in other arenas, such as family life.

Among mental health counselors, there is increased concern about licensure. As practitioners expand their practice into industry and other community settings, there is an accompanying need to establish credibility among these groups for whom the opportunity for mental health care is a new reality. Mental health counselors are seeking equal status with other health providers in the delivery of mental health services (Anderson & Parenté, 1980). With this growing emphasis on licensure, continuing education efforts have grown to assist professionals to enhance their knowledge and meet the standards established for licensure. Recent bills have been introduced in Congress to make mental health counselors recognized core providers of mental health services under Medicare and Medicaid. As noted before, certification for mental health counselors was begun in 1979 (Messina, 1979).

Short-term treatment is receiving a renewed emphasis, as this form of care can be more economical and provides the opportunity for many more people to receive mental health services. This is related to ethical concerns about the relative effectiveness of long-term treatment and to the emerging associated issues of professional and social accountability.

A final trend is a greater awareness of the role of prevention in promoting positive mental health. This includes promoting positive lifestyles, restructuring the environment to reduce stress, and building personal competencies in such areas as decision making, problem solving, and coping with transient crises.

The current field of mental health counseling is the result of many and varied emerging issues and social trends in the history of mental health care. Advances in treatment, the cyclical nature of government funding, and changing societal conditions have contributed to the directions in which the field of mental health counseling has evolved. This field comprises a fairly diverse group of helping practitioners, distinct perhaps in their training and in their work settings, but generally united in their concern to assist individuals to attain optimal life adjustment. It is a field that will continue to show diversity as social and government priorities and the needs of the population change, and as newer treatment approaches are developed.

THE PROFESSION OF MENTAL HEALTH COUNSELING

By definition, every occupation must possess two things: first, a specialized body of knowledge, skills, and attitudes; and second, a recognized group of practitioners of that body of knowledge, skills, and attitudes. Mental health counseling contains both of these elements, which we will now briefly examine. For an occupation to qualify further as a profession, it must also fill a recognized societal need (as we have already discussed) and be self-regulating as to what constitutes appropriate practices and qualifications of practitioners. This, as has also been noted, is the case with mental health counseling.

Characteristics of Mental Health Counseling

The events reviewed earlier in this chapter have had considerable impact on the philosophy and practice of mental health counseling as a distinct helping profession. Thus, mental health counseling has sought to be:

1. Need-responsive—to deal with specifically defined and targeted needs of its clients (individuals, groups, or communities), rather than attempting to change ill-defined states of malaise.
2. Developmental—to promote healthy growth, rather than focusing on eliminating pathology.
3. Integrative—to recognize the interrelatedness of all life areas—social, emotional, work, and learning—and to understand that what occurs in one of them will inevitably affect the others.
4. Environment-sensitive—to recognize that the client's behavior is a function of both the person and the client's environment, and that the counselor can neither assess nor change behavior without involving both factors.
5. Enabling—to assist the client to help him/herself, rather than trying to impose "a cure."
6. Asset oriented—to identify and to mobilize client strengths as the basis for coping.
7. Skill based—to assist clients to develop skills for coping that have use beyond the immediate issue that brought them into counseling.
8. Eclectic—to use counseling techniques from any theoretical model if they are appropriate to the client's situation.
9. Evaluation driven—to utilize only those techniques and methods that have been shown through empirical research to be effective.

Seiler and Messina (1979) proposed an alternate list of the characteristics of mental health counseling including:

1. A focus on inducing high level well-being, rather than just the absence of pathology;

2. The use of the counseling relationship to help clients: (a) modify behavior patterns, (b) restructure the environment, (c) build competences, and (d) improve decision making;
3. A holistic focus on physical, emotional, social, and spiritual aspects of the person, the environment, and their interaction;
4. An interdisciplinary approach, drawing on the relevant findings of other disciplines;
5. A multifaceted approach, prepared to utilize both physical and mental approaches to intervention (for example, relaxation training);
6. A commitment to promote healthy lifestyles and to have clients assume responsibility for doing so for themselves;
7. Identification of stressors in clients' lives and of clients' functional levels in a way that avoids labeling and promotes coping; and
8. The development of proactive, self-help problem-solving skills in clients.

It should be noted that Seiler and Messina's list is totally compatible with the list suggested by the authors of this book.

Qualifications of Mental Health Counselors

As professionals, mental health counselors must possess the knowledge, skills, and attitudes necessary for the practice of their profession and must continually engage in evaluation and research to improve themselves and their field.

The knowledge and skills of mental health counseling are determined by client needs and interpreted by professional credentialing bodies. The profession of counseling, as represented by the National Board for Certified Counselors (NBCC), has determined that all counselors must possess knowledge about human growth and development; group dynamics; social, cultural, and environmental factors affecting human behavior; lifestyle and career development; the helping process (individual and group counseling, consultation); appraisal of clients; research and evaluation procedures; and professional ethics and practices. Counselors must also demonstrate skills in appraisal, helping, and research and evaluation. In addition to these general counseling skills and knowledge, mental health counselors must:

1. Possess the required education in a recognized body of specialized knowledge and skills relevant to mental health issues. At this time, the minimum education required of entry-level practitioners is at the graduate (master's degree) level.
2. Meet a standard of proficiency in those skills set by the profession and accepted by the broader society. That is, mental health counselors must demonstrate that they can effectively apply what they have learned at a

level of competence sufficient for their profession to certify their right to this title and for society to accept that certification as a valid credential for practice.
3. Hold a set of professional attitudes, including: (a) that they work for the legitimate interests of their clients; (b) that they serve society by the practice of their profession and by protecting that society from destructive behavior of clients and colleagues; and (c) that they place their professional obligations (to clients, the profession, and society) above personal gain and advancement.
4. Accept the obligation to: (a) continually evaluate current knowledge and skills; (b) seek to add to the body of knowledge and to improve the skills within themselves and within their profession.

The issues of professionalization of mental health counseling alluded to here will be discussed in detail in chapter 3.

Practice Settings of Mental Health Counselors

In addition to the brief survey of the history and philosophy of mental health and mental health counseling just provided, an overview of the range of settings in which mental health counselors work and of how they are distributed across this range should also be helpful in orienting the reader to the field. In the early years of the American Mental Health Counselors Association (AMHCA), the majority of the members worked in community mental health centers. For example, Weikel and Taylor (1979) found, in a 1978 survey of members of AMHCA, that 39% worked in community mental health centers, 18% were in private practice, and between 7% and 9% worked in each of the other categories of settings listed (college counseling center, private agency, state agency, college teaching, and other). Weikel (1985) reported that now the largest single group of AMHCA members consists of those working in private practice (22%). About 13% work in private counseling centers, 13% in colleges and universities, 11% in community mental health centers, and 4% in community agencies. The rest work for rehabilitation agencies (5%), state or local government (4%), parochial or private institutions (3%), secondary schools (3%), elementary schools (3%), junior colleges (2%), business and industry (2%), the federal government (2%), and "other settings" (13%). This shift of preferred work settings has promoted an increased emphasis on a holistic view of health, a reconceptualization of some traditional professional practices, and the emergence of new roles for the mental health counselor (e.g., McCollum, 1981).

In another relevant study conducted in 1985, Burtnett (1986) surveyed 351 mental health agencies concerning their professional staffing patterns. Of these agencies, over 57% had mental health counselors on their professional staff. About 90% of these mental health counselors held masters' degrees, and the remainder held doctorates. Mental health counselors occupied 11% of the total professional staff positions (the rest being held by psychiatrists and other physicians, nurses, psychologists, and social workers). Burtnett (1986) concluded, "This study clearly reveals that the mental health counselor is present and performing mental health services in agencies and organizations across the United States" (p. 6).

Thus, mental health counselors work in a vast array of agencies and programs. This variety will increase as new client needs emerge from the country's population. The mental health counseling profession is a flexible field of human service delivery, responsive to the changing environment and open to the development of new intervention approaches.

SUMMARY

In summary, mental health counselors are professionals who apply the knowledge and skills of counseling to assist individuals, groups, organizations, and communities to determine and to attain their optimal level of psychosocial functioning.

With its focus on helping its clients to cope with the demands of living, mental health counseling is related to several other professions, such as psychiatry, clinical psychology, psychiatric social work, and psychiatric nursing. It differs from these fields, however, in that they primarily seek to eliminate pathological behavior, whereas mental health counseling seeks to promote healthy development and functioning by mobilizing the client's assets. This difference in orientation has been termed the distinction between the medical (illness-oriented) model and the developmental (asset-oriented) model. This distinction determines how one appraises clients (looking for pathology versus looking for strengths) and how one intervenes (eliminating pathological behavior versus promoting healthy behavior). Mental health counseling asserts that mental health is more than the absence of "mental illness"; that it involves positive growth and development in the client's ability to cope with life by utilizing the assets and skills that the client possesses. Mental health counseling gives equal emphasis to the effects of the environment on behavior and recognizes that changing the environment, rather than the client, can be an effective intervention. In summary, mental health counseling tries to consider the total person in context and to help that person develop ways of coping that will be useful not only in the present situation, but also in the future. As such, it is entitled to use the name "mental health."

REFERENCES

Adler, P. T. (1982). An analysis of the concept of competence in individuals and social systems. *Community Mental Health Journal, 18*(2), 34–35.

Allport, G. W. (1955). *Becoming: Basic considerations for a psychology of personality.* New Haven: Yale University Press.

Anderson, J. K., & Parenté, F. (1980). AMHCA members forecast the future of the mental health profession. *AMHCA Journal, 2,* 4–12.

Anderson, T. P. (1975). An alternative frame of reference for rehabilitation: The helping process versus the medical model. *Archives of Physical Medicine and Rehabilitation, 56,* 101–104.

Beigel, A., & Sharfstein, S. (1984). Mental health care providers: Not the only cause or only cure for rising costs. *American Journal of Psychiatry, 141*(5), 668–671.

Brickman, P., Rabinowitz, V. C., Karuza, J., Jr., Coates, D., Cohn, E., & Kidder, L. (1982). Models of helping and coping. *American Psychologist, 37,* 368–384.

Burtnett, F. E. (1986). *Staffing patterns in mental health agencies and organizations.* Unpublished report, American Association for Counseling and Development, Alexandria, VA.

Caddy, R. G. (1981). The development and current status of professional psychology. *Professional Psychology, 12,* 377–384.

Dumas, R. G. (1983). Social, economic, and political factors and mental illness. *Journal of Psychosocial Nursing and Mental Health Services, 21*(3), 31–35.

Dunn, H. L. (1977). What high-level wellness means. *Health Values: Achieving High Level Wellness, 1*(1), 9–16.

Eberst, R. M. (1984). Defining health: A multidimensional model. *Journal of School Health, 54*(3), 99–103.

Ewalt, J. R. (1975). The birth of the community mental health movement. In W. E. Barton & C. J. Sanborn (Eds.), *An assessment of the community health movement* (pp. 13–20). Lexington, MA: D. C. Heath & Co.

Farber, B. A. (Ed.). (1983). *Stress and burnout in the human service professions.* Elmsford, NY: Pergamon Press.

Gottlieb, B. H. (1979). The primary group as supportive milieu: Applications to community psychology. *American Journal of Community Psychology, 7,* 469–480.

Hamburg, D. A., & Adams, J. E. (1967). A perspective on coping behavior: Seeking and utilizing information in major transitions. *Archives of General Psychiatry, 17,* 277–284.

Hollander, R. (1980). A new service ideology: The third mental health revolution. *Professional Psychology, 11,* 561–566.

Hudson, L. (1975). *Human beings: The psychology of human experience.* Garden City, NY: Anchor Books.

Jahoda, M. (1959). *Current concepts of positive mental health.* New York: Basic Books.

Leighton, A. H. (1982). *Caring for mentally ill people: Psychological and social barriers in historical context.* Cambridge: Cambridge University Press.

Lewis, J. A., & Lewis, M. D. (1984). Preventive programs in action. *Personnel and Guidance Journal, 62,* 550–553.

Maslow, A. H., & Mittelmann, B. (1951). *Principles of abnormal psychology.* New York: Harper & Bros.

McCollum, M. G. (1981). Recasting a role for mental health educators. *American Mental Health Counselors Association Journal, 3*(1), 37–47.

Mechanic, D. (1980). *Mental health and social policy* (2nd ed.). Englewood Cliffs, NJ: Prentice-Hall.

Mental disorders may afflict 1 in 5. (1984, October 3). *Washington Post,* p. A1.

Messina, J. J. (1979). Why establish a certification system for professional counselors? A rationale. *AMHCA Journal, 1,* 9–22.

Moffic, H. S., Adams, G. L., Rosenburg, S., Blattstein, A., & Chacko, R. (1983). *Boom areas: Implications for mental health care systems.* Amherst, MA: Human Science Press.

Musto, D. (1975). The community mental health center movement in historical perspective. In W. E. Barton & C. J. Sanborn (Eds.), *An assessment of the community mental health movement* (pp. 1–11). Lexington, MA: D. C. Heath & Co.

Naisbitt, J. (1982). *Megatrends.* New York: Warner Communications Company.

Offer, D., & Sabshin, M. (1966). *Normality: Theoretical and clinical concepts of mental health.* New York: Basic Books.

Rogers, C. R. (1959). A theory of therapy, personality, and interpersonal relationships, as developed in the client-centered framework (pp. 184–256). In S. Koch (Ed.), *Psychology: A study of a science. Vol. 3.* New York: McGraw-Hill.

Saccuzzo, D. P. (1977). The practice of psychotherapy in America: Issues and trends. *Professional Psychology, 8*(3), 297–303.

Seiler, G., & Messina, J. J. (1979). Toward professional identity: The dimensions of mental health counseling in perspective. *AMHCA Journal, 1,* 3–8.

Smith, M. B. (1961). Mental health reconsidered: A special case of the problem of values in psychology. *American Psychologist, 16,* 299–306.

Sprafkin, R. (1977). The rebirth of the moral movement. *Professional Psychology, 8*(2), 161–168.

Weikel, W. J. (1985). The American Mental Health Counselors Association. *Journal of Counseling and Development, 63,* 457–460.

Weikel, W. J., & Taylor, S. S. (1979). AMHCA: Membership profile and journal preferences. *AMHCA Journal, 1,* 89–94.

Zilboorg, G. A. (1941). *History of medical psychology.* New York: Norton.

2 Characteristics of Effective Mental Health Counselors*

All mental health counselors must have certain personal and professional characteristics if they are to perform effectively with clients (individuals, groups, and organizations) who have a wide range of problems. These characteristics can be categorized as: (a) professional and personal attitudes, values, and beliefs regarding human nature, the dynamics of the helping process, and the conditions under which people change; (b) professional knowledge; (c) professional skills; and (d) personal characteristics or traits that are in part a reflection of the counselor's underlying personality structure. This structure also includes personal values.

As noted elsewhere in this book, the counselor assumes various roles depending on the type of intervention planned (e.g., counseling, consultation, advocacy, etc.) and the level of intervention required (e.g., individual, small group, or large group). Regardless of role, intervention, strategy, or clientele, the person of the counselor, apart from any discrete skills or competencies, will be an important factor in the change process. In addition, the change process is interactive and depends to a great extent not only on what the counselor is able to provide in the way of intervention, but also on the ways that the counselor is perceived by the client and the client's expectations that change can and will occur.

The person of the mental health counselor is the primary tool that facilitates change in the counseling process. This person — the counselor — holds certain attitudes, beliefs, and values about human beings, the lifelong process of emotional and spiritual growth, and the counseling relationship. The personal characteristics of the counselor, in combination with skills and the ability to develop a working relationship, will activate desired outcomes.

This chapter will discuss the characteristics exemplified by the competent

---

*This chapter was written by Marita Danek.

mental health counselor, including how the person of the counselor is used to facilitate change; examine the theoretical and empirical basis for our assumptions about these characteristics; and review potential impediments to the effective delivery of services, such as burnout and cross-cultural issues. Although the primary emphasis in this chapter will be on counselor characteristics that facilitate the individual and group counseling process, many of these characteristics are also essential to other counselor roles and interventions.

This chapter will begin with an examination of how the person of the counselor, through the use of interpersonal influence, can be used in the counseling process.

INTERPERSONAL INFLUENCE

Interpersonal influence involves the ways that the client and counselor interact and how the person of the counselor is used to develop, support, and maintain a facilitative and growth-inducing relationship. There is considerable research in the area of counselor interpersonal influence (Dell, 1973; Strong, 1968, 1970; Strong & Dixon, 1971). Interpersonal influence theory assumes that not only the real but also the perceived characteristics of the counselor have an impact on the nature and quality of the counseling relationship. Under this theory, clients are liable to perceive the counselor as more or less expert, trustworthy, or attractive; and this perception will determine the degree to which counselor and client can work together. To a certain extent, the interpersonal influence of the counselor is a type of power that can be used to influence the client and facilitate change (Strong & Matross, 1973). This power is a function both of the client's perceived needs of what other resources in the client's environment are available to meet these needs, and how well the counselor is expected to meet these needs. These perceptions can also interact with other counselor characteristics. For example, age, sex, or physical characteristics can be determinants of interpersonal influence for some counselors with some clients. There is also some evidence that male and female counselors will use different methods of influence, based on what are perceived to be the most appropriate methods for facilitating change with same- or different-gender clients. Along similar lines, in terms of clients' perceptions, Wiggins (1980) found that overweight counselors (both male and female) were rated as less capable in terms of perceived cognitive effectiveness, empathy, warmth, leadership qualities, and overall counseling effectiveness.

ATTITUDES, VALUES, AND BELIEFS

Counselor attitudes that are conducive to client growth and development include positive attitudes toward self, others, and the change process. These attitudes provide one cornerstone for the counseling relationship and are common to effective counselors of varying theoretical orientations. In general, regardless of theoretical or philosophical orientation, effective counselors see themselves as identified with rather than separate from others, adequate, worthy, and trustworthy. Similarly, effective counselors perceive others as capable and dependable. They see the change process as a growth-producing, developmental progress toward human actualization and goal attainment.

Counselors' Attitudes Toward Themselves

Counselor's beliefs about themselves, their personal efficacy as counselors, and their professional competencies are crucial to inducing positive change in their clients. Counselors must see themselves as:

1. *Identified with rather than separate from others.* Although counselors must have a strong sense of personal identity (Erikson, 1968) which provides a unique, integrated, cohesive sense of self, they must also be able to identify with the essential human feelings and responses of clients (Jackson & Thompson, 1971). Counselors might not and frequently do not share the same value or belief systems as their clients; however, they should be able to respect each individual's right to choose from a plurality of belief systems. This identification with others, and a sense of oneness with the world is, in essence, considered the hallmark of self-actualized individuals (Maslow, 1954).

2. *Trustworthy.* There must be a sense of trust between the counselor and client. The counselor is aware of personal motivations, does not have hidden agendas, and does not use the counseling relationship to satisfy his or her own needs. This is communicated to the client both verbally and nonverbally as one dimension of personal integrity.

3. *Adequate.* Counselors should understand and accept their own limitations in the helping relationship (Brammer, 1973). Effective counselors recognize that their personal and professional growth is a lifelong, ongoing process (Carkhuff, 1969) and that adequacy and competency in the counseling relationship must be continuously monitored.

4. *Caring.* Good counselors care what happens to their counselees because the individual as a human being is respected regardless of personal strengths and limitations. Counselors demonstrate caring by attending to and maintaining involvement with their clients and being constantly aware of the content and affect of their clients' statements.

Counselors' Attitudes Toward Human Nature

Effective counselors must have a positive attitude of acceptance toward clients, and believe that these clients are worthwhile as individuals, worthy of receiving help, and that the counseling relationship will provide an opportunity for growth. The following attitudes and beliefs regarding human nature should be held by the counselor:

1. *Belief in an individual's ability to change.* This belief is central to the work of the counselor. If people are incapable of change, why work with them? Counselors must enter a counseling relationship with a positive expectation that the counselee is capable of succeeding in attaining all or most of his or her goals. This should be communicated to the counselee through the counselor's expression of caring, support, and encouragement. Some empirical evidence exists that this characteristic distinguishes superior from average counselors (Boyatzis & Burruss, 1977).

2. *Belief in the worth of each individual.* The counselor must hold the attitude that the client is worthy of positive regard because the client is human, has individual strengths and limitations, and possesses the capacity to live more effectively (Egan, 1982).

3. *Freedom from prejudice.* This belief is concomitant to valuing the worth of each individual. Counselors and clients frequently differ in terms of educational level, social status, ethnic or cultural group, sex, and other characteristics. The counselor must not permit these differences to become the basis for stereotypical or biased attitudes toward or outright rejection of the client. Although there will always be some clients with whom the counselor will feel more comfortable, the counselor should have a high level of awareness of personal attitudes regarding clients they perceive as different. If it appears that attitudes toward a client or type of client will interfere with the relationship, the counselor has the responsibility to refer the client to another helping professional. Similarly, if a client's belief system is markedly divergent from the counselor's in a way that will impede progress toward goals, the relationship should be terminated.

4. *Right to be different.* Counselors must remain open-minded toward idiosyncratic differences in clients. Only in this way can full acceptance be achieved.

Counselors' Attitudes Toward the Change Process

Mental health counselors also hold beliefs about the nature of the helping and change process and the dynamics of the counseling relationship. Good counselors are more likely to perceive the helping relationship as freeing rather than controlling (Pietrofesa, Hoffman, & Splete, 1984). This means that the relationship exists not to manipulate or to dominate the client, but to facilitate the client's movement toward unique, personalized goals. Good counselors believe that events are interrelated and causal, and that broader meanings may be uncovered and explored from specific events. Finally, they believe in the counseling process as a mechanism for change. They know that if both counselor and client are committed toward change, such change will occur. They have a positive view toward the outcomes of counseling. However, the counselor must do more than present facilitative conditions—such conditions are necessary but not sufficient for counselee change. The counselor must demonstrate appropriate skill in helping clients define accurate and attainable goals and appropriate strategies to reach these goals. The counselor must confront when necessary, support the client's efforts to change, respect the client's need to grow at his/her own pace, and preserve the confidentiality of the counseling relationship. When facilitative conditions are buttressed with competent service and the counselee recognizes progress toward mutually agreed-upon goals, the relationship is developed and maintained.

SKILLS AND COMPETENCIES OF AN EFFECTIVE COUNSELOR

These are both global, highly complex skills and more discreet, distinct counseling skills. The latter can be developed through training and are open to observation and measurement, and are most frequently utilized in individual counseling. The former are also acquired through training, but they are usually refined through continued counseling experiences. The global skills will now be discussed.

Ability to Develop and Maintain a Relationship

The counseling relationship actually begins before the initial contact. Both counselor and counselee bring certain preconceptions (conscious or unconscious) to the first counseling session. Whether the counselee is self- or other-referred, whether the prospect of counseling is eagerly anticipated or dreaded, whether the counselee is an unwilling or reluctant partner in the prospective relationship, whether the counselor's reputation and perceived expertness are known to the counselee, whether the counselee has been previously involved in a helping relationship and the outcome of that relationship—all these factors will provide a perceptual framework against which the counselee evaluates the initial contact. Similarly, the counselor, from written or verbal referral information or perhaps inquiries from the counselee, will have developed a sense of what motivates the client to seek help and what issues or concerns need to be resolved.

During the initial counseling session, the counselor works on developing a relationship with the counselee by using specific techniques and strategies: attending and listening skills; the clarification of mutual expectations; and an open discussion of structural issues such as fees, a time frame for intervention, and how progress toward goals will be monitored. Additionally, during the initial session the counselor communicates a positive attitude about the change process, motivates the client to accept the responsibility to work with the counselor toward change, and helps him or her begin thinking about ways these changes may be accomplished. These skills are clarified further in a later section.

The counseling relationship is begun in the initial session and built upon incrementally in subsequent sessions as the counselee comes to realize that the counselor is trustworthy, accepting, nonjudgmental, caring, and competent.

Empathy

There is a tendency today for people to see each other in terms of differences, not similarities. The mental health counselor may, therefore, be challenged by a client on the basis of these differences, for example, sex, social class, age, ethnic group, and so on. The question is raised, "How can you truly understand how I feel when you are not (married, gay, middle-aged, etc.) or have never experienced (infidelity, discrimination, an identity crisis, etc.)." The response, of course, is that no human being ever experiences the same life conditions and circumstances as any other human being. Even if we did experience almost identical life circumstances, the personal meaning derived from such experiences would be unique. However, we all have or can develop the capacity to experience the intense, often very painful feelings associated with these life circumstances or situations.

Empathy is the sensitivity a counselor feels toward the counselee's concerns and problems. It involves the experiencing of the counselee's feelings and the ability to communicate accurately such experiencing (Carkhuff & Berenson, 1967). It has often been described as putting ourself in the shoes of another and relating to the feelings a situation may evoke, regardless of whether the counselor has personally encountered such a situation.

Just as empathy is a personal and relatively stable characteristic of the counselor, the term *accurate empathy* relates to the counselor's ability to perceive sensitively what the client is experiencing and communicate back both the content and affect of the client's message. Both cognitive and affective empathy are important. Cognitive empathy refers to the accurate perception of the content of what the client is communicating; affective empathy relates to the feelings associated with the content.

Certain human emotions know no cultural, geographic, racial, or sexual boundaries. Despair, depression, grief, joy, love, anger, hatred—these feelings are shared by all members of the human race and are not situation-specific. Indeed, certain situations may evoke entirely different emotional responses in two different individuals. For example, divorce may elicit the deepest despair in some individuals, an enormous sense of relief in others, and a numbness and deadening of affect in yet another group. In a similar manner, although the counselor may never have been married, she or he should be able to experience with the client the overwhelming and often conflicting emotions that accompany the dissolution of a meaningful relationship.

Carl Rogers (1951) listed the capacity to empathize as one of the most important personal qualities the counselor brings to the relationship. He defined it as the ability of the counselor to "sense and express the client's felt meaning, catching what the client communicates as it seems to the client" (Rogers, Gendlin, Keisler, & Truax, 1967, p. 10). However, it is important that the counselor simultaneously maintains his or her separateness from the counselee. Although he or she feels as the counselee feels, this is a temporary condition and the counselor maintains a separate identity.

It should be noted, however, that research in counseling effectiveness has not always demonstrated the relationship between counselor empathy and counselee outcome (Horwitz, 1974; Payne, 1971; Thoreson, 1977). Some theorists have speculated that a certain amount of empathy is necessary but too much with a particular type of client and under certain conditions may be contraindicated (Gelso & Carter, 1985; Gladstein, 1983). The inexact definition of empathy and how it is expressed most probably accounts for the inconclusive research findings.

Positive Regard

The term *unconditional positive regard* was first coined by Carl Rogers (1961) but subsequent theorists have tended to minimize the element of "unconditional." It is virtually impossible for all counselors to experience an attitude of caring for all clients under *all* conditions. As human beings with unique backgrounds and experiences, counselors will be influenced by certain conditions surrounding the counseling process. However, an attitude of respect for the client as a person, regardless of the behaviors exhibited by him or her at any given time, should be experienced by the counselor and communicated either verbally or nonverbally to the client.

The expression of positive regard, of an acceptance of the client, also means that any judgmental or evaluative behavior toward the client is avoided; the client's resources are considered sufficient for self-understanding and positive change. The client, under the condition of positive regard, is assumed to internalize this perception and this perception becomes part of an overall feeling of self-worth.

Genuineness

This refers to the congruence or perceived authenticity of the counselor. The counselor's ability to be real and to respond in a genuine fashion to the client provides the client with a basic sense of trust.

Most humanistic approaches to counseling consider genuineness to be the pivotal agent of client change — the openness of the counselor and willingness to share that provides the relationship with a sense of aliveness. The counselor does not assume a "role" such as counselor or therapist. Rather, he or she acts in a way that is consistent with his or her feelings. This does not imply that all feelings or responses are explored, but rather that there is a correspondence between the counselor's words and feelings (congruence) and a lack of phoniness (authenticity) (Schulman, 1982).

Intentionality

Intentionality means that the counselor brings a sense of purpose to the counseling relationship. The counselor provides structure to an essentially unstructured relationship; a systematic approach to an open process; and an element of choice to what might otherwise become a session filled with chance and haphazard rumination (Schmidt, 1984).

Ivey (1983) defined intentionality as "acting with a sense of capability and deciding from a range of alternative actions. The intentional individual has more than one action, thought, or behavior to choose from in responding to changing life situations" (p. 3). Counselor intentionality is different from and goes beyond what might be referred to as counselor intentions. Intentions refer to specific behaviors that are chosen to assist the client in the counseling process, whereas intentionality refers to a level of awareness that integrates those behaviors and the counselor's assessment of client and environmental feedback into a helping relationship.

Providing Support

The provision of support to the client extends beyond mere encouragement. It can, and does, include providing the client from without what he or she lacks within. For example, offering specific suggestions, providing an orientation to reality where distractions exist, and structuring the counseling sessions are all forms of support. Support is also provided when the counselor conveys a belief in the client's potential for change, reinforces those behaviors and attitudes that are growth producing, and accepts powerful feelings as capable of being mastered.

Instructing

Psychoeducation has only recently become valued by counselors as a significant strategy for client change. The emerging importance of instructing or informing the client is recognized, in part, because of the counselor movement of the 1970s and, in part, because such assistance provides the client with additional insight, personal mastery, and growth toward greater independence. The partnership of the counselor and client is an egalitarian one; therefore, the counselor has the responsibility to inform the client not only about the change process in general, but also about personal dynamics and universal phenomena that contribute to change.

Reduction of Overwhelming Affect

Major presenting complaints of many clients in individual counseling are their strong negative feelings, which can range from incapacitating to merely inconvenient. Affective concerns include depression, a sense of hopelessness, anxiety, hostility, and anger.

To assist the client in dealing with these concerns, the counselor may employ a variety of strategies including: (a) ventilation of feeling (the ability to show or describe strong affect in itself contributes to a subjective feeling of relief among clients who frequently are not permitted or do not permit themselves to express such feeling in daily life); (b) investigating the antecedents (events or thoughts) of such affect and the meaning that these antecedents have for the client; (c) direct intervention with environmental precipitants of such affect; and (d) providing specific strategies to help the client deal with the affect (e.g., relaxation training, systematic desensitization, covert modeling, etc.).

Reducing or Increasing Specific Client Behaviors

All individuals develop a repertoire of behaviors to respond to specific situations or life circumstances. Some behaviors may be maladaptive or contribute to diminished personal competence, for example, specific phobias, lack of assertiveness, undeveloped social skills, indecisiveness, obsessive or compulsive behavior, frigidity or impotence, and so on. Behavioral and cognitive approaches are useful in treating such behaviors (which may or may not be symptomatic of more pervasive underlying concerns). For example, assertiveness or social skills training may provide the client with an opportunity to practice alternative and more adaptive behaviors. Similarly, all individuals possess unique strengths. The counselor can reinforce such strengths or competencies when they are expressed or exhibited by the client.

Restructuring Client Perceptions

Clients can frequently be victims of their own thoughts regarding personal standards of behavior that are rigid or excessively high. These thoughts can be translated into negative "self-talk" (Ellis, 1962, 1973) which is critical and discouraging. In addition to frequent negative self-statements, clients will often reveal a low frequency of positive self-evaluation. The counselor can intervene with negative client "self-talk" by helping the client to identify and restructure such thoughts (Beck, 1976).

Ability to Self-disclose

Therapists have frequently emphasized the basic neutrality, near-anonymity of the helping professional. Almost always, this kind of helping professional was a psychiatrist who adhered to the medical model and was trained in a classical analytical tradition. In more recent years, particularly among mental health counselors, self-disclosure on the part of the counselor has been recommended as another strategy to assist the client in achieving appropriate goals (Halpern, 1977). The counselor should maintain focus and be selective in the use of self-disclosure and have a rationale for its use (e.g., to model disclosing behaviors, to overcome resistance, or to work through transference). It should always be used in the context of helping to meet client needs and not those of the counselor.

Self-disclosure is different from a similar construct labeled "immediacy" (Carkhuff & Berenson, 1967). Whereas self-disclosure provides the factual information about the counselor to the client, immediacy is the personalization of the nature of the counseling relationship. That is, immediacy is concerned with the "here and now" of what is occurring at any given time between the counselor and the client.

Ability to Recognize and Cope with Resistance

The concept of resistance is associated with psychoanalytic theory, yet it has usefulness in counseling practice, for it describes a phenomenon that frequently occurs regardless of the theoretical orientation of the counselor. Many theorists believe that resistance is always present to some extent and at some time during the counseling relationship.

Resistance can be seen as a type of reluctance. Reluctance is a characteristic of clients who are unmotivated to change and who do not wish to enter into a counseling relationship. Patterson and Eisenberg (1983) stated, "the reluctant client is any person who, if given the choice, would choose not to be in the presence of a counselor and who would prefer not to talk about self" (p. 153). Although counseling philosophies emphasize the voluntariness of counseling, many clients are not self-referred and feel coerced to "go for counseling." Typical of these clients would be students referred because of adjustment problems, a marital partner who does not wish to save the marriage, individuals in an institution who must comply with the system's wishes and, indeed, a large proportion of those individuals served by mental health clinics and public agencies. Vriend and Dyer (1973) noted that clients are reluctant for various reasons: an inability to admit inadequacy, a resentment toward authority, or a desire to gain approval or acceptance from peers.

Resistance usually occurs in clients who appear to want counseling but then become intimidated by the necessity for increasing levels of self-disclosure, insight, and self-awareness. These clients usually engage in behaviors that sabotage the counseling process and yet they are not usually aware of their motivations for doing so. When confronted with the reality of their resistance, they frequently will deny it.

Reluctance, on the other hand, is usually obvious from the time of the client's first encounter with the counselor. Clients can refuse to speak or provide minimal responses. Sometimes the client will express the reluctance directly, "I didn't want to come here, but they told me I should." At other times, clients can be more subtle and ostensibly comply or be over-agreeable and yet still be reluctant. Resistance can also be expressed by the client focusing on trivial or insignificant events or feelings, focusing on others, canceling or coming late to appointments, or not coping with the expression of strong feelings (anxiety or dependency). The various types of resistance displayed by involuntary or reluctant clients, and as identified by Ritchie (1986), can be summarized into three types: (a) the client does not admit having a problem, (b) the client acknowledges the problem but does not want to change, and (c) the client acknowledges the problem and wants to change but is unable to change because he or she does not know how or is afraid to try.

There are several ways that counselors can cope with the reluctant client or the otherwise motivated client who experiences periodic resistance. The effectiveness of a particular technique depends on the cause of the client's reluctance (Ritchie, 1986). The following approaches may assist in reducing resistance:

1. Increase client's motivation and right to self-determination by encouraging clients to set goals, particularly attainable, realistic intermediate goals rather than unachievable long-term goals. When the reluctant client does admit to having a problem and expresses a desire to work on it, setting both long-term and intermediate goals may help minimize resistance by reducing the change process into small steps (Riordan, Matheny, & Harris, 1978; Ritchie, 1986).
2. Provide structure and direction rather than ambiguity in the counseling process. Ambiguity can be extremely threatening to clients who lack an internal sense of direction and control (Riordan, Matheny, & Harris, 1978).
3. Provide reinforcement for small successes so that the client can perceive the change process positively and develop an expectancy for personal empowerment. Many clients do not attempt change because of learned helplessness (Seligman, 1975). Unless their belief in personal efficacy is bolstered, they feel powerless to effect any lifestyle or behavioral changes (Riordan, Matheny, & Harris, 1978).
4. Interpret the resistance based on its behavioral manifestations (e.g., silence, defensiveness, etc.) and describe it as a normal part of the change process. Sometimes, with some clients, the counselor may explore the rea-

sons for the resistance. At other times, it is helpful to move to a less threatening focus (Riordan, Matheny, & Harris, 1978).

5. Determine what payoffs maintain the problem behavior. An abused wife, for example, may refuse to leave her husband for fear of being alone. Frequently, allowing the client to remain passive is not in the client's best interest. The counselor may have to consider trying a more direct approach (Ritchie, 1986).

In summary, then, resistance and reluctance are similar phenomena. Reluctance refers to a general disinclination to participate in the counseling process or to change dysfunctional attitudes or behaviors. Resistance refers to an often unconscious process in an otherwise motivated client who is unable to proceed (usually temporarily) with behavioral or attitudinal changes. The counselors' skill in acknowledging and modifying resistance is important if the counseling process is to continue.

The classification of global skills such as empathy, genuineness, or positive regard is perhaps somewhat misleading, because they may also be considered personal attributes of the counselor. These behaviors can, however, be taught. Similarly, the ability to self-disclose or deal with resistance defines a complex set of learned skills that are put into action in response to client verbal or nonverbal behaviors, usually in individual or small group sessions.

Counseling Process Skills

In addition to global, highly complex skills, there are additional skills utilized by the counselor that are more discreet, distinct, can be developed through training, and are open to observation and measurement. These skills are most frequently utilized in individual counseling.

Attending Skills
This includes physical and psychological attending. Physical attending involves the arrangement of the environment as well as the counselor's body posture and other nonverbal cues. Psychological attending has to do with the reflection of content and feeling so that the client's meaning is understood.

Personalization of Meaning
To be helpful, the counselor must go beyond the reflection of content and feeling. The counselor must accurately add meaning to what the client has expressed. The counselor can then move to *personalizing* the client's problems and goals or the expected outcomes of counseling. This means that the unique, *special* meaning that a circumstance or event holds for a client is recognized relative to the meaning it takes and the response it elicits in the client.

Initiating Action

Once the client's feelings and the meaning attached to the feelings have been thoroughly explored and personalized and goals have been described, the counselor helps the client develop strategies to reach these mutually agreed upon goals. The counselor supports and encourages the client to take needed steps to achieve these goals.

IMPEDIMENTS TO THE EFFECTIVE
DELIVERY OF COUNSELING SERVICES

Although there are many impediments to the effective delivery of counseling services, this section will discuss two that are currently of concern to counselors and human-service systems. These impediments are burnout and cross-cultural issues, both of which can be disruptive to the change process.

Burnout

Although much has been written in recent years on burnout in human services occupations, there are some indications that burnout presents a potential occupational hazard for most white-collar workers. In a recent study (Golembiewski, 1986), 45% of all organizational employees were found to suffer from burnout.

Burnout was first defined by Freudenberger (1974) and has subsequently been the subject of serious scrutiny by many authors in the helping professions (Boy & Pine, 1980; Daley, 1979; Larson, 1981; Ursprung, 1986). Burnout is a pervasive, all-encompassing phenomenon that arises from the unique interaction of an individual's personality with the work environment (Watkins, 1983) and results in a loss of motivation, enthusiasm, and energy and decreased performance in every area of the individual's life (Forney, Wallace-Schutzman, & Wiggers, 1982). Burnout is not merely the tedium and stress associated with work that dissipates after hours; it permeates the individual's entire lifestyle and waking hours and has specific behavioral and somatic symptoms.

The risk of experiencing burnout is particularly high for counselors and other human-service professionals due to the ambiguity and high energy involved in working intensely with individuals. Unpredictable or ambiguous outcomes, lack of adequate supervision and peer support, difficult or large case loads, inadequate preparation for work demands, stress, lack of control over working conditions, personality characteristics such as unrealistic expectations for performance and consequent guilt, and lack of reinforcement for performance all contribute to burnout (Maher, 1983; Watkins, 1983).

The symptoms of burnout fall into four general categories: physical, psychological, social, and systems (Carroll, 1979). Physical symptoms include exhaustion, sleep disturbances, eating disturbances (too much or too little),

somatic complaints (e.g., headaches, gastrointestinal symptoms), and suscepti-
bility to illness. Psychological symptoms frequently involve anger, irritability,
depression, boredom, lack of trust, cognitive rigidity, reduced self-esteem, and
an overall negative attitude toward work. For mental health counselors, dis-
tancing and detachment from clients and a feeling of helplessness or of losing
control may be particularly debilitating.

Social symptoms include the disruption of long-term relationships, and
withdrawal from or conflict with family members or co-workers. Overall systems symptoms include absenteeism, poor morale, high turnover rates, problems involving turf and competition issues, and less effective and efficient
work styles.

There are three major categories of burnout:

1. That which affects individuals who are "vulnerable personalities." These
   individuals either place themselves in high-stress work situations or have
   insufficient coping mechanisms with which to deal with periodic work
   stressors.
2. Acute burnout as a result of psychic trauma that may or may not be associated with working conditions.
3. Chronic burnout, which is the long-term continuing response to working
   conditions and demands, the type that is most commonly associated with
   the term.

Regardless of the type, individuals with burnout tend to: feel powerless
about their work roles and responsibilities; feel that they are not or cannot be
recognized for competent behavior within the work setting; and feel their jobs
lack challenges or opportunities for continued growth. Conversely, reduced
levels of burnout in human service or mental health settings appear to be
related to commitment to the agency's philosophy and objectives.

The most appropriate intervention for burnout is prevention; that is, maintaining within the system and within the individual the conditions for optimal
professional growth. These conditions include a variety of work tasks with
varying levels of stress, a strong administrative and peer support system, and
an even distribution of risks and rewards related to each work role.

Once burnout occurs, there are two possible approaches: (a) change or modify the environment (system), or (b) change and modify the individual's
response to the system. System changes would emphasize reducing stressors
such as heavy case loads, long hours, and lack of staff involvement in the system. Changes to the individual's response to the system include interventions
that provide more effective coping strategies such as systematic problem-solving training; participation in support groups (Spicuzza & DeVoe, 1982); free
private time to engage in pleasurable, avocational activities (Dowd, 1981;
Freudenberger & Robins, 1979); and enrichment of family and social relationships.

Mental health counselors, particularly, need to take time for themselves and their spiritual and emotional renewal. The energy required to provide competent service to individuals with varying ends must be continuously replenished. The tendency to over-commit and become over-involved is very seductive; only by continuous monitoring of affect, values and behaviors can counselors avoid slipping into the burnout syndrome.

Corey (1982) suggested various strategies that counselors can use to prevent burnout (pp. 287–288); by utilizing these strategies and maintaining a high level of self-awareness, mental health counselors can avoid the threat of burnout that affects all human service professionals.

1. Finding other interests besides work.
2. Thinking of ways to bring variety into work.
3. Taking the initiative to start new projects that have personal meaning and not waiting for the system to sanction this initiative.
4. Promoting health through diet, adequate sleep, exercise, and meditation.
5. Developing social relationships that are characterized by mutuality of giving and receiving.
6. Learning how to ask for what one wants, though not always expecting to get it, and learning to deal with not always getting what is asked for.
7. Learning to work for intrinsic rather than extrinsic rewards (self-validation as opposed to other-validation).
8. Seeking new experiences through travel, hobbies, or attending classes or workshops for professional renewal.
9. Taking the time to evaluate the meaningfulness of one's projects to determine where professional investment and time will continue to be spent profitably.
10. Avoiding assuming the burden of responsibility that is properly the responsibility of others.
11. Exchanging jobs with a colleague for a short period or asking a colleague to join forces in a common work project.
12. Forming a support group with colleagues to share openly feelings of frustration and to find better ways of approaching the reality of certain job situations.

Cross-Cultural Issues

Counselor objectivity may be lacking or impaired when the client is from a different social class, or ethnic or cultural group. The United States has always embraced the ideal of cultural pluralism, that is, the right of all citizens to retain their ethnic traditions while maintaining equal rights and access to opportunity. Regardless of this ideal, counselors frequently lack exposure to cross-cultural experiences or have not been adequately trained or prepared to work with cultural minorities (Hall, 1981; Vontress, 1976). Increasingly, there is acknowledgment of the previous impact of the cultural environment on the client's understanding and response to problems in living for ethnic minorities (Pedersen, 1984).

Most counselors are members of the majority American culture: white, middle class, and Anglo-Saxon or European in heritage. A wave of immigration from Third World countries over the past 20 years has brought to our country individuals with markedly different world views, strategies for coping with problems in living, and attitudes toward societal helping systems and their processes.

The tendency to stereotype these culturally different individuals should be avoided; however, the unique cultural perspectives that characterize many cultural minorities must be understood by counselors who wish to work with them effectively. Counselors must be particularly knowledgeable about attitudes, values, and behaviors in certain cultural groups that might pose certain limitations on a formal counseling relationship.

Ruiz and Padilla (1977), for example, noted several similar patterns among individual members of various Latino subcultural groups. The most common unifying factor among Latino subgroups is a strong adherence to the Spanish language as a source of personal identity. Although most Latinos must use English in their everyday lives outside of the family, it is not the preferred language because it is frequently perceived as the language of the "oppressor." Counselors who work with Latinos must be aware of and sensitive to these attitudes toward the use of English and the potential for communication breakdown or resistance to the use of English as a counseling modality.

Another characteristic of Latino culture is the central importance of the family and the extended family in the life of the individual; highly defined sex roles with a dominant father and nurturing, compliant mother; and a preference for personal contact when dealing with agencies or societal institutions rather than the "chain of command" approach used by Anglos (Ruiz & Padilla, 1977). This means that physical touch such as a handshake or even a hug is expected from the counselor and that first names rather than formal titles should be used.

Sue (1977) made some additional observations about cultural factors in other Third World minorities. Asian Americans share the Latino emphasis on a family orientation, but are more highly restrained in the expression of their feelings. To Asian Americans, the counselor is an authority figure, and interaction is usually one-way, with silence a mark of respect, and advice-giving as the major modality of counseling. There is a strong sense of pride and also shame and disgrace when behavioral expectations are not met; most Asian Americans use the family as a support system in times of crisis and prefer not to go to societal institutions such as a counseling service (Sue, 1977).

American Indians are characterized by a cooperative rather than competitive attitude, a present-time orientation, and a creative/intuitive approach to life with many supernatural explanations for individual or environmental crises. Black Americans are more action-oriented with a sense of "peoplehood" and an emphasis on nonverbal behavior.

Many of these cultural values are in conflict with traditional counseling approaches, which emphasize the use of verbal communication, usually in standard English; middle class values such as strict time schedules and long-range goals; and American cultural values such as an emphasis on cause and effect, verbal expressiveness, openness and intimacy, and a separation between physical and mental well-being.

The counselor must recognize that the American perception and acceptance of counseling services for problems in living is contrary to most Third World cultural values. Trust in a stranger who represents authority cannot be assumed and may be a real barrier to sustained involvement in counseling (LaFromboise & Dixon, 1981; Vontress, 1976). Lack of trust and an awkwardness about the level of self-disclosure required in counseling might account for the high levels of termination (up to 50% after one counseling contact) observed among Asian Americans, blacks, Latinos, and native Americans (Sue & McKinney, 1975; Sue, Allen, & Conaway, 1975).

It is also necessary for the counselor not to overgeneralize and stereotype from the characteristics of cultural minorities presented in this section. There is a great deal of heterogeneity among cultural minorities along with varying degrees of acculturation. However, the counselor should remain sensitive to cultural differences as a means of understanding the individual and as a guideline for tailoring counseling approaches.

Counseling approaches that appear to have the highest potential for success with Third World individuals include those that emphasize immediate, short-term goals and utilize a concrete, tangible, structured approach. It is imperative that the counselor recognize and respect cultural factors that impede the client from expressing strong emotions or high levels of self-disclosure.

An additional caveat is in order: Some of the cultural characteristics of Third World individuals could also be incorrectly attributed to reluctance or resistance, as described previously in this chapter. Although many Third World individuals are, indeed, reluctant to enter into a counseling relationship, the behaviors they may exhibit in counseling (silence, short responses, diffidence to authority) are not, per se, an indication of resistance, but are considered to be culturally appropriate responses to that type of social interaction.

In summary, then, it appears that counseling services are under-utilized by Third World individuals because of cultural sanctions against going outside the family or community for help or because the helping process with its emphasis on verbal interaction, insight, and long-range goals is truly an alien process. Counselors need to become familiar with general cultural norms and sanctions regarding help-seeking behaviors and modify their counseling strategies to meet the needs of clients who come from other cultures.

REFERENCES

Beck, A. T. (1976). *Cognitive therapy and the emotional disorders.* New York: International Universities Press.

Boy, A. V., & Pine, G. J. (1980). Avoiding counselor burnout through role renewal. *Personnel and Guidance Journal, 59,* 161-163.

Boyatzis, R. E., & Burruss, J. A. (1977). *Validation of a competency model for alcoholism counselors in the navy.* Boston, MA: McBee & Co.

Brammer, L. M. (1973). *The helping relationship.* Englewood Cliffs, NJ: Prentice-Hall.

Carkhuff, R. R. (1969). *Helping and human relations.* New York: Holt, Rinehart & Winston.

Carkhuff, R. R., & Berenson, B. G. (1967). *Beyond counseling and therapy* (2nd ed.). New York: Holt, Rinehart & Winston.

Carroll, J. F. K. (1979). Staff burnout as a form of ecological dysfunction. *Contemporary Drug Problems, 8,* 207-227.

Corey, G. (1982). *Theory and practice of counseling and psychotherapy.* Monterey, CA: Brooks/Cole.

Daley, M. R. (1979). Burnout: Smouldering problem in protective services. *Social Work, 24,* 375-379.

Dell, D. M. (1973). Counselor power base, influence attempt, and behavior change in counseling. *Journal of Counseling Psychology, 20,* 399-405.

Dowd, E. T. (Ed.). (1981). Leisure counseling [Special issue]. *Counseling Psychologist, 9*(3).

Egan, G. (1982). *The skilled helper: A model for systematic helping and interpersonal relating.* Monterey, CA: Brooks/Cole.

Ellis, A. (1962). *Reason and emotion in psychotherapy.* New York: Lyle Stuart.

Ellis, A. (1973). *Humanistic psychotherapy.* New York: Julian Press.

Erikson, E. H. (1968). *Identity: Youth and crisis.* New York: W. W. Norton.

Forney, D. S., Wallace-Schutzman, R., & Wiggers, T. T. (1982). Burnout among career development professionals: Preliminary findings and implications. *Personnel and Guidance Journal, 60,* 435-439.

Freudenberger, H. J. (1974). Staff burnout. *Journal of Social Issues, 30,* 159-165.

Freudenberger, H. J., & Robbins, A. (1979). The hazards of being a psychoanalyst. *Psychometric Review, 66,* 275-296.

Gelso, C., & Carter, J. (1985). The relationship in counseling and psychotherapy. *The Counseling Psychologist, 13*(2), 155-244.

Gladstein, G. (1977). Empathy and counseling outcome: An empirical and conceptual review. *Counseling Psychologist, 6*(4), 70-79.

Gladstein, G. (1983). Understanding empathy: Integrating counseling, developmental, and social psychology perspectives. *Journal of Counseling Psychology, 80,* 467-482.

Golembiewski, R. (1986). Nearly half of employees in major study suffer burnout. *Behavior Today, 17*(3), 1-3.

Hall, L. K. (1981). Dimensions in mental health: Availability, accessibility, and accountability. In E. R. Myers (Ed.), *Race and culture in the mental health service delivery system.* Washington, DC: University Press of America.

Halpern, T. P. (1977). Degree of client disclosure as a function of past disclosure, counselor disclosure, and counselor facilitativeness. *Journal of Counseling Psychology, 24,* 41-47.

Horwitz, L. (1974). *Clinical prediction and psychotherapy.* New York: Jason Aronson.

Ivey, A. (1983). *International interviewing and counseling.* Monterey, CA: Brooks/Cole.

Jackson, M., & Thompson, C. (1971). Effective counselor: Characteristics and attitudes. *Journal of Counseling Psychology, 18*(3), 249-254.

LaFromboise, T. D., & Dixon, D. N. (1981). American Indian perceptions of trustworthiness in a counseling interview. *Journal of Counseling Psychology, 28*, 135-139.

Larson, C. (1981). Psychologists ponder ways to help troubled colleagues. *APA Monitor, 16*, 50.

Maher, E. L. (1983). Burnout and commitment: A theoretical alternative. *Personnel and Guidance Journal, 6*(7), 390-393.

Maslow, A. H. (1954). *Motivation and personality.* New York: Harper & Row.

Myers, E. R. (Ed.) (1981). *Race and culture in the mental health service delivery system.* Washington, DC: University Press of America.

Patterson, L. E., & Eisenberg, S. (1983). *The counseling process* (3rd ed.). Boston: Houghton Mifflin.

Payne, P. A. (1971, April). *A reconsideration of empathy in counselor effectiveness.* Paper presented at the American Personnel and Guidance Association Convention, Atlantic City, NJ.

Pedersen, P. B. (1984). The cultural complexity of mental health. In P. B. Pedersen, N. Starorius, & A. J. Marsella (Eds.), *Mental health services: The cross-cultural context* (pp. 13-25). Beverly Hills, CA: Sage.

Pietrofesa, J., Hoffman, A., & Splete, H. (1984). *Counseling: An introduction.* Boston: Houghton Mifflin.

Riordan, R. J., Matheny, K. B., & Harris, C. W. (1978). Helping counselors minimize client reluctance. *Counselor Education and Supervision, 18*, 6-13.

Ritchie, M. H. (1986). Counseling the involuntary client. *Journal of Counseling and Development, 64*, 516-518.

Rogers, C., Gendlin, E., Keisler, D., & Truax, C. (1967). *The therapeutic relationship and its impact.* Westport, CT: Greenwood Press.

Rogers, C. R. (1951). *Client-centered therapy.* Boston: Houghton Mifflin.

Rogers, C. R. (1961). *On becoming a person.* Boston: Houghton Mifflin.

Ruiz, R. A., & Padilla, A. M. (1977). Counseling Latinos. *The Personnel and Guidance Journal, 56*, 401-408.

Schmidt, J. J. (1984). Counselor intentionality: An emerging view of process and performance. *Journal of Counseling Psychology, 31*(3), 383-386.

Schulman, E. (1982). *Intervention in human services.* St. Louis, MO: C.V. Mosby.

Seligman, M. E. (1975). *Helplessness: On depression, development, and death.* San Francisco: W. H. Freeman.

Spicuzza, F. J., & DeVoe, M. W. (1982). Burnout in the helping professions: Mutual aid groups as self-help. *Personnel and Guidance Journal, 61*(2), 95-99.

Strong, S. R. (1968). Counseling: An interpersonal influence process. *Journal of Counseling Psychology, 15*, 215-224.

Strong, S. R. (1970). Causal attribution in counseling and psychotherapy. *Journal of Counseling Psychology, 17*, 388-399.

Strong, S. R., & Dixon, D. N. (1971). Expertness, attractiveness, and influence in counseling. *Journal of Counseling Psychology, 18*, 562-570.

Strong, S. R., & Matross, R. P. (1973). Change processes in counseling and psychotherapy. *Journal of Counseling Psychology, 20*(1), 25-37.

Sue, S. (1977). Community mental health services to minority groups. *American Psychologist, 32*, 616-624.

Sue, S., Allen, D., & Conaway, L. (1975). The responsiveness and equality of mental health care to Chicanos and native Americans. *American Journal of Community Psychology, 6*, 137-146.

Sue, S., & McKinney, H. (1975). Asian Americans in the community mental health care system. *American Journal of Orthopsychiatry, 45*, 111-118.

Thoreson, C. E. (1977). Constructs don't speak for themselves. *Counselor Education and Supervision, 16*(4), 296–303.

Ursprung, A. W. (1986, March). Burnout in the human services: A review of the literature. *Rehabilitation Counseling Bulletin,* 190–199.

Vontress, C. E. (1976). Counseling the racial and ethnic minorities. In G. S. Belkin (Ed.), *Counseling: Directions in theory and practice* (pp. 417–431). Dubuque, IA: Kendall/Hunt.

Vriend, J., & Dyer, W. (1973). Counseling the reluctant client. *Journal of Counseling Psychology, 20,* 240–246.

Watkins, C. E. (1983). Burnout in counseling practice: Some potential professional and personal hazards of becoming a counselor. *Personnel and Guidance Journal, 6*(5), 304–308.

Wiggins, J. D. (1980). Effectiveness ratings of counselors by coached clients related to attractiveness–fitness variables. *American Mental Health Counselors Association Journal, 2*(2), 83–87.

3 The Profession of Mental Health Counseling

At what point an occupation, that is, an activity by which a person may earn a living, becomes a "profession" is a topic that has been studied by sociologists. Professions are a subclass of occupations, a subclass that implies a relatively high degree of social prestige and public trust. Therefore, many occupations have sought to present themselves as professions, in hopes of cashing in on these benefits of professional status. These occupations include everything from real-estate salespersons to stock-and-bond dealers to funeral directors. Because so many varying lists of professions have been compiled to reflect different criteria or to serve different purposes, it is best that we turn instead to the sets of objective standards compiled by some of the sociologists who have studied the topic of professions and professionalization of occupations.

Gross (1958) suggested the criteria by which to judge how far an occupation had moved toward professional status as being:

1. An unstandardized product is dealt with; that is, "general knowledge is applied to solve particular problems, each of which is different from all other such problems" (p. 77).
2. "A special relation of confidence between professional and client or patient is involved" (p. 78).
3. The practitioner possesses a specialized body of knowledge not possessed by the client.
4. The professional is "expected to use only the best or the most efficient techniques and not merely the traditional or dramatic one" (p. 79).
5. Professionals have a strong sense of identification with their colleagues, as represented through admissions qualifications, professional associations, codes of practice, and sanctions for deviations from those codes.
6. "The professional's activities tend to be regarded as either vital to society or else involving a high degree of trust" (p. 80).

Gross pointed out that each of these criteria represents ideals and that no profession fully meets them all.

Greenwood (1962) suggested that the characteristics that all professions appear to possess are: "(1) systematic theory, (2) authority, (3) community sanction, (4) ethical codes, and (5) a culture" (p. 207). "Authority" refers to the same attribute as Gross's second criterion, the special confidence placed in the professional by the client because of the professional's specialized knowledge and skills. The professional "culture," according to Greenwood, involves the process of enculturation of the candidate into the profession, including the adoption of the profession's set of symbols (e.g., terminology), values, behavior norms, organizational memberships, and career pattern.

Although other sociologists have developed other lists of attributes of professions, these two are sufficient to reflect the most commonly stated criteria. Much of the rest of this book has been devoted to an examination of the "specialized body of knowledge" and "systematic theory" of mental health counseling. Also included have been discussions of the counselor–client relationship and of the profession's relationship to the broader society. We will now examine the other, more specific attributes of professional status that have been evolved by mental health counseling in its movement toward professionalization. As suggested by the sociologists cited earlier, these attributes include ethical codes, credentialing, professional organizations, professional literature, and professional training. As suggested by Gross, to the extent that mental health counseling has achieved each of the listed criteria, it is to that extent entitled to be called a profession.

ETHICS

A code of ethics for mental health counselors has been developed and adopted by the American Mental Health Counselors Association. Other codes with which mental health counselors should be familiar are the code of ethics of the National Board for Certified Counselors (1983), the standards for providers of psychological services (American Psychological Association, 1977), and the ethical standards for rehabilitation counselors (National Rehabilitation Counselors Association, 1972). Because it is of most direct relevance to the practice of mental health counseling, the "Code of Ethics for Mental Health Counselors" of the American Mental Health Counselors Association is presented here. Because this code forms the explicit basis for the ethical practice of mental health counseling, it is given in its entirety as an appendix to this chapter. This code should be studied with care by anyone preparing to enter the profession of mental health counseling. This code is adapted from the ethical standards of the American Association for Counseling and Development (formerly, the American Personnel and Guidance Association [APGA]) and the code of the Virginia Board of Licensed Professional Counselors.

CREDENTIALING

Credentialing by professions takes several forms. Individuals who undergo prescribed training, demonstrate professional knowledge and/or skills on an examination set by the profession, and have no history of relevant legal or moral turpitude may become *certified* by their profession. That is, the profession acknowledges them as fellow professionals. Many professions, including counseling (Messina, 1979), have established related bodies to *accredit* the academic programs in which professionals are educated. Some professions (not including counseling) will only certify graduates of accredited programs, whereas most other professions (including counseling) require significantly greater experience in the field for individuals who did not graduate from accredited programs but who are seeking certification. Finally, states have a legal process of *licensing* or *certifying* members of certain professions. Licensure generally provides those practitioners with the exclusive right to engage in certain activities that constitute the practice of their profession, whereas certification laws only provide those certified with the exclusive right to call themselves by the name of the profession. All licensure or certification laws incorporate the standards set by the profession. Professional certification, program accreditation, and legal licensure or certification all are intended for one principal purpose: to notify the public as to who is qualified to practice a given profession. Thus, these processes are intended to protect those seeking professional help from charlatans. Coincidentally, some professions have been accused of using these credentialing processes to limit the supply of qualified practitioners, in order to keep the incomes of those within the profession high. This accusation has, however, frequently come from those excluded from the field and has lost even more of its credibility as economic and population shifts have produced surpluses of professionals in the very professions most often accused of using this tactic to control their numbers.

Professional Certification

Within the field of mental health counseling, two types of professional certification are available. The National Board for Certified Counselors, established by the American Association for Counseling and Development, offers a certification procedure for all counselors, including those in mental health. This procedure leads to the designation of National Certified Counselor (NCC). The procedure involves a review of academic credentials and of references by already qualified professionals and the passing of an examination covering the areas of: (a) human growth and development; (b) social and cultural foundations of counseling; (c) the helping relationship (counseling and consultation theory and practices); (d) group dynamics, processes, and counseling; (e) lifestyles and career development; (f) appraisal of individuals; (g) research and evaluation; and (h) professional orientation (ethics, roles, practices). Graduates of programs accredited by the Council for Accreditation of Counseling and Related Educational Programs (CACREP, to be discussed later under accreditation) may take the examination immediately upon graduation. Others with graduate degrees in counseling from nonaccredited programs must have 2 years of supervised professional counseling experience following their degree in order to be qualified to sit for the examination. Moreover, their academic program must have included a course in counseling theory, a supervised counseling practicum, and courses in at least six of the eight areas covered on the examination. Although the NCC certification process certifies an individual as having the knowledge and experience required of a professional counselor, it does not distinguish among types of counselors (mental health counselors, school counselors, career counselors, etc.)

The American Mental Health Counselors Association, a division of the American Association for Counseling and Development, established the National Academy of Certified Clinical Mental Health Counselors (CCMHC) to individuals who meet its educational and experience requirements, pass its written examination and work sample, and receive recommendations from fellow professionals (colleagues and/or supervisors). The minimum educational requirements for the CCMHC are somewhat higher than those for the NCC, a 45-credit master's degree as opposed to a master's degree of unspecified length (and hence possibly as low as 30 credits). The experiential requirements for the CCMHC are considerably more extensive than for the NCC. The CCMHC requires at least 3,000 hours of post-master's supervised clinical work spread over at least 2 years and at least 100 hours of documented, face-to-face supervision, preferably by a CCMHC, over this period. If the applicant's master's degree program included a 1-year long, 1,000 hour supervised internship, that may be substituted for 1 year of the required 2 years of post-master's experience. Both CCMHC and NCC requirements recognize CACREP-approved programs (which must be at least 48 credits in length; see the section on academic program accreditation), but post-master's experience is waived for graduates of CACREP-approved programs only in the case of the NCC. (Graduates of CACREP-approved programs would, of course, qualify for the 1 year substitution if their program included a 1,000-hour internship; but this will not always be the case, because CACREP standards allow a shorter minimum internship.) The CCMHC process also requires the submission of a work sample (an audio tape-recorded interview with a client) and a self-evaluation of this sample. Thus, the CCMHC designation, which denotes specific certification as a mental health counselor, involves a more extensive set of requirements than does the general certification as a counselor (without specialty designation), which is represented by the NCC.

As is evident from the preceding discussion, the NCC and CCMHC certification processes have not been coordinated with each other. This, no doubt, results from the fact that the CCMHC specialty certification was developed before the NCC general certification came into being. In the case of career counseling, a specialty certification (Nationally Certified Career Counselor, NCCC) that was established following the foundation of the NCC, has recently been integrated with the NCC. Thus, a counselor now can attain the general NCC certification and, having demonstrated generic knowledge, can then gain certification within the specialty of career counseling. In that way, the specialty need not repeat the evaluation of general competence, but can focus completely on assessing the candidate's knowledge and skills in the specialty area. This process appears to be both logically and economically superior to that of the parallel but uncoordinated certification processes that now exist in mental health counseling. It is to be hoped that in the near future the two certifying bodies will be able to work out an arrangement similar to the one established with career counseling. In that case, the NCC would certify a general knowledge of the field of counseling, and those possessing this certification could then go on to attain the CCMHC as an indication of their specialized experience, knowledge, and skills in mental health counseling. This coordination should be facilitated by the fact that both certifying bodies eventually relate to the same parent organization, the American Association for Counseling and Development, and both have their offices in the association's headquarters building.

It should also be noted that once certified as an NCC or a CCMHC, the counselor must maintain this certification by taking continuing professional education and documenting the required number of hours of approved training to the certifying agency. This assures clients that certified counselors will remain up-to-date as to the knowledge base, techniques, and practices within their profession.

As of spring 1985, there were 13,970 counselors who held the NCC credential (NBCC News Notes, 1985), and 1,000 who held the CCMHC certification (Messina, 1985).

Finally, it should be noted that both certifying bodies periodically publish registers listing the names and addresses of those who have been certified, so that the public and third party payers can be aware of who is considered qualified by the profession. This practice is followed by most professional certifying groups.

Academic Program Accreditation

Established at the beginning of the 1980s under the auspices of the American Association for Counseling and Development, the Council for Accreditation of Counseling and Related Educational Programs (CACREP) is an independent body that accredits (that is, approves as meeting the standards set by the professions) counselor education programs in colleges and universities.

Currently, only master's degree level programs in school counseling, college student personnel, and mental health counseling in community and agency settings and doctoral programs in counselor education are evaluated for accreditation. To qualify for accreditation, an academic program must submit an extensive self-study (frequently running several hundred pages), documenting that it meets all of the standards of the accrediting body. Then, a team of site visitors comes to the campus to speak with program faculty, students, alumni, field supervisors, employers of graduates, and university administrators about their views of the program. The site visitors prepare a written report, to which the program may respond. Then, the self-study, the site visitors' report, and the program's response to that report are evaluated by the CACREP board. The board may vote to give full or provisional accreditation or to deny accreditation to the program. Full accreditation means that the program has substantially met all of the standards. Provisional accreditation means that the program has met most of the standards, including all major ones, and can be expected to meet the remaining ones within several years. Denial of accreditation means that the program has failed to meet one or more major standards and/or so many minor standards that it is improbable that it could remedy its deficiencies within several years.

Although there are a large number of explicit standards, some central ones are that a master's program must be at least 2 years (48 semester hours or 72 quarter hours) in length and include a supervised practicum and a supervised internship of specified length. The academic program must include courses in the eight core areas of human growth and development, social and cultural foundations of counseling, the helping relationship (counseling and consultation theory and practice), group dynamics and counseling, lifestyle and career development, appraisal of individuals, research and evaluation, and professional orientation (ethics and professional practices). Standards relating to faculty size, student–faculty ratios, admissions and student evaluation procedures, program resources and support staff, and so on, must also be met.

For specific accreditation in mental health counseling in community and agency settings, the program must also demonstrate that through the curriculum and field experiences, students become knowledgeable about: (a) clinical psychopathology and assessing mental status; (b) psychopharmacology and medications management; (c) history and philosophy and trends of mental health counseling; (d) training and curriculum in mental health; (e) mental health care and the community environment; (f) administration, supervision, and management in mental health services; (g) budget and finance in mental health care systems; (h) ethics, standards, and legal aspects of mental health counseling; (i) assessing mental health needs; (j) mental health program development and evaluation; (k) crisis intervention and emergency care; (l) quality assurance; (m) mental health consultation, education, and outreach; (n) utilization of community resources, information, and referral; (o) client advocacy and patients' rights; (p) case management, treatment planning, and information systems; (q) outpatient, inpatient, partial treatment, and aftercare services; and (r) mental health promotion and prevention. The program curriculum must include three courses specific to mental health counseling, as well as the eight core courses, and the fieldwork must be in mental health settings and supervised by mental health counselors or, if none are available, by their equivalents from other mental health professions, such as psychiatrists, clinical psychologists, master's degree–level psychiatric social workers, or master's degree–level psychiatric nurses.

As of July 1, 1985, there were 31 programs that had received full or provisional accreditation from CACREP and a number of others in various stages of review by CACREP (Wittmer, 1985). Many of these programs offered specialization in mental health counseling. Because many more programs will have completed the accreditation process by the time this book appears in print, it is pointless to give the list of those approved.*

Licensure and Legal Status

Licensure is the process by which a state enacts a law recognizing a profession's exclusive right to engage in certain activities ("licensure") or to use a certain name in designating qualified practitioners of the profession ("certification"). Thus, in a state with a licensing law, counselors are given exclusive rights, or rights along with certain other professions, to perform certain specified activities (for example, individual and group counseling, client appraisal, etc.). Anyone not licensed under a profession that is authorized to perform a particular activity, but who engages in that activity, is subject to prosecution by the state for practicing a profession without a license. It is generally the profession that defines what activities are within its domain, although in developing laws, legislatures must consider the claims of other groups to perform some of these activities. Similarly, the profession ordinarily provides the legislature with the standards for training and the appropriate methods of evaluating those seeking to become licensed under the law. Such laws set up licensing boards, consisting of both members of the profession and members of the public, to carry out the law. Licensing boards serve to admit or retain only those who meet the standards established by the law and to remove those with licensure who violate those standards. The aim of these boards is to protect the public, who are presumed to lack the specialized knowledge to be able to distinguish between qualified and unqualified practitioners on their own.

---

*For the most up-to-date listing of approved programs, one should write to: Dr. Joe Wittmer, Executive Director, Council for Accreditation of Counseling and Related Educational Programs, 1215 Norman Hall, University of Florida, Gainesville, Fl 32611.

Similarly, certification laws establish educational, experience, and examination criteria (generally as dictated by the profession). Those who qualify under these criteria may use a certain title (for example, professional mental health counselor) to designate their expertise to the public; and anyone not so qualified who uses that title is subject to legal prosecution for misrepresentation. The structure of the licensing boards in states with certification laws and in states with licensure laws are generally similar to each other.

Obviously, most professions prefer licensure to certification laws, because the former give the profession exclusive rights to engage in certain activities, and thus to control the accepted practice and the marketplace for those services. As more and more professions claiming overlapping expertise develop, it becomes harder to define exclusive domains of activity. For example, physicians and nurses, clergy, lawyers, clinical and counseling psychologists, social workers, and a wide variety of other occupations all do some counseling in the course of their work. Thus, it would be practically impossible to establish a law giving any one profession exclusive rights to engage in this activity. Consequently, many state legislatures prefer to pass certification laws than to get into the interprofessional territorial disputes that almost inevitably come up in seeking to define what activities should be exclusively reserved for a given profession.

As of the end of 1985, 16 states had passed some form of counselor licensure or certification law. These included: Alabama, Arkansas, Florida, Georgia, Idaho, Maryland, Mississippi, Missouri, Montana, North Carolina, Ohio, Oklahoma, South Carolina, Tennessee, Texas, and Virginia (Licensure tops, 1986). Most of the remaining states have counselor licensure or certification bills under development or at some stage of consideration by their legislature. Some of these laws specify mental health counselors; others do not distinguish among counseling specialties. It is up to the individual counselor to find out what the law is in the state in which he or she plans to practice.

It may be pointed out that the attainment of licensure laws is not an unmixed blessing for professionals, because it opens the practitioner to greater likelihood of suits for malpractice, now that a law exists defining what appropriate professional practice should be. Thus, court decisions have in part come to determine the counselor's obligations and duties. For example, in the case of *Tarasoff v. Regents of the University of California* (1976), the principle was established that if during a client's discussion with a counselor the client threatens to harm someone and the counselor determines (or the standards of the profession indicate) that there is a serious danger of violence to that person, then the counselor is obliged to use reasonable care to protect the intended victim from that danger. Generally, this is taken to mean warning the intended victim. This obligation, of course, places a limit on the confidentiality of the counselor–client relationship. It must, of course, be pointed out that the confidentiality of the counselor–client relationship (privileged communication) is only fully protected by law if specifically recognized within the laws of the state. Otherwise, it may become a debatable issue concerning which the counselor should seek advice from a lawyer (in the instance, for example, of a counselor who is called to testify in a law case involving a client, such as a child custody battle).

Other legal issues that affect counseling practice include informed consent (Did the counselor explain to the client what procedures and risks were entailed in all parts of the counseling process and get the client's agreement to participate?) and malpractice (Did the counselor deviate from accepted professional practice in a way that caused harm or injury to the client?). These are issues on which a counselor is most liable to be sued as a consequence of practicing the profession. For a comprehensive discussion of the legal issues relating to the practice of counseling, see Hopkins and Anderson (1985) or Van Hoose and Kottler (1985).

PROFESSIONAL ORGANIZATIONS

In 1976, the American Mental Health Counselors Association (AMHCA) was initiated as an independent organization. A year later, the membership voted by a close margin in favor of affiliating with the American Personnel and Guidance Association (subsequently renamed the American Association for Counseling and Development), and in 1978, AMHCA became a division of this larger counseling organization. The AMHCA originally claimed 1,500 members, but it has grown at an extremely rapid rate, surpassing older divisions until today it is the largest division within the American Association for Counseling and Development (AACD), reaching a membership of 9,669 in September 1985 (*AMHCA News*, 1985).

The AMHCA established the mental health counselor certification body, the National Academy of Certified Clinical Mental Health Counselors, discussed previously, and began publication of a professional journal, the *AMHCA Journal*, which will be discussed in the following section. In those ways, AMHCA has moved mental health counseling toward fulfilling the criteria for professional status by providing a professional organization, a certifying process, and a specialized professional literature (as well as a code of ethics, discussed earlier). Issues with which AMHCA concerns itself currently include: licensure laws for mental health counselors in those states that do not yet have them, obtaining third-party payment (for example, from health insurance plans) for services rendered by mental health counselors, defining private practice standards for mental health counselors, obtaining full parity for mental health counselors with other "core providers" of mental health services (psychiatrists, clinical psychologists, psychiatric social workers, and psychiatric nurses), and the treatment of special populations (for example, the elderly, the mentally retarded, etc.). The organization has also established a toll-free phone line for members to use in contacting the organization's central office, has developed a scholarship program for graduate students in mental health counseling, and has created a network of members to lobby their congressional delegations on issues relevant to mental health and mental health counseling, as well as employing several professional lobbyists on a part-time basis. Finally, AMHCA has contributed to its parent organization, the American Association for Counseling and Development (AACD), and participated in supporting the National Board for Certified Counselors, which AACD established as its professional credentialing body (Weikel, 1985).

Clearly, AMHCA has been a particularly active and effective professional organization. It deserves much of the credit for advancing the professionalization and public acceptance of mental health counseling. The current bylaws of the organization are printed in the January 1982 *AMHCA Journal*.

PROFESSIONAL LITERATURE

To quality as a profession, a field must have a body of literature and, usually, a unique journal or group of journals in which current findings and practices are reported to others within the profession. This literature documents the profession's having "knowledge of a specialized technique" (Gross, 1958, p. 78) and "systematic theory" (Greenwood, 1962, p. 207). In mental health counseling, the most immediately relevant journal is the *AMHCA Journal*. This journal has been published since 1979, with issues in January and July for the first four volumes (1979–1982) and quarterly (January, April, July, and October) since 1983 (Volume 5). In reviewing the contents of the first 13 issues (January 1979 to January 1984), Seligman and Weinstock (1984) found that the largest single category of articles dealt with counseling models and skills (18 articles), followed by articles on the future of the profession and credentialing (11 articles), counseling outcome criteria (9 articles), and marriage and family (8 articles). There were between one and four articles on each of the following topics: accountability, computer use in counseling, consultation, counseling adults, counseling men, counseling older adults, counseling women, counseling youth, counselor training programs, crisis counseling, and testing and assessment. The articles printed reflect the interests both of those within the profession who are engaged in scholarly work and of the journal editors, who decide which articles, among all that are submitted, will get published. As may have been seen from its content, the *AMHCA Journal* is oriented primarily toward the interests of practitioners in the field of mental health counseling. This is highly appropriate, given the membership and purposes of AMHCA.

Of almost equal importance to mental health counselors is the journal published by AMHCA's parent organization, the American Association for Counseling and Development. The *Journal of Counseling and Development* (formerly entitled the *Personnel and Guidance Journal*; and before that, *Occupations*) carries more theoretical articles and studies of interest to all counselors, regardless of specialty. Every member of AMHCA receives both of these journals by virtue of membership in AMHCA (which also requires being a member of its parent organization). Subscriptions to both these journals are available to nonmembers from the American Association for Counseling and Development, 5999 Stevenson Avenue, Alexandria, Virginia 22304.

Mental health counselors will also find articles of relevance to their field in the journals published by the other divisions of the American Association for Counseling and Development and several of the journals published by other mental health fields (see Table 3.1). Although the sources a mental health counselor would seek out would, of course, depend on the topic under investigation, mental health counselors will benefit from regularly perusing any and all of the journals in Table 3.1.

Surveys of journal articles published on a topic of interest may be carried out by using *Psychological Abstracts*, which is published by the American Psychological Association and is available at research libraries, or by purchasing a computerized search of the topic from any of several services, also generally available through research libraries. These sources provide the titles and reference citations, and frequently abstracts to all articles on a particular topic of interest that were published in journals indexed by the service. Usually, these journals account for most of what one would hope to find on a topic, although some important articles (for example, those in certain foreign or marginally related journals) may be missed by these searches.

In addition to journals, mental health counselors should keep up with books and other published sources of information of relevance to their profession. Many new publications are reviewed in the professional journals (such as the *Journal of Counseling and Development*). The American Association for Counseling and Development (address given previously) also publishes a catalog of books, films, and videotapes on counseling, which may be obtained from the organization. Finally, a good way to keep up with newly published books is to check *Books in Print*, which is available at any library or book store. By looking under the topics of "counseling," "mental health," and the other topics to which these two topics refer the reader, one can rapidly learn the authors, titles, publishers, and prices of new or unread books of relevance to mental health counseling.

EDUCATION OF PROFESSIONALS

Professions set expectations as to what sort of educational preparation those seeking to enter the profession should possess. Indeed, this is the first major step in inducting the candidate into the culture of the profession (Greenwood, 1962). As noted under the topic of accreditation, CACREP has established the

TABLE 3.1. Journals Containing Relevant Articles for Mental Health Counselors

JOURNAL CATEGORY	JOURNALS
Those published by other divisions of the American Association for Counseling and Development	*Counseling and Values* *Counselor Education and Supervision* *Elementary School Guidance & Counseling* *Journal for Specialists in Group Work* *Journal of College Student Personnel* *Journal of Employment Counseling* *Journal of Multicultural Counseling* *Journal of Offender Counseling* *Measurement and Evaluation in Counseling and Development* *Rehabilitation Counseling Bulletin* *The Journal of Humanistic Education and Development* *The School Counselor* *The Career Development Quarterly*
Specialized counseling journals published by other groups	*Behavioral Counseling Quarterly* *International Journal for the Advancement of Counseling*
Those published by the American Psychological Association or its divisions	*American Journal of Community Psychology* *Journal of Abnormal Psychology* *Journal of Consulting and Clinical Psychology* *Journal of Counseling Psychology* *Professional Psychology: Research and Practice* *Psychotherapy: Theory, Research, and Practice* *The Counseling Psychologist* *Psychology of Women Quarterly*
Journals published in the other mental health fields	*Administration in Mental Health* *American Journal of Family Therapy* *American Journal of Orthopsychiatry* *Behavioural Psychotherapy* *Community Mental Health Journal* *Crisis Intervention* *Family Therapy* *Hospital and Community Psychiatry* *International Journal of Family Therapy* *International Journal of Group Psychotherapy* *Journal of Community Psychology* *Journal of Health and Social Behavior* *Journal of Marital and Family Therapy* *Journal of Primary Prevention* *Journal of Psychosocial Nursing and Mental Health Services* *Mental Retardation* *Prevention in Human Services* *Psychosocial Rehabilitation Journal* *Schizophrenia Bulletin* *Social Work*

following criteria for master's degree (professional entry level) programs in mental health counseling in community and agency settings:

1. Must be at least 2 years (48 semester hours or 72 quarter hours) in length.
2. Must include a supervised practicum and internship of specified length in a mental health setting, preferably supervised by a mental health counselor.
3. Must include courses in: (a) human growth and development; (b) social and cultural foundations of counseling; (c) the helping relationship (counseling and consultation theory and practice); (d) group dynamics, processes, and counseling; (e) lifestyle and career development; (f) appraisal of individuals; (g) research and evaluation; (h) professional orientation (ethics and professional practices); (i) at least three courses specific to mental health counseling.
4. Must demonstrate that it prepares the graduate in: (a) clinical psychopathology and assessing mental status; (b) psychopharmacology and medications management; (c) history and philosophy and trends of mental health counseling; (d) training and curriculum in mental health; (e) mental health care and the community environment; (f) administration, supervision, and management in mental health services; (g) budget and finance in mental health care systems; (h) ethics, standards, and legal aspects of mental health counseling; (i) assessing mental health needs; (j) mental health program development and evaluation; (k) crisis intervention and emergency care; (l) quality assurance; (m) mental health consultation, education, and outreach; (n) utilization of community resources, information, and referral; (o) client advocacy and patient's rights; (p) case management, treatment planning, and information systems; (q) outpatient, inpatient, partial treatment, and aftercare services; (r) mental health promotion and prevention.

Needless to say, this represents an extremely demanding program and one that would be very difficult to cover within the minimum program length (48 semester hours or 72 quarter hours). It is therefore not surprising that a subgroup of counselor educators, the Committee on Community Counseling of the Association for Counselor Education and Supervision (another division of the American Association for Counseling and Development), recently concluded that within several years, the standard for professional preparation should be raised to 60 semester hours of course work and 1,000 hours of fieldwork (practicum plus internship) (Hayes, 1984). This group went on to suggest that education of community counselors should emphasize a particular approach and orientation (developmental, educative, aware of environmental effects, empowering and advocating for clients) first and foremost. Only then should the counseling student be taught to apply this approach to a particular client population (for example, mental health clients).

An interesting alternative approach to determining what should go into counselor education was taken by DeRidder, Stephens, English, and Watkins

(1983). Instead of starting from theoretical premises, these authors surveyed the directors of a wide range of agencies that employ mental health or related counseling graduates (aged, alcohol and drug, children and youth, community action, employment, mental health, mental retardation, probation, public health, public welfare, and vocational rehabilitation agencies). A total of 345 agency administrators, spread across these 11 types of agencies, ranked 13 skill areas that they wished new counselors they hired to possess. Skills were rated as essential [3], of possible value [2], or of little value [1]. Somewhat surprisingly, all agency directors across all settings agreed that four competencies from the list were essential. These were: (a) an understanding of human growth and development and of the barriers to learning and adjustment; (b) skills in individual, group, and family counseling across diverse socioeconomic and cultural groups for varied personal, educational, and career issues; (c) knowledge of ethics; and (d) ability to write clear, coherent, usable reports. All also agreed that statistics and research was the least essential skill from among those listed for the entry level counselor. Among the other eight skills on the list, the 21 mental health agency directors in the study rated all, on average, 2.5 or above except career development and job placement. The other skills rated an average of 2.5 or higher by the mental health agency directors included: knowledge of personality theory; knowledge of substance and child abuse; client assessment; group counseling; consulting; knowledge of and ability to use resources; and applying knowledge gained from supervised experiences (practicum and internship). It should be pointed out that with the exception of the four high and one low competences that all the respondents had in common, the other competences varied in ranking depending on the work setting of the respondents. Thus, career development and job placement, ranked next to last by the mental health agency directors, was ranked at the top by the samples of employment agency directors and of vocational rehabilitation agency directors. Through studies of this sort, counselor educators can determine what content to include and to emphasize in preparing counselors for work in various types of settings, such as mental health agencies. This assumes, of course, that the samples of agency directors polled were representative and that other factors, such as future directions in which the profession will probably move, are also taken into consideration.

Thus, we have reviewed several approaches to designing a curriculum for mental health counselors: one evolving from the theory that underlies that field, and the other based on the empirically determined expectations of the employers of graduates. It would be inappropriate to lose sight of either set of guidelines in developing a curriculum. A program that neglected the theoretical base of the field will produce technicians, rather than professionals. A program that, conversely, neglected practical considerations will produce sophisticated but unemployable graduates. Therefore, any appropriate curriculum must incorporate both theoretical and practical considerations.

Lewis and Lewis (1983) suggested a number of additional principles in training community counselors that are applicable to mental health counselor education. These include: training counselors to be open to working with paraprofessionals and volunteers; developing skills in needs assessment and in program development and evaluation; developing knowledge of the full range of service delivery systems; developing skills in working as a member of a team; having student counselors learn about social systems and the principles of social change; having students learn to be trainers, consultants, and mental health educators, as well as direct service providers; and having students examine how their values, attitudes, and goals affect their practice of their profession.

It should also be noted that the master's level professional entry programs we have been discussing are not the only educational route into the field. One may enter mental health counseling by way of a career ladder, starting with on-the-job and in-service training as an aide (high school graduate) and working up to paraprofessional status as a mental health technician through a 2- or 4-year undergraduate degree program. These career roles are discussed in chapter 14, Co-professionals and Co-helpers. For individuals who have accumulated experience moving up a career ladder, the formal education provided at the professional entry master's level should be different from that provided to career entrants with no prior work experience in the field. How the content should differ would depend on the nature and extent of the career ladder student's prior experience.

Among Lewis and Lewis's (1983) criticisms of current counselor education practices, they cogently observed that most academic programs train students for traditional, idealized roles as professionals. Therefore, graduates of these programs tend to lack the skills to adapt creatively to conditions in the ever changing "real world" of professional practice, and both the graduates and their supervisors are frustrated because actual day-to-day professional practice does not match the idealized picture the graduates were taught to expect during their academic program. A number of counselor educators and supervisors see these inappropriate aspects of training as contributing to the phenomenon of "burnout" among counselors. It is to be hoped that the increased fieldwork requirement that has been mandated for professional entry programs by the CACREP standards will help resolve this concern by allowing more reality-testing of the actual practice of counseling before the novice counselor enters the role of practitioner. On this point, it is of interest that in DeRidder et al.'s (1983) study of counseling agency directors' ranking of desired competencies for entry level counselors, discussed earlier, the mental health agency directors sample ranked applying knowledge gained from practicum and internship–supervised experience as the most essential competency among the eight, which varied from setting to setting. This item was ranked an average of 3.0 on a 3-point scale by the mental health agency directors, as high as the items that were universally agreed upon as essential. Feedback from graduates of the authors' professional preparation programs is also consistent with these trends, because former students consistently rank the fieldwork segments of their graduate education as most helpful in teaching them the applied skills they are called upon to use in their work as counselors. Counselor educators can console themselves with the fact that without prior didactic coursework, students would be unable to function in or benefit from fieldwork experiences.

It should be pointed out, in the context of this discussion of professional education, that mental health counseling is an emerging profession. As such, most of those now working in the field were not trained in programs designed specifically to teach the principles and practices of the profession as it is currently evolving. Therefore, the expectations of the profession that mental health counselors must engage in continuing professional education in order to maintain their certification are extremely important. At this time, NCCs are required to document 100 clock hours of approved continuing education every 5 years, and CCMHCs are required to meet a similar standard for certification maintenance. These continuing education experiences provide an opportunity for practicing professionals to gain skills in coordination of community and environmental resources, program development and evaluation, mental health education, needs assessment, client advocacy, and some of the other roles and functions that have been introduced into the field of mental health counseling as it has developed. Moreover, mental health counselors must keep up-to-date on developments in such long-recognized topics as psychotropic medications, least restrictive environments, new techniques of counseling and consultation, and methods of client appraisal.

ASSESSMENT: IS MENTAL HEALTH COUNSELING A PROFESSION?

At the beginning of this chapter we presented the criteria developed by several sociologists (Greenwood, 1962; Gross, 1958) to assess whether an occupation qualified to claim the status of a profession. These criteria included: (a) a specialized body of knowledge, (b) systematic theory, (c) a special relationship between practitioner and client, (d) that the professional activity requires that each client be treated differently from all others in the application of professional services and principles, (e) societal approval, (f) standards for admitting and for policing practitioners, (g) a code of ethics, and (h) professional organizations and other similar indicia of a professional "culture" to which members of the profession are expected to conform.

It is the judgment of the authors that although no profession fully meets all of these criteria, mental health counseling has sufficiently fulfilled each of these criteria to justify its claim to professional status. The greater part of this book has been devoted to presenting the position of the field of mental health counseling on criteria (a) through (d). Clearly, mental health counseling has a body of knowledge and systematic theory, and a body of literature in which these are documented. The counselor–client relationship is special, in that it is only operational if trust is present. No mental health counselor can treat any two clients the same, because each client's constellation of personality and problems is different from every other client's. Counseling only works if it is individualized (a virtue in qualifying for professional status, but a nuisance in carrying out research and evaluation studies). Mental health counseling is gaining societal approval (criterion [e]), as evidenced by more and more states adopting counselor licensure laws and by efforts in Congress to include mental health counseling as a mental health "core provider" profession. With the procedures for certifying and certification maintenance for mental health counselors (NCC and CCMHC) and for accrediting academic preparation programs for mental health counselors (CACREP) now in operation, criterion (f) appears to be met. Mental health counseling has a code of ethics, presented in its entirety in the appendix to this chapter, and professional organizations (the American Mental Health Counselors Association and its parent body, the American Association for Counseling and Development), thus addressing criteria (g) and (h).

Based on this analysis, we may conclude that mental health counseling has achieved the status of a profession.

REFERENCES

American Psychological Association. (1977). *Standards for providers of psychological services.* Washington, DC: Author.

AMHCA News. (1985). 9(1), 2.

By-laws of the American Mental Health Counselors Association. (1982, January). *AMHCA Journal, 4,* 41–48.

DeRidder, L. M., Stephens, T. A., English, J. T., & Watkins, C. E., Jr. (1983). The development of graduate programs in community counseling: One approach. *AMHCA Journal, 5,* 61–68.

Greenwood, E. (1962). Attributes of a profession. In S. Nosow & W. H. Form (Eds.), *Man, work, and society* (pp. 206–218). New York: Basic Books.

Gross, E. (1958). *Work and society.* New York: Crowell.

Hayes, R. L. (1984, March). Report on community counseling. *ACES Newsletter, 44*(3), 15.

Hopkins, B. R., & Anderson, B. S. (1985). *The counselor and the law* (2nd ed.). Alexandria, VA: American Association for Counseling and Development.

Lewis, J. A., & Lewis, M. D. (1983). *Community counseling: A human services approach* (2nd Ed.). New York: Wiley.

Licensure tops counseling advances. (1986, January 9). *AACD Guidepost, 28*(10), 11.

Messina, J. J. (1979). Why establish a certification system for professional counselors? A rationale. *AMHCA Journal, 1,* 9–22.

Messina, J. L. (1985). The National Academy of Certified Clinical Mental Health Counselors: Creating a new professional identity. *Journal of Counseling and Development, 63,* 607–608.

National Academy of Certified Clinical Mental Health Counselors. (1985). *Application instructions and information.* Alexandria, VA: Author.

National Board for Certified Counselors. (1983). *Certification Application* packet. Falls Church, VA: Author.

National Rehabilitation Counseling Association. (1972). *Code of ethics for rehabilitation counselors.* Washington, DC: Author.

NBCC News Notes. (1985, Spring). *2*(2).

Seligman, L., & Weinstock, L. D. (1984). The *AMHCA Journal*: A review of the last 5 years and future possibilities. *AMHCA Journal, 6,* 106–113.

Standards for providers of psychological services. (1974). Washington, DC: American Psychological Association.

Tarasoff v. Regents of the University of California, 17 Cal. 3rd 425, 551 P. 2d. 334, 131 Cal. Rptr. 14 (1976).

Van Hoose, W. H., & Kottler, J. A. (1985). *Ethical and legal issues in counseling and psychotherapy: A comprehensive guide* (2nd ed.). San Francisco: Jossey-Bass.

Weikel, W. J. (1985). The American Mental Health Counselors Association. *Journal of Counseling and Development, 63,* 457–460.

Wittmer, J. (1985, Fall). CACREP accreditation: An update. *ACES Access,* 16–17.

APPENDIX: CODE OF ETHICS FOR MENTAL HEALTH COUNSELORS*

Preamble

Mental health counselors believe in the dignity and worth of the individual. They are committed to increasing knowledge of human behavior and understanding of themselves and others. While pursuing these endeavors, they make every reasonable effort to protect the welfare of those who seek their services or of any subject that may be the object of study. They use their skills only for purposes consistent with these values and do not knowingly permit their misuse by others. While demanding for themselves freedom of inquiry and community, mental health counselors accept the responsibility this freedom confers: competence, objectivity in the application of skills and concern for the best interests of clients, colleagues, and society in general. In the pursuit of these ideals, mental health counselors subscribe to the following principles.

Principle 1. Responsibility

In their commitment to the understanding of human behavior, mental health counselors value objectivity and integrity, and in providing services

---

*This code is an adaptation of the code of the Board of Licensed Professional Counselors in Virginia and APGA Code of Ethics and is reprinted with permission of the American Mental Health Counselors Association.

they maintain the highest standards. They accept responsibility for the consequences of their work and make every effort to insure that their services are used appropriately.

(a) Mental health counselors accept ultimate responsibility for selecting appropriate areas for investigation and the methods relevant to minimize the possibility that their finding will be misleading. They provide thorough discussion of the limitations of their data and alternative hypotheses, especially where their work touches on social policy or might be misconstrued to the detriment of specific age, sex, ethnic, socioeconomic, or other social categories. In publishing reports of their work, they never discard observations that may modify the interpretation of results. Mental health counselors take credit only for the work they have actually done. In pursuing research, mental health counselors ascertain that their efforts will not lead to changes in individuals or organizations unless such changes are part of the agreement at the time of obtaining informed consent. Mental health counselors clarify in advance the expectations for sharing and utilizing research data. They avoid dual relationships that may limit objectivity, whether theoretical, political, or monetary, so that interference with data, subjects, and milieu is kept to a minimum.

(b) As employees of an institution or agency, mental health counselors have the responsibility of remaining alert to institutional pressures which may distort reports of counseling findings or use them in ways counter to the promotion of human welfare.

(c) When serving as members of governmental or other organizational bodies, mental health counselors remain accountable as individuals to the Code of Ethics of the American Mental Health Counselors Association (AMHCA).

(d) As teachers, mental health counselors recognize their primary obligation to help others acquire knowledge and skill. They maintain high standards of scholarship and objectivity by presenting counseling information fully and accurately, and by giving appropriate recognition to alternative viewpoints.

(e) As practitioners, mental health counselors know that they bear a heavy social responsibility because their recommendations and professional actions may alter the lives of others. They, therefore, remain fully cognizant of their impact and alert to personal, social, organizational, financial, or political situations or pressures that might lead to misuse of their influence.

(f) Mental health counselors provide reasonable and timely feedback to employees, trainees, supervisors, students, clients, and others whose work they may evaluate.

Principle 2. Competence

The maintenance of high standards of professional competence is a responsibility shared by all mental health counselors in the interest of the public and the profession as a whole. Mental health counselors recognize the boundaries of their competence and the limitations of their techniques and only provide services, use techniques, or offer opinions as professionals that meet recognized standards. Throughout their careers, mental health counselors maintain knowledge of professional information related to the services they render.

(a) Mental health counselors accurately represent their competence, education, training, and experience.

(b) As teachers, mental health counselors perform their duties based on careful preparation so that their instruction is accurate, up-to-date, and scholarly.

(c) Mental health counselors recognize the need for continuing training to prepare themselves to serve persons of all ages and cultural backgrounds. They are open to new procedures and sensitive to differences between groups of people and changes in expectations and values over time.

(d) Mental health counselors with the responsibility for decisions involving individuals or policies based on test results should know and understand literature relevant to the tests used and testing problems with which they deal.

(e) Mental health counselors/practitioners recognize that their effectiveness depends in part upon their ability to maintain sound interpersonal relations, that temporary or more enduring aberrations on their part may interfere with their abilities or distort their appraisals of others. Therefore, they refrain from undertaking any activity in which their personal problems are likely to lead to inadequate professional services or harm to a client, or, if they are already engaged in such activity when they become aware of their personal problems, they would seek competent professional assistance to determine whether they should suspend or terminate services to one or all of their clients

(f) The mental health counselor has a responsibility both to the individual who is served and to the institution with which the service is performed to maintain high standards of professional conduct. The mental health counselor strives to maintain the highest levels of professional services offered to the individuals to be served. The mental health counselor also strives to assist the agency, organization, or institution in providing the highest caliber of professional services. The acceptance of employment in an institution implies that the mental health counselor is in substantial agreement with the general policies and principles of the institution. If, despite concerted efforts, the member cannot reach agreement with the employer as to acceptable standards of conduct that allow for changes in institutional policy conducive to the positive growth and development of counselees, then terminating the affiliation should be seriously considered.

(g) Ethical behavior among professional associates, mental health counselors and nonmental health counselors, is expected at all times. When information is possessed that raises serious doubt as to the ethical behavior of professional colleagues, whether association members or not, the mental health counselor is obligated to take action to attempt to rectify such a condition. Such action shall utilize the institution's channels first and then utilize procedures established by the state, division, or the association.

(h) The mental health counselor is aware of the intimacy of the counseling relationship and maintains a healthy respect for the personhood of the client and avoids engaging in activities that seek to meet the mental health counselor's personal needs at the expense of the client. Through awareness of the negative impact of both racial and sexual stereotyping and discrimination, the member strives to ensure the individual rights and personal dignity of the client in the counseling relationship.

Principle 3. Moral and Legal Standards

Mental health counselors' moral, ethical, and legal standards of behavior are a personal matter to the same degree as they are for any other citizen, except as these may compromise the fulfillment of their professional responsibilities, or reduce the trust in counseling or counselors held by the general public. Regarding their own behavior, mental health counselors should be aware of the prevailing community standards and of the possible impact upon the quality of professional services provided by their conformance to or deviation from these standards. Mental health counselors should also be aware of the possible impact of their public behavior upon the ability of colleagues to perform their professional duties.

(a) To protect public confidence in the profession of counseling, mental health counselors will avoid public behavior that is clearly in violation of accepted moral and legal standards.

(b) To protect students, mental health counselors/teachers will be aware of the diverse backgrounds of students and, when dealing with topics that may give offense, will see that the material is treated objectively, that it is clearly relevant to the course, and that it is treated in a manner for which the student is prepared.

(c) Providers of counseling services conform to the statures relating to such services as established by their state and its regulating professional board(s).

(d) As employees, mental health counselors refuse to participate in employer's practices that are inconsistent with the moral and legal standards established by federal or state legislation regarding the treatment of employees or of the public. In particular and for example, mental health counselors will not condone practices that result in illegal or otherwise unjustifiable discrimination on the basis of race, sex, religion, or national origin in hiring, promotion, or training.

(e) In providing counseling services to clients, mental health counselors avoid any action that will violate or diminish the legal and civil rights of clients or of others who may be affected by the action.

(f) Sexual conduct, not limited to sexual intercourse, between mental health counselors and clients is specifically in violation of this code of ethics. This does not, however, prohibit the use of explicit instructional aids including films and videotapes. Such use is within accepted practices of trained and competent sex therapists.

Principle 4. Public Statements

Mental health counselors in their professional roles may be expected or required to make public statements providing counseling information, professional opinions, or supply information about the availability of counseling products and services. In making such statements, mental health counselors take full account of the limits and uncertainties of present counseling knowledge and techniques. They represent, as objectively as possible, their professional qualifications, affiliations, and functions, as well as those of the institutions or organizations with which the statements may be associated. All public statements, announcements of services, and promotional activities should serve the purpose of providing sufficient information to aid the consumer public in making informed judgments and choices on matters that concern it.

(a) When announcing professional services, mental health counselors limit the information to: name, highest relevant degree conferred, certification or licensure, address, telephone number, office hours, cost of services, and a brief explanation of the types of services offered but evaluative as to their quality of uniqueness. They will not contain testimonials by implication. They will not claim uniqueness of skill or methods beyond those acceptable and public scientific evidence.

(b) In announcing the availability of counseling services or products, mental health counselors will not display their affiliations with organizations or agencies in a manner that implies the sponsorship or certification of the organization or agency. They will not name their employer or professional associations unless the services are in fact to be provided by or under the responsible, direct supervision and continuing control of such organizations or agencies.

(c) Mental health counselors associated with the development or promotion of counseling devices, books, or other products offered for commercial sale will make every effort to insure that announcements and advertisements are presented in a professional and factually informative manner without unsupported claims of superiority, and must be supported by scientifically acceptable evidence or by willingness to aid and encourage independent professional scrutiny or scientific test.

(d) Mental health counselors engaged in radio, television, or other public media activities will not participate in commercial announcements recommending to the general public the purchase or use of any proprietary or single-source product or service.

(e) Mental health counselors who describe counseling or the service of professional counselors to the general public accept the obligation to present the material fairly and accurately, avoiding misrepresentation through sensationalism, exaggeration, or superficiality. Mental health counselors will be guided by the primary obligation to aid the public in forming their own informed judgments, opinions, and choices.

(f) As teachers, mental health counselors ensure their statements in catalogs and course outlines are accurate, particularly in terms of subject matter to be covered, bases for grading, and nature of classroom experiences.

(g) Mental health counselors accept the obligation to correct others who may represent their professional qualifications or associations with products or services in a manner incompatible with these guidelines.

Principle 5. Confidentiality

Mental health counselors have a primary obligation to safeguard information about individuals obtained in the course of teaching, practice, or research. Personal information is communicated to others only with the person's written consent or in those circumstances where there is clear and imminent danger to the client, to others, or to society. Disclosures of counseling information are restricted to what is necessary, relevant, and verifiable.

(a) All materials in the official record shall be shared with the client, who shall have the right to decide what information may be shared with anyone beyond the immediate provider of service and to be informed of the implications of the materials to be shared.

(b) The anonymity of clients served in public and other agencies is preserved, if at all possible, by withholding names and personal identifying data. If external conditions require reporting such information, the client shall be so informed.

(c) Information received in confidence by one agency or person shall not be forwarded to another person or agency without the client's written permission.

(d) Service providers have a responsibility to insure the accuracy and to indicate the validity of data shared with their parties.

(e) Case reports presented in classes, professional meetings, or in publications shall be so disguised that no identification is possible unless the client or responsible authority has read the report and agreed in writing to its presentation or publication.

(f) Counseling reports and records are maintained under conditions of security and provisions are made for their destruction when they have outlived their usefulness. Mental health counselors insure that privacy and confidentiality are maintained by all persons in the employ or volunteers, and community aides.

(g) Mental health counselors who ask that an individual reveal personal information in the course of interviewing, testing, or evaluation, or who allow such information to be divulged, do so only after making certain that the person or authorized representative is fully aware of the purposes of the interview, testing, or evaluation and of the ways in which the information will be used.

(h) Sessions with clients are taped or otherwise recorded only with their written permission or the written permission of a responsible guardian. Even with guardian written consent, one should not record a session against the expressed wishes of a client.

(i) Where a child or adolescent is the primary client, the interests of the minor shall be paramount.

(j) In work with families, the rights of each family member should be safeguarded. The provider of service also has the responsibility to discuss the contents of the record with the parent and/or child, as appropriate, and to keep separate those parts that should remain the property of each family member.

Principle 6. Welfare of the Consumer

Mental health counselors respect the integrity and protect the welfare of the people and groups with whom they work. When there is a conflict of interest between the client and the mental health counselors' employing institution, the mental health counselors clarify the nature and direction of their loyalties and responsibilities and keep all parties informed of their commitments. Mental health counselors fully inform consumers as to the purpose and nature of any evaluative, treatment, educational, or training procedure, and they freely acknowledge that clients, students, or subjects have freedom of choice with regard to participation.

(a) Mental health counselors are continually cognizant both of their own needs and of their inherently powerful position "vis-à-vis" clients, in order to avoid exploiting the client's trust and dependency. Mental health counselors make every effort to avoid dual relationships that might impair their professional judgment or increase the risk of client exploitation. Examples of such dual relationships include treating an employee or supervisor, treating a close friend or family relative, and sexual relationships with clients.

(b) Where mental health counselors' work with members of an organization goes beyond reasonable conditions of employment, mental health counselors recognize possible conflicts of interest that may arise. When such conflicts occur, mental health counselors clarify the nature of the conflict and inform all parties of the nature and directions of the loyalties and responsibilities involved.

(c) When acting as supervisors, trainers, or employers, mental health counselors accord recipients informed choice, confidentiality, and protection from physical and mental harm.

(d) Financial arrangements in professional practice are in accord with professional standards that safeguard the best interests of the client and that are clearly understood by the client in advance of billing. This may best be done by the use of a contract. Mental health counselors are responsible for assisting clients in finding needed services in those instances where payment of the usual fee would be a hardship. No commission or rebate or other form of remuneration may be given or received for referral of clients for professional services, whether by an individual or by an agency.

(e) Mental health counselors are responsible for making their services readily accessible to clients in a manner that facilitates the client's ability to make an informed choice when selecting a service provider. This responsibility includes a clear description of what the client may expect in the way of tests, reports, billing, therapeutic regime and schedules, and the use of the mental health counselor's Statement of Professional Disclosure.

(f) Mental health counselors who find that their services are not beneficial to the client have the responsibility to make this known to the responsible persons.

(g) Mental health counselors are accountable to the parties who refer and support counseling services and to the general public and are cognizant of the indirect or long-range effects of their intervention.

(h) The mental health counselor attempts to terminate a private service or consulting relationship when it is reasonably clear to the mental health counselor that the consumer is not benefiting from it. If a consumer is receiving services from another mental health professional, mental health counselors do not offer their services directly to the consumer without informing the professional persons already involved in order to avoid confusion and conflict for the consumer.

(i) The mental health counselor has the responsibility to screen prospective group participants, especially when the emphasis is on self-understanding and growth through self-disclosure. The member should maintain an awareness of the group participants' compatibility throughout the life of the group.

(j) The mental health counselor may choose to consult with any other professionally competent person about a client. In choosing a consultant, the mental health counselor should avoid placing the consultant in a conflict of interest situation that would preclude the consultant's being a proper party to the mental health counselor's efforts to help the clients.

(k) If the mental health counselor is unable to be of professional assistance to the client, the mental health counselor should avoid initiating the counseling relationship or the mental health counselor terminates the relationship. In either event, the member is obligated to suggest appropriate alternatives. (It is incumbent upon the mental health counselor to be knowledgeable about referral resources so that a satisfactory referral can be initiated.) In the event the client declines the suggested referral, the mental health counselor is not obligated to continue the relationship.

(l) When the mental health counselor has other relationships, particularly of an administrative, supervisory, and/or evaluative nature, with an individual seeking counseling services, the mental health counselor should not serve as the counselor but should refer the individual to another professional. Only in instances where such an alternative is unavailable and where the individual's situation definitely warrants counseling intervention should the mental health counselor enter into and/or maintain a counseling relationship. Dual relationships with clients that might impair the member's objectivity and professional judgment (such as with close friends or relatives, sexual intimacies with any client, etc.) must be avoided and/or the counseling relationship terminated through referral to another competent professional.

(m) All experimental methods of treatment must be clearly indicated to prospective recipients, and safety precautions are to be adhered to by the mental health counselor instituting treatment.

(n) When the member is engaged in short-term group treatment/training programs, for example, marathons and other encounter-type or growth groups, the member ensures that there is professional assistance available during and following the group experience.

Principle 7. Professional Relationship

Mental health counselors act with due regard to the needs and feelings of their colleagues in counseling and other professions. Mental health counselors respect the prerogatives and obligations of the institutions or organizations with which they are associated.

(a) Mental health counselors understand the areas of competence of related professions and make full use of other professional, technical, and administrative resources that best serve the interests of consumers. The absence of formal relationships with other professional workers does not relieve mental health counselors from the responsibility of securing for their clients the best possible professional service; indeed, this circumstance presents a challenge to the professional competence of mental health counselors, requiring special sensitivity to problems outside their areas of training, and foresight, diligence, and tact in obtaining the professional assistance needed by clients.

(b) Mental health counselors know and take into account the traditions and practices of other professional groups with which they work, and cooperate fully with members of such groups when research, services, and other functions are shared or in working for the benefit of public welfare.

(c) Mental health counselors strive to provide positive conditions for those they employ and they spell out clearly the conditions of such employment. They encourage their employees to engage in activities that facilitate their further professional development.

(d) Mental health counselors respect the viability, reputation, and the proprietary right of organizations they serve. Mental health counselors show due regard for the interest of their present or prospective employers. In those instances where they are critical of policies, they attempt to effect change by constructive action within the organization.

(e) In the pursuit of research, mental health counselors give sponsoring agencies, host institutions, and publication channels the same respect and opportunity for giving informed consent that they accord to individual research participants. They are aware of their obligation to future research workers and insure that host institutions are given feedback information and proper acknowledgment.

(f) Credit is assigned to those who have contributed to a publication, in proportion to their contribution.

(g) When a mental health counselor violates ethical standards, mental health counselors who know firsthand of such activities should, if possible, attempt to rectify the situation. Failing an informal solution, mental health counselors should bring such unethical activities to the attention of the appropriate state, and/or national committee on ethics and professional conduct. Only after all professional alternatives have been utilized will a mental health counselor begin legal action for resolution.

Principle 8. Utilization of Assessment Techniques

In the development, publication, and utilization of counseling assessment techniques, mental health counselors follow relevant standards. Individuals examined, or their legal guardians, have the right to know the results, the interpretations made, and where appropriate, the particulars on which final judgment was based. Test users should take precautions to protect test security but not at the expense of an individual's right to understand the basis for decisions that adversely affect that individual or that individual's dependents.

(a) The client has the right to have and the provider has the responsibility to give explanations of test results in language the client can understand.

(b) When a test is published or otherwise made available for operational use, it should be accompanied by a manual (or other published or readily available information) that makes every reasonable effort to describe fully the development of the test, the rationale, specifications followed in writing items analysis or other research. The test, manual, record forms, and other accompanying material should help users make correct interpretations of the test results and should warn against common misuses. The test manual should state explicitly the purposes and application for which the test is recommended and identify any special qualifications required to administer the test and to interpret it properly. Evidence of validity and reliability, along with other relevant research data, should be presented in support of any claims made.

(c) Norms presented in test manuals should refer to defined and clearly described populations. These populations should be the groups with whom users of the test will ordinarily wish to compare the persons tested. Test users should consider the possibility of bias in tests or in test items. When indicated, there should be an investigation of possible differences in validity for ethnic, sex, or other subsamples that can be identified when the test is given.

(d) Mental health counselors who have the responsibility for decisions about individuals or policies that are based on test results should have a thorough understanding of counseling or educational measurement and of validation and other test research.

(e) Mental health counselors should develop procedures for systematically eliminating from data files test score information that has, because of the lapse of time, become obsolete.

(f) Any individual or organization offering test scoring and interpretation services must be able to demonstrate that their programs are based on appropriate research to establish the validity of the programs and procedures used in arriving at interpretations. The public offering of an automated test interpretation service will be considered as a professional-to-professional consultation. In this the formal responsibility of the consultant is to the consultee but his/her ultimate and overriding responsibility is to the client.

(g) Counseling services for the purpose of diagnosis, treatment, or personalized advice are provided only in the context of a professional relationship, and are not given by means of public lectures or demonstrations, newspapers or magazine articles, radio or television programs, mail, or similar media. The preparation of personnel reports and recommendations based on test data secured solely by mail is unethical unless such appraisals are an integral part of a continuing client relationship with a company, as a result of which the consulting clinical mental health counselor has intimate knowledge of the client's personal situation and can be assured thereby that his or her written appraisals will be adequate to the purpose and will be properly interpreted by the client. These reports must not be embellished with such detailed analysis of the subject's personality traits as would be appropriate only for intensive interviews with the subjects.

Principle 9. Pursuit of Research Activities

The decision to undertake research should rest upon a considered judgment by the individual mental health counselor about how best to contribute to counseling and to human welfare. Mental health counselors carry out their investigations with respect for the people who participate and with concern for their dignity and welfare.

(a) In planning a study, the investigator has the personal responsibility to make a careful evaluation of its ethical acceptability, taking into account the following principles for research with human beings. To the extent that this appraisal, weighing scientific and humane values, suggests a deviation from any principle, the investigator incurs an increasingly serious obligation to seek ethical advice and to observe more stringent safeguards to protect the rights of the human research participants.

(b) Mental health counselors know and take into account the traditions and practices of other professional groups with members of such groups when research, services, and other functions are shared or in working for the benefit of public welfare.

(c) Ethical practice requires the investigator to inform the participant of all features of the research that reasonably might be expected to influence willingness to participate, and to explain all other aspects of the research about which the participant inquires. Failure to make full disclosure gives added emphasis to the investigator's abiding responsibility to protect the welfare and dignity of the research participants.

(d) Openness and honesty are essential characteristics of the relationship between investigator and research participant. When the methodological requirements of a study necessitate concealment or deception, the investigator is required to insure as soon as possible the participant's understanding of the reasons for this action and to restore the quality of the relationship with the investigator.

(e) In the pursuit of research, mental health counselors give sponsoring agencies, host institutions, and publication channels the same respect and opportunity for giving informed consent that they accord to individual research participants. They are aware of their obligation to future research workers and insure that host institutions are given feedback information and proper acknowledgment.

(f) Credit is assigned to those who have contributed to a publication, in proportion to their contribution.

(g) The ethical investigator protects participants from physical and mental discomfort, harm, and danger. If the risk of such consequences exists, the investigator is required to inform the participant of that fact, secure consent before proceeding, and take all possible measures to minimize distress. A research procedure may not be used if it is likely to cause serious and lasting harm to participants.

(h) After the data are collected, ethical practice requires the investigator to provide the participant with a full clarification of the nature of the study and to remove any misconceptions that may have arisen. Where scientific or humane values justify delaying or withholding information, the investigator acquires a special responsibility to assure that there are no damaging consequences for the participants.

(i) Where research procedures may result in undesirable consequences for the participant, the investigator has the responsibility to detect and remove or correct these consequences, including, where relevant, long-term aftereffects.

(j) Information obtained about the research participants during the course of an investigation is confidential. When the possibility exists that others may obtain access to such information, ethical research practice requires that the possibility, together with the plans for protecting confidentiality, be explained to the participants as a part of the procedure for obtaining informed consent.

Principle 10. Private Practice

(a) A mental health counselor, where permitted by legislation or judicial decision, should assist the profession in fulfilling its duty to make counseling services available in private settings.

(b) In advertising services as a private practitioner, the mental health counselor should advertise the services in such a manner so as to accurately inform the public as to services, expertise, profession, and techniques of counseling in a professional manner. A mental health counselor who assumes an executive leadership role in the organization shall not permit his/her name to be used in professional notices during periods when not actively engaged in the private practice of counseling. The mental health counselor may list the following: highest relevant degree, type and level of certification or license, type and/or description of services, and other relevant information. Such information should not contain false, inaccurate, misleading, partial, out-of-context, or deceptive material or statements.

(c) The mental health counselor may join in partnership/corporation with other mental health counselors and/or other professionals provided that each mental health counselor of the partnership or corporation makes clear the separate specialties by name in compliance with the regulations of the locality.

(d) A mental health counselor has an obligation to withdraw from a counseling relationship if it is believed that employment will result in the violation of the code of ethics, if their mental capacity or physical condition renders it difficult to carry out an effective professional relationship, or if the mental health counselor is discharged by the client because the counseling relationship is no longer productive for the client.

(e) A mental health counselor should adhere to and support the regulations for private practice of the locality where the services are offered.

(f) Mental health counselors are discouraged from deliberate attempts to utilize one's institutional affiliation to recruit clients for one's private practice. Mental health counselors are to refrain from offering their services in the private sector, when they are employed by an institution in which this is prohibited by stated policies reflecting conditions for employment.

(g) In establishing fees for professional counseling services, mental health counselors should consider the financial status of clients and locality. In the event that the established fee structure is inappropriate for a client, assistance should be provided in finding services of acceptable cost.

Principle 11. Consulting

(a) The mental health counselor acting as consultant must have a high degree of self-awareness of his or her own values, knowledge, skills, and needs in entering a helping relationship that involves human and/or organizational change and that the focus of the relationship be on the issues to be resolved and not on the person(s) presenting the problem.

(b) There should be understanding and agreement between the mental health counselor and client for the problem definition, change goals, and predicted consequences of interventions selected.

(c) The mental health counselor must be reasonably certain that she or he or the organization represented has the necessary competencies and resources for giving the kind of help that is needed now or may develop later and that appropriate referral resources are available to the consultant, if needed later.

(d) The mental health counselor relationship must be one in which client adaptability and growth toward self-direction are encouraged and cultivated. The mental health counselor must maintain this role consistently and not become a decision maker or substitute for the client.

(e) When announcing consultant availability for services, the mental health counselor conscientiously adheres to professional standards.

(f) The mental health counselor is expected to refuse a private fee or other remuneration for consultation with persons who are entitled to these services through the member's employing institution or agency. The policies of a particular agency may make explicit provisions for private practice with agency counselees by members of its staff. In such instances, the counselees must be apprised of other options open to them should they not seek private counseling services.

Principle 12. Client's Rights

The following apply to all consumers of mental health services, including both in- and outpatients in all state, county, local, and private care mental health facilities, as well as patients/clients of mental health practitioners in private practice.

The client has the right:

(a) to be treated with consideration and respect;

(b) to expect quality service provided by concerned, competent staff;

(c) to a clear statement of the purposes, goals, techniques, rules of procedure, and limitations as well as potential dangers of the services to be performed and all other information related to or likely to affect the ongoing counseling relationship;

(d) to obtain information about their case record and to have this information explained clearly and directly;

(e) to full, knowledgeable, and responsible participation in the ongoing treatment plan, to the maximum feasible extent;

(f) to expect complete confidentiality and that no information will be released without written consent;

(g) to see and discuss their charges and payment records; and

(h) to refuse any recommended services and be advised of the consequences of this action.

II THEORETICAL AND EMPIRICAL FOUNDATIONS

4   Persons and Their Problems

As was discussed in part I, mental health counseling seeks to assist clients—individuals, families, groups, organizations, or communities—to determine and to attain their optimal level of psychosocial functioning. Most mental health counselors spend the majority of their time working with individual clients on a one-to-one basis; and in the final analysis, each of the other categories of clientele is made up of individuals, as well. Therefore, it is appropriate to consider the individual first. In doing so, we will first survey a few of the conceptualizations of individual development over the life span that have been evolved by behavioral scientists. We shall then review some of the systems that have been used to categorize the problems of living that occur in the course of that development. Finally, we shall consider some of the goals of intervention that have been proposed for assisting individuals to deal with these problems of living. In general, it has been assumed that these problems represent natural or unusual occurrences in the course of development. Therefore, the way in which one conceptualizes individual development determines how one conceptualizes problems of living; and this, in turn, determines how one seeks to deal with those problems. For example, if one believes that over the course of their lives people move away from demonic possession and toward divine grace, then a problem of living must mean that one is still possessed by demons. The solution to the problem must then be to drive out the demons. If, on the other hand, one believes that people act the way they have learned to act, then problems of living must represent improper learning. In this case, the solution to the problem of living would be to teach the person how to act correctly in the problematic situation. If one accepted the view that demonic possession caused the problem, one would not conclude that teaching the person to act differently would be of any help in overcoming the problem. Thus, the counselor's views of the nature of development, of problems of living, and of how to resolve those problems are inevitably interrelated and must form a coherent system.

MODELS OF HUMAN DEVELOPMENT

In the behavioral and social sciences, innumerable models of human development have been created. Some models focus on just one stage of life, such as childhood (for example, the psychoanalytic theory of psychosexual development or Piaget's theory of cognitive development); adolescence (see Muuss, 1975, for a survey of these theories); or adulthood (for example, Levinson, Darrow, Klein, Levinson, & McKee, 1978). Some theories are based on the study of atypical individuals, such as Freud's evolution of psychoanalytic theory from his treatment of neurotic (primarily hysterical) patients. In the case of this and a number of other theories evolved by mental health professionals, the logical–deductive sequence just discussed was reversed. The theorist started with a treatment approach that seemed to work and from that, evolved a model of problems of living from which, in turn, a model of human development was derived. This process raises questions as to how generally applicable such theories are. Is a view of human development that is derived from the study of persons with problems the best basis upon which to proceed? Not if, as in the case of this book, one posits that healthy development can proceed once the client is enabled to cope with the problem of living. Therefore, we shall focus here on theories of human development that were derived from the study of essentially mentally healthy persons. We shall discuss four such theories (or models; the terms will be used interchangeably here, although there are some differences between them that are not of significance in this discussion; see Marx, 1976). Havighurst's (1972) compendium of developmental tasks and learning theory–based models are among the formulations of human development that have their roots in the learning/teaching domain. Erikson's (1963, 1968) theory of epigenetic stages and Maslow's (1954, 1962) hierarchy of needs are essentially psychodynamic theories, in that each assumes the existence of a built-in specific sequence of development, such that the completion of one event (stage or need satisfaction) inevitably brings into focus the next event in the posited series. Thus, whereas Havighurst and the learning theory–based models are based on the premise that one develops by learning appropriate and effective patterns of behavior, Erikson and Maslow posited that human beings possess a preprogrammed sequence of development in which each subsequent stage or level is triggered by the substantial completion of the prior one.

Havighurst's Compendium of Developmental Tasks

Havighurst (1972) believed that certain life skills are best taught at a particular time of life; and if that "teachable moment" is missed, it becomes much more difficult for an individual to learn that life skill. Therefore, as a guide for educators, Havighurst compiled a list of the tasks that, through his research, he believed were the major learnings for each stage of life. In that way, parents and/or teachers could teach each life skill at the teachable moment, rather than too early or too late. This list of life skills provides an excellent reference point for the mental health counselor to use in assessing a client's assets and age-appropriate competencies.

Havighurst's (1972) compendium of developmental tasks, by stage of life, is as follows: *

I   Infancy and early childhood
 1. Learning to walk
 2. Learning to take solid foods
 3. Learning to talk
 4. Learing to control the elimination of body wastes
 5. Learning sex differences and sexual modesty
 6. Forming concepts and learning language to describe social and physical reality
 7. Getting ready to read
 8. Learning to distinguish right and wrong and beginning to develop a conscience
II   Middle childhood (about ages 6-12)
 1. Learning physical skills necessary for ordinary games
 2. Building wholesome attitudes toward oneself as a growing organism
 3. Learning to get along with age-mates
 4. Learning an appropriate masculine or feminine social role
 5. Developing fundamental skills in reading, writing, and calculating
 6. Developing concepts necessary for everyday living
 7. Developing conscience, morality, and a scale of values
 8. Achieving personal independence
 9. Developing attitudes toward social groups and institutions
III Adolescence (about ages 12-18)
 1. Achieving new and more mature relations with age-mates of both sexes
 2. Achieving a masculine or feminine social role
 3. Accepting one's physique and using the body effectively
 4. Achieving emotional independence of parents and other adults
 5. Preparing for marriage and family life
 6. Preparing for an economic career
 7. Acquiring a set of values and an ethical system as a guide to behavior — developing an ideology
 8. Desiring and achieving socially responsible behavior
IV   Early adulthood (about ages 18-30)
 1. Selecting a mate
 2. Learning to live with a marriage partner
 3. Starting a family
 4. Rearing children

*Note. From *Developmental Tasks and Education* (3rd ed.) by Robert J. Havighurst, 1972, New York, David McKay Co. Copyright 1972 by Longman Inc. All rights reserved. Reprinted with permission.

    5. Managing a home
    6. Getting started in an occupation
    7. Taking on civic responsibility
    8. Finding a congenial social group
V   Middle age (about ages 30–60)
    1. Assisting teenage children to become responsible and happy adults
    2. Achieving adult social and civic responsibility
    3. Reaching and maintaining satisfactory performance in one's occupational career
    4. Developing adult leisure-time activities
    5. Relating to one's spouse as a person
    6. Accepting and adjusting to the physiological changes of middle age
    7. Adjusting to aging parents
VI   Later maturity
    1. Adjusting to decreasing physical strength and health
    2. Adjusting to retirement and reduced income
    3. Adjusting to death of spouse
    4. Establishing an explicit affiliation with one's age group
    5. Adopting and adapting social roles in a flexible way
    6. Establishing satisfactory physical living arrangements

By developing this list of age-related tasks, Havighurst has created a useful tool for the mental health counselor to use in assessing a client's skills (both assets and deficits) and level of functioning.

Learning Theory–Based Models

Unlike the other three theories of human development presented here, learning theory is not uniquely associated with a single theorist and does not present its conceptualization in terms of specific, necessarily sequential stages. We shall review two models that derive from learning theory, the basic premise of which is that all behavior (except possibly instinctive behaviors) is learned (i.e., comes to be repeated more or less frequently as a result of being positively or negatively rewarded) and hence can be modified by learning. We shall look briefly at two approaches from among the many that start from this premise: social learning theory and cognitive–behavioral theory. Although several writers, such as Rotter (1954) and Bandura and Walters (1963), are particularly associated with the term *social learning*, the concept evolved over an extended period, beginning with attempts in the early 1940s to reconceptualize Freud's ideas about personality development into the terms of learning theory. That is, these were early attempts to show that behavior patterns that Freud had concluded were innate were actually learned, shaped by the things one's parents and the broader society rewarded or punished. In essence, social learning theory posits that human behavior is learned (as does all learning theory), but it goes on to posit that complex social behaviors may be learned through such processes as imitation, modeling, or identification with the teacher of the behavior, rather than only through simple, direct, immediate reward or punishment for trying out a particular behavior (the classical learning theory position). Social learning theory also goes beyond classical learning theory in the social learning assertion that many behaviors are acquired but not exhibited until later. Reinforcement for a behavior may be self-reinforcement or vicarious (observing the consequences to others when they exhibit the behavior), rather than only the classically defined, externally administered kind.

Cognitive-behavioral approaches (e.g., Beck, 1976; Ellis, 1962) generally share most of the ideas and premises of social learning theory, but add a distinction between internal mental process (thoughts and emotions) and overt behaviors (actions). Thoughts, emotions, and actions interact. What people think affects how they feel and how they act; how they act affects their thoughts and feelings, and so on. In this view, people learn in all three domains as they develop over their lives. Problems of living occur when incorrect learning takes place in one or more of these three domains, which then may go on to affect behavior in the other two domains. These incorrect learnings may involve erroneous ideas, faulty associations, distorted perceptions, and so on, which may be remedied by having the client recognize the faulty learning and learn to replace it with an appropriate thought, feeling, or action. Both logical (getting the client to recognize the error) and behavioral (role playing, skill training, modeling, self-reinforcement, etc.) techniques may be used to correct the error.

Learning theory is of relevance to mental health counselors not only in offering one consistent explanation of a client's behavior (how it developed, became problematic, and can be changed), but also as a basis for helping a client to learn new skills, a topic that will be discussed in the next chapter.

Erikson's Epigenetic Stages

Erik H. Erikson (1963, 1968), an art teacher who underwent psychoanalytic training and became a psychotherapist, proposed that normal human development takes place in eight successive stages. Based on his studies of other cultures, he claimed that these eight stages are universally valid. Although the stages are typically age-related, each stage must be substantially accomplished in order for the individual to move on to the next stage. Each stage is concerned with the resolution of a particular issue, the positive outcome of these being: (1) trust, (2) autonomy, (3) initiative, (4) industry, (5) identity, (6) intimacy, (7) generativity, and (8) integrity. Thus, the infant must develop *trust* in its parents and its surroundings before it can take the risk to try to function autonomously. Once, however, it gains *autonomy* of functioning, the young child can feel secure enough of its self-control to be able to *initiate* actions affecting its environment. Having proved to itself that it can have an impact on its surroundings, the child learns the habits and skills (*industry*) necessary for survival as a productive member of its society, that is, how to have an effective, goal-directed impact on its environment. By adolescence, the individual has a clear enough picture of personal strengths and weaknesses to develop a particular social, sexual, and vocational *identity* by which one is uniquely recognizable to oneself and to other people. Having established a secure identity, the young adult can become intimately involved with a significant other (person, career, and/or cause) without fear of loss of selfhood. *Intimacy* generates products—children, artistic creations, ideas, business ventures, and so on—which must be nourished and developed through the years of middle adulthood (the period of *generativity*). Finally, as one moves toward the end of life, one should be able to look back over one's life as a whole and see it as a positive, *integrated,* fulfilled experience, thereby freeing one to face death (the final passage) with equanimity.

In this theory, a series of successive, age-related life stages are defined. As with Havighurst's system, the mental health counselor may use Erikson's model to suggest the skills and concerns a client typically could be expected to have at a particular time of life. Moreover, if a client is dealing with the issue of a stage that should have been resolved earlier in life, the counselor may infer at what point in life the client's problem began. Erikson has also defined the *unsuccessful* outcome that may occur at each stage; this may be used as an indicator of when the individual's problems of living arose. These negative outcomes for each stage are, respectively: (1) mistrust (failure to develop trust), (2) shame and doubt (failure to achieve autonomy), (3) guilt (failure to achieve initiative), (4) inferiority (failure to develop industry), (5) identity confusion (failure to form an identity), (6) isolation (inability to achieve intimacy), (7) stagnation (failure to attain generativity), (8) despair (lack of integrity).

Another point made by Erikson that is of importance to mental health counselors is that each culture develops institutions (such as rites of passage, role expectations, etc.) that serve to assist an individual to progress through the life stages. One example is the moratorium provided by the college years, which allows the late adolescent a relatively unpressured time in which to consolidate an identity. It is incumbent on the counselor to be aware of the particular institutions in the general culture and in the client's subculture that can support and facilitate the client's growth. The counselor should regularly utilize these institutions as sources of environmental support in working with the client.

Maslow's Need Hierarchy

Abraham Maslow (1954, 1962), based on his study of highly successful people, proposed that all people have a hierarchy of needs, such that each level of need must be substantially satisfied before the next level can be recognized and attended to. This hierarchy consists of the following, starting from the most basic level:

1. Physiological needs (food, shelter, clothing, etc.)
2. Safety needs
3. Needs for love and belonging
4. Need for esteem
5. Need for self-actualization
6. Need for cognitive understanding

For example, if one is starving (facing physiological need), one will take risks (not be driven by safety needs) in order to get food; and so on, up the hierarchy. As one moves up the hierarchy, one moves from survival needs to growth needs. Numbers 1 and 2 are clearly survival needs; numbers 5 and 6, clearly growth needs (Maslow, 1962). Most people never achieve the higher levels of the hierarchy because their needs at a lower level are never sufficiently met. Nonetheless, from the point of view of the mental health counselor, this model suggests a way of categorizing a client's problem, suggesting what has to be provided to resolve it, and predicting what needs will arise once that problem is solved (that is, once that level of need is met).

Hershenson (1982) has proposed a model that combines Erikson's stages and Maslow's levels into a single system of six sequential developmental trends: survival, growth, communication, recognition, mastery, and understanding. Survival encompasses Maslow's physiological and safety needs and Erikson's issue of trust. As its name implies, this trend concerns the biological, psychological, and social survival and continuity of the individual. Growth encompasses Maslow's point of shift from survival needs to needs involving growth and Erikson's issues of autonomy and initiative. Having survived, the individual can manifest the trend of growth—physically, emotionally, intellectually, and socially. It may be noted that writers in a wide range of fields, from biology to sociology, have attributed the trends of survival and growth to all organisms, from single-celled plants and animals to large human organizations and societies. Communication encompasses Maslow's needs for love and belonging and Erikson's issue of intimacy. The trend of communication entails the receiving and giving of love, closeness, and social interchange. Berelson and Steiner (1964, p. 65) stated, as one of the few scientifically verified findings concerning human behavioral development: "Normal adult human behavior develops only through the stimulation of other people." Recognition encompasses Maslow's need for esteem and Erikson's issue of identity. Recognition involves the acceptance by the person and by significant others of the person's individuality and worth. It involves self-respect and respect by and for others. Mastery encompasses Maslow's need for self-actualization and Erikson's issues of industry and generativity. Mastery involves the development of the ability to cope with one's environment in a competent, productive, and satisfying manner. Finally, understanding encompasses Maslow's need for cognitive understanding and Erikson's issue of integrity. This trend involves the development of a personally meaningful conception of one's world and of one's place within it. It may be noted that the first of these two trends (survival and growth) relate particularly to the person's self, the next two (communication and recognition) relate to interpersonal functioning, and the last two (mastery and understanding) relate to task performance. The mental health counselor may use this sequence of trends as a framework within which to place a client's level of development and consequently to conceptualize the client's problem of living. For example, a client may have a problem with mastery in an area of life because of never having satisfactorily achieved recognition for the unique set of talents and abilities that identify the client as a capable individual, worthy of respect (self-respect and by others).

We have briefly looked at four models of human development from among the many that exist. Two of these models have their roots primarily in learning theory, that is, in the assumption that behavior is learned, and therefore its development will depend on the individual's experiences. The other two models, either individually or as combined, assume that there is a preordained sequence of stages, levels, or trends through which the individual will move during the course of development. It is in the nature of any theory or model in any field of science to focus on only one aspect of the complexity of the real world, intentionally disregarding other aspects so that the object of study is reduced to a size that can be comprehended by the human mind (Marx, 1976). Therefore, one need not conclude that the two schools of thought represented by the four theories of development presented here are necessarily in conflict with each other. Rather, each school has focused on a different aspect so as to reduce the problem of describing human development to manageable proportions. We may, therefore, seek to reintegrate these models or to draw from each of them. For example, it may be argued that Maslow's needs, Erikson's issues, or Hershenson's trends are really learned, rather than innate behavior patterns. Likewise, it may be argued that learning is not the purely individualized process that strict learning theory posits, but necessarily follows certain patterns (stages? trends?) dictated by human biological capacities and cultural norms for different life stages. Explicitly or implicitly, each mental health counselor must develop a working theory of human development by which clients can be understood, their problems put into a context, and solutions to those problems suggested. Moreover, this theory must be flexible enough to allow the counselor to try other alternatives systematically, if the one first suggested by the theory does not work. Without such a framework, based on a model of human development, counseling becomes a haphazard activity, without validity or chance for improvement. The counselor must not, however, use the theory of human development as a procrustean bed, to which the client must be stretched or crushed, regardless of how well the theory really fits.

PROBLEMS OF LIVING: BASES FOR A DEFINITION

Problems of living imply aberrations and/or natural rough spots as one moves through the course of life-span development. The mental health disciplines have evolved a number of ways of conceptualizing and categorizing these problems. We shall deal first with the conceptual bases and then with systems for categorization. Some of these conceptual approaches are taxonomic, that is, concerned with identifying, describing, and classifying types of problems (just as biologists have classified species of plants or animals as a first step to understanding them). Other conceptual approaches are developmental, concerned not with the overt signs or symptoms of the problem but rather with identifying the issue in the course of development that provides the underlying cause of the problem. The advocates of the taxonomic approaches argue that unless one establishes a typology, any attempt to remedy problems of living will be like trying to bail out the ocean one drop at a time. Without categories, one cannot apply what one has learned from one's past successes or mistakes, and each new case must be approached in total ignorance about what will work. Conversely, the advocates of the developmental approaches argue that the same problematic behavior may have any of a large number of causes, and one must find and treat the cause (not the symptom) if the problem is to be resolved. Thus, in a medical analogy, one does not get rid of every fever by taking out a person's appendix. Behaviorally, psychosis and adolescent acting-out may underlie behaviors (symptoms) that appear indistinguishable from each other, but that does not mean that they require the same treatment.

Taxonomic Approaches

We shall now review some of the more common bases upon which systems of taxonomic classification of problems of living have been based and then offer some observations about developmental approaches to categorizing problems of living. Developmental approaches are necessarily tied to specific theories of development, that is, they represent the antithesis of what each of these theories posits to be the healthy course of development. For example, as noted earlier, Erikson defined failure for each of the eight stages through which, according to his model, the individual passes (mistrust as the failure to develop trust, shame and doubt as the failure to develop autonomy, and so on). Similarly, every other developmental theory suggests its own system for classifying and understanding problems of living, always based on failure to achieve some aspect of appropriate development, as defined by the theory. Taxonomic systems, however, are generally more independent of specific theories of human development. Frequently, they treat problems of living as a phenomenon in its own right, rather than as a by-product of some theory of development or of some approach to treatment. Most taxonomic approaches start from one or more of three bases for defining problems of living: (a) statistical deviance; (b) social disruption; or (c) subjective discomfort.

Statistical Deviance

Statistical deviance is the extent to which a particular behavior departs from the behavior of most people in general when faced with a similar situation. Behavioral scientists generally assume that most human characteristics, including behaviors, follow a normal distribution. That is, they tend to cluster around a most common (average) value; and the further one gets from that average, "normal" (i.e., the norm) value, the fewer the number of cases that will exist. For example, if the average height for adult men is 5'10", there will be many who are 5'9" or 5'11", fewer who are 5'6" or 6'2", and far fewer who are 4'10" or 6'10". Similarly, if most adults go out in public and maintain decorum (thus, "normal" behavior), then those who refuse ever to go out in public and those who go out but who shout threats or curses at strangers deviate from the statistical norm and are, therefore, considered to have a problem. One difficulty with this approach is in defining how far from the norm a behavior must be before it is considered problematic. This decision is largely influenced by cultural and subcultural expectations. For example, in some cultures hallucinations are seen as a sign of divine grace; whereas in others, they are seen as evidence of severe problems. Another difficulty with this approach to a definition is that sometimes the norm changes. Once one would have been considered to have a serious problem if he or she professed a belief that the earth was round; now the reverse is true, and those who assert that the earth is flat are viewed as problematic. A third difficulty is that, typically, the greater any departure is from the norm, the more it is assumed a priori to be problematic. The average or "normal" is, however, not necessarily the optimal state for a given characteristic. It may be that one extreme tail of the distribution of the characteristic is actually better, rather than worse than the norm (for example, intelligence). Thus, what was apparently a quantifiable, objective basis for defining problems of living is, in practical application, quite subjective.

Social Disruption

A second approach to defining problems of living is based on a criterion that, by its very nature, has even less potential for quantification or objectivity than statistical deviance. That criterion is social disruption. By this approach, a behavior is defined as a problem of living if it causes danger or annoyance to a significant number of others in the environment of the person who is exhibiting the behavior. Thus, inflicting physical harm, making threats, or standing on a street corner shouting at an invisible object are all classifiable as problems of living, albeit of progressively less public concern. The greater the public menace, the more problematic the behavior is generally perceived to be and the more immediate the pressure to remove the perpetrator or to force that person to change the offending behavior. This, however, is one problem with that approach, in that the most menacing behavior need not reflect the presence of the most serious problem within the client. Indeed, the reverse may be true, as in the withdrawal (no menace to anyone else) that frequently precedes a suicide. Another problem with this approach is the cultural relativity of definitions of what constitutes social disruption. Behaviors that appear totally acceptable to one age, ethnic, socioeconomic, or educational group may be seen as socially disruptive to another group living within the same society. Who determines whether a given behavior is defined as problematic? Usually, it is the group with the most power to enforce their standards. From the point of view of the mental health counselor, however, a problem arises in attempting to get a client to change a behavior from one that is accepted and sometimes reinforced in the client's own reference group (among whom the client may well spend the most time) to one that is approved by those who set the standards of what is socially acceptable. This conflict becomes even more intense when the dominant social group accepts the inevitability of certain behaviors it has designated as disruptive (and, hence, should be changed) and offers reinforcement for those who exhibit that behavior. Examples of this include use of addictive drugs, unwed parenthood, illegal immigration, chronic unemployment, and homelessness. These behaviors are publicly deplored by the arbiters of standards for the broader society; are widely accepted, prevalent practices within some subgroups of the society; and are supported by apparatus (for example, welfare services) set up by the very group that declared the behaviors disruptive in the first place. A dilemma arises for mental health counselors, who are frequently employed in agencies funded by those in power, that is, by those who decide which behaviors are disruptive and must be changed. It is difficult for mental health counselors to "bite the hand that feeds them" by pointing out to those in the power structure their role in creating (if only by designating the behavior as disruptive) and sustaining the very behaviors they have employed the mental health counselor to change. (For a recent, extensive discussion of the role of society in creating and defining problems of living for certain of its subgroups, see Cochrane, 1983.)

Subjective Discomfort

A third basis for defining behaviors (which includes thoughts and feelings, as well as overt actions) as problematic is subjective discomfort, that is, the degree to which they cause pain or distress to the person exhibiting the behavior. This would seem to be a reasonable basis for defining problems of living, comparable to using physical pain as a sign that one has a medical problem. There are, however, several inherent problems in using subjective distress as the defining characteristic of problems of living. One problem is that some persons (frequently labeled as "psychopaths" or "sociopaths") feel no discomfort or remorse for behaving in ways that are both statistically deviant and socially disruptive. If one uses only the criterion of subjective discomfort, these individuals (including some mass murderers) would have to be defined as problem-free. Another problem with this criterion is its subjectivity. People have different thresholds for discomfort. Therefore, is a behavior to be defined as problematic if only one individual out of a million finds that it causes personal distress? Also, how uncomfortable must a person be made by the behavior before it can be defined as causing "discomfort"? Because all perceptions are, by their very nature, subjective, it is inevitable that this basis for defining problematic behavior is a difficult one to apply consistently. This criterion is, however, of relevance to a particular counselor working with a particular client. If the client reports that a behavior causes subjective discomfort, it is clearly a problem for that client, even if no one else feels that way about that behavior.

We have briefly reviewed three widely used bases for defining problems of living: statistical deviance, social disruption, and subjective discomfort. Although each has some degree of validity, there are clearly limitations to applying any of these bases as the sole criterion for deciding if a behavior is problematic. A better (that is, more consistent, less open to exceptions) basis may be found in requiring that at least two of these criteria be met, that is, a behavior must be statistically deviant and socially disruptive, statistically deviant and cause subjective discomfort, or socially disruptive and cause subjective discomfort before it is to be considered problematic. This approach is not without its own limitations; for example, how much deviance, disruption, or discomfort is necessary to meet the combined criteria? Because there is no absolutely objective basis possible, the counselor must arrive at a definition that is both as objective as possible (that is, can be described to and applied by others) and fits best into the counselor's conceptual system of human development—problems of living—intervention.

Developmental Approaches

Developmental systems for defining problems of living start from the premise that such problems represent departures from "normal, healthy development," as defined by the particular theory of human development. For example, by Erikson's schema, failure to move from autonomy to initiative means that one is left with the problem of shame and doubt. One difficulty with this approach is that it assumes that everyone (including the client) necessarily moves directly from autonomy to initiative. In this view, no one can move from autonomy right to industry. There is some evidence that Erikson's sequence is not necessarily as universal as he claimed, but may be at least to some extent culture-bound (Hershenson, 1964). Another difficulty with this approach is the assumption that failure to achieve autonomy is the only cause of shame and doubt. Could not shame and doubt also result from failure to attain industry, identity, intimacy, or generativity? Thus, all developmental approaches are only as good as that group of persons to whom the theory of development actually applies; and it is not always possible for the mental health counselor to determine immediately whether the client belongs to that group. Also, many of the links between developmental processes and specific problems of living are tenuous, at best. Therefore, it may be hazardous for the counselor to base the treatment plan on these assumptions. On the other hand, the theoretical models of development/problems that are used most commonly by mental health professions are those that were derived from clinical practice (such as psychoanalytic or client-centered approaches). Because such approaches create a logically circular process (practice X is used to generate theory Y, which is then used to justify practice X), they are of little use to the scientifically oriented mental health counselor.

Hence, the counselor is faced with a serious dilemma. The counselor needs a system for categorizing clients' problems, so that they can be approached systematically. Without such a system, the counselor can only flail about, treating each new problem of each client as a unique, random event. In that case, the counselor forfeits any claim to systematic knowledge or professional expertise. On the other hand, existing theories of human development and approaches to classifying problems of living are neither universally applicable nor totally valid. Therefore, the most effective and efficient solution to this dilemma may be for the counselor to use the concept of "failure to cope," with the reasons for that failure specified. As long as these reasons can be reliably given and suggest an appropriate intervention, this rather simplistic approach may well be the best alternative of any of the currently available bases for defining problems of living.

PROBLEMS OF LIVING: SYSTEMS OF CATEGORIZATION

The system of categorization most widely used in the United States is the *Diagnostic and Statistical Manual of Mental Disorders* put out by the American Psychiatric Association (1980). This manual, now in its third edition, is popularly known as *DSM-III*. Medicine, as a field of applied biology, has always approached problems with the belief that they had to be described and classified as a first step to the understanding and, eventually, treatment of them. Considerable support for this approach may be derived from the progress medicine has made using it in the realm of organic disease. When, however, one attempts to apply this approach to problems of living (in medical terms, mental illness), one runs into severe difficulties because of the issues of multicausality (more than one cause for the same symptom) and of individual differences in the way that any single cause is expressed. One cannot arrive at the neat generalizations possible in biological medicine, for example, that fever usually is symptomatic of infection. In the behavioral realm, for example, hallucinations may result from any of a number of causes, including organic brain damage, certain drugs, psychosis, adolescent turmoil, lack of food or sleep, sensory deprivation, and so on. Nonetheless, since the time of the ancient Greek physician Hippocrates, physicians have tried to categorize "mental illnesses" as a basis for treating them, and those who follow the medical model have found these systems of categorization useful (or at least comforting to have available). It may, moreover, be noted that even if a mental health counselor does not accept the premises of the medical model, it is still useful to be familiar with the *DSM-III* system, because many insurance forms used by third-party payers require that a diagnosis be submitted in terms of *DSM-III* categories.

Webb, Di Clemente, Johnstone, Sanders, and Perley (1981) have published a training manual for using the *DSM-III*, which was itself published in 1980. *DSM-I* was published in 1952; and *DSM-II* in 1968. *DSM-III* is significantly different from the earlier editions in that it redefines major conditions based on research findings; adds new categories, more explicit diagnostic criteria, and a formal definition of "mental disorder"; and presents a multiaxial system for classification. Five axes of this system involve: (a) clinical syndromes and additional codes, (b) personality disorders and specific developmental disorders, (c) physical disorders and conditions, (d) psychosocial stressors, and (e) highest level of adaptive functioning in the past year (Webb et al., 1981). There are 16 groups of conditions that comprise the first axis, including: (a) disorders usually first evident in infancy, childhood, or adolescence; (b) substance use disorders; (c) organic mental disorders; (d) schizophrenic disorders; (e) psychotic disorders not elsewhere classified; (f) paranoid disorders; (g) affective disorders; (h) anxiety disorders; (i) dissociative disorders; (j) somatoform disorders (involuntary physical symptoms with no organic basis); (k) factitious disorders (voluntarily controllable physical symptoms with no organic basis); (l) psychosexual disorders; (m) disorders of impulse control not elsewhere classified; (n) adjustment disorders; (o) psychological factors affecting physical conditions; and (p) codes for conditions not attributable to a mental disorder. These, along with the two groups on the second axis, comprise the 18 categories of psychiatric diagnosis defined by *DSM-III*. Thus, an attempt has been made to develop a classification system that can be more accurately applied, universally accepted, and clinically relevant than was the case with the earlier editions of *DSM*.

One serious problem with the earlier editions of *DSM* was that psychiatrists and others who used it showed relatively poor agreement in classifying patients. Zigler and Phillips (1961) found identical symptoms in cases placed in different diagnostic categories and low correlations between individual symptoms and diagnostic decisions made. Although there is reason to hope that the revised approach used in *DSM-III* will improve the reliability of diagnoses made according to this system, there is no reason to expect that these changes will have eliminated the subjective factors that render this system less than sufficiently reliable to meet scientific standards.

Another interesting approach to categorizing the problems for which clients seek counseling was proposed by Celotta and Teglasi-Golubcow (1982). They suggested that problems can be categorized as being on one of five levels:

Level 1 — General expectation problems (the client sees self as the passive victim of a hostile environment).

Level 2 — General cognition problems (the client is making broad maladaptive statements about self or others, on a conscious or an unconscious level).

Level 3 — Specific cognition problems (the client is conflicted by ideas, attitudes, or beliefs that seem to affect the problem with which the client is trying to cope).

Level 4 — Information problems (the client lacks necessary information or facts).

Level 5 — Behavioral problems (lack or excess of some type of behavior).

As one moves up the hierarchy from Level 5 to Level 1, the problems: (a) increase in the general distress they cause the client, (b) have a longer history over the client's life, (c) affect more roles in the client's life (worker, student, friend, family member, etc.), (d) appear as more disturbed interpersonal behavior, and (e) will be less accessible to the client's awareness. The authors further suggested that different interventions may be appropriate for different levels, although this aspect of the model had yet to be validated.

A third approach of interest to the mental health counselor is that adopted by Holmes and Rahe (1967), who have obtained average rankings from approximately 400 people of how stressful 43 events in a person's life are perceived to be. Thus, counselors can be aware of the probable impact of certain events on their client or on those who might, as a consequence of the stress caused by these events, become their clients (Bloom, 1985). The events they rated, in descending order of stressfulness, are given in Table 4.1. Obviously, for any given individual, the order and relative magnitude of stressfulness of these events will vary; and Leong, Tseng, and Wu (1985) have shown that the order of stressfulness varies systematically across different cultures and even across different regions within a single country. Nonetheless, the list of events and the rankings generated by Holmes and Rahe are of value to counselors.

Prevalence and Incidence

Related to the question of classification is that of frequency of occurrence of a given problem. In public health terms, this breaks down into two factors: prevalence and incidence. Prevalence refers to the number of cases of a given condition found to be existing in the general population or a sample of that

TABLE 4.1. Stressfulness of Life Events

RANK	LIFE EVENT	MEAN VALUE
1	Death of spouse	100
2	Divorce	73
3	Marital separation	65
4	Jail term	63
5	Death of close family member	63
6	Personal injury or illness	53
7	Marriage	50
8	Fired at work	47
9	Marital reconciliation	45
10	Retirement	45
11	Change in health of family member	44
12	Pregnancy	40
13	Sex difficulties	39
14	Gain of new family member	39
15	Business readjustment	39
16	Change in financial state	38
17	Death of close friend	37
18	Change to different line of work	36
19	Change in number of arguments with spouse	35
20	Mortgage over $10,000	31
21	Foreclosure of mortgage or loan	30
22	Change in responsibilities at work	29
23	Son or daughter leaving home	29
24	Trouble with in-laws	29
25	Outstanding personal achievement	28
26	Wife begin or stop work	26
27	Begin or end school	26
28	Change in living conditions	25
29	Revision of personal habits	24
30	Trouble with boss	23
31	Change in work hours or conditions	20
32	Change in residence	20
33	Change in schools	20
34	Change in recreation	19
35	Change in church activities	19
36	Change in social activities	18
37	Mortgage or loan less than $10,000	17
38	Change in sleeping habits	16
39	Change in number of family get-togethers	15
40	Change in eating habits	15
41	Vacation	13
42	Christmas	12
43	Minor violations of the law	11

Note. From "The Social Readjustment Rating Scale," by T. H. Holmes and R. H. Rahe, 1967, *Journal of Psychosomatic Research, 11*, p. 216. Copyright 1967 by Pergamon Press Ltd. Reprinted with permission.

population. Incidence refers to new cases of a condition that come into being within a certain time frame. Prevalence is measured in terms of number of cases per hundred or per thousand persons, whereas incidence indicates number of new cases that develop within a specified population within a given time span. In a landmark study of the prevalence of mental health problems,

Srole, Langner, Michael, Opler, and Rennie (1962) surveyed a random sample of more than 1,600 residents of a section of Manhattan in New York City during the mid-1950s, asking them to report all past and present physical and mental conditions and the degree to which any resultant symptoms interfered with their lives. Based on their self-reports, less than a quarter of the sample was judged to be "well" and almost 20% was judged to be psychologically "incapacitated." These results were shocking to many, including a large number of professionals, who had been estimating the prevalence of mental health problems as being much lower.

Within the overall issues of prevalence and incidence, the mental health counselor should be aware of the factors that have been shown to relate to the presence or frequency of certain mental health problems. These factors include socioeconomic status, sex, age, race, ethnicity, and urban-versus-rural community. In a famous study, Hollingshead and Redlich (1958) demonstrated that psychiatric diagnosis in the New Haven, Connecticut area was related to social class, in that those of higher class status were more frequently diagnosed as neurotic, whereas those belonging to lower socioeconomic classes were more frequently diagnosed as psychotic. This phenomenon may reflect class differences in behavior patterns, including patterns of problematic behavior; or it may reflect the economics of treatment, in that psychiatrists could collect fees from upper class outpatients and hence gave them diagnoses that kept them out of the hospital, but could only get paid for treating lower class patients who were hospitalized, and so gave them diagnoses that would allow them to be hospitalized. Race, ethnicity, and urban–rural differences are often confounded with socioeconomic class, although Murphy, Wittkower, Fried, and Ellenberger (1963) showed ethnic, religious, social and urban–rural differences in the frequency with which particular symptoms were exhibited by schizophrenics in different cultures, in some cases apparently regardless of socioeconomic class. Age has been related to type and distribution of mental health problems in several ways, including (a) the biologically based senile degenerative conditions associated with aging, such as Alzheimer's disease, and (b) frequent reports of a higher incidence of certain mental problems among older persons. For example, Butler and Lewis (1983) cited studies indicating that the incidence rate for psychoses among those age 75 and over is double that of 35- to 44-year-olds and five times that of 15- to 24-year-olds. Obviously, likewise, adolescent turmoil is a phenomenon of the adolescent years. Finally, some mental health problems have been associated with traditional sex-role differences within the culture. For example, hysteria is more common in women (so much so that the name *hysteria* itself derives from the classical Greek word for womb), probably reflecting sex-role behaviors that were traditionally expected of women (emotionality, irrationality, seductiveness).

GOALS OF INTERVENTION

We have now reviewed several models of human development and several ways of conceptualizing and categorizing the things that can go wrong in the course of development. Taken together, these provide bases for suggesting appropriate intervention to get development back on the proper course and for determining what that course should be. Insofar as mental health counseling takes an educational, developmental approach to intervention, it is particularly important that the mental health counselor have a "lesson plan" that spells out the goals of each intervention.

Broad sets of goals for intervention have been defined along several different dimensions. For example, one set of alternative goals follows the distinction between the learning theory and the psychodynamic conceptions of human development outlined in the first section of this chapter. Using this context, the goals of intervention may be seen as either (a) behavior change or (b) adjustment or actualization. Another set of alternative goals reflects the three criteria for defining problems of living discussed in the second section of this chapter: statistical deviance, social disruption, and subjective discomfort. In this context, the goals of intervention may be defined as (a) cure, (b) social adaptation, or (c) comfort, respectively. We shall briefly examine each of these five criteria and then look at the goal of intervention as defined by mental health counseling, that is, coping.

Behavior change as a goal is most closely linked with the view that behaviors are learned and that intervention therefore consists of assisting the client to learn a better behavior than the one representing the problem of living. Defining the goal of intervention in this way has the advantages of giving the counselor an integrated system of human development (learned behaviors)—problems (bad learning)—interventions (improve that learning). Also, as emphasized by John Krumboltz (1966), a strong advocate of behavioral counseling, this approach allows one to define a problem of living in terms of concrete, objective behaviors and thus to assess accurately how much the intervention has helped to change those behaviors. Thus, if the problem of living is defined in terms of being plagued by repetitive thoughts about one's worthlessness, then the effectiveness of a particular intervention can be measured in terms of how many fewer times per day the client has such thoughts. If, however, the problem is merely defined as the client's feeling worthless, the counselor cannot say to what extent a client's global report of feeling better resulted from the intervention used, to what extent it was the client's desire to please the counselor, to what extent it reflected fluctuations in the client's mood, and so on. Thus, the fact that a learning theory–based goal (behavior change) requires an explicit definition of the behavior to be changed is one of the great virtues of this approach. One may, however, apply this principle and require an explicit definition of the problem (which by its very nature suggests an approach to change and a measure of that change) even if one does not otherwise adopt the premises and procedures of learning theory. The principal difficulty with the learning theory approach is, in general, that the more complex the problem behavior is, the less able this system is to explain and to offer techniques for changing it. Thus, although this system seems to work well with relatively specific, easily defined problems (for example, fear of snakes), it does not succeed any better than other approaches in working with broader, more pervasive problems, such as generalized feelings of anxiety. From the viewpoint of the psychodynamic theorists, moreover, those who define the goals of intervention in terms of behavior change are inappropriately focusing on symptoms, rather than causes. In this view, the personality is seen as a worn inner tube, such that if a patch is put over one leak (symptom), a new and possibly more serious leak will only spring up at another spot. Thus, to seek to treat only the symptom, rather than the cause, may well do more harm than good. Needless to say, the literature is full of arguments between behaviorists who claim to have changed a problem behavior (treated a symptom) without other problems arising and psychodynamicists who argue that the problem was a trivial one, the behaviorist did not know where to look for the new symptom, or the behaviorist did not wait long enough for the new symptom to appear.

Adjustment or actualization are the goals of intervention that derive from the psychodynamic model. The difference between these goals is that "adjustment" refers to meeting the minimal-to-average expectations set by the model, whereas "actualization" refers to fulfilling and exceeding those expectations. Thus, if the problem has to do with passing a course in physics, the goal of attaining a grade of at least C– would represent adjustment; the goal of winning a Nobel prize would be actualization. To some extent, the choice between these goals is dictated by: (a) what the theory states is sufficient, (b) the personality and level of aspiration of the counselor, and (c) the severity of the client's problem. In some instances, adjustment would be the most one could hope for; in others, anything short of actualization would leave the client unfulfilled. The argument against these goals is that they are too vague and subjective to be scientifically meaningful and so cannot be used as the criteria for a scientifically oriented approach to counseling. On what basis can a client and/or counselor assert that "adjustment" or "actualization" has been attained? To what extent is the decision a self-fulfilling fantasy: because I want to believe it, it must be true? To what extent is it a rationalization: If I declare that the goal is achieved, I can quit this painful process? Another problem is that even if one can accurately assess "adjustment" or "actualization" in terms of a specific psychodynamic theory, who is to say that that particular theory and what it prescribes are appropriate for the given client in the particular life situation? Is a client who lives in a dangerous neighborhood better adjusted if he or she reduces the levels of suspiciousness and aggression in the personality, as is called for by some psychodynamic theories?

Defining the goals of intervention as cure, social adaptation, or comfort reflect the problems with the specific criteria for defining problems of living to which each of them relates. Thus, "cure" (the goal of the medical model of problems of living) faces the same problems as a goal of intervention that "statistical deviance" faced as a criterion for defining problems of living. That is, norms are not absolute, but vary with social and historical context, nor are norms necessarily the same as optimum states. Thus, what constitutes a cure is a relative decision cloaked in absolute terms. Not only are the terms misleading, but the choice of "cure" as the goal implies acceptance of the unproven assumption that problems of living are a form of disease. This assumption is rejected by mental health counselors and others who do not have a vested interest in bringing problems of living exclusively within the treatment domain of the medical profession.

The goal of "social adaptation," like the criterion of social disruption to which it relates, is even less objective and more relativistic than "cure" (although not necessarily more objectionable to mental health counselors). The counselor must always consider the norms to which the client is being expected to adapt and whether those norms are truly adaptive for the client's life situation and personal objectives. Thus the goal of social adaptation may be disastrous for the client, if it is actually attained.

The goal of "comfort," like the criterion of "subjective discomfort," is by its very nature totally subjective and so of little use in a scientific approach to counseling. This is not meant to imply that one does not wish to help the client to feel better, but rather to suggest that feeling better is a consequence of living more effectively rather than a sufficient goal in and of itself.

Having seen the benefits and limitations of five of the most commonly espoused goals of intervention, we may turn to the goal generally espoused by mental health counselors: assisting the client to cope with the problems of living for which help was sought. Coping generally entails:

1. *Mobilizing* one's *assets* that are relevant to dealing with the problem at hand,
2. *Developing* necessary but currently unavailable *skills* for dealing with the problem, and
3. *Modifying* the *environment* so that it is maximally supportive and minimally detrimental to dealing with the problem.

Is it possible to derive a summary, integrated model for mental health counseling from the variety of theories of human development, problems of living, and goals of intervention presented in this chapter? No doubt a number of such models may be derived, and each counselor should construct and amplify upon one that seems valid in light of that counselor's professional experience.

To be valid, the model must be constantly subjected to evaluation. Does it help the counselor to help the client? If not, it is merely an intellectual exercise and of no practical significance. However, as Kurt Lewin has been frequently quoted as saying, "There is nothing more practical than a good theory."

We may suggest the following model as one possible theory:

1. As people grow, they learn from their family, peers, subcultural group, and culture how to deal with certain situations. For dealing with many of these situations, these groups have evolved standardized patterns of behavior (responses) that seem to work at least much of the time. Many of these responses relate to matters that arise at a particular time in life and so are learned at that time.

2. Problems arise when the person confronts a new situation to which he or she has not learned how to respond or confronts an apparently familiar situation on which the known response does not produce the expected effect.

3. Coping comes through the person's analyzing the problem and calling up or developing responses that will achieve the desired result and/or changing the situation so that the person's responses will produce that result.

4. Mental health counseling assists the client to cope by: (a) defining and analyzing the problem; (b) determining and selecting among possible solutions, based on employing available or potential assets and skills within the client or on changing the situation; (c) implementing that solution; and (d) evaluating its effectiveness (and if necessary, repeating the process).

Obviously, the first important step is defining the problem in such a way that it can be analyzed, dealt with, and evaluated. This issue, and the subsequent steps in this process, will be discussed in the following chapters.

REFERENCES

American Psychiatric Association. (1980). *Diagnostic and statistical manual of mental disorders, DSM III* (3rd ed.). Washington, DC: Author.

Bandura, A., & Walters, R. (1963). *Social learning and personality development.* New York: Holt, Rinehart & Winston.

Beck, A. T. (1976). *Cognitive therapy and the emotional disorders.* New York: International Universities Press.

Berelson, B., & Steiner, G. A. (1964). *Human behavior: An inventory of scientific findings.* New York: Harcourt, Brace & World.

Bloom, B. L. (1985). *Stressful life event theory and research: Implications for primary prevention.* Rockville, MD: National Institute of Mental Health.

Butler, R. M., & Lewis, M. I. (1983). *Aging and mental health: Positive psychosocial approaches.* St. Louis: C.V. Mosby.

Celotta, B., & Teglasi-Golubcow, H. (1982). A problem taxonomy for classifying clients' problems. *Personnel and Guidance Journal, 61,* 73–76.

Cochrane, R. (1983). *The social creation of mental illness.* New York: Longman.

Ellis, A. (1962). *Reason and emotion in psychotherapy.* Secaucus, NJ: Lyle Stuart.

Erikson, E. H. (1963). *Childhood and society* (2nd ed.) New York: Norton.

Erikson, E. H. (1968). *Identity: Youth and crisis.* New York: Norton.

Havighurst, R. J. (1972). *Developmental tasks and education* (3rd ed.) New York: McKay.

Hershenson, D. B. (1964). *Erikson's "Sense of Identity," occupational fit, and enculturation in adolescence.* Unpublished doctoral dissertation, Boston University.

Hershenson, D. B. (1982). A formulation of counseling based on the healthy personality. *Personnel and Guidance Journal, 60,* 406–409.

Hollingshead, A. B., & Redlich, F. C. (1958). *Social class and mental illness.* New York: Wiley.

Holmes, T. H., & Rahe, R. H. (1967). The social readjustment rating scale. *Journal of Psychosomatic Research, 11,* 213–218.

Krumboltz, J. D. (1966). *Revolution in counseling: Implications of behavioral science.* Boston: Houghton Mifflin.

Leong, F. T. L., Tseng, W. S., & Wu, D. Y. H. (1985). Cross-cultural variations in stressful life events: A preliminary study. *AMHCA Journal, 7,* 72–77.

Levinson, D. J., Darrow, C. N., Klein, E. B., Levinson, M. H., & McKee, B. (1978). *The seasons of a man's life.* New York: Ballantine Books.

Marx, M. H. (1976). Formal theory. In M. H. Marx & F. E. Goodson (Eds.), *Theories in contemporary psychology* (2nd ed., pp. 234–260). New York: Macmillan.

Maslow, A. H. (1954). *Motivation and personality.* New York: Harper.

Maslow, A. H. (1962). *Toward a psychology of being.* Princeton, NJ: Van Nostrand.

Murphy, H. B. M., Wittkower, E. D., Fried, J., & Ellenberger, H. (1963). A cross-cultural survey of schizophrenic symptomatology. *International Journal of Social Psychiatry, 9,* 237–249.

Muuss, R. E. (1975). *Theories of adolescence* (3rd ed.) New York: Random House.

Rotter, J. B. (1954). *Social learning and clinical psychology.* Englewood Cliffs, NJ: Prentice-Hall.

Srole, L., Langner, T. S., Michael, S. T., Opler, M. K., & Rennie, T. A. C. (1962). *The Midtown Manhattan Study: Mental health in the metropolis* (Vol. I). New York: McGraw-Hill.

Webb, L. J., Di Clemente, C. C., Johnstone, E. E., Sanders, J. L., & Perley, R. A. (1981). *DSM-III training guide.* New York: Brunner/Mazel.

Zigler, E., & Phillips, L. (1961). Psychiatric diagnosis and symptomatology. *Journal of Abnormal and Social Psychology, 63,* 69–75.

5   Models of Counseling*

The practice of mental health counseling represents a philosophical and prag-
matic departure from other human service and mental health professions.
Philosophically, mental health counseling differs in the way that human
growth and development is conceptualized and in its approach to preventing or
remedying problems of living. Pragmatically, mental health counseling differs
from other mental health professions in terms of basic professional identification, type and length of academic preparation, and the way intervention strategies are determined.

This chapter will focus on the practice of mental health counseling and
examine several practice models that may be used to guide and formulate
intervention strategies. Rather than focus on the abundance of counseling theories currently in existence (references provided in chapter 7), this chapter
will focus on larger frameworks or models used to integrate divergent theoretical approaches. The emphasis here is on approaches that pertain essentially to
counseling in nature, as opposed to therapy.

A counseling approach differs from a therapeutic approach in that it is devel-
opmental/educational in orientation, time limited, and has specific behavioral
or attitudinal outcomes as the goal. In addition, as noted in chapter 1, the mental health counseling approach: (a) takes into account the individual within the
environment; (b) focuses on the client's assets rather than deficits; (c) is oriented toward developmental and preventive rather than remedial needs; (d)
assumes an egalitarian relationship between counselor and counselee; (e)
responds to the counselee's conscious needs rather than his or her unconscious
drives and motivations; (f) emphasizes the counselor's use of discreet, observable skills in assisting the counselee to achieve desired outcomes; (g) conceptualizes appropriate counseling outcomes as involving improved counselee

---

*This chapter was written by Marita Danek.

coping skills, increased personal mastery over life tasks, an enhanced sense of self-esteem, and improved problem-solving ability; (h) continuously monitors counselee's progress toward goals and modifies approaches, when necessary, to expedite the achievement of such goals.

BASIC ASSUMPTIONS REGARDING HUMAN NATURE

These assumptions regarding the nature of mental health counseling are derived from more basic assumptions on the part of the counselor regarding human nature and how change can occur through a helping relationship. In choosing a framework for conceptualizing counseling interventions, the counselor should be aware that this choice involves two basic assumptions regarding human nature. These assumptions concern the issues of nature versus nurture and of cognition versus emotion.

Nature-Nurture Issues

The nature-nurture issue looks at individual characteristics—physical, mental, and emotional—and makes assumptions regarding whether these characteristics are due largely to the environment or largely to genetic (inherited) factors.

It is obvious that certain physical characteristics such as eye and skin color, height, and overall physical appearance are inherited. Although sometimes the transmission of these characteristics can be traced to parents, frequently characteristics appear that are not apparent in parents or other blood relatives. These characteristics, which appear to spring from nowhere, actually have their basis in recessive genes that depend on genes from both parents for overt expression. This explains how two brown-eyed individuals can have a blue-eyed child: The gene for blue eyes is recessive.

The heritability of behavioral characteristics is not quite so obvious, because behavior cannot be identified and quantified as easily as physical appearance. However, there is increasing evidence that certain behavioral dysfunctions such as schizophrenia, alcoholism, bipolar depression, and sociopathic tendencies are, at least in part, genetically determined. Current research indicates that other, less categorized dysfunctions such as impulsive behavior, learning disabilities, and generalized emotional instability may be inherited (Cantwell, 1972; Gershon, Bunney, Leckman, van Eerdewegh, & De Bauche, 1976; Loehlin & Nichols, 1976; Vaillant & Milofsky, 1982). The actual manifestation of behavioral dysfunction might possibly be triggered by environmental factors when an individual possesses the genetic predisposition toward dysfunction.

The nurture approach to behavioral differences assumes that all behavior is caused by or is an effect of various environmental factors such as quality of parenting and family life, early childhood experiences, the resolution of developmental tasks, social class, or stressful life experiences.

Most theoretical approaches do not adhere to a unitary position, that is, that either environmental or genetic influences are the sole determinants of behavior. Rather, they tend to emphasize the relative importance of one factor over another, while considering nature and nurture interactively. Adherents of the more traditional medical model will, for example, perceive behavioral dysfunctions as symptomatic of mental illness, and therefore more apt to be biologically based. Counselors who follow a problem-solving or ecological model will perceive the environment as interacting with and having an impact on the individual. Therefore, these models emphasize interventions that take into account the individual within the environment. They also emphasize prevention at the individual and systems level.

Cognition versus Emotion

The nature–nurture issue is closely paralleled by the consideration of the relative roles of cognition and emotion. Both cognition (thought) and emotion (affect or mood) are considered to be precursors of behavior. However, the question that arises is: Which comes first, mood or cognition? Does an individual's mood or feeling state predispose him or her to certain thoughts? For example, if a person feels depressed, does this mood lead to feelings of hopelessness or worthlessness? Conversely, if a person believes he/she is not worthy, does this thinking pattern lead to a state of depression?

Those who believe that mood precedes cognition take the somatogenic approach—that is, they believe that there is a biological, constitutional basis for affect (Zajonc, 1984). They believe that a feeling state can develop independently of any particular thoughts and that this mood will, in turn, lead to certain negative or positive thoughts. Those who believe that cognition precedes mood (Lazarus, 1984) take a psychogenic approach.

A related approach, that of learned helplessness, was developed by Milton Seligman (1975). Based on initial experiments with dogs, Seligman believed that individuals can develop expectations that their actions are ineffective in making changes in their lives. This belief system may occur because of overwhelming trauma or an unreinforcing social environment, which leads to a generalized feeling of helplessness that has been learned through reinforcement. Depression is the consequence of this belief.

The treatment of affective disorders by those who choose the biologically oriented approach (that is, mood precedes cognition) is through chemotherapy or long-term psychotherapy. These treatments are the prerogative of psychiatrists or other physicians. However, to the extent that depression can be caused by cognition, it can also be relieved by cognition. Over the past two decades, counselors and other nonmedical mental health professionals have become interested in cognitive–behavioral approaches to managing anxiety, depression, and other affective disorders. By taking affective disorders out of the exclusive purview of medical personnel, counselors can provide nonchemical, short-term strategies for relief and even teach clients how to manage the subjective experience of emotional pain.

Neuroses are another medical category of defined disorders that are mainly learned and maintained through cognition, although the symptoms may be affective. Examples include phobias or obsessive–compulsive neurosis, which are amenable to intervention strategies provided by mental health counselors.

Major psychoses such as schizophrenia are mainly disruptions of cognition with affective consequences including emotional withdrawal. Because psychoses are assumed to have an organic basis, they are considered (by most researchers) to be mental illnesses and therefore most amenable to drug therapy. Most mental health counselors do not work with individuals in the acute stages of psychoses and, indeed, the efficacy of "talking treatment" for actively psychotic individuals is questionable.

These issues of nature versus nurture and emotion versus cognition are philosophically linked to conceptual models of practice that integrate major perspectives on human nature, the role of the mental health counselor, and the change process. The conceptual models that are most linked philosophically to mental health counseling are the counseling ecology model (Conyne, 1981, 1985), the developmental/problem management model (Egan, 1982) and the change agent model. These models are not totally independent of each other because most adhere to the main tenets of mental health counseling, but they have enough differences to be described separately. A fourth model, the medical model, is used as a point of reference because it follows closely the pathology orientation of most traditional intervention approaches. By describing this model in some detail, the contrast between its philosophical constructs and the mental health counseling orientation will become more apparent.

No conceptual model is based on an assumption of a pure position either on nature versus nurture or on cognition versus emotion. This is as it should be, because in reality both nature and nurture and both cognition and emotion intertwine and have an effect on behavior. The four models presented here do, however, differ in their relative positions along these two dimensions. The counseling ecologist model assumes a position closer to the nurture and cognitive ends of these dimensions. The medical model is closer to the nature and emotional ends. The assumptions underlying the developmental/problem management model are somewhat closer to the nature and cognitive ends of these dimensions. Finally, the change agent represents a nurture–cognitive position that is even further toward the cognitive pole than is the counseling ecologist model.

THE COUNSELING ECOLOGIST MODEL

Definition

The counseling ecologist model was first proposed by Conyne & Rogers (1977) and Conyne (1985), although contributions to this conceptualization include Lewin (1936) and his life space model of behavior and the social ecology discipline of Insel and Moos (1974). Kurt Lewin first described behavior as a function of persons interacting with their environment and developed the formula $B = f(P \times E)$ to represent this relationship. Much later, Insel and Moos (1974) derived their social ecology model from both ecology and human ecology emphases. The science of ecology is concerned with the interrelationship of the environment with the organism. Human ecology applies this concept to human populations. Social ecology, although based on the previous ecological definitions, goes beyond both of these with a value orientation toward the actual promotion of effective human functioning.

The counseling ecologist model (Conyne, 1985), in contrast to other models of practice described in this chapter in which systems change or persons change are the predominant emphases, is a more comprehensive model that is adhered to by many contemporary mental health counselors (Huber, 1983) and community or mental health counselor training programs. This model combines both the systems and persons change emphases and promotes individual competence through a focus on a person-by-environment perspective. Individuals are seen as moving through environments that nurture or support certain kinds of competencies but hinder others. Using this approach, the creation of developmentally responsive environments is a parallel goal with that of promoting individual competence. Personal competence and environmental characteristics are in a continuously reciprocal relationship (Conyne, 1985).

The Dual Focus of Interventions

The ecological perspective of counseling provides sharp contrast to the traditional clinical psychology emphasis, which is almost exclusively on intrapsychic (what goes on within the individual) dimensions. Instead, this model provides a broader framework of intervention that encompasses the development of the "necessary conditions" for individual growth and for change within society.

Crucial to the counseling ecologist model, therefore, is a dual and complimentary focus of intervention involving both person and environment. The person as a target of intervention includes three possible levels: (a) individual, which would involve the life space concerns of one individual as traditionally addressed in individual counseling; (b) small groups such as those that naturally occur (families, small organizations) or those that are brought together for a common purpose (support, self-help, or counseling groups); (c) large groups such as institutions or communities, which may occur naturally (e.g., ethnic enclaves in cities) or artificially (e.g., mental hospitals, residential schools, or jails). These levels are never considered without viewing their relationship to the total environment and its components (Conyne, 1981; Steele, 1973).

The environmental components of a person's life space include social, physical, political, economic, and cultural realities. Although all of these components interact to form a total system that is greater than the sum of its parts (Conyne, 1985) they may be conceptualized as follows: (a) social: the characteristics of an individual or groups and surroundings, including demographic features and prevailing norms of behavior; (b) physical: both natural and artificial factors such as weather and climate, housing and shelter, population density, and geographic features such as terrain; (c) political: the explicit and implicit (codified or otherwise) laws that govern and moderate human behaviors; (d) economic: the distribution of resources including goods and money and the perceived access of the person to such resources; (e) cultural: prevailing intellectual, aesthetic, and leisure and recreational opportunities available to the individual and groups of individuals.

Intervention Methods

Intervention in the counseling ecology model always targets the relevant level of the person and the environment simultaneously or sequentially. Intervention strategies result from the combination of a specific method (either direct or indirect) with a specific purpose (remedial, developmental, or preventive).

Methods involve either direct or indirect approaches. Direct methods involve a direct, face-to-face contact between the counselor and the individual or system. Included would be individual or group counseling, psycho-education, or crisis intervention. Indirect methods effect change through other individuals or through instrumentation. Such methods would include advocacy, assessment, program development and evaluation, consultation, and professional training and environmental design. Several of these methods are discussed in detail in chapters 10–12; however, they will be reviewed briefly here within the context of the counseling ecology model.

Advocacy involves fostering developmental rights in the environment and proposing change strategies to meet the needs of individuals and groups over the life cycle as they move through environmental settings. The philosophical underpinning of the use of advocacy as a method of change is a belief in the right of individuals and groups to participate in decisions affecting their lives and that such participation is possible through access to relevant information.

Assessment can be defined as a multilevel process that involves various functions of information-gathering and organization. Two models of assessment exist that take an ecological approach. The Ivey–Simek-Downing model (1980) takes into account the person and the environment and incorporates standardized test results, observational data, self-report inventories, and other methods of determining client competencies. The Cormier and Cormier model (1979) provides an eclectic method for measuring and assessing intervention outcomes. This is a three-dimensional model involving six types and methods of measurement, and four times the measurement data may be obtained. The types of measurement are verbal, self-reports, frequency counts, duration counts, rating scales, and checklists. The methods are interviews, self-monitoring, self-report inventories or survey schedules, role-play procedures, and various observation-by-others techniques. The four times are prior to, during, and after intervention, as well as a follow-up assessment (Cormier & Cormier, 1979, pp. 206–227).

Consultation is the provision of technical assistance by the mental health counselor to an individual or group within an agency regarding programmatic and human relations concerns.

Training involves professional preparation to acquire the requisite knowledge and skills to function competently. According to Conyne (1985), the training of mental health counselors is posited most frequently on the following ecologically oriented principles: (a) counseling interventions are based on the perspective that people interact with their environment; (b) developmental-preventive interventions are more efficient than remedial ones; (c) a community-ecological change model is more efficient than an individual-clinical one; (d) efficient helping services are based on an active rather than passive orientation; and (e) a multifaceted-services approach is more efficient than a single-service approach. Competencies related to the preceding philosophy include: (a) helping skills; (b) knowledge of social skills and change; (c) program development; (d) education and training; (e) consultation; (f) program administration; (g) program evaluation; and (h) environmental assessment.

Environmental design as an intervention method focuses on manipulating the environment in growth-inducing ways so that it provokes lessened stressor loads on individuals and institutions at risk, encourages individuals to avoid exposure to stressors, and enhances coping mechanisms in times of crisis.

Two kinds of research are of potential use as intervention methods in the counseling ecology model: process research and outcome research. Process research studies the ongoing process or procedures used to facilitate individual and environmental objectives. It is concerned with strategies, techniques, theoretical approaches, and other variables relating to the particular intervention goal or purpose. Outcome research determines how well and to what degree intervention goals have been accomplished. Research can be applied and have practical applications, but frequently it is basic, theoretical, or focuses on theoretical constructs. To the extent that research involves determining the effectiveness of intervention methods, it is similar to evaluation. Evaluation is a broader concept that incorporates needed adjustments, if any, to intervention methods. It is practical and always related to individual, programmatic, or systems concern. Several evaluation strategies exist. Cormier and Cormier (1979) proposed a behavioral approach to evaluation that determines overt and covert behavioral changes, including type, degree, and direction of change.

The purpose (preventive, developmental, or remedial) of intervention is related to the choice of method. The counseling ecology model focuses on prevention and development primarily and on remediation secondarily. Both preventive and developmental approaches are concerned with intervening before corrective action is needed. Conyne (1985) noted that they are both futuristic, but differ to the extent that prevention focuses on "at risk" target populations or on individuals who are considered to be highly susceptible or vulnerable to a particular type of dysfunction. Prevention activities are targeted to this particular population so that the effects of their personal deficits or environmental stressors can be reduced or modified. Developmental interventions are targeted at the population as a whole and are designed to enhance coping skills and overall functioning over time. Remediation is perceived as necessary in response to crises and debilitating problems of living; however, the counseling ecology emphasis remains primarily developmental and preventive.

The entire intervention process is mediated as individuals interact with the environment. The way an individual will respond to an environment is determined by such factors as cognitive appraisal, motivation, and dominant coping strategies. One individual's mediation processes may be far different from another's. Because intervention strategies must take into account possible mediation processes, the active involvement by target persons in intervention design is recommended.

Because the emphasis on prevention is pivotal to the counseling ecology model, some considerations relative to what is preventable will be explored here. Hollister (1977) noted that a distinction needs to be made regarding what is preventable; we don't know how to prevent major psychoses or character disorders; however, we can prevent social incompetence, over-response to stress, and other difficult life situations. Although these problems might be "fuzzy" or of minor importance to some theorists (Lamb & Zusman, 1979), they do result in impaired functioning, even though such impediments do not always occur in discrete diagnostic categories (Justice, 1982).

According to Hollister (1979), a stress model should be kept in mind when conceptualizing primary prevention strategies. Stress may be defined as the "internal response we experience when subjected to stimuli that threaten our survival or emotional needs" (Justice, 1982, p. 211).

The four major primary prevention strategies are: (a) stressor management, which controls, moderates, and defuses stimuli before they have an impact on the person or group; (b) stressor avoidance, which removes vulnerable individuals or groups from feeling the impact of specific stimuli; (c) stress resistance building, which develops the capacity to resist the effects of stress through strength building experience; and (d) stress reaction management, which occurs after the onset of stress but before it has progressed into debilitation and dysfunction.

Stressor management is involved in prevention programs that identify very specific (rather than global), limited and observable stressors that may effect high-risk individuals or groups. One example is Broussard's (1977) approach with first-born children of high-risk mothers, which involved support groups and instruction in parenting skills.

Stressor avoidance interventions are based on removing vulnerable individuals from potentially stressful situations or environments. An example of this kind of placement would be the removal of a younger child from a home in which an older child has been subjected to physical, mental, or sexual abuse.

Building stress resistance is a third type of prevention strategy. There are several ways that an individual's resistance to stressors can be strengthened. One strategy, anticipatory guidance, involves providing information about potentially threatening events. Social support from self-help groups or natural support systems (families, or civic or religious organizations) are another way of building stress resistance. Studies have shown that individuals lacking a support system are prone to higher levels of emotional disturbance, especially when many previous negative or few positive life-changing events had occurred. Conversely, persons who are currently involved in an intimate relationship are less vulnerable to potential stressors (Brown & Harris, 1978; Brown, Harris, & Peto, 1983; Jacobs & Charles, 1980; Lynch, 1977). The explanation for this appears to be that such individuals feel esteemed, can ventilate feelings, and confirm perceptions. Regardless of the reasons, the existence of such support systems or relationships appears to provide stress resistance. Another approach to stress resistance is the development of specific coping skills in the individual. These skills might include interpersonal problem-solving skills (Spivack & Shure, 1977), social interaction skills, or other competency-based approaches to giving individuals the tools by which they can understand the stress acting on them.

The fourth strategy for prevention—stress reaction management—is an effort to prevent a person from reacting to unavoidable or already occurring stressors. Social support networks have been again found useful in this approach, particularly during times of life transition (Schlossberg, 1984). Such transitions may include role changes that may be unanticipated, for example, widowhood; work responsibilities (gains or losses); or other personal, interpersonal, or occupational changes. For those individuals who do not have access to a natural support system, mutual help groups seem to be particularly instrumental in providing the necessary support to work through stressful situations (Silverman, 1972; Goldston, 1977).

THE MEDICAL MODEL: A COMPARISON

In contrast to the counseling ecology model is the medical model, which has been the predominant mode of conceptualizing mental health and "mental illness" (problems of living) over the past century.

The medical model differs from the counseling ecology model on several important dimensions: (a) it focuses almost exclusively on the individual rather than the person(s) within the environment; (b) it adheres to a deficit model of human functioning rather than a competency model; (c) its concern is remedial rather than preventive or developmental; and (d) it considers the helping professional (usually a medical person) as the "expert" rather than as a partner in a process of growth and change.

Perhaps the most questioned aspect of the medical model is its illness paradigm of mental functioning. Albee (1980) and others contended that "mental illness" is not based on objective facts and is not consistently and reliably diagnosed. Further, they believe that medicine, in general, is more concerned with remediation (treatment and cure) than with prevention primarily because of economic reasons.

Philosophically, the deficit (medical) and competency (counseling ecology) models perceive persons in very different ways. The competency model presupposes an egalitarian perspective in which each person has a right to grow and the potential for such growth, and can develop personal competencies to deal with stress. The deficit model assumes that the cause or causes of dysfunction are rooted within the individual and, therefore, the cure can be accomplished through the administration of drugs or intensive intrapsychic therapy. The individual is a passive recipient of such treatments rather than an active participant in the change process.

Finally, the illness model identifies a wide range of human problems in terms of pathology, and thus the focus is negative rather than positive. Deviations from the norm are given labels. This is most apparent in the use of the *Diagnostic and Statistical Manual of Mental Disorders* (American Psychiatric Association, 1980) nosology, which provides 222 labels for a broad range of human behavior, although such labeling does not appear to be related to any attempt to differentially intervene or "treat." Indeed, the diagnosis in physical medicine may be entirely appropriate because it helps determine the mode of treatment; however, this is not the case in the mental health professions, in which the pre-existing theoretical training of the therapist is much more likely to influence the choice of an intervention strategy.

EGAN'S DEVELOPMENTAL/PROBLEM MANAGEMENT MODEL

Definition

The developmental problem management model is a conceptual framework for a systematic and integrative approach to the broad category of therapies that fall under the cognitive and coping skills methods of intervention (Egan, 1982, p. 9).

The problem management framework is basically an eclectic, practical, and operational approach rather than a theoretical one. It holds a deficiency rather than a pathology perspective on human behavior, as noted by D'Zurilla and Goldfried (1971). In this model maladaptive behavior is merely ineffective or inefficient in terms of the person's energy, or the costs of coping inadequately are actually creating additional problems.

Using this perspective, the helping process is considered, in part, an educational process of providing clients with a working knowledge about themselves, others, and the world, as well as training in the kind of skills that are necessary to cope with problems in living. The model makes assumptions about the requisite counselor skills to effect change as well as the skills and knowledge clients learn through the various stages of the problem-solving models.

Counselor Skills

The development of counselor skills consists of four interrelated stages, according to Egan (1982, p. 10). The first is a *conceptual understanding* of appropriate helping skills and how they are manifested. The second is a *behavioral feeling* for these skills, which comes from observing them in practice with a counselee. At this stage, intellectual understanding is combined with a sense of how these skills may be used. The third stage involves *initial mastery*, in which the counselor begins to use the skills previously learned. *Further mastery* is obtained through continuous refinement of these skills through supervision. The specific skills counselors may utilize are described in more detail in the section on the stages of intervention.

Counselee Skills

The developmental/problem management model assumes that clients have the personal resources and strengths to manage their problems and determine appropriate lifestyles choices throughout the various periods of their lives. The goal of counseling is to reduce client dependence on external sources of support and increase self-reliance. The tools that permit clients to become independently functioning individuals are the skills and working knowledge of themselves obtained through the counseling relationships. These tools provide clients with a sense of self-efficacy, that is, an expectation that behaviors will lead to certain outcomes and a belief that they are capable of engaging in such behaviors. Counselors help clients develop self-efficacy in several ways: by challenging self-defeating beliefs and disabling self-talk (Ellis, 1962, 1973), by helping to reduce the client's fears and anxieties that keep them from using their resources, and by encouraging them to take reasonable risks.

Stages of the Problem Management Process

The problem management model has three stages which build upon each other in a developmental (systematic and cumulative) fashion. Stage I is preparatory to Stage II, and the successful resolution of Stage III depends on how well the work in Stages I and II has progressed. Of course, counseling does not always proceed in a forward fashion and sometimes it is necessary to circle back to complete some overlooked work in former stages. The purpose of conceptualizing counseling as stages is to provide an organized approach to what needs to be done in counseling.

Stage I: Problem Clarification

Most individuals are capable of handling most problems they encounter in the ordinary course of daily living. However, due to skill or knowledge deficits, some individuals find they either are not coping well or are expending too much energy on the process of coping. Other individuals may periodically be faced with a succession of stressors or a major traumatizing event that taxes their available coping skills. Individuals who are aware of their problems or who are made aware of their problems by others will turn to a helping professional if the problem is sufficiently incapacitating and if they believe that they can be helped.

The goal of Stage I is clarifying the problem for both the counselor and the client. This is accomplished by establishing a good working relationship that is characterized by respect and an appropriate degree of warmth. To orient themselves toward their clients, counselors need to use the skills of attending, listening, responding, and probing. As discussed more fully in chapter 2, attending involves maintaining eye contact and posture, and letting clients know the counselor is available and aware. Active listening means hearing the messages that are conveyed by the content of what the client says, but also noting nonverbal communication such as pauses, facial expression, and so on. Responding indicates to the client that the counselor understands how the client perceives his or her problem; this understanding must not merely be felt, it must also be communicated. Probes help the client express a problem in more specific and concrete ways. Probing means using open questions; restating the problem in a way that makes the client clarify the situation; requesting a restatement of the problem; providing minimal prompts (Hackney & Cormier, 1979); and otherwise providing additional concreteness to the process of clarifying the problem.

Stage II: Setting Goals Based on Dynamic Understanding

In Stage II, there are three major tasks. One is to assist the counselee in putting the "pieces" or threads of insight together and seeing the broader picture. The second is to help the client become more objective about the reality by overcoming distortions in the way the counselee perceives the problem situation. When objectivity regarding the problem situation is developed, goals that appear reasonable to both counselor and counselee can be set. The third task of Stage II is actual goal-setting based on the counselee's broadened and integrated understanding of the problem situation.

According to Egan's model, several additional sets of counselor skills are utilized in Stage II of the process. These skills, which do not replace but are built upon the skills used in Stage I, include the following: the skill of integrating the data, challenging skills, and goal-setting skills.

The ability to integrate the data involves helping the counselee to take new perspectives, put them into a broader conceptualization of his or her life, and look beyond to new possibilities regarding goals and ways of managing problems. Challenging skills (also called confrontational skills by other theorists) are used to assist counselees in broadening a narrow or distorted viewpoint and becoming more objective about the problem situation. Egan listed five challenging skills as essential. The first, information-sharing, provides counselees with basic knowledge and information they may lack. New or additional information can, in itself, assist counselees to see the problem situation in a different way. Advanced accurate empathy is the second skill and consists of providing clients with an understanding of what they are really saying either verbally, through hints or implications, or nonverbally, through facial expressions and bodily posture.

Direct confrontation is a challenging skill that identifies discrepancies and distortions in a client's life by pointing out, for example, inconsistencies between what the counselee thinks or believes and how he/she acts. Self-sharing (called self-disclosure by other theorists) is the fourth skill. This means helping clients understand themselves by the counselor's sharing his or her experiences, which may be similar. The fifth skill is immediacy, which is defined (chapter 2) as the exploration of the "here and now" of the counselor-client relationships. Finally, the counselor needs to use goal-setting skills in Stage II. Goals are defined as what the counselee decides to do about the problem situation; goals should be measurable, specific, and concrete rather than a vague decision to change.

In addition to skills counselors need in Stage II, Egan identified skills that clients need. These include nondefensive listening, dynamic understanding (defined as understanding with a commitment to take action), and choosing goals (based on counselee's decisions regarding what to do about the problem situation). Counselors should assist clients in developing those skills by reinforcing and supporting them as well as modeling them.

Because these Stage II skills place greater demands on the client, they must be used judiciously and not until the client is ready to move into Stage II.

Stage III: Facilitating Action

In Stage III, skills used in the two previous stages continue to be used. However, there are three additional skills specific to this stage: program-development skills, facilitating-action skills, and evaluation skills.

As defined by Egan, programs are methods or strategies that will help the counselee achieve previously identified goals. Program development skills include two types: helping the client choose possibilities among various strategies and then helping the client choose among programs and determine the most appropriate and realistic method or combination of methods. To facilitate this stage, counselors need to help clients prepare for action while reasonably considering all possible obstacles. They also need to provide challenge and support so that the client does not become discouraged with the program. During this stage, clients will learn to overcome resistance and reluctance by cooperating in the planning and implementation of their program.

Evaluation is considered a crucial component in Egan's model of helping. There should be ongoing evaluation of the process rather than waiting until termination. The following evaluation questions should be asked by counselor and client at appropriate times during the process (Egan, 1982, p. 47): (a) What is the quality of client's participation in the program? Is the client truly committed to working through the program? (b) What is the quality of the program itself? Is the client moving toward established goals? If not, perhaps the program needs to be redesigned. (c) What are the quality of the goals? If goals have been reached, do they appear to resolve the problem situation? If problems persist or do not become more manageable, then perhaps new goals should be set.

The Egan helping model depends to a great extent on sharing what the process is about with the client. In this way, clients can fully participate with a sense of personal mastery over where they are going and can utilize the model to deal with future problem situations.

The counseling ecologist model, as noted previously, focuses on the person within the environment; whereas the problem-solving model places more emphasis on the development of individual competence that will in turn permit that individual to function more effectively within a system. In contrast to both these models, the change agent is concerned primarily with creating environments that encourage and nurture the individual's growth and development. This framework for helping also differs markedly from the traditional medical model, which seeks to help individuals adapt to their environments rather than environments to the individual.

CHANGE AGENT MODEL

The change agent framework for counseling identifies the level of intervention as the environment, rather than the individual (Cook, 1971; Pine, 1976; Shoben, 1962). Implicit in this approach is the recognition that certain societal institutions—governments, communities, schools, and even mental health treatment programs—have bureaucratic characteristics that tend to depersonalize the individual. For example, system goals are placed ahead of individual goals and interpersonal relationships are hierarchical and often undemocratic.

The potentially destructive impact of a system on an individual or group of individuals' development can be seen in the empirically documented concept of learned helplessness (Seligman, 1975). Learned helplessness, as described previously, demonstrates how repeated negative reinforcement from the environment can predispose the individual to believe that personal action is ineffective in changing a situation.

To create conditions that will benefit the individual, the change agent model posits that the system level is the most effective one at which to intervene. Frequently it is not enough to assist individuals to cope with their existing problem; rather the problem can be prevented at its source, which is at the systems or environmental level. Counselors who target intervention—either prevention or remediation—at the systems level must first understand systems theory.

Overview of Systems Theory

A system can be defined as any "entity made up of interconnected parts, with recognizable relationships that are systemically arranged to serve a perceived purpose" (Kurpius, 1985, p. 369). Systems theory has its origins in the biological sciences, which view human organisms as consisting of mutually dependent and interacting parts and processes (Von Bertalanffy, 1968).

As applied to human beings, a system is a community institution or other aspect of the total environment that consists of individuals involved in ongoing reciprocal relationships. Concepts that are basic to systems theory include (a) mutual dependence, (b) mutual interaction, (c) homeostasis, (d) ecosystems, (e) subsystems, and (f) boundaries.

Mutual dependence means that individuals function as part of a system when they partially provide for other individuals' needs within the system. These needs might include social, emotional, or financial support. Mutual interaction occurs when individuals influence and are influenced by another's behaviors and by feedback from the environment. A change in any part of the system will change the whole system. An example of this is the alcoholic husband who stops drinking only to have his wife leave him once he is sober. The husband's alcoholism met a need in the wife; once this need was no longer met, the "system" or marriage became dysfunctional (or more dysfunctional).

A related concept is that of homeostasis, which relates to the "balance" within the system or the way system-wide relationships are organized. Systems struggle to maintain homeostasis (the "status quo") and will develop methods of responding to imbalance and returning to a former state of functioning. The ecosystems or ecological approach, as noted previously, looks at an individual's functioning within the context of the environment.

The subsystems concept refers to component parts within a system. For example, an educational institution such as a college might be divided into academic affairs and student life subsystems. The academic subsystem would consist of faculty, whereas the student life subsystem would consist of staff who provide support services such as housing, social activities, financial assistance, and so on. Students would interact with both subsystems directly. Although the subsystems themselves would not necessarily directly interact with each other, an imbalance in one might influence the functioning of the other. Repeated false fire alarms in a dormitory, for example, would interfere with students' studying, class participation, ability to pass exams, and so on.

The boundary concept relates to the rules of behavior that govern the system and its component subsystems. When boundaries are vague or poorly defined, the individuals within a system do not function competently because expectations and roles are unclear.

Crisis intervention, as discussed in chapter 7, is frequently conceptualized on the systems level. A hazardous event occurs (either anticipated or accidental) that threatens a vulnerable system, subsystem, or individual and disrupts its homeostasis. An active state of crisis ensues that includes both cognitive and affective components (e.g., feelings of guilt, reliving the experience, restlessness, a disturbance of bodily functions, an inability to concentrate, and possible suicidal ideation). Although, obviously, individuals or systems (families, communities) can go into crisis, the change agent model perceives the most effective crises intervention strategy as prevention on a systems-wide level. The theory underlying this is that many individual crises are predictable (developmental) or are precipitated by the environmental system. Individual crises are almost endemic in our society. Predictable individual crises include developmental tasks or transitions (any event or nonevent) as well as "marker events" (Sheehy, 1976) such as marriage, divorce, or the "empty-nest" syndrome. Situational crises include environmental catastrophes such as floods, fires, war, and so on; exposure to life-threatening pollutants; or personal catastrophes such as financial loss, illness, injury, or death. These occur randomly and are seldom anticipated (Schneidman, 1973).

The counselor as change agent would provide preventive activities such as advocacy or community organization, education (or training), or consulting so that populations at risk could plan and prepare for anticipated crises or cope with unanticipated crises. These functions will be discussed briefly in the following section, and many of these functions have been explained more fully in chapter 11.

Functions of a Change Agent

Advocacy

The advocacy function is integral to the change agent model of intervention. Advocacy refers to the reduction of system-wide inequities that deny individuals or groups of individuals certain basic human rights, encourage differential access to goods and services, and undermine the capacity of healthy growth (Knitzer, 1980). When engaged in advocacy, the counselor must consider the target for change as well as strategies. The target for change includes both the system and that aspect of the system (policies, rules, norms, etc.) that should be modified.

One approach to classifying strategies of advocacy involves the categories of case and class advocacy. Case advocacy occurs on a smaller scale and incorporates collaborative activities to enlist the cooperation of individuals within a system, as well as possible adversarial techniques such as legal action (Knitzer, 1980). Class advocacy is broader in scale and is used to change public policy. It includes legislative, administrative, legal, and monitoring activities. Legislative techniques involve identifying appropriate laws that have an impact on specific populations and modifying, replacing, or strengthening such laws as needed. Administrative advocacy intervenes with bureaucracies to insure that policies are appropriate and fairly carried out. Legal strategies call for litigation that can force major societal changes. The final advocacy technique, monitoring, involves checking on the progress of previously won changes so that systems are actually doing what they have been empowered to do and that they are in compliance with the law.

In summary, the advocacy function within the change agent framework assumes that systems can become competent and serve the needs of both individuals and subsystem by actively changing dysfunctional structures and processes.

Consultation

This second major function has received considerable attention elsewhere in this text. As considered from the change agent framework, the counselor as consultant focuses on what Caplan (1970) would term program-centered consultation. The assumption is that changes can be made within a program or activity by collaborative efforts on the part of the consultant and individuals within the system. Consultation differs from advocacy in that there is a shared perception of programmatic issues that must be resolved and a mutual explanation of such issues or concerns. In many cases, the consultant can increase the power base or effectiveness of the consultee, but direct advocacy efforts are not used to change a system and the consultant function is mainly advisory.

Education/Training

As change agents, counselors can impart the knowledge and skills that systems need in order to function more competently. Carkhuff's (1976) systematic human resource development (HRD) model, for example, uses an educational approach to changing a system by training all levels of individuals in the skills that are necessary to function within that system. Skill development for individuals within a system would include interpersonal problem-solving and program development skills such as provided by workshops and structured groups on parent education training, assertiveness skills, wellness education, stress-reduction education, lifestyle decision-making processes, and the like. The purpose of an educational or training function is to provide individuals with the tools that they can use in a variety of lifelong tasks.

Program Development

This function is closely related to the following one, organizational development. Both functions focus on permitting individuals within a system to develop the capacity to use their cumulative resources to change a system. Lewis and Lewis (1983) noted that program planning and development must include: (a) assessing system needs, (b) setting priorities, (c) identifying resources, and (d) developing appropriate programs to meet the needs. An integral part of the counselor's role is to insure that program development is done by and with those who will use the program's services, that linkages with existing services are established, and that the rights of all involved are protected.

Organizational Development

This systems change intervention is widely used within business and industry. It is based, to a large extent, on group decision-making processes and theories of how groups can function as change agents within organizations. The T-group and sensitivity training movements of the 1960s originated within the context of organizational development (Bradford, Gibb, & Benne, 1964).

As a system, organizations are composed of people with different work roles as well as personal values, beliefs, and behaviors. They comprise subsystems with different goals, technologies, and structures. The relationship between these subsystems varies according to organizational norms, "culture," or, in systems theory, boundaries. The boundaries of an organization are where intervention occurs. These boundaries are shared assumptions about rules, work, and the amount of participatory decision-making that individuals are allowed.

Two general intervention strategies are used to change or modify organizational boundaries (Friedlander & Brown, 1974). The sociotechnical method attempts to increase job satisfaction through redesigning a job task or role so that it is enlarged and the worker can derive satisfaction from seeing a product completed and obtain a sense of contributing to the whole rather than a part. For example, autoworkers have traditionally been assigned one very specific task that is performed on every car that comes down the assembly line. By redesigning the job so that a worker performs a variety of tasks until a car is completed, the worker can derive some satisfaction from seeing a broader goal achieved. The second approach, labeled "human processual," helps to increase the workers' participation in the organization's processes and decisions. Some of the techniques used would be providing feedback through surveys and other research that is summarized and presented to the group. The group then makes specific recommendations regarding necessary changes. Another technique would be team-building (Argyris, 1982), which seeks to change attitudes within an organization by setting mutually agreed-upon goals, building interpersonal relations, and clarifying roles and responsibilities. A third technique would be developing the relationships between subsystems by engaging in problem-solving activities.

The mental health counselor as a change agent can be either a part of the organization or function as an outside consultant. For example, if the counselor were providing employee assistance service (see chapter 13) from either an internal or external role, these services could be expanded from an individual to an organizational focus of intervention. However, caveats must be made about changing a system from within: Many times the counselor can become enmeshed in the system and responses can become subjective rather than objective in relation to the system's concerns. If potential role conflicts can be overcome, the mental health counselor who is part of an organization, whether it is business and industry, an educational institution, or governmental agency, can assume responsibility for organizational development interventions.

In summary, the change agent model for the mental health counselor is derived from an ecological, preventive perspective that is wholly consistent with the philosophical approach to mental health counseling presented in this book. It perceives the most efficient level of intervention as that of a system (communities or governments, families, educational institutions, and places of employment), and seeks to facilitate change through the functions of advocacy, consultation, education, program and organization development, and similar strategies.

CONCLUSION

As stated earlier, the practice of mental health counseling considers the individual within the environment, focuses on the client's assets rather than deficits, and is oriented toward developmental and preventive rather than remedial needs. Basic to understanding these assumptions is the counselor's viewpoint regarding human nature and how change occurs through a helping relationship. Once this viewpoint is identified, the counselor can then appreciate the importance of selected conceptual models that have been explained in this chapter. Each model provides guidelines for mental health counseling intervention.

REFERENCES

Albee, G. (1980). A competency model to replace the defect mode. In M. S. Gibbs, J. R. Lachenmeyer, & J. Sigal (Eds.), *Community psychology: Theoretical and empirical approaches* (pp. 213–238). New York: Gardner Press.

American Psychiatric Association. (1980). *Diagnostic and statistical manual of mental disorders (DSM-III).* Washington, DC: Author.

Argyris, C. (1982). *Interpersonal competence and organizational effectiveness.* Homewood, IL: Irwin.

Bradford, L. P., Gibb, J. R., & Benne, K. D. (1964). *T group theory and laboratory method.* New York: Wiley.

Broussard, E. R. (1977). Primary prevention program for newborn infants at high risk for emotional disorder. In D. C. Klein & S. E. Goldston (Eds.), *Primary prevention: An idea whose time has come* (pp. 63–75). Washington, DC: U.S. Government Printing Office.

Brown, G. W., & Harris, T. (1978). *Social origins of depression.* London: Tavistock.

Brown, G. W., Harris, T. O., & Peto, J. (1983). Life events and psychiatric disorders. Part II: Nature of the causal link. *Psychological Medicine, 3,* 159–176.

Cantwell, D. P. (1972). Psychiatric illness in the families of hyperactive children. *Archives of General Psychiatry, 70,* 414–417.

Caplan, G. (1970). *The theory and practice of mental health consultation.* New York: Basic.

Carkhuff, R. R. (1976). The development of systematic human resource development models. In G. S. Belkin (Ed.), *Counseling: Directions in theory and practice* (pp. 210–219). Dubuque, IA: Kendall/Hunt.

Conyne, R. K. (1981). *Environmental assessment and design: A new tool for the applied behavioral scientist.* New York: Praeger.

Conyne, R. K. (1985). The counseling ecologist: Helping people and environments. *Counseling and Human Development, 18*(2), 1–12.

Conyne, R., & Rogers, R. (1977). Psychotherapy as ecological problem-solving. *Psychotherapy: Theory, research and practice, 14*(3), 298–305.

Cook, D. R. (Ed.). (1971). *Guidance for education in revolution.* Boston: Allyn & Bacon.

Cormier, W. H., & Cormier, L. S. (1979). *Interviewing strategies for helpers: A guide to assessment, treatment, and evaluation.* Monterey, CA: Brooks/Cole.

D'Zurilla, T. J., & Goldfried, M. R. (1971). Problem solving and behavior modification. *Journal of Abnormal Psychology, 78,* 107–126.

Egan, G. (1982). *The skilled helper: Model, skills, and methods for effective helping.* Monterey, CA: Brooks/Cole.

Ellis, A. (1962). *Reason and emotion in psychotherapy.* New York: Lyle Stuart.

Ellis, A. (1973). *Humanistic psychotherapy: The rational-emotive approach.* New York: Julian Press.

Friedlander, F., & Brown, L. D. (1974). Organizational development. *Annual Review of Psychology, 25,* 313–341.

Gershon, E. S., Bunney, W. E., Leckman, J. F., van Eerdewegh, M., & DeBauche, B. A. (1976). The inheritance of affective disorders: A review of data and of hypotheses. *Behavior Genetics, 6,* 227–261.

Goldston, S. E. (1977). An overview of primary prevention programming. In D. C. Klein & S. E. Goldston (Eds.), *Primary prevention: An idea whose time has come* (pp. 23–40). Washington, DC: U.S. Government Printing Office.

Hackney, H., & Cormier, L. S. (1979). *Counseling strategies and objectives (2nd ed.).* Englewood Cliffs, NJ: Prentice-Hall.

Hollister, W. G. (1977). Basic strategies in designing primary prevention programs. In D. C. Klein & S. E. Goldston (Eds.), *Primary prevention: An idea whose time has come.* Washington, DC: U.S. Government Printing Office.

Huber, C. H. (1983). A social–ecological approach to the counseling process. *American Mental Health Counselors Association Journal, 5*(1), 4–11.

Insel, P., & Moos, R. (1974). Psychological environments: Expanding the scope of huma ecology. *American Psychologist, 29*(3), 179–188.

Ivey, A. E., & Simek-Downing, L. (1980). *Counseling and psychotherapy: Skills, theories, and practice.* Englewood Cliffs, NJ: Prentice-Hall.

Jacobs, T., & Charles, E. (1980). Life events and the occurrence of cancer in children. *Psychosomatic Medicine, 42,* 11–23.

Justice, B. (1982). *Crisis intervention.* Beverly Hills: Sage.

Knitzer, J. (1980). Advocacy and community psychology. In M. S. Gibbs, J. R. Lachenmeyer, & J. Sigal (Eds.), *Community psychology: Theoretical and empirical approaches.* New York: Gardner Press.

Kurpius, D. J. (1985). Consultation interventions: Successes, failures and proposals. *The Counseling Psychologist, 13*(3), 368–389.

Lamb, H. R., & Zusman, J. (1979). Primary prevention in perspective. *American Journal of Psychiatry, 136,* 12–17.

Lazarus, R. S. (1984). On the primacy of cognition. *American Psychologist, 39*(2), 124–130.

Lewin, K. (1936). *Principles of topological psychology.* New York: McGraw-Hill.

Lewis, J. A., & Lewis, M. D. (1983). *Community counseling: A human services approach* (2nd ed.). New York: John Wiley & Sons.

Loehlin, J. C., & Nichols, R. C. (1976). *Heredity, environment and personality.* Austin, TX: University of Texas Press.

Lynch, J. (1977). *The broken heart.* New York: Basic Books.

Pine, G. J. (1976). Troubled times for school counselors. *Focus on Guidance, 8,* 1–16.

Schlossberg, N. (1984). *Counseling adults in transition: Linking practice with theory.* New York: Springer.

Schneidman, E. (1973). Crisis intervention: Some thoughts and perspectives. In G. Specter & W. Claiborn (Eds.), *Crisis intervention* (pp. 9–15). New York: Behavioral Publications.

Seligman, M. E. P. (1975). *Helplessness: On depression, development and death.* San Francisco: Freeman.

Sheehy, G. (1976). *Passages: Predictable crises of adult life.* New York: E. P. Dutton.

Shoben, E. J. (1962). Guidance: Remedial function or social reconstruction? *Harvard Educational Review, 32,* 431–443.

Silverman, P. R. (1972). Widowhood and preventive intervention. *The Family Coordinator, 21,* 95–102.

Spivack, G., & Shure, M. B. (1977). Preventively oriented cognitive education of preschoolers. In D. C. Klein & S. E. Goldston (Eds.), *Primary prevention: An idea whose time has come* (pp. 79–82). Washington, DC: U.S. Government Printing Office.

Steele, F. (1973). *Physical settings and organizational development.* Reading, MA: Addison-Wesley.

Trist, E. L. (1969). On sociotechnical systems. In W. G. Bennis, K. D. Benne, & R. Chin (Eds.), *The planning of change.* New York: Holt, Rinehart & Winston.

Vaillant, G. E., & Milofsky, E. S. (1982). The etiology of alcoholism: A prospective viewpoint. *American Psychologist, 37*(5), 494–503.

Von Bertalanffy, L. (1968). *General systems theory: Foundations, development, applications.* New York: George Braziller.

Zajonc, R. B. (1984). On the primacy of affect. *American Psychologist, 39*(2), 117–123.

6 Research on Counseling Effectiveness

The growth of the mental health professions has resulted in increased attention on the effectiveness of clinical services. Whether impelled by the emphasis on professionalization or compelled by increasing public and governmental pressure, practitioners now face the task of demonstrating accountability for their services (Butcher, Scofield, & Baker, 1984; Riggs, 1979). The agencies of the federal government, local governing boards, and consumers have begun to show considerable interest in the efficacy of mental health counseling. The ability to demonstrate effectiveness of the therapeutic process will continue to be of the utmost necessity and concern to the profession (Baruth & Huber, 1985). Many people who have high hopes and have offered strong support for mental health services in past years are now wondering whether the needs they saw—and still see—are being met. The word *accountability*, which was rarely heard in the 1960s, is in common use in the 1970s and 1980s.

Remer (1981) stated that counselors need research relevant to their effectiveness because they "have an ethical, if not legal and moral responsibility to both their clients and the public to know the effects and limits of the tools and techniques they use" (p. 569). Bridging the gap between outcome research and the practice of mental health counseling is a special concern in the 1980s. Lewis and Hutson (1983) explained that Congress and the agencies of the federal government have considerable interest in the efficacy of counseling and psychotherapy. These authors wrote:

> The 1980 Senate Bill 3029 included a section to create a 13 member national professional mental health commission to study the safety and efficacy of various mental health treatment approaches. A similar bill, S.647, was introduced in 1981. The ability to demonstrate the effectiveness of counseling will be important for the future of our profession. (p. 532)

Mental health counseling is both an art and a science (Seligman, 1985). Though there is very little conclusive evidence currently available to indicate that existing counseling activities are worth doing, many emotional and hard-fought struggles have been waged regarding effectiveness (Eysenck, 1978; Hurvitz, 1974). There is no easy answer to the question, "Is counseling effective?" (Lewis & Hutson, 1983). But studies have been reported that suggest reliable approaches to evaluate counselor productivity. They will be discussed later in this chapter.

Moreover, although much has been written about the training of different types of mental health professionals, that is, psychiatric workers, substance abuse counselors, marriage and family therapists, and so on, the mental health professions have given little attention to the evaluation of mental health personnel after they are trained. The reasons are many. Mental health workers in agencies with high case loads simply do not have the time to build evaluation efforts into their work. Agency rewards for doing evaluation are few. Also, many mental health professionals may feel threatened by an evaluation of their programs or clinical work. They may be so emotionally attached to a pet project or a theoretical point of view that any kind of accountability or evaluation is perceived as a personal threat to one's competence or professional reputation. Finally, a further reason for few existing evaluation efforts is the lack of evaluation methodology in mental health training programs. Today most mental health counselors have come from a variety of disciplines, such as community counseling, psychology, social work, rehabilitation counseling, and nursing. A majority of practicing mental health workers have finished an undergraduate or graduate program in which they completed a course in elementary statistics and perhaps a course in basic research. Though these individuals may have an overview of sophisticated research methodologies, they usually do not receive instruction on how to evaluate their work in the context of the difficulties and obstacles encountered in the real world of mental health counseling practice.

The efforts since 1980 to develop certification and licensure requirements for mental health counselors, and to maintain these guidelines, represent considerable improvements in enhancing accountability and effectiveness of these professionals. But accountability and effectiveness are broad concepts, and they include, beyond defined credentialing guidelines, the assumed responsibility for the evaluation of "professional" or clinical success and failures, and the translation of this information into constructive decisions that may modify current services (Crabbs, 1984). Yet there is a movement toward establishing measurable criteria for evaluating counseling endeavors (Henjum, 1982; Hiebert, 1982; Martin & Hiebert, 1982). Several procedures for collecting such data are presented in the literature (Hiebert, 1982).

This chapter will identify the relevant issues concerned with the effectiveness of mental health counselors, and explain the different approaches that have been developed to evaluate the effectiveness of counseling. A relationship will be indicated between these approaches and current mental health practice. Importantly, however, the reader should be aware that the words *accountable* and *effective* will be used often in this chapter. They have different meanings, for accountability refers both to a process of responsibility and a periodic awareness of this same responsibility. On the other hand, effective means the quality of one's counseling and professional work. It includes the product of one's efforts. Yet in any efforts that the mental health counseling field may employ to enhance its clinical practice, both terms come under active consideration.

ISSUES CONCERNED WITH THE CONTENT OF COUNSELOR EFFECTIVENESS

One important finding of outcome research is the differential effectiveness among counselors (Lewis & Hutson, 1983). All counselors do not develop the same relationships with clients even when they presume to be operating from the same frame of reference and are presumably using the same techniques (Diamond & Shapiro, 1973; Lieberman, Yalom, & Miles, 1973). Moreover, the majority of studies do not clearly define counseling effects, and they fail to show consistent outcomes (Lewis & Hutson, 1983). There are many issues, consequently, that have an impact on counselor effectiveness. They represent factors that can determine the quality of counseling outcome, and should be considered before the different approaches are identified that measure the success or failure of counseling efforts. They also suggest the many difficulties when evaluating counseling effectiveness. These issues are: (a) the role of the counselor, (b) certification and licensure, (c) measurability of results, (d) the counselor as a person, (e) therapeutic credibility, (f) counselor skills, (g) voluntary client involvement, (h) the degree counseling meets the client's needs, and (i) client awareness of the impairing problem.

Role of Counselor

Each mental health counselor is unique, "bringing his or her own personality and mood to whatever tools and techniques are used, individualizing them to suit both counselor and client" (Seligman, 1985, p. 2). The role of the mental health counselor is being stated, restated, interpreted, and reinterpreted until a point is reached where counselors can become fearful of being evaluated by administrators who may do little or no counseling themselves. The role of the mental health counselor, moreover, has not been and may never be clearly delineated. But efforts continue in the areas of identifying "ideal" counselor personality characteristics as well as credentialing of the counselor through certification or licensure (Riggs, 1979).

The fiscal austerity of the late 1970s and early 1980s and the attendant demands for accountability have highlighted the need for a clarification of the counselor's role. Do counselors only perform clerical and record-keeping functions? Ibraham, Helms, and Thompson (1983) reported a study in which administrators, school counselors, parents, and the business community associated with 23 schools were surveyed for an identification of school counselor roles and functions. With 1,017 surveys completed, the results indicated that school counselors and administrators considered counseling, helping parents and families, and public relations of great importance; in contrast, parents and the business community rated educational and occupational planning as more important.

Though mental health counselors are employed in many other settings than schools, this study suggests that there are different role perceptions of counselor roles. These varied perceptions can influence any attempt at evaluating counseling effectiveness, for the question can be asked: "What is to be assessed—clerical functions, clinical work with the client, public relations efforts, or a relationship with agency administrators?" So the effort to define the role of the mental health counselor continues.

Certification and Licensure

The movement toward counselor certification has far-reaching implications for counselor effectiveness. In March 1978, the American Mental Health Counselors Association (AMHCA) elected to establish a national certification system for mental health counselors, utilizing guidelines that were developed from reading federal government research concerning credentialing of health-related professions (Messina, 1985). The National Academy of Certified Clinical Mental Health Counselors was developed by the AMHCA as an effort to firmly establish the role and identity of mental health counselors in the field of counseling as well as in the field of mental health. The academy promotes regulatory guidelines and standards for those who practice under the title of "counselor." Yet definite criteria have not been developed for the "effective" mental health counselor. What has been done is to establish guidelines that could facilitate effectiveness in clinical, community practice.

Measurability of Counseling Results

This issue is concerned with such questions as: How can effectiveness be measured? . . . Does client satisfaction, or observable client change, or a counselor's career promotion represent expressions of counselor effectiveness? Positive responses to these questions may suggest that the mental health counselor is performing well, but cause and effect are the basic ingredients for any measurement exercise (Humes, 1972). The difficulty that arises for counseling, particularly from the standpoint of the practitioner, is that the cause, or input, is frequently so fuzzy or unstructured that there is no way of defining its effect, or output. There are many components of mental health services, and counselor evaluation activities have only focused on outcome. Not much consideration has been given to other counseling dimensions, such as referral information, occupational knowledge, and client assessment conducted as a preliminary step to actual counseling.

The difficulties inherent in the measurability of counselor effectiveness become apparent when determining client satisfaction. The criterion of consumer satisfaction is often used as one, important guideline for counselor quality. The assessment of consumer satisfaction with mental health services is a recent and growing phenomenon (Heath, Hultberg, Ramey, & Ries, 1984). The evaluation of consumer satisfaction can document the benefit of services (Lebow, 1982), and can provide useful information to aid in the decision-making process (Larson, Attkisson, Hargreaves, & Nguyen, 1979). But client satisfaction surveys have also not elicited many suggestions or complaints from patients and former patients when they have been asked to give open-ended comments on services (Justice & McBee, 1978). There may be an inclination on the part of clients to express satisfaction because of a hidden fear that if they do not, present or future institutional services may be withdrawn. Also, a number of researchers believe that counselors and clients must have similar perceptions of the therapeutic relationship if a satisfying outcome is to be achieved (Strong, 1968; Zarski, Sweeney, & Barcikowski, 1977).

Studies on client satisfaction have suggested, therefore, that the evaluation of counselor effectiveness should be done from a variety of perspectives, that is, supervisor, client, independent judge, and on several dimensions. These dimensions might include: (a) an evaluation of the counselor's conceptual knowledge of counseling dynamics and interaction patterns, (b) an assessment of the counselor's agency from the perspective of the supervisor and an objective observer, and (c) an assessment of counseling outcome (Zarski, Bubenzer, & Walter, 1980).

Quality of the Counselor as a Person

Boy and Pine (1978) believe that the counseling process has little hope of producing positive results unless it flows from the qualities of the counselor as a person. Frank (1979) explained that "the results of outcome research strongly suggest that more of the determinants of therapeutic success lie in the personal qualities of the patient and the therapist and in their interaction than in the therapeutic method" (p. 311). These qualities include age, sex, race, empathy, genuineness, respect, and a willingness to listen to the client's problem. But for purposes of measuring counselor effectiveness, these qualities can not be mathematically identified. The quality of the counselor as a person is an often unresearchable influence. Also, each client is unique, and the encounter with the counselor is unique.

Mental health counselors, consequently, are as different from each other as all other people are different from each other, but the one trait that all good counselors have in common is sincerity in their relationships with other people. The counselor must also be one who understands the background and training of the people with whom he or she works, has an understanding of these people's problems, and behaves in a way that shows he or she really cares for people and wants to help them help themselves (Siegel, 1969). Yet the problem of determining who qualifies as the "good" mental health counselor remains basically unsolved. Perhaps the evaluation of a counselor's worth must be self-evaluation (Siegel, 1969).

Intimately associated with the qualities of a counselor are values. The influence of the values of mental health professionals is recognized in the literature, especially the potential effect of these values on the process and outcome of counseling (Margolin, 1982; Strupp, 1980). To explore whether different mental health workers have similar or divergent values, Khan and Cross (1984) conducted a survey of 58 psychiatrists, 173 psychologists, and 282 social workers. They found that the three groups of mental health professionals all stressed the desirability of being honest, loving, and broad-minded and emphasized the importance of inner harmony, wisdom, and mature love. But the psychologists placed more emphasis on values associated with individual development (i.e., ambitious, independent); the social workers placed more importance on values reflecting a better life (i.e., cheerfulness, equality); and the psychiatrists tended to support values that suggest the maintenance of the status quo (i.e., obedience, national security). Given the pervasive influence of the therapist's values in any therapeutic change process (Margolin, 1982), Khan and Cross (1984) believed that on the basis of their study, each of the professional groups could be expected, in the context of working with a client, to pursue different perspectives. These viewpoints may be an important factor in the outcome of individual counselor–client relationships.

Counselor Therapeutic Credibility

Boy and Pine (1978) explained that clients must believe in the counselor's ability to render therapeutic assistance. In other words, clients must have faith in the actual or potential productivity of the relationship. This credibility may be communicated in many ways, such as the ongoing, positive reputation of the mental health worker; the counselor's recognized educational and training background; the organizational involvement of the worker (i.e., professional associations and memberships); and the factors of credentialing and licensure. Credibility can also be communicated through the counselor's total caring attitude toward the client. The client may sense the existence of this caring attitude and then respond to it with a keen awareness that the counselor possesses therapeutic credibility.

Skills of the Counselor

The counselor usually has certain discernible and positive counseling skills. These skills include the ability to attend to the client, be empathic, listen effectively, and respond both to the client's feelings and the content of the verbal message. Client complaints and even satisfaction are related to the counselor's ability to utilize these skills.

Voluntary Client Involvements

Many clients are referred to a mental health counselor by agencies or the courts. Counseling is mandated, and the referral source expects that the services provided by the mental health counselor will assist the client to correct wrongdoing and follow the law. Yet counseling can be far more productive when the client is voluntarily involved in a relationship with a counselor. Persons tend to invest themselves in experiences that are freely chosen and tend to resist experiences not voluntarily chosen (Boy & Pines 1978).

Since 1970, specific developments in the delivery of helping services have encouraged the voluntary participation of the client in the way services are provided. Public Law 94-142 and the necessity of the Individualized Education Plan (IEP), the Rehabilitation Amendments of 1973, and the mandate for the Individualized Written Rehabilitation Plan (IWRP) have prompted counselors to examine carefully their relationships with clients so that participation can be ensured. This client involvement lays the groundwork for a more productive, effective counseling outcome. If clients freely consent to the plans for the implementation of services, then there is a greater possibility for both client satisfaction and an outcome that responds to client needs. Moreover, the legislative and agency push for this client participation is an expression of the mental health counselor's respect for the dignity and worth of the person.

Degree Counseling Meets Client Needs

It should be self-evident that the counseling process should meet the needs of clients. Yet often many mental health counselors approach a helping situation with the attitude: "I know what is best for you," or, "all that matters is your label," or, "I am here to save you." A counselor may also project a certain theoretical bias to all clients, and does not pay attention to the different needs of clients who did not fit the theoretical model (Boy & Pine, 1978). These attitudes can even be subtle influences that deflect the mental health counseling process toward the counselor's needs, and not those of clients. Inattention to client needs is frequently a reflection of the counselor's lack of basic communication and relationship skills, such as listening and attending.

An aspect of this avoidance of client needs occurs when, for a variety of reasons, the referral service designates that certain persons should undergo counseling while being inattentive to whether these persons actually do need counseling. Occasionally, clients are referred to a mental health agency that specializes in meeting certain client needs in a particular problem area although these referred clients possess no latent or actual needs that can be met by this particular agency.

Client Awareness of Impairing Problem

Mental health counselors spend much time convincing their clients that certain behaviors must change. Often these clients are referred by sources that have identified specific behavior problems that interfere with the effective functioning of these clients. Both the referral source and the counselor agree that a problem exists for the client, but the client does not possess the same awareness. Yet the counselor may simply go ahead and apply the required skills for the treatment of the identified problem. But the client does not change. Yet when the client understands both the existence of a behavior problem, and its implications for appropriate, daily functioning, then this person may be motivated to continue in a counseling relationship and perhaps expend the energy necessary to solve the problem (Carkhuff & Anthony, 1979). Effective counseling can flow from this understanding.

Though there could be additional influences or issues that have an impact on counselor effectiveness, such as counselor intelligence or a counselor's administrative authority that might inhibit clients from being honest, open, and revealing in a counseling relationship, the preceding issues suggest causes that may determine a positive outcome to helping efforts. Yet each cause is most difficult to measure mathematically and a definite relationship between each cause and outcome is only suggested, not definitely established. Despite the difficulties in identifying precisely what produces effective counseling, approaches still need to be considered that will provide a direction to evaluating effective counseling. These approaches will be discussed in the next chapter.

APPROACHES TO EVALUATE COUNSELOR EFFECTIVENESS

The literature has indicated that when evaluating mental health counseling there are certain basic guidelines to follow (Henjum, 1982; Hiebert, 1982; Krumboltz, 1974; Lipsett, 1971). Hiebert (1982) and Krumboltz (1974) have particularly contributed to the development of these guidelines. Hiebert (1982) believed that counseling effectiveness is a broad concept, extending beyond the traditional limits and program evaluation, and should include data on the counselor's intervention behaviors, client adherence to the counseling intervention, and client change. He also explained that a well-defined and implemented effectiveness model is (a) systematic and planned, with recognized time lines; (b) continuous and concurrent with counselor and agency activities; (c) comprehensive in embracing all important functions of the counselor's work; (d) linked with both the counselor's and agency's philosophy and objectives; and (e) inclusive of formal and informal data gathering and record-keeping techniques.

Krumboltz (1974), in discussing an accountability model for counselors, explained five criteria that must be met if an accountability approach is to produce the desired results. They are:

1. When defining the domain of counselor responsibility, the general goals of counseling must be agreed to by all concerned parties. Identifying these goals is difficult, however, for one goal might be rigidly preset, and other problems are overlooked. For example, a general goal for returning the de-institutionalized client to paid employment might be important, but it could bypass a more immediate goal, such as a suitable adjustment to daily living demands.

2. Counselor accomplishments must be stated in terms of important, observable, behavior changes by clients. Krumboltz (1974) emphasized that outcomes for each individual client must be potentially observable, tailored to individual circumstances, and agreed to by both client and counselor. If a counselor, for example, wishes to reduce a client's substance abuse behavior, the term *reduction* must be carefully defined. In other words, will it mean a 100%, 80%, or 60% cutback in drug intake?

3. An accountability system must be constructed to promote professional effectiveness and self-improvement, not to cast blame or punish poor performance. The approaches to measure counselor effectiveness should be wholeheartedly supported by everyone involved, that is, administrators and supervisors.

4. In order that accurate reporting may be achieved, reports of failures and unknown outcomes must be permitted and never punished. Many of the outcomes of mental health counseling may not be known for years. All counselors experience failure, for success cannot be achieved with every client. Knowledge of failures must also be accurately reported.

5. Any system of accountability must be developed by all those who are going to use it. Representation of all constituents is necessary in order to obtain everyone's ideas and insure cooperation (Krumboltz, 1974).

The types of evaluative data collected by counselors, moreover, include such things as the number of visits, the type of clients, the type of referring problems, agency performance, and some general index of overall client satisfaction (Henjum, 1982). But when this type of information is used in effectiveness and accountability arguments, it is not surprising that administrators are usually not convinced. Also, counselors are often evaluated favorably because their intervention or program fits into established procedures, or because a certain intervention has appeared well and traditionally worked in other settings, such as a job-club group or assertiveness training. But can a counselor be judged as effective by simply utilizing these methods without exploring whether they actually are relevant to a specific population? Further, counselors are often judged as effective because their interventions have helped one particular person, and they have not been attempted on other clients.

There are other, perhaps more practical problems that must be solved in order to implement a useful accountable plan. For example, once it is accepted that evaluation of counselors is desirable, it is necessary to identify evaluative criteria. In other words, what are the parameters for excellence in doing mental health counseling? Lipsett (1971) believed that evidence of counselor effectiveness may be found in requests for consultation, in volunteering professional services, and in broader aspects of participation such as adviserships and committee memberships. But even with these criteria, such questions remain as: "How good are one's counseling interviews?" "How effective are one's reports?" "How will counselors record their daily activities?" "How will information about the outcomes of counseling be collected?" "What safeguards will be needed to preserve client confidentiality and prevent abuse of the information?" In attempting to resolve these questions, the costs may outweigh the benefits.

All of the preceding guidelines strongly indicate that special approaches are needed when evaluating counselor effectiveness. A medical approach, in which a licensed practitioner is subject to no evaluation or control unless one is found to violate some law or ethic, cannot be followed. There is too much societal pressure for accountability that would preclude any waiting for an ethical violation. Nor can an industrial model be utilized for measuring counselor effectiveness, because in this approach employees tend to be evaluated in relation to their contribution to profits. Yet direct measurement of the productivity of professional workers such as mental health counselors is seldom possible. Other models or approaches must be developed, therefore. The literature does contain both theoretical approaches or designs from which evaluation directions can evolve, and particular approaches that have been formulated in counseling practice. The theoretical designs will be discussed now, and approaches that have evolved from these designs and reported in the literature will then be explained.

DESIGNS

Many experimental and quasi-experimental designs have been used in social research. Six models that bear the simple-case, quasi-experimental, interrupted time series, and goal attainment labels will be briefly explained.

They all have relevance to evaluating counselor effectiveness. Ethical considerations, as will be stated, prevent the utilizations of other designs, such as an
untreated control group design with pretest and posttest, or a removed treatment design with pretest and posttest. Moreover, much of the following material is taken from Cook and Campbell (1979), who have written on
quasi-experimentation and its analysis for field settings. Their material, however, is being applied here for consideration in measuring counselor effectiveness.

Single-Case Designs

Hiebert (1984) explained that since 1980 some authors have suggested the
use of single-case designs to evaluate counseling effect. The practicing mental
health counselor is in a position to make almost every interview applicable to
counseling research. When procedures for differential diagnosis are systematic (Hutchins, 1982) and treatment is well documented, it is possible to
approximate a multiple baseline design across clients with similar presenting
problems. Hiebert (1984) stated that "If client changes occur in similar patterns across similar cases that use similar interventions, then a strong argument can be made that a causal influence of the counseling interaction is
producing the change" (p. 599).

One-Group Posttest-Only Design

This approach involves making observations only on persons who have
undergone a treatment, and then only after they have received it. A client
experiencing depression, for example, is referred to a mental health counselor.
After the intervention, the counselor ascertains what progress the client has
made in alleviating the depression. One basic deficiency is the lack of pretest
observations from persons receiving the treatment. As a result, one cannot
easily infer that the treatment is related to any kind of change (Cook & Campbell, 1979). Also, a second deficiency is the lack of a control group of persons
who did not receive the treatment. Yet in most mental health clinical settings,
a control group is not possible. To obtain the control group, one would have to
deny clients necessary treatment, or delay it for a future time. Such denial or
delays may not be possible.

It is important to note that this design is not the same as the "one-shot case
study." Explained earlier, single-setting, one-time period case studies occur in
settings where many variables or characteristics can be identified and perhaps
even measured. Then the counselor, in attempting to evaluate the effectiveness
of the intervention, may have enough information to rule out alternative possi-

bilities. For example, the difference in the client's mental condition after intervention is not due to chance, or solely to such environmental influences as the client's family or occupation. A case study analysis of these factors has provided enough information to the counselor to eliminate them as the main causes of the client's improved mental state.

One-Group Pretest–Posttest Design

This approach is one of the more frequently used designs in the social sciences (Cook & Campbell, 1979). It supposes that pretest observations are recorded on a single group of persons, who later receive a treatment, after which posttest observations are made. A group of clients, for example, may be referred to a community mental health center or a vocational rehabilitation program for the acquisition of job-finding and job-keeping skills. The counselor, before the intervention begins, decides to assess the clients' skill levels in these two employment-related areas. This could be done through structured, validated questionnaires. Then the treatment is given, such as group training, and following this intervention, the same questionnaire is given again to the same clients.

Of course, in appraising the value of this design, the counselor could infer that perhaps other events may have taken place outside of the intervention, that is, during group training time, that might affect skill acquisition. Some of the clients might be employed part-time in a sheltered workshop and learn a few basic job-keeping skills. In order to eliminate this, or other possibilities, the counselor has to make his or her case as to whether or not such possibilities are plausible. Experience and information are required for buttressing the argument of implausibility (Cook & Campbell, 1979).

In many mental health clinical situations, however, it may not be possible to obtain "pretest" information. The counselor may not be knowledgeable about ways to gain this information, or the nature of the presenting problem simply makes it too difficult. A crisis situation, for example, in which one is interviewing a married couple who have just lost, through a sudden accident, their only child, may not lend itself to using standardized questionnaires. Apart from impressionistic observations, the counselor may not be able to identify just how much difference one's intervention made in the couple's change of mood or life-adjustment. Other factors, such as other positive influences on the couple or simply the passage of time, might be strong causal determinants of the clients' change. Consequently, unless the counselor has a valid pretreatment measure, and is working with novel outcomes and in short pretest–posttest time intervals, causal inferences to the "why" of client change must be made cautiously (Cook & Campbell, 1979).

The Repeated-Treatment/Intervention Design

When the mental health counselor has access to only a single population, such as those, for example, who have been recently released from long-term (2–4 years) confinement in a mental institution, it may sometimes be possible to introduce the intervention, fade it out, an then re-introduce it at a later date. This approach is most viable in contexts where the initial effects of the intervention are transient or do not prevent the treatment from having an even stronger effect when it is re-introduced (Cook & Campbell, 1979). A counselor, for example, may develop a psychoeducational group to teach community living skills to these clients. The initial effects of this intervention may only be temporary, as it may be difficult for the clients either to retain or to implement consistently the training. When the training is re-introduced, it may have a stronger impact for the clients' community living skills. Regarding the value of this design, however, Cook & Campbell (1979) believe that this approach is best when the re-introductions of the intervention are frequent and randomly distributed across time blocks.

Simple Interrupted Time Series

This is the most basic time-series design and requires either one client or one group of clients and multiple observations before and after an intervention. A counselor, for example, may be treating a client or a group of clients for the alleviation of a specific problem, such as shyness. With a questionnaire, the counselor may be able to determine the intensity of the problem as indicated by behavioral deficits, and then after the particular intervention the client may return periodically to give feedback to the counselor. At this time, the questionnaire may be repeated.

Though the design may appear attractive as a possible way to determine if the counselor's efforts are making a difference, it is usually unrealistic to expect either that most clients will return to provide feedback, or, that a counselor has the time to locate clients for evaluative purposes. Of course, another threat to the internal validity of this design is intervening history, namely, the possibility that forces other than the counselor's intervention came to influence, for example, the reduction of shyness. The client may have read an article in the paper on how to reduce shyness, or a friend may have spent considerable time with the client in teaching assertiveness skills. Yet if careful records are kept of all plausible effect-causing events that could influence the client during the intervention, it could be possible to assess whether any of them were operative between the last questionnaire and the first questionnaire. If they were not, intervening history is less plausible as a threat (Cook & Campbell, 1979).

Goal Attainment Scaling

Paritzky and Magoon (1982) believed that another procedure for collecting systematic data that is comparable across clients is goal attainment scaling. This is a procedure whereby clients identify specific counseling objectives and criterion descriptors that would be evidence of varying degrees of outcome expectation, typically ranging from much better than expected, to as expected, to much worse than expected (Hiebert, 1984). Clients rate their current level of behavior at the beginning of treatment and also at the end of treatment. Hiebert (1984) explained that "using this procedure, it is possible to have some measure of counseling effectiveness that is comparable across different clients with different problems" (p. 599).

The six designs discussed in the preceding sections represent different frameworks for the development of approaches for evaluating counselor effectiveness. Each design has its own difficulties regarding threats to external and internal validity. Yet each design or framework has provided a structure or direction for selected approaches that have been utilized in counseling practice. Six of these approaches will now be explained.

COMMUNICATION-BASED MODEL

Pulvino and Sanborn (1972) proposed a program of accountability based on communication theory. All those involved in the evaluation must be able to transmit and receive information that is relatively unencumbered by the transmission process. The concept of feedback is central to their theory, for without feedback the total system would be inoperative, counselors would be isolated, and accountability would not exist (Pulvino & Sanborn, 1972). Their accountability approach includes the following five phases.

Dialogue with the Public

Achievement of mental health counseling goals is a joint responsibility of the professional and one's public. The public would comprise such people as the counselor, the clients themselves, the administration, and perhaps significant others of the client. As the counselor provides expertise and follow-through activity, so the public provides demands or needs. A communication system must be developed whereby the public and the counselor come to a mutual understanding of the needs to be met, agreement on goals, and sharing of responsibility based on realistic role expectations for each person included in the public. Pulvino and Sanborn (1972) explained that counselors must be willing to alter their own services and be able to effect changes in the activities of others so that the relevant needs of the public may be realized.

Joint Development of Measurable Objectives

Because counseling is a joint responsibility, it is imperative that all partici-pants help to establish goals (Pulvino & Sanborn, 1972). Further, it is impor-tant that these goals be stated in operational terms, and once these goals are specific, then the counselor should provide an understanding of how one's competencies and those of other relevant persons, that is, administrators and the client's significant others, can be used to achieve the goals. This again necessitates two-way communication.

The Counseling Process

The particular counseling process that is selected may include not only activities of the counselor, but also responsibility and action of the client and others who are involved by virtue of their association with the client (Pulvino & Sanborn, 1972). In this accountability approach, however, the authors emphasized that counselors must help individuals to develop the ability to use feedback procedures. In other words, during the counseling process, clients must feel free to give feedback to their counselors. Client needs may change. For example, in helping a client to secure employment, initial discussions may focus on personal attitudes toward work and the availability of jobs, whereas later discussions may be the individual's job behavior. During this helping process, the client should be encouraged to discuss previous job-oriented behaviors so that this input could be a source for developing a program for any necessary modification of job performance behaviors.

Evaluation

In this phase, counselors must be concerned with whether they are achiev-ing objectives that they, with the client and significant others, have found to be important. Another focus of evaluation must be on the process employed in reaching the stated objectives. For example, was individual counseling as effective as group counseling in helping parents work through the losses accruing from their children's handicaps? Again, feedback from the client or relevant components of the "public" is a valuable part of the evaluative mecha-nism. Through feedback, counselors can determine if stated goals are actually appropriate, if clients have made progress toward desired goals, and if the process used to achieve goals leads to desired changes (Pulvino & Sanborn, 1972).

Communication of Evaluation Results

It is through this phase that the counselor determines whether evaluative procedures are appropriate for measuring counseling outcomes and processes and whether the counseling program is meeting the needs of the individual and achieving expectations previously agreed on with others in the client's environment.

Pulvino and Sanborn (1972) believed that accountability will be the natural result of effective utilization of the five phases or steps just listed. And the process of accountability will help to answer the question: "What difference did counseling processes make in the lives of the individuals with whom mental health counselors work?"

COGNITIVE STRUCTURES MODEL

A second approach to evaluating counselor effectiveness is based on the premise that during the course of successful counseling, clients gradually make a transition from a state of incompetence in the face of current life experiences to a state of relative competence with respect to these same events (Martin, 1985). Martin (1985) believed that as clients learn to act in ways that exert a desired influence on their current life circumstances, they are able to progress toward their personal goals. "Underlying such performative competences, however, are structures and processes of cognition that mediate clients' responses to the situations in which they find themselves" (Martin, 1985, p. 556). What Martin (1985) proposed is that when assessing counseling outcomes, researchers consider measures of clients' cognitive structures as data sources. Such measures range from simple frequency count measures of extent, for example, number of conceptual responses to individual memory probes, to more complex, computed measures of shape and integration.

Although much of the content in this approach is quite complicated, the fundamental direction of the model is accessing and representing cognitive structure in such a way that a client's cognitive competence is captured by the knowledge that the client has gained from counseling itself. For example, in counseling, the client is equipped with relevant information concerning a particular problem, which may include knowledge of community resources that have been developed to meet the specific problem. The acquisition of this information may reduce such emotions as guilt, fear, and hopelessness, which initially accompanied the client's problem. Also, this new knowledge increases the client's options. All in all, a change takes place during counseling, a change that Martin (1985) explained is in the client's conceptual knowledge. In other words, the client's cognitive competence increases.

Yet cognitive structure is a hypothetical construct that attempts to capture something of the organization of concepts in memory, and one of the ways for the counselor to measure one's effectiveness is to monitor changes in this competence over the course of counseling. This approach, of course, does not discourage the use of other innovative methods or more traditional methods of gaining access to change processes in counseling. Martin (1985) shared the belief with other counseling researchers that "probably the most complete picture of counseling outcomes can be obtained only through the sensible use of multiple methods" (p. 559).

THE EGAN APPROACH

A third approach has been developed by Egan (1982), who proposes three principal areas of inquiry to guide counseling evaluation efforts: quality of participation, quality of intervention strategies, and quality of problem resolution.

Client Participation

Is the client participating in the intervention efforts? To what extent? To illustrate this step, let us suppose that a client named Jack has been unemployed for 3 months. He enters counseling because he is discouraged and depressed over his inactivity in pursuing job leads or developing job options. Increasing his job options is one of Jack's counseling goals. Progressively increasing his job options by developing two job leads per day constitutes his process goal. Jack and the counselor devise a schedule for gradually increasing these options. Jack has maintained the schedule, increasing his job leads to one every 2 days in pursuit of the process goals. Clearly, he is fully participating in the intervention efforts.

Intervention Effectiveness

Are the agreed-to outcome and process goals being accomplished through the client's participation in intervention efforts? (The emphasis here is not necessarily on total goal attainment, but progress toward goal achievement.)

For example, Jack's outcome goal is to find suitable employment. His process goal is to gradually increase his job leads until reaching the objective of developing two job leads a day and then maintaining that until he has obtained a job. Jack has maintained his scheduled increase of leads. His progress and the effectiveness of the current intervention strategy are readily recognizable.

Problem Resolution

Is the problem that was originally defined being satisfactorily handled through achievement of the goals that had been established? To what degree? (This is the ultimate inquiry, for it deals with the reason for beginning therapy in the first place.)

Jack entered counseling because he saw himself as a failure. He possessed little motivation to find employment. The developing job leads program was geared not just to helping Jack find a job, but also to improve his self-confidence. Jack may find that increasing his job leads has a generalization effect; namely, he can feel more self-confident and his outlook could be more of the focus: "I can" instead of "I give up."

Baruth and Huber (1985) believed that evaluation via the Egan model may seem relatively simple given only three very basic areas of inquiry to pursue. Although they explain that evaluation can be easily conceptualized, it often is not viewed that way because of the difficulty many counselors have in systematically gathering evaluation data. Information that falls into Egan's (1982) three areas of inquiry, for example, can be gathered in such a way that the client's functioning at Point A (minimally, prior to intervention) can be compared against that same functioning at Point B (minimally, after intervention). Cormier and Cormier (1979) identified the different ways this information can be collected.

Verbal Self-report

Client verbal self-reports are likely the easiest and most convenient type of evaluation data to gather. Although client verbal reports are not typically regarded as the most reliable measure of evaluation data, "From a purely clinical perspective, measurement that is independent of the patient's report is superfluous." (Tasto, 1977, pp. 153–154). Client verbal self-reports are often too vague, however, to offer enough information to make accurate comparisons. For example, a client may report after intervention strategies have been implemented that "I'm feeling less depressed now." The client may be unable to identify how much his or her depression has actually decreased. For this reason, client verbal self-reports are frequently supplemented with other types of measurement that produce more concrete and quantifiable data (Cormier & Cormier, 1979).

Frequency Counts

Frequency counts reflect the number of times (how many, how often) that specific types of functioning occur. The number of anxiety attacks, self-denigrating thoughts, or inappropriate behaviors experienced within a given time are examples of forms of client functioning that can be assessed with frequency counts.

Duration Counts

Duration counts reflect the length of time a particular response or collection of responses occurs. For example, the amount of time spent speaking with another person, how long depressive thoughts are compulsively repeated, and the length of time an anxiety attack lasts are forms of client functioning that can be appropriately measured using duration counts (Baruth & Huber, 1985).

Egan (1982) explained that frequency counts and duration counts are commonly obtained in two ways: continuous recording and time-sampling. In continuous recording, the client records each time the specified response occurs. Often, this is impossible, particularly when the response occurs frequently or when its onset and ending are difficult to ascertain. Time-sampling is, therefore, usually the procedure of choice. In time-sampling, a client keeps track of the frequency or duration of the selected response only during specific time intervals. For example, a client might record the number of self-denigrating thoughts he or she had from 10 to 11 a.m., 3 to 4 p.m., and 8 to 9 p.m. each for a specified period. Time-sampling is not as precise as continuous recording in that many responses will possibly be missed; however, the former is clearly the more practical.

Rating Scales

Baruth and Huber (1985) emphasized that the intensity or degree of specific responses can be assessed with a rating scale. For example, the intensity of anxious feelings might be measured by using a rating scale with gradations from 1 (calm) to 5 (panic-stricken). Cronbach (1970) suggested in regard to rating scales that what is to be rated should be well-defined. For example, if a client is to rate self-denigrating thoughts, examples of what constitutes these types of thoughts should be concretely identified and agreed to (e.g., "I hate myself," "I'm no good," etc.). Cronbach (1970) also emphasized the importance of descriptions for each point on a rating scale. Episodes of depression, for example, might be graded from 1 to 5 and described as 1 (no depression), 2 (some depression), 3 (moderate depression), 4 (severe depression), and 5 (incapacitating depression). Finally, rating scales should have at least four gradations and no more than seven. Cronbach proposed that "less than four points limits a client's capacity to discriminate and more than seven cannot be rated reliably because too many discriminations are called for" (p. 274).

Checklists

Checklists are somewhat similar to rating scales. The type of judgment required, however, differs. Rating scales assess degree or intensity. Checklists simply seek to determine the presence or absence of a certain response. For instance, consider the client seeking to display more assertive behaviors in interactions with others. The verbal and nonverbal behaviors associated with assertive action would be listed on a checklist. If the client demonstrates a specific assertive behavior in an observed setting, it is recorded on the checklist.

These five methods of gathering information about possible client change can facilitate the usefulness of the Egan model. They also imply that the counselor should have a rather comprehensive knowledge of measuring "devices" that could be utilized for evaluative purposes.

A COMPETENCY-BASED APPROACH

A fourth approach utilized to evaluate counselor effectiveness is formulated on a competency-based, criterion-referenced perspective. Master's degree counselor education programs often use a competency-based assessment method in developing their curriculum (Gavilan & Ryan, 1979). These programs identify instructional activities, resources, and experiences, as well as terminal and enabling objectives. One particular method is rooted in the following definition of evaluation: "Evaluation is the process of delineating, obtaining, and providing useful information or judging decision alternatives" (Stufflebeam, 1968, p. 113). The emphasis is on decision making, and is described in terms of the settings in which decisions occur.

The term *competency-based* includes knowledge and skill acquisition (Gavilan & Ryan, 1979). Using behavioral objectives, such a program is evaluated by assessing the overt skill performance of the counseling students. The ultimate criterion of effectiveness for this program is stated in terms of the effects on the clients of counselors who have completed the training program. When conducting this evaluation, there are usually four steps:

1. Decisions are made regarding the competencies required of students or counselors. These decisions may be based on competencies derived from explicit role behaviors described in the standards of professional organizations and the literature.
2. Courses are then established that include content relevant to the required competencies. The behavioral domains in each course are validated by a panel of experts in a particular counselor education program.
3. Process information is obtained, for example, from student input. Standardized course and instructor evaluations are completed by counseling students at the end of a particular term. The data from the questionnaires provide information for the refinement and modification of the courses, field placements, and instructors.
4. The final step in this evaluative approach may be accomplished by a survey of the counseling graduates to assess, for example, whether they have obtained jobs in (a) their area of expertise, (b) a related area, (c) a nonrelated area, and (d) no job at all.

The implementation of a competency-based counseling program is perceived as a continuous process. Yet this approach doesn't really answer the question: "Are counselors effective when working with clients?" It appears that this method is concerned with whether planned competencies are acquired by future counselors. Yet with modification this approach could also be used to assess counselor impact on clients.

AN INSTRUCTIONAL APPROACH

This approach to evaluating counselor effectiveness assumes that the role of the counselor should be to instruct. It also emphasizes the interaction between counselor and client, for together they establish goals, determine the most appropriate course of intervention, and decide how the intervention will be implemented. Also, the counselor's task is to arrange the kinds of experiences that will result in the desired learning for a particular client (Hiebert, 1984). Developed basically by Hiebert (1984), this model comprises the following steps:

1. The counselor and client reach a consensus concerning the goal of counseling.
2. A pre-assessment is made of client strengths and weaknesses, skills and skill deficits, and past attempts at achieving the present counseling goal, all with a view for formulating specific intervention hypotheses for future action.
3. Specific instructional objectives are identified, which address: who will be doing what, to what extent or level will it be done, and how will it be measured.
4. The instructional activities designed to achieve the objectives are begun.
5. The counseling effects are evaluated in terms of the criteria and measurement systems specified in the objectives.

A STAGES–SKILLS APPROACH

In emphasizing a different perspective to program evaluation activities, Cohen, Anthony, Pierce, and Spaniol (1979) have developed a model that focuses on mental health practitioners designing goals important to their job, monitoring their performance, and using the results of the evaluation to formulate a new direction. Specifically, these authors described this process as comprising

> (1) developing and establishing priorities for client and administrative goals, (2) operationalizing the highest priority goals and their related intermediary goals, (3) monitoring performance on the goals, (4) organizing and using the monitoring results, and (5) recycling the evaluation process to generate new client and administrative goals. (Cohen et al. 1979, p. 2)

An important contribution of this approach is that it can assist mental health workers to be directly informed about their areas of effectiveness and ineffectiveness. Such feedback enables them to modify and improve their delivery of services. It can be used once the helping process in mental health has been implemented. For example, practitioners can evaluate their performance at any time during the diagnostic interviewing, assessment, or programming process (Cohen, et al., 1979). As the authors stated, "The point at which practitioners evaluate their performance depends on the priorities of their client and administrative goals as well as on the amount of time the practitioner has available to focus on the evaluation" (p. 5).

To illustrate this approach, consider a mental health practitioner who is assisting patients recently released from a mental institution to make a satisfactory life adjustment in a halfway, transitional home. The particular mental health agency in which one is working has both administrative and client goals. The administrative goals include client satisfaction, cost effectiveness, increasing the availability of services, improving the relationships with many community resources, generating positive community opinion, and prevention of client rehospitalizations. Many of the clients' goals are:

1. Appearing regularly for scheduled appointments;
2. Contacting the worker when there is a crisis;
3. Learning independent living skills, and demonstrating that they can live independently for at least 1 year;
4. Achieving the other goals identified from initial assessment and planning, which may include learning job seeking skills or being aware of their own strengths and deficits.

Once all of these goals have been identified, then priorities for goal attainment can be established. Criteria for the priorities may include urgency to the client or the agency, benefit to the client or the agency, and consistency with the practitioners' job description (Cohen, et al., 1979). Once priorities have been established, the worker needs to select the highest priority goals for evaluation. The number of goals selected will depend on the practitioner's evaluation skills and the amount of time available for evaluation efforts. With this example, suppose that the prioritized goals are: (a) appearing regularly for scheduled appointments, (b) learning independent living skills, and (c) cost effectiveness.

Intermediary goals will then both be developed for each of the preceding prioritized goals and will be operationalized. Using the goals identified here as an example, operationalized, intermediary goals would be:

1. The number of times clients appear for regularly scheduled interviews in a month at the mental health agency;
2. The number of times clients fail to show up for or cancel an appointment with the worker;
3. The percentage of clients who, within a prescribed number of sessions, achieve independent living goals written in client files.

Following these steps, a monitoring plan would be developed that comprises: (a) specifying the person whose behavior is to be monitored, (b) specifying the person who is to do the monitoring, (c) specifying the monitoring device, (d) specifying the appropriate time and dates for the monitoring, (e) specifying where the monitoring is to occur, and (f) determining how the monitoring results will be retained.

To organize the results, Cohen et al. (1979) have developed a useful format that can both indicate current client and worker performance and suggest new directions. The format includes a scale that explores such questions as: What amount of the goal would be considered optimum, what amount of the goal would be considered average, and what amount of the goal would be considered undesirable? Administrative demands, practitioner judgment, knowledge of the literature, and analyzing present performance are a few of the ways to determine levels of performance. Scales help the worker to understand in detail how each goal can be evaluated.

A sample format, using suggested scales with operationalized goals, is shown in Table 6.1.

With the development of observable, operationalized, client goals, the mental health worker has a useful way to evaluate one's performance. This particular approach, moreover, can also be accomplished with the cooperation of others. For example, a group of practitioners may wish to work together to explore the goals important to their delivery of mental health services (Cohen, et al., 1979). Through collaboration, priorities for client and agency goals can be established, an operational definition for each goal could be developed, monitoring plans identified, and scales devised that would determine the levels of achievement.

The preceding six theoretical designs and the six approaches that have been influenced by these designs illustrate the diversity of evaluative methods for measuring counseling outcomes. What all of these approaches have in common is: (a) the necessity to generate feedback from the client, agency, and relevant public in order to identify what effectiveness is and the criteria by which it can be assessed; (b) the possible need for use of multiple methods when planning an approach for evaluating counselor effectiveness; and (c) the importance of specificity about client outcomes if credible results of effectiveness are to be obtained. All of the approaches that have been discussed not only highlight the many difficulties in methodology when designing assessment approaches, but also at the same time strongly suggest that counselor effectiveness can be evaluated.

TABLE 6.1. Sample Evaluation Using Scales and Operationalization of Goals

GOAL	OPERATIONALIZED GOAL	LEVEL	SCALE
Number of clients interviewed	The number of times clients appear for regularly scheduled interviews in a month at the mental health agency	5	20 or more
		4	16-19
		3	11-15
		2	7-10
		1	0-6
Client independent living	Percentage of clients who, within a prescribed number of sessions, achieve independent living goals written in client files	5	30-40
		4	20-29
		3	10-19
		2	5-9
		1	0-4

CONCLUSION

The evaluation of mental health counseling efforts is usually done to learn whether an intervention strategy is helping a client as it was designed to and whether the client is using the strategy accurately and productively. Evaluating the effectiveness of intervention strategies helps the client and counselor determine the type, direction, and amount of change in functioning demonstrated by the client. As stated in this chapter, an assessment of counseling effectiveness can yield valuable information though many of the evaluation approaches are not as rigorous as evaluations conducted under carefully controlled experimental conditions. But it was not the purpose of this chapter to discuss evaluation as it relates to detailed experimental research design. Rather, the objective here was to provide an overview of issues that are relevant to assessing counselor effectiveness, to identify selected models that have been developed to explore counselor effectiveness, and to suggest some approaches that could be utilized when evaluating counseling effectiveness. Evaluation not only indicates the extent to which therapeutic goals are achieved; it also provides continuing encouragement to client and therapist alike as progress is clearly seen.

REFERENCES

Baruth, F., & Huber, C. (1985). *Counseling and psychotherapy: Theoretical analysis and skills applications.* Columbus, OH: Charles E. Merrill.

Boy, A. V., & Pine, G. J. (1978, December). Effective counseling: Some proportional relationships. *Counselor Education and Supervision*, pp. 137–144.

Butcher, E., Scofield, M. E., & Baker, S. B. (1984, October). Validation of a standardized simulation for assessment of competence in mental health counseling. *American Mental Health Counselors Association Journal*, pp. 162–172.

Carkhuff, R. R., & Anthony, W. A. (1979). *The skills of helping.* Amherst, MA: Human Resource Development Press.

Cohen, M., Anthony, W., Pierce, R., & Spaniol, C. (1979). *The skills of professional evaluation.* Amherst, MA: Carkhuff Institute of Human Technology.

Cook, T. D., & Campbell, D. T. (1979). *Quasi-experimentation: Design and analysis issues for field settings.* Chicago: Rand McNally.

Cormier, W., & Cormier, L. (1979). *Interviewing strategies for helpers: A guide to assessment, treatment, and evaluation.* Monterey, CA: Brooks-Cole.

Crabbs, M. A. (1984, February). Reduction in force and accountability: Stemming the tide. *Elementary School Guidance and Counseling*, pp. 167–175.

Cronbach, C. (1970). *Essentials of psychological testing.* New York: Harper & Row.

Diamond, M., & Shapiro, J. (1973). Changes in locus of control as a function of encounter group experiences, *Journal of Abnormal Psychology, 82*, 514–518.

Egan, G. (1982). *The skilled helper: Models, skills, and methods for effective helpers.* Monterey, CA: Brooks/Cole.

Eysenck, H. J. (1978). An exercise in meta-silliness. *American Psychologist, 33*, 517.

Frank, J. (1979). The present status of outcome studies. *Journal of Consulting and Clinical Psychology, 47*, 310–316.

Gavilan, M. R., & Ryan, C. A. (1979, December). A competency-based program in counselor education. *Counselor Education and Supervision*, pp. 146–151.

Heath, B. H., Hultberg, R. A., Ramey, J. M., & Ries, C. S. (1984). Consumer satisfaction: Some new twists to a not so old evaluation. *Community Mental Health Journal, 20,* 123-133.

Henjum, R. (1982). The criterion problem in the evaluation of guidance. *The School Guidance Worker, 38,* 5-10.

Hiebert, B. (1982). *Preparing vocational counselors* (NATCON 2). Ottawa: Employment and Immigration Canada.

Hiebert, B. (1984). Counselor effectiveness: An instructional approach. *Personnel and Guidance Journal, 62,* 597-601.

Humes, C. W. (1972). Accountability: A boon to guidance. *Personnel and Guidance Journal, 51,* 21-26.

Hurvitz, N. (1974). Manifest and intent functions in psychotherapy. *Journal of Consulting and Clinical Psychology, 42,* 301.

Hutchins, D. (1982). Ranking major counseling strategies with the TFA/Matrix system. *Personnel and Guidance Journal, 60,* 417-430.

Ibraham, F., Helms, B., & Thompson, P. (1983). Counselor role and function: An appraisal by consumers and counselors. *Personnel and Guidance Journal, 61,* 597-601.

Justice, B., & McBee, G. (1978). A client satisfaction survey as one element in evaluation. *Community Mental Health Journal, 14,* 18-25.

Khan, J. A., & Cross, D. G. (1984, January). Mental health professionals: How different are their values? *American Mental Health Counselors Association Journal,* 42-51.

Krumboltz, J. D. (1974). An accountability model for counselors. *Personnel and Guidance Journal, 52,* 639-646.

Larson, D. L., Attkisson, C. C., Hargreaves, W. A., & Nguyen, T. D. (1979). Assessment of client/patient satisfaction: Development of a general scale. *Evaluation and Program Planning, 2,* 197-207.

Lebow, J. (1982). Consumer satisfaction with mental health treatment. *Psychological Bulletin, 91,* 244-259.

Lewis, W. A., & Hutson, S. P. (1983). The gap between research and practice on the question of counseling effectiveness. *Personnel and Guidance Journal, 61,* 532-535.

Lieberman, M., Yalom, I., & Miles, M. (1973). *Encounter groups: First facts.* New York: Basic Books.

Lipsett, L. (1971). Evaluating the performance of service agency counselors. *Vocational Guidance Quarterly, 19,* 206-210.

Margolin, G. (1982). Ethical and legal considerations in marital and family therapy. *American Psychologist, 37,* 788-801.

Martin, J. (1985). Measuring client's cognitive competence in research on counseling. *Journal of Counseling and Development, 63,* 556-559.

Martin, J., & Hiebert, B. (1982). *Instructional counseling.* Vancouver: University of British Columbia, Centre for Studies in Curriculum.

Messina, J. (1985). The National Academy of Certified Clinical Mental Health Counselors: Creating a new professional identity. *Journal of Counseling and Development, 63,* 607-608.

Paritzky, R. S., & Magoon, T. M. (1982). Goal attainment scaling models for assessing group counseling. *Personnel and Guidance Journal, 60,* 381-384.

Pulvino, C. J., & Sanborn, M. P. (1972). Feedback and accountability. *Personnel and Guidance Journal, 51,* 15-20.

Remer, R. (1981). The counselor and research: Introduction. *Personnel and Guidance Journal, 59,* 567-571.

Riggs, R. C. (1979). Evaluation of counselor effectiveness. *Personnel and Guidance Journal, 58,* 54-59.

Seligman, L. (1985, January). The art and science of counseling. *American Mental Health Counselors Association Journal*, 2-3.

Siegel, B. (1969, March). Evaluating a guidance counselor. *The School Counselor*, pp. 309-311.

Strong, S. R. (1968). Counseling: An interpersonal influence process. *Journal of Counseling Psychology*, *15*, 215-224.

Strupp, H. (1980). Humanism and psychotherapy: A personal statement of the therapeutic essential values. *Psychotherapy: Theory, Research and Practice*, *17*, 396-400.

Stufflebeam, D. L. (1968). *Evaluation as enlightenment for decision-making*. Columbus: Ohio State University. (ERIC Document Reproduction Service No. ED 048 333)

Tasto, D. (1977). Self-report schedules and inventories. In A. Ciminero, K. Calhoun, & H. Adams (Eds.), *Handbook of behavioral assessment*. New York: Wiley.

Zarski, J. J., Bubenzer, D. L., & Walter, D. C. (1980, September). Counseling effectiveness and trainee helping qualities: Another view. *Counseling Education and Supervision*, pp. 15-21.

Zarski, J. J., Sweeney, T. J., & Barcikowski, R. J. (1977). Counseling effectiveness as a function of counselor social interest. *Journal of Counseling Psychology*, *24*, 1-5.

III CLIENTS AND INTERVENTIONS

7 Counseling Individuals

In chapter 4, we reviewed some of the conceptualizations of human development, of the problems of living that arise in the course of that development, and of the goals for intervention in those problems. The mental health counselor must integrate these three elements into a consistent, personally useful system by which to select the specific procedures to be used in working with a client. As stated in chapter 1, four broad principles underlie the mental health counseling orientation:

1. Behavior can only be understood in context; it must be considered as a function of both the person and that person's environment.
2. Problems of living represent an individual's failure to cope with a particular set of circumstances. Once this failure has been overcome and its effects have been undone, normal growth can proceed.
3. To help the client to cope with a problem of living, the mental health counselor may work with the client to:
   (a) identify or develop personal strengths and skills in the client that will allow him/her to deal with the particular problem, and/or
   (b) change the environment to mitigate the problem or facilitate the client's dealing with it.
4. In working with the client toward these purposes, the counselor utilizes scientifically validated techniques.

Within this framework, each counselor must establish his/her own logically derived and empirically validated basis for determining which scientifically validated techniques should be used (or at least tried first) in helping a given client to cope with a particular problem of living.

EFFECTING CHANGE

Implicit in any resulting conceptualization of the mental health counseling process is the aim of helping a client to change (coping capacity and/or the situation). Therefore, another necessary consideration for the counselor in formulating his/her systematic approach to intervention is knowledge about how the process of change occurs. As with most of the broad-based phenomena that have been considered by the social sciences, a large number of competing models of the change process have been proposed. These models generally were developed out of different contexts, and consequently any one of them may be better or worse than other models in explaining change in a particular situation. (Presumably, the closer the particular situation is to the context in which the model was originally developed, the better the model will work in accounting for the situation. For example, a model derived from studying change in lower socioeconomic class Hispanic women would probably do better at predicting change in a client of that gender, ethnic, and socioeconomic group than would a model derived from studying upper class, Anglo-Saxon men.) In analyzing change in organizations, Beckhard and Harris (1977) proposed a principle that is equally applicable to individuals. This principle is that there is a natural tendency to resist change, even in an uncomfortable situation ("Better the devil you know than the devil you might meet"). Change will only occur when the present situation is felt to be sufficiently untenable that the person is moved to attain the necessary state of both high readiness and high capability for that change. Therefore, in some instances in which a change seems appropriate to both the client and the counselor, it may be necessary for the counselor to increase, rather than to diminish, the client's anxiety or discomfort in order to precipitate the desired change. (Naturally, care must be taken that the anxiety or discomfort is not raised so high that it immobilizes the client.) Similarly, Wheelis (1975), a psychoanalyst, has proposed a sequence of steps that he believes are necessary for change: "The sequence is suffering, insight, will, action, change" (p. 102).

Once the inertia has been overcome, it is necessary for the counselor to have a model to guide his/her handling of the change process. One model of change in human systems (that is, individuals, families, groups, organizations, or communities) was proposed by Capelle (1979). This model suggests that change involves a nine-step process, these successive steps being:

1. Analyze the situation
2. Assess the potential for change
3. Set outcome criteria
4. Generate alternative solutions
5. Make a decision
6. Develop a plan
7. Implement the plan
8. Evaluate performance
9. Reward performance, following which, return to Step 1, analyze the changed situation, and proceed through the successive steps.

PHASES OF TREATMENT

In most mental health professions, the nine steps just listed are usually collapsed into four phases of the treatment process: (a) appraisal (Steps 1, 2, and 3); (b) planning (Steps 4, 5, and 6); (c) intervention (Step 7); and (d) evaluation (Steps 8 and 9).

The specific direction taken in these four phases by any mental health professional is determined by:

1. The ethos of the particular profession to which the professional belongs (thus, psychiatrists think in terms of diagnosing, treating, and curing an illness; mental health counselors, in terms of improving coping capacities and changing the environment to promote growth and development);
2. The professional's own conception of mental health, mental health problems, and the aims of intervention within the framework provided by the ethos of the profession;
3. The context of the particular client–counselor relationship (for example, is the client there voluntarily or under compulsion; are there other constraints on the counseling process, etc.); and
4. The characteristics of the client, the client's problem, and the client's life situation.

Given these stipulations, we may now examine the four phases of the treatment process.

Appraisal

For the mental health counselor, the questions to be explored in the appraisal process include:

1. What motivates the client to seek to change at this time?
2. How does the client see his/her problem?
3. How do I conceptualize the client's problem in terms that I as a professional can work with?
4. Are Questions 2 and 3 compatible with each other?
5. What does the client seek as the outcome of counseling?
6. What can I ethically and realistically work toward as the outcome of counseling?
7. Are Questions 5 and 6 consistent with each other?
8. Can this outcome be put in terms of measurable goals?
9. What are the client's perceptual, defense, and reasoning processes?
10. What is the impact of these processes on how the client sees the problem and on the desired outcome?
11. What is needed in order to attain the agreed-upon outcome?
12. What assets and skills does the client have that can be used in attaining

that outcome?
13. What supports in the client's environment may be brought into play to support the desired change?
14. What additional skills must the client develop and/or what environmental changes must be effected in order to attain the desired outcome?
15. Are these changes in the client and/or the client's environment realistically possible?
16. Is the client sufficiently motivated to do what is necessary to bring about these changes?
17. Do the client and I feel that we will be able to work together effectively?
18. Can we define the problem, the possible ways to deal with it, and the criteria for determining how well it has been dealt with in terms that we both find acceptable?
19. What are the probable and the possible consequences for the client if counseling is not successful? That is, do the risks of failure outweigh the benefits of success? If so, should counseling still be undertaken?

Planning

If the client and counselor can agree on these issues, then they may move on to the planning phase. In this phase, the client and counselor consider the advantages and disadvantages of each possible alternative approach to solving the problem, agreeing on one as worth trying first, and arranging the sequence of actions to be implemented. The choice of approach may be based on the one judged most likely to succeed, the one with the fewest negative consequences of failure, or the one that can be accomplished in the least time. The choice will at least in part depend on the nature of the problem and the client's capacity to deal with failure or with delay of gratification.

Brickman et al. (1982) pointed out that both the counselor's and the client's views of who is responsible for the problem (the client or someone else) and of who is responsible for the solution (the client or someone else) determine the approach that will be selected in trying to solve the problem. An incorrect attribution as to the responsibility for either the problem or its solution will lead to the choice of an inappropriate (and therefore probably ineffective) strategy of intervention.

Intervention

Once the problem has been defined in a way that it can be attacked (that is, in terms of specified behaviors to be changed and, where possible, the sources of those behaviors within the client and the client's environment) and a plan of attack has been agreed upon, it can be carried out. Naturally, no plan is ever able to foresee all the effects of each of its elements. Thus, evaluation of an intervention must be done along with, as well as at the completion of, the intervention phase. Where the ongoing evaluation indicates the need for it, the intervention may have to be modified or replaced and the plan may have to be changed.

Evaluation

Assuming that no contraindications arose and the intervention was pursued to its completion, its results can then be evaluated. This evaluation should be structured in terms of how effective the intervention was in remedying the problem as originally defined (that is, the extent to which the originally specified behaviors changed in the desired direction).

As is implicit in the preceding paragraph, the method used for initially appraising the extent of the problem may sometimes also be used to evaluate how much the problem has changed following the intervention. It may be noted that one cannot necessarily attribute that change to the intervention. Conditions in the client's life outside of counseling may have changed, thus precipitating a change in the client's problematic behavior or removing the source of the problem. The client may have been ready to change on his/her own, and seeking counseling was a way to justify or to celebrate the change rather than to make it occur. Nonetheless, if the desired change has occurred, one must conclude that the aims of the counseling were fulfilled.

The relationship among the four phases of the treatment process we have just described may be diagrammed as in Figure 7.1.

In pursuing the four phases of the treatment process, three established sets of professional tools are available to the counselor: (a) methods for appraising the client, the setting, and the problem; (b) techniques for intervening; and (c) methods of evaluation. The rest of this chapter will be devoted to a discussion of the first two of these topics; the third topic — methods of evaluation — is discussed in detail in chapter 12.

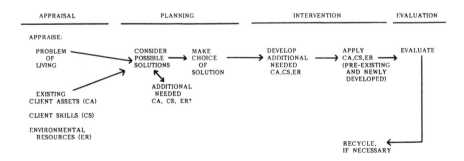

FIGURE 7.1. Phases of the treatment process.

It doubtless will not have escaped the reader's notice that there is no section devoted to a discussion of the planning phase. This is because the systematic study of this phase is just beginning (for example, Seligman, 1986). Butcher, Scofield, and Baker (1985) have recently examined the effects of the counselor's problem-solving style on a simulated treatment planning task. This is a promising development in this literature. In their review of the state of knowledge on this subject prior to their study, Butcher et al. (1985) stated that research to date indicates that counselors tend to decide on a treatment strategy very early in their contact with a client; that counselors rarely consider more than a few alternative intervention approaches; that counselors resist changing their initial assessments, even when faced with contradictory evidence; and that competence in planning is not consistent but seems to vary with the nature of the case. These conclusions strongly point to the need for concerted study of the planning phase, so that effective techniques and skills of planning can be developed and incorporated into counselor education and counseling practice.

METHODS OF APPRAISAL

To summarize the earlier discussion of the topic, the appraisal phase of the treatment process seeks to determine three categories of information:

1. The nature, extent, and (if possible) causes of the client's problem;
2. The potential for changing the client and/or the client's environment in such a way as to mitigate the problem and/or to enable the client to cope with it;
3. The criteria to be used to evaluate the effectiveness of the intervention.

Among the methods used by counselors to appraise clients are: (a) observation, (b) interviews, (c) life history, (d) psychometric instruments, (e) behavioral assessment, and (f) functional assessment. Observation begins from the moment the client first contacts the counselor. The counselor may be able to observe how the client approaches the process of making an appointment for a first visit. Is the client tentative or assertive, self-effacing or self-assured, vascillating or decisive? When the client comes for the first meeting, how does he/she present him/herself: on time, early, or late; well-groomed or poorly groomed; neatly dressed or slovenly? Does the client walk in with assurance? Is his/her handshake firm, too firm, or tentative; moist from anxiety or dry? As the counseling process proceeds, the counselor must observe the client's body language, whether the client distances him/herself from the counselor, when the client is tense, when relaxed, and so on. Observation is essential in understanding the client and the client's impact on others. The counselor must always be careful not to impose her/his personal values on the client's appearance or actions but must place them in the context of the client's own reference group.

Interviews may be structured (the questions and their order are all set ahead of time) or unstructured. Structured interviews are, of course, less spontaneous; but they allow the counselor to gather specific information in an expeditious manner, and they provide a consistent frame of reference within which to compare the client's responses and way of responding with other people's behavior in the same situation. Much of the counseling process is conducted in a relatively unstructured interview format, with only the rules of the counseling technique being used and the conditions of professional practice determining the limits of how the interview is conducted and what it will cover.

The life history is important in establishing the client's strengths and limitations, past problems and how they were coped with, and what sorts of situations are problematic for the client. Family history, medical history, educational record, work history, past and continuing social relationships, and past problems and how they were handled are all necessary parts of understanding the client. They provide the counselor with some insight into the actual facts of relevance to the client's life; and through the way in which the client tells these facts, they also provide insight into how the client feels about what he/she reports. Depending on the nature of the client's problem, the counselor will seek greater detail concerning relevant areas in the client's past. For example, if the client's problem relates to his/her relationship to his/her boss at work, the client's work history and relationship to past authority figures would ordinarily be examined in greater detail than the client's social friendships. Other, apparently unrelated areas of the client's life should not be disregarded, because they may offer suggestions as to how the client has coped successfully in the past and because problems in one area may really be the expression of deeper problems in some other area of life. For example, family violence may stem from frustration at work.

Psychometric tests are generally classified as objective (questions with a correct and incorrect answer or at least a structured response, such as yes, no, or don't know) or projective (no structured response is provided, so that the client will reveal him/herself by how he/she approaches the task as well as by the answer given). Projective tests may be thought of as a form of structured interview, in which the client's approach to a novel task can be compared to other people's approach to the same task. Objective tests, by their very nature, have more interrater reliability (two independent scorers are more likely to come up with the same number when scoring a client's responses). Although there have been some attempts to develop relatively "objective," reliable scoring systems for responses to projective tests, most of these systems fall short of acceptable levels of reliability. Generally, objective tests are of the paper-and-pencil variety (mark one alternative) or, less frequently, require the person being tested to perform a certain task within a specified time period. Objective tests generally measure abilities and achievements (for example intelligence, critical reasoning, vocabulary tests), although a few instruments use the objective test format to assess career interests (such as the Strong–Campbell Interest Inventory or the Kuder Occupational Interest Survey) or personality (the Minnesota Multiphasic Personality Inventory, the Personal Orientation Inventory, the Sixteen Personality Factors, the Myers–Briggs Type Indicator, adjective checklists, etc.). Generally, mental health counselors use tests much less commonly than clinical psychologists (who are uniquely skilled in the use of projective tests such as the Rorschach inkblots, the Thematic Apperception test, and the Draw-a-Person), but mental health counselors very often are required to read and understand test reports that psychologists have written concerning a client. It behooves the mental health counselor to familiarize her/himself with the items and psychometric properties (reliability and validity) of the tests used by the psychologist in preparing the appraisal, in order to assess the limits of the conclusions one may draw from the report. (Reliability refers to the probability that the test-taker will answer the same item the same way on different occasions and to the probability that different scorers, looking at the same set of responses, will arrive at the same score. Validity is the extent to which a test measures what it purports to measure. For example, does a test purporting to measure potential for heroic acts actually predict who will be a hero, or is it really a measure of boastfulness?) Shertzer and Linden (1979) have provided an excellent survey of the principles and techniques of assessment commonly used by counselors.

Behavioral assessment frequently involves the client's keeping a record of when and under what circumstances a particular behavior occurs. For example, if a client is trying unsuccessfully to stay on a diet, the counselor may instruct the client to keep a record of when and in what room of the house the urge to overeat occurs. Is it always after 8:30 p.m., in the kitchen, that hunger and/or binge eating occurs? If so, the client may be instructed to stay out of the kitchen after dinner.

Finally, functional assessment is a newer approach of particular relevance to mental health counselors. Cohen and Anthony (1984) have pointed out that psychiatric diagnosis or symptoms do not correlate with either a client's skills or rehabilitation outcome. On the other hand, skills do correlate with rehabilitation outcome. Therefore, a measure of skills is both one of the better predictive devices and a way of determining what assets the client has available and what assets the client needs to develop in order to solve the problem of living. Granger (1984) called functional assessment

> a method for describing abilities and activities in order to measure an individual's use of the variety of skills included in performing the tasks necessary to daily living, vocational pursuits, social interactions, leisure activities, and other activities, and other required behaviors. (p. 24)

Halpern and Fuhrer (1984) defined functional assessment as "the measurement of purposeful behavior in interaction with the environment, which is interpreted according to the assessment's intended uses" (p. 3). They cautioned, however, that "the results of functional assessment cannot automatically be assumed to generalize across different environments" (p. 4). They went on to note that a wide array of functional assessment instruments and procedures have been developed, and the rate of development of new measures is increasing. Measurement of skills has been one of the most prolific areas of activity in the field of functional assessment, particularly as represented by the many activities of daily living scales that have emerged over the years. Given the focus on skills that is present in mental health counseling, functional assessment represents a particularly relevant appraisal method for mental health counselors to become familiar with and to use.

In addition to appraisal of the client, the counselor must appraise the client's environment in which the problem takes place. Cohen and Anthony (1984) went so far as to state that functional assessment is only of value if accompanied by and coordinated with an environmental assessment. Do the human and inanimate environments really help the client to cope or do they complicate the client's life? Environments are often assessed by what people do in them, how people react to them, and how they are compared with other environments by those engaged in certain activities. Barker (1968) developed the concept of behavior settings, that is, the observation that certain environments elicit particular behaviors not elicited by other places; and Moos (1976) has investigated how the structure of various environments (college dormitories, hospital wards, prisons, classrooms) affect how people interact and react in them.

Finally, one must consider how the counselor is to integrate and make use of all the information about a client and the client's environment that has been gathered through the appraisal process. Without such a framework, the mass of information confronting the counselor appears overwhelming, disorganized, and irrelevant. Appraisal is, however, intended to guide the selection and planning of the intervention. For mental health counselors, information about the client's coping skills, patterns, and deficits and information about the client's environmental interactions are particularly to be sought out and examined in formulating the plan for intervention. A model for integrating this information is presented in Figure 7.2.

This model was adapted from Kurt Lewin's (1936) pioneering work on diagramming person–environment interaction.

For the current purposes, this model represents a "time slice" of the client and the client's environment. During the counseling process, several such time slices are necessary: (a) a time slice taken at the start of counseling; (b) a projected time slice as to what the situation should become, on which to base the strategy of intervention; and (c) a time slice taken after the intervention, in order to evaluate its success.

The model consists of a rectangle, representing the client's *actual* human and impersonal *environment* (that is, the supports and barriers to coping, as objectively assessed during the appraisal process). Within this rectangle is an oval, representing the client. This oval is divided into four parts that touch each other and are separated by broken lines, to represent their interaction. Also, one end of the oval is represented by a broken line, to represent the interaction between the actual environment and the *perceived environment* existing within the client, on the basis of which the client is functioning. One goal of counseling may have to be to bring the actual and perceived environments into closer correspondence with each other by changing one or both of them. Also within the client are areas representing *dispositions* (the client's ways of perceiving, thinking, feeling, and acting); *competencies* (the client's existing skills, abilities, aptitudes, and effective coping mechanisms); and *goals* (in terms of how well-formulated, appropriate, and firmly held they are by the client). The information on dispositions, competencies, and goals is gained during the appraisal process. Naturally, information in each of the categories is attended to in proportion to how it bears on the client's problem. At the same time, other life areas of good coping should not be overlooked, as they may suggest ways of solving the existing problem. Finally, the diagram includes two other constructs (represented by arrows) that must be considered in the appraisal process: *satisfaction* (that is, how well the client preceives she/he is coping with the problem); and *effectiveness* (that is, how well an objective observer, such as the counselor, sees the client as coping). The counseling process will be evaluated by the changes in satisfaction and effectiveness from the beginning to the end of the process.

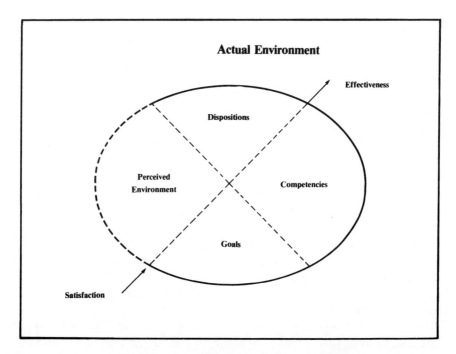

FIGURE 7.2. A model for integrating appraisal data.

TECHNIQUES OF INTERVENTION

As a result of the appraisal, the mental health counselor has a picture of the client's problem of living, the environmental context of that problem, and the resources the client has available or can develop that will allow him/her to cope with that problem. The nature and extent of a problem determine the overall goals of an intervention, which may be for:

1. Prevention: avoiding a problem that has not yet occurred but is likely to if no steps are taken,
2. Facilitation: smoothing the path of normal development so that the individual's maximum potential in a given area can be realized,
3. Remediation: stopping the continued operation of a problem,
4. Rehabilitation: overcoming the residual effects of a problem that is no longer creating new difficulties, or
5. Enhancement: improving the client's life situation above its present level (which may be good or bad).

The intervention for any of these levels may involve: (a) mobilizing and applying assets that already exist in the client toward overcoming the problem, (b) developing those other skills in the client that are necessary for coping with the problem, and/or (c) changing the environment to mitigate the problem and/ or to facilitate its solution.

Particularly important to the mental health counseling orientation is the mobilization and the development of skills. A number of authors (Anthony, 1979; Goldstein, 1981; Hersen & Bellack, 1976; Jacobs, Kardashian, Kreinbring, Ponder, & Simpson, 1984; L'Abate, 1980; to name just a few) have proposed lists of necessary skills and ways of helping to develop them in clients who are experiencing mental health problems. In the introduction to his book, Goldstein (1981) catalogued about 30 prior articles by various authors, each of which lists a different compendium of skills. These skills include everything from problem solving to communicating, from assertiveness to empathy, from listening to negotiating. Goldstein himself compiled a list of 50 separate skills needed by mental health clients, which he grouped into five categories: (a) social skills, (b) skills for dealing with feelings, (c) skill alternatives to aggression, (d) skills for dealing with stress, and (e) planning skills. Goldstein went on to indicate how these skills could be taught to mental health clients, using such social learning theory techniques as modeling, role-playing, feedback, transfer of training, and self-reward.

A discussion of techniques of skill building would be misleading if one did not recall to the reader the message of the second chapter of this book, that techniques are only as effective as the capacity of the counselor to enlist the client's active participation in learning and applying these skills. Thus, the mental health counselor must possess two sets of skills if interventions of the type discussed here are to be effective: (a) the skills of relating to the client so that the client takes an active role in the counseling process, and (b) the skills to teach needed techniques to the client.

In addition to mobilizing and, where needed, developing skills, the mental health counselor always has under consideration the option of changing the client's environment to mitigate the problem being worked on. Is the client in a destructive living arrangement, in an overly stressful work setting, or facing economic collapse? Will helping the client effect a change in the situation be enough, on its own, to resolve the problem?

The counseling relationship provides a setting for exploring these alternatives. In the past, numerous "schools" of counseling (i.e., systems of theory and methods of intervention) were formulated by practitioners who found them to be personally effective systems. The counseling literature contains a number of books that survey the theories and methods proposed by the better known schools (psychoanalytic, client-centered, behavioral, humanistic, etc.). The more recent of these books include those by Belkin (1984); Gilliland, James, Roberts, and Bowman (1984); Patterson (1986); and Wallace (1986). The literature also contains an even larger number of books by the founders or the proponents of individual schools, presenting (and often extolling) their own particular approaches to intervention. Many of these are listed in the survey books just named.

In recent years, counselors have tended to move away from blind allegiance to a single school, and have instead tried to pick and choose specific methods or concepts from a variety of schools, applying them where it appears appropriate to do so. Eclecticism, however, has its own set of hazards, as indicated in the paper by Brabeck and Welfel (1985) and the rejoinders to it by Patterson (1985) and Rychlak (1985). Certainly, there were limits to the old approach of strict adherence to one school, even to the extent that in some instances counselors abandoned clients who did not respond to their approach as being "unmotivated" or "resistant" rather than questioning the appropriateness of the principles and practices of their school for that client. The danger of eclecticism, however, is that unless the counselor has a systematic basis for selecting among the wide range of available techniques, the choice of technique becomes haphazard and therefore not susceptible to scientific evaluation. Without knowing which technique is effective at what point in the counseling process with what sort of client facing what problem in what context, the choice of technique becomes random and the counselor loses any claim to professional expertise. Therefore, a number of systems have been proposed for organizing techniques and suggesting when to apply them. Among the more recent of these are the ones proposed by Bruce (1984), Frey and Raming (1979), Hershenson (1982), L'Abate (1981), and Ponzo (1976).

Another approach to this problem has been to develop texts that emphasize general principles of relating to clients, rather than specific techniques. Carkhuff, Pierce, and Cannon (1980); Corey (1986); Egan (1986); Ivey (1980); Kottler and Brown (1985); and Shertzer and Stone (1980) are among the more recent books that have adopted this approach.

Finally, some authors have attempted to tease out one essential issue in the counseling process that transcends schools or techniques, to study that element in detail, and then to suggest an approach to counseling based upon it. Thus, Janis and Mann (1977) studied the decision-making process; and based on their findings, Janis (1983) proposed a model for counseling about personal decisions. Likewise, Schlossberg (1984) studied adult life transitions, and she and others (Elliot, 1985) have written on counseling about these transitions.

It should be noted that the books and articles named here are representative, rather than exhaustive listings. Finally, it should also be noted that if the reader is left with the impression that a bewildering array of theories, principles, methods, and techniques of intervention coexist (and sometimes compete) within the field of counseling, the reader need not worry, for she/he has perceived the state of affairs accurately. At this point in the development of the field, systematic studies are needed to determine which of these elements are effective under what particular combination of client, counselor, problem, and setting variables. This is a never-ending process, because people and conditions are forever changing; but we cannot establish even broad principles unless we approach the task systematically. The counseling profession is now making a concerted effort on this task, as most recently indicated by Forsyth and Strong (1986). There is every reason to expect that if properly controlled studies are done and appropriate outcome evaluation techniques are used, the field will be able to develop an empirically validated system for selecting and using particular interventions, based on relevant, clearly specified parameters.

SPECIAL ISSUES IN INTERVENTION

One cannot end a discussion of intervention without mentioning a few special issues that come up with great frequency in the practice of mental health counseling. These include: (a) crisis intervention, (b) substance abusers, (c) psychoactive medication, (d) rehabilitation procedures, and (e) case management.

Crisis Intervention

Ordinarily, one thinks of seeking counseling as the result of a carefully thought out decision, arrived at over time. There are, however, crisis situations that bring people to counselors with no prior preparation. Gerald Caplan (1964), one of the major contributors to the field of community mental health, noted this phenomenon and developed the concept of crisis intervention to address this need. Killilea (1982) summarized Caplan's conception of crisis as "a period of disequilibrium accompanied by psychological and physical distress of a relatively limited duration which temporarily taxes a person's ability to cope competently or to achieve mastery. Crisis can be predictable or unpredictable" (p. 164). Marriage, the birth of a child, retirement, or many of the other items on Holmes and Rahe's (1967) list given in chapter 4 are predictable crises. Violence, spouse or child abuse, accidents, natural disasters (floods, earthquakes), acts of terrorism, the sudden death of a loved one, or an unplanned marital separation are unpredictable crises. It may be noted that the term *crisis* has been overused recently by politicians and by the media, so that now *a crisis* has come to mean little more than an event that has risen to sufficient significance to merit being given attention. As Caplan used the term *crisis intervention*, however, it had more far-reaching implications. These implications included the potential for the counselor to use the crisis to improve the client's coping by assisting the client cognitively to take the following steps (Killilea, 1982):

1. Appraise the threat and actual danger in the situation;
2. Seek new information and perspectives about the situation, including new ways for dealing with it;
3. Seek appropriate role models for how to behave;
4. Reassure oneself that the situation can be mastered by referring to analogous past experiences that had been mastered;
5. Link the current situation to personal competencies that had been demonstrated in the past;
6. Obtain feedback about one's behaviors, plans, and goals;
7. Modify one's level of aspiration;
8. Acquire growth-promoting skills.

Thus, a crisis may provide growth experiences, by using it as a learning experience and as an opportunity to expand the range of experiences in which the client has been able to cope successfully. Hence, the notion of a *crisis* may be restructured into a positive experience, rather than merely be viewed as a potentially disastrous event.

Substance Abusers

Alcohol and drug abuse (to which some would add smoking, habitual overeating, compulsive gambling, and any other addictive, self-destructive behavior patterns) are personal problems that have direct social consequences (accidents caused by drunk drivers, crime by drug addicts seeking money to support their habits, dissolution of families and loss of work productivity due to drugs and alcohol). Although this is not a book on substance abuse or the treatment of substance abusers (which range from some countries that supply drugs to addicts at government expense to others that jail or even execute them), and although separate specialized courses and certification procedures for alcoholism counselors exist in the United States, mental health counselors are nonetheless very likely to encounter clients with one or another of these addictions.

Working with individuals with addiction problems raises particular problems for many mental health professionals for several reasons. One of these reasons is that most mental health professionals subscribe at some emotional level to a middle class ethic, which states that in last analysis, people have some personal responsibility for their actions. Addictions are generally seen as problems that one has gotten oneself into, because they involve the introduction of a substance into the body. Therefore, at some level, many mental health professionals (psychiatrists, clinical psychologists, psychiatric social workers and nurses, as well as mental health counselors) find addicts to be morally reprehensible people. Thus, the professional may unconsciously treat such clients in a less helpful, more punitive way. Coupled with this phenomenon is the fact that for many addicts, the attraction of remaining on the substance exceeds the appeal of getting off it. Therefore, these clients may act consciously or unconsciously to sabotage any treatment aimed at helping them get rid of the addiction. Many addicts have arrived at mental health facilities under duress, where the alternative given to them was to go to jail. Needless to say, the combination of a disapproving counselor and an unwilling client does not make the chances for successful outcome very great.

Therefore, frequently those individuals with drug or alcohol problems who are motivated to overcome their addiction have turned to professionals who had themselves had the addiction and are therefore more likely to be sympathetic and nonjudgmental in their approach, or to nonprofessional self-help groups. Groups such as Alcoholics Anonymous and, in the case of drug addicts, Synanon or Daytop, appear to have been more successful than professionals in helping many persons with addiction problems. Professionals, of course, have often tended to attack these conclusions, basing their attacks on the fact that these groups do not follow scientific procedures in substantiating their claims of success. Thus, professionals argue that because of the anonymity practiced by some of these groups, successes get counted over and over while failures drop out and cannot be traced.

Today, however, the territorial warfare between these self-help groups and the professions seems to have largely cooled off. Each side recognizes that the other has something to contribute to helping the person with an addiction. Therefore, mental health counselors should do all they can to link a client with an addiction problem to an appropriate self-help group, so that the client can gain the benefits of both professional and self-help interventions in a coordinated way. It is, however, important that the counselor be familiar with the self-help group to which the client is referred, so that the match is a good one. For example, inner city and suburban chapters of Alcoholics Anonymous may be totally different from each other in membership and in approach. Just to tell a client to "go to AA meetings" may do that client a disservice, if the client happens to come from a poverty-level environment and ends up at a meeting peopled by only upper income, highly educated suburbanites.

Psychoactive Medication

Although medicine (including psychiatry) is the only profession legally allowed to prescribe psychoactive medications, it is essential for a mental health counselor to know if a client is receiving such medications. Appraisal or intervention without that information would be totally ill-advised. There are numerous books and journal articles devoted to the topic of psychoactive medication, which focus on the chemical structure, physiological effects, and/or clinical use of these drugs. The principal concern for the mental health counselor, however, is the effects of these drugs on the client's functioning both within and outside of the counseling process. Goldsmith (1977) and Ponterotto (1985) have particularly focused on this issue. Ponterotto (1985) emphasized the responsibility of the counselor to contact the physician prescribing the medication (after obtaining the client's permission to do so) in order to: (a) gain specific information needed for the conduct of the counseling process, (b) gain needed information about the action and side-effects of the drug as they appear to be manifesting themselves in the counseling situation, and (c) coordinate the counseling with the chemotherapy so that they do not work at cross-purposes. It is incumbent on the mental health counselor to know exactly what information is needed and why it is needed before contacting the prescribing physician. It is essential that the counselor and the physician work cooperatively toward goals that are agreed upon by the client, counselor, and physician. For example, it would be counterproductive if the physician was prescribing heavy doses of an antianxiety medication at a time at which the counselor was attempting to mobilize and channel the client's anxiety toward a productive goal, such as going to work. Thus, a balance may have to be sought between too much anxiety for the client to be functional and too little for the client to be motivated. This may require an adjustment in the client's medication that only the physician can make.

In general, psychoactive medications are divided into three major categories: (a) antipsychotic drugs, (b) antidepressants, and (c) antianxiety drugs. Antipsychotic drugs are those that reduce or control the symptoms of schizophrenia, manic–depressive psychoses, or psychotic depression. These include, among other drugs, the phenothiazines and lithium salts (the latter specific to manic–depressive conditions). Antidepressants, the two major classes of which are tricyclics and monoamine oxidase inhibitors (MAO inhibitors), relieve depression; they do not, however, cause happiness or euphoria. There are three major classes of antianxiety drugs: barbiturates, benzodiazepines, and antihistamines. These drugs are intended to relieve anxiety, fear, or tensions. (See Ponterotto, 1985, for an excellent summary of the effects, side-effects, and counseling implications of these drugs.)

A final point on this topic is in order. Not all medications have the same effect on all clients. Thus, for some persons, a particular antianxiety drug may actually increase the person's feelings of tension or foreboding. In such cases, a different medication may be called for. If the counselor observes this phenomenon of contrary effects of a medication being given to a client, the counselor should have the client (or if that is not possible, the counselor should) inform the prescribing physician immediately.

Rehabilitation Procedures

The area of mental health rehabilitation is gaining continuously increasing attention, particularly in work with clients who have had more severe mental health problems and/or who have been out of the mainstream of society because of institutionalization or incapacity. It is of interest that the earliest writings on mental health rehabilitation (e.g., Davis, 1946) focused on helping the client adjust to the mental hospital setting, whereas the current focus (e.g., Anthony, 1979; Anthony, Howell, & Danley, 1984; Lamb, 1971) is almost exclusively on adjustment to the community. This, of course, reflects the shift from long-term hospitalization to deinstitutionalization, which has taken place over this time period. Moreover, Anthony (1979) has marshalled evidence to show that traditional psychodiagnosis, psychotherapy, or measures of hospital inpatient behavior are not predictive of rehabilitation outcome in the community. Therefore, Anthony has developed a system for assessing and acquiring the skills and the environmental supports a client will need for successful adjustment to living, learning, and working in the community. As a skill-based model, Anthony's approach is entirely consistent with the approach to mental health counseling espoused throughout this book. It is, indeed, even difficult to draw a clear line between the roles of the mental health counselor and of the rehabilitation counselor when they are working in this area, other than that the rehabilitation counselor usually has greater responsibility for the client's vocational functioning (preparing for, obtaining, and keeping a job). Even so, a competent mental health counselor must understand the area of work and career behavior, and a competent mental health rehabilitation counselor must understand psychosocial functioning as well as work. Anthony, Cohen, and Pierce (1979) have produced (along with additional co-authors on several of the individual volumes) a set of six manuals, plus an instructor's guide, which comprise the *Psychiatric Rehabilitation Practice Series*. These manuals cover the skills the counselor needs in: (a) diagnostic planning,

(b) rehabilitation programming, (c) professional evaluation, (d) career counseling, (e) career placement, and (f) community service coordination. The authors of the series assert that these are the empirically determined skills needed in order to be an effective practitioner of mental health rehabilitation. In turn, the counselor's skills attained through this series are used to assess and promote client skills and environmental supports needed for coping in the community setting. For example, the client skills needed to live in a halfway house may include skills in hygiene, relaxation, nutrition (self-selection of diet), responsibility (e.g., to take own medication), punctuality, interpersonal relationships, and dealing with crises. Other skills may be necessary for getting or keeping a job. The counselor must be able to work with the client to prepare a list of skills needed to achieve a particular goal, to structure a way for the client to gain those skills that he/she does not already have, and to assist the client in learning to apply those skills in the current situation. At the same time, the counselor, along with the client, must assess the environmental supports and barriers and work to maximize the former and to eliminate or compensate for the latter. Thus, mental health rehabilitation (like rehabilitation of persons with physical disabilities) seeks to help the client achieve independent living and productive employment by building on the client's residual assets and by creating an environment that will help the client to succeed. Rehabilitation is more and more becoming recognized as a necessary part of the mental health counseling process.

Case Management

The term *case management* is brought up here because in some settings, this function is distinguished from counseling. Thus, case management refers to the monitoring of the client's progress through the intake, appraisal, planning, intervention, evaluation, follow-up, and closure steps of the agency's routine and the coordination of resources outside the agency that have been enlisted on the client's behalf. In some settings, the term may also include the counselor's time management and paperwork flow. Marlowe, Marlowe, and Willets (1983) listed the case management tasks of the mental health counselor as: assessment, planning, linking, monitoring, and advocacy. Very often, however, the distinction between counseling and case management (in those situations in which this distinction is even made) is an administrative rather than a clinical one. It may, however, be used in circumscribing the role of supervision in the agency. Thus, one may have a senior counselor supervising one's counseling techniques and an administrator overseeing the case management aspects of one's case load. In many settings, however, this distinction is not made.

In addition to case management (the management of individual cases), the mental health counselor is also required to engage in case-load management, that is, the organization of one's workload. Greenwood (1982) listed the tasks of case-load management as: (a) planning for effective allocation of one's time and skills across one's caseload; (b) managing the plan to make best use of one's skills, resources, and time; and (c) reviewing client progress periodically to assess the effectiveness of services. To carry out these tasks, the counselor must have at least five sets of knowledge and skills: (a) knowledge of counselor roles and functions, (b) knowledge of planning procedures, (c) decision-making skills, (d) time management skills, and (e) administrative skills.

SUMMARY

In this chapter, we have reviewed some of the knowledge and applied skills all mental health counselors must have in order to work with a client. These included knowledge about and skills in appraisal, intervention, and a range of specialized techniques (crisis intervention, mental health rehabilitation, case management) and frequently encountered issues (substance abuse, psychoactive medication). All of these considerations are also applicable to working with families, groups, and communities, which will be covered in the following three chapters.

REFERENCES

Anthony, W. A. (1979). *The principles of psychiatric rehabilitation*. Amherst, MA: Human Resources Development Press.

Anthony, W. A., Cohen, M. R., & Pierce, R. M. (1979). *The psychiatric rehabilitation practice series* (Vols. 1-6 plus instructor's guide). Amherst, MA: Carkhuff Institute of Human Technology.

Anthony, W. A., Howell, J., & Danley, K. S. (1984). Vocational rehabilitation of the psychiatrically disabled. In M. Mirabi (Ed.), *The chronically mentally ill: Research and services* (pp. 215-237). New York: Spectrum.

Barker, R. G. (1968). *Ecological psychology: Concepts and methods for studying the environment of human behavior.* Stanford, CA: Stanford University Press.

Beckhard, R., & Harris, R. T. (1977). *Organizational transitions: Managing complex change.* Reading, MA: Addison-Wesley.

Belkin, G. S. (1984). *Introduction to counseling* (2nd ed.). Dubuque, IA: Wm. C. Brown.

Brabeck, M. M., & Welfel, E. R. (1985). Counseling theory: Understanding the trend toward eclecticism from a developmental perspective. *Journal of Counseling and Development, 63,* 343-348.

Brickman, P., Rabinowitz, V. C., Karuza, J., Jr., Coates, D., Cohn, E. & Kidder, L. (1982). Models of helping and coping. *American Psychologist, 37,* 368-384.

Bruce, P. (1984). Continuum of counseling goals: A framework for differentiating counseling strategies. *The Personnel and Guidance Journal, 62,* 259-263.

Butcher, E., Scofield, M. E., & Baker, S. B. (1985). Clinical judgment in planning mental health treatment: An empirical investigation. *AMHCA Journal, 7,* 116-126.

Capelle, R. G. (1979). *Changing human systems.* Toronto: International Human Systems Institute.

Caplan, G. (1964). *Principles of preventive psychiatry.* New York: Basic Books.

Carkhuff, R. R., Pierce, R. M., & Cannon, J. R. (1980). *The art of helping IV.* Amherst, MA: Human Resources Development Press.

Cohen, B. F., & Anthony, W. A. (1984). Functional assessment in psychiatric rehabilitation. In A. S. Halpern & M. J. Fuhrer (Eds.), *Functional assessment in rehabilitation* (pp. 79-100). Baltimore: Paul H. Brookes.

Corey, G. (1986). *Theory and practice of counseling and psychotherapy* (3rd ed.). Monterey, CA: Brooks/Cole.

Davis, J. E. (1946). *Rehabilitation: Its principles and practice* (rev. ed.). New York: Barnes.

Egan, G. (1986). *The skilled helper: A systematic approach to effective helping* (3rd ed.). Monterey, CA: Brooks/Cole.

Elliott, T. R. (1985). Counseling adults from Schlossberg's adaptation model. *AMHCA Journal, 7,* 133-141.

Forsyth, D. R., & Strong, S. R. (1986). The scientific study of counseling and psychotherapy: A unificationist view. *American Psychologist, 41,* 113-119.

Frey, D. H., & Raming, H. E., (1979). A taxonomy of counseling goals and methods. *Personnel and Guidance Journal, 58,* 26-33.

Gilliland, B. E., James, R. K., Roberts, G. T., & Bowman, J. T. (1984). *Theories and strategies in counseling and psychotherapy.* Englewood Cliffs, NJ: Prentice-Hall.

Goldsmith, W. (1977). *Psychiatric drugs for the non-medical mental health worker.* Springfield, IL: Charles C Thomas.

Goldstein, A. P. (1981). *Psychological skill training: The structured learning technique.* Elmsford, NY: Pergamon.

Granger, C. V. (1984). A conceptual model for functional assessment. In C. V. Granger & G. E. Gresham (Eds.), *Functional assessment in rehabilitation medicine* (pp. 14-25). Baltimore: Williams & Wilkins.

Greenwood, R. (1982). Systematic caseload management. In R. T. Roessler & S. E. Rubin (Eds.), *Case management and rehabilitation counseling: Procedures and techniques* (pp. 159-172). Baltimore: University Park Press.

Halpern, A. S., & Fuhrer, M. J. (Eds.). (1984). *Functional assessment in rehabilitation.* Baltimore: Paul H. Brookes.

Hersen, M., & Bellack, A. S. (1976). Social skills training for chronic psychiatric patients: Rationale, research findings, and future directions. *Comprehensive Psychiatry, 17,* 559-580.

Hershenson, D. B. (1982). A formulation of counseling based on the healthy personality. *Personnel and Guidance Journal, 60,* 406-409.

Holmes, T. H., & Rahe, R. H. (1967). The social readjustment rating scale. *Journal of Psychosomatic Research, 11,* 213-218.

Ivey, A. E. (1980). *Counseling and psychotherapy: Skills, theories, and practices.* Englewoods Cliffs, NJ: Prentice-Hall.

Jacobs, H. E., Kardashian, S., Kreinbring, R. K., Ponder, R., & Simpson, A. R. (1984). A skills-oriented model for facilitating employment among psychiatrically disabled persons. *Rehabilitation Counseling Bulletin, 28,* 87-96.

Janis, I. L. (1983). *Short-term counseling: Guidelines based on recent research.* New Haven, CT: Yale University Press.

Janis, I. L., & Mann, L. (1977). *Decision making: A psychological analysis of conflict, choice, and commitment.* New York: Free Press.

Killilea, M. (1982). Interaction of crisis theory, coping strategies, and social support systems. In H. C. Schulberg & M. Killilea (Eds.), *The modern practice of community mental health* (pp. 163-214). San Francisco: Jossey-Bass.

Kottler, J. A., & Brown, R. W. (1985). *Introduction to therapeutic counseling.* Monterey, CA: Brooks/Cole.

L'Abate, L. (1980). Toward a theory and technology for social skills training. *Academic Psychology Bulletin, 2,* 207-228.

L'Abate, L. (1981). Classification of counseling and therapy theorists, methods, processes and goals: The E-R-A model. *Personnel and Guidance Journal, 59,* 263-265.

Lamb, H. R. & Associates. (1971). *Rehabilitation in community mental health.* San Francisco: Jossey-Bass.

Lewin, K. (1936). *Principles of topological psychology.* New York: McGraw-Hill.

Marlowe, H. A., Jr., Marlowe, J. L., & Willetts, R. (1983). The mental health counselor as case manager: Implications for working with the chronically mentally ill. *AMHCA Journal, 5,* 184-191.

Moos, R. H. (1976). *The human context: Environmental determinants of behavior.* New York: Wiley-Interscience.

Patterson, C. H. (1985). New light for counseling theory. *Journal of Counseling and Development, 63,* 349-350.

Patterson, C. H. (1986). *Theories of counseling and psychotherapy* (4th ed.). New York: Harper & Row.

Ponterotto, J. G. (1985). A counselor's guide to psychopharmacology. *Journal of Counseling and Development, 64,* 109-115.

Ponzo, A. (1976). Integrating techniques from five counseling theories. *Personnel and Guidance Journal, 54,* 415-419.

Rychlak, J. F. (1985). Eclecticism in psychological theorizing: Good and bad. *Journal of Counseling and Development, 63,* 351-353.

Schlossberg, N. K. (1984). *Counseling adults in transition: Linking practice with theory.* New York: Springer.

Seligman, L. (1986). *Diagnosis and treatment planning in counseling.* New York: Human Sciences Press.

Schertzer, B., & Linden, J. D. (1979). *Fundamentals of individual appraisal: Assessment techniques for counselors.* Boston: Houghton Mifflin.

Shertzer, B., & Linden, J. D. (1979). *Fundamentals of individual appraisal: Assessment techniques for counselors.* Boston: Houghton Mifflin.

Wallace, W. A. (1986). *Theories of counseling and psychotherapy: A basic issues approach.* Boston: Allyn and Bacon.

Wheelis, A. (1975). *How people change.* New York: Harper Colophon.

8   Counseling Families

The family has been the cornerstone of society since the origins of humanity. Whatever the variation in its structure and function, the family is and will continue to be a social system that has functioned over time to fulfill the emotional, physical, and intellectual needs of its members. The way it functions, establishes roles, and communicates and negotiates differences between members, has numerous implications for the theory and practice of mental health counseling. In fact, the family is an important environment to consider when planning interventions for mental health care.

Because the family is the social group most immediately affected by illness and mental health treatment, individual problems are also family concerns (Power & Dell Orto, 1980). It could also be the social group most damaged by the client's problem or the group that must be mobilized to help the client recover from the problem. Because the family has the potential to be the mental health counselor's greatest ally in treatment, it should be an important focus of attention in the delivery of mental health services.

The goal of this chapter is to help the reader to appreciate that effective mental health counseling demands an understanding not only of the individual, but also of family dynamics and how family members can influence the individual's life adjustment. To gain this appreciation the following topics will be discussed: (a) a definition of *family*; (b) a portrait of the "modern" family and its implications for the practice of mental health counseling; (c) selected ways of understanding the family; and (d) the different approaches that have been developed for helping families. Each topic area blends with the others to form a picture illustrating the relationship between mental health and the family. A knowledge of the family today suggests issues that can receive attention from mental health counselors. In turn, these factors come into sharper focus when several theoretical approaches to understanding the family are explained. These approaches then generate a background for explaining briefly the history of family therapy and for identifying the leading, established directions in family therapy. The roles and functions of the mental health counselor when assisting families can be more cogently understood when we become aware of the varied ways that a family can be helped.

WHAT IS THE FAMILY?

Family today conveys many meanings to different people. Such structures as the open marriage, group and multilateral marriages, the communal family, and the one-parent family are identified as viable styles of family life. The U.S. Census Bureau defines the family as two or more people who are related by blood, marriage, or adoption and who live in the same dwelling (Doherty & Baird, 1983). But this definition leaves out members of the extended family who may live close by and who have considerable influence on family life. Robischon and Smith (1977) define the family as an interdependent group system that may consist of the biological or adoptive family and/or influential others. Such a definition allows one to understand a family as a group of intimates who provide continuing social support and to whom one turns for physical and emotional assistance in time of trouble.

The term *family*, consequently, can have multiple definitions, all appropriate in some contexts and for some purposes. Rakel (1977) suggested a clearer perspective for the varied perception of family when he outlined family forms in the following way:

1. Nuclear family: husband and wife and their children,
2. Extended family: a family extended to include parents and sometimes other relatives,
3. Alternate family: single-parent families, married adults without children, unmarried adults (heterosexual and homosexual), communes, others.

Historically, in America the so-called nuclear family was the widespread family form. Consisting of husband, wife, and children it emerged as the 20th century began. This form tends to be child-centered and emphasizes the family as a center of nurture and affection. Though Shorter (1975) has observed that the nuclear family is as much a state of mind as it is a formal structure, this type of family reached its peak in popular acclaim and social influence in the years following World War II and continuing through the 1950s (Conger, 1981).

Between the mid-1960s and the early 1970s, however, a series of cultural shocks took place in America, such as the assassinations of John and Robert Kennedy and Martin Luther King, Watergate, the forced resignations of Spiro Agnew and Richard Nixon, and the war in Vietnam. The war issue alone significantly contributed to dividing the nation and to alienating many bright and promising young people from their elders. The authority of the adult culture became compromised in the eyes of many adolescents, and the authority derived by parents from their position as family representatives of this culture was compromised along with it (Conger, 1981). All in all, this period challenged the integrity of the "nuclear family."

From the early 1970s there was an acceleration in the development of different family forms. Many rootless, alienated, and confused young adults found it difficult to make the type of commitment that generates the nuclear family. Different styles of life were attempted, resulting in the kaleidoscopic picture of "family" as we know it today.

A "PORTRAIT" OF THE MODERN FAMILY

The family today in American society has many characteristics. Some of these have caused a weakening of family functions; others "point to the contemporary travails of families as labor pains before a brave new birth" (Melson, 1980, p. 33). These main family characteristics and their implications for mental health workers are listed in the following paragraphs.

The Shrinking Family

Though marriage continues to be a nearly universal experience for adults, the size of the American family has decreased. Parents are having fewer children. Coupled with the increased life expectancy of people in the United States, a lower fertility rate has lengthened by 14 years the period in which the average couple lives together without children (Glick, 1977, 1979). Women of childbearing age are delaying the onset of childbearing and having fewer children. In addition, there is increasingly less likelihood that the household will include individuals outside the nuclear family (Melson, 1980).

Changing Incidence and Status of Divorce

Dissatisfaction with the institution of marriage itself has not risen; only the willingness to do something about an unsatisfactory marriage has increased. In 1978, divorces numbered 1,122,000, a rate of 22 divorces per 1,000 married women, indicating that 2.2% of marriages ended in divorce that year (U.S. Bureau of the Census, 1979a). Divorce figures since 1978 indicate the rate of divorce is continuing to climb in the early 1980s, although the rate of increase per year has slowed down (Doherty & Baird, 1983).

As a phenomenon related to these divorce statistics, another important reality is the increase of the single-parent household, particularly that headed by a female. This family change has been steadily increasing since 1980. The trend from 1960 has been for percentages of white female-headed households to increase at a relatively greater rate than nonwhite, which have actually decreased (Melson, 1980). There may be joint custody of children or, in a minority of single-parent families, the father may have custody of his children. When all single-parent households are considered, including those resulting from separation, widowhood, and single-parent adoption, at least 10% are headed by men (U.S. Bureau of the Census, 1979b).

Moreover, divorce is no longer considered a symptom of a society's moral decay or social instability. Of course, whether divorce is a disruptive factor or a useful adjustment depends upon the culture and one's point of view. If a mental health professional sees the family's chief purpose as the nurture of the young, then divorce and the often resulting single-parent family may be viewed with great concern. Four of ten children born in the 1970s will spend time in a single-parent household during the course of their coming of age. It is estimated that the proportion will rise to half for children born in the 1980s (Strickland, 1985). For others, however, divorce may not be a sign of failure but a creative passage on the way to psychological maturity.

Dual Employment

The pivotal year for mothers of infants through teens was 1979, the year in which more mothers worked than stayed at home on a full-time basis (American Council of Life Insurance, 1980). Financial reasons, expanding career options, the increased educational attainment of women, the isolation of the homemaker from an extended family and support system, and changing marital status, that is, divorced or widowed, have all been identified as influences for mothers to enter the work place (Robinson, Rotter, & Wilson, 1982). The dual-earner couple has become the norm in American society. In 1978 there were more dual-earner couples (both persons working) than couples in which only the husband was employed. This included 51% of all wives aged 18 to 24, 43% of all mothers, and 41% of mothers with a child 2 years of age or younger (U.S. Bureau of the Census, 1979a).

Increased occupational and financial pressures are also potential dangers to family stability. Particularly among middle-class career professionals, work and career demand a commitment of time and energy far beyond a nine-to-five routine (Melson, 1980). Also, the blue collar husband-father has equally serious work pressures that affect his family life. He may have to take two jobs to make ends meet and thus work as long as the career professional.

Division of Labor and Authority

The traditional American family was highly patriarchal. But today an increasing number of family members share duties that in the past were customarily reserved for the husband/father or wife/mother. For example, the wife may perform such functions as paying the bills and managing the family budget, and the husband may spend much time doing the family shopping or taking care of the children. Fathers are beginning to be more involved in the emotional care of children and wives, as well as the older generation (Bretto-Kelly, 1979).

Implications for Mental Health Professionals

The increase of family variations, the growing incidence of divorce, changing family roles, and the occupational pressures affecting the family have implications for mental health counselors. For example, as new adult roles continue to emerge within the family, counselors who work with families could spend a great portion of their time dealing with the examination and re-definition of roles and expectations that individuals have about marriage, masculinity, femininity, and parenthood (Bretto-Kelly, 1979). Individuals will also experience much more role conflict. The employed wife and mother, for example, may be torn by the incompatible demands of various roles. Husbands may want a full-time traditional wife, but then learn that they are married to women who want a professional career.

With the development of new adult roles, power struggles within the family may increase in a greater number and intensity. As men and women share more tasks that previously were sexually exclusive, problems relating to decision making will emerge. Mental health counselors may spend more time in assisting people to learn how to negotiate, to divide responsibilities, to make joint decisions, to solve problems, and to compromise (Bretto-Kelly, 1979).

As family forms increase in their diversity, mental health counselors will have to enlarge their repertoire of techniques and models to deal with more varied and complex family systems. Sparked by the diversification of family forms, new types of family counseling may have to be developed. This offers a serious challenge for mental health counseling.

Separation and divorce can precipitate a host of problems for the family. Mothers who retain custody of their children are likely to find themselves in severe economic straits within a few years after divorce (Melson, 1980). Child-support payments may dwindle to nothing, and it is very difficult to prosecute defaulting ex-husbands. Sixty-two percent fail to comply within the first year and 42% make no payments at all. After 10 years, 79% of all ex-husbands are in noncompliance (Weitzman, 1974). "The single mother's precipitous fall in economic status is translated for the child into a new neighborhood and new school, fewer toys, treats, and outings, and perhaps communication of abiding resentment against the one-time provider" (Melson, 1980, p. 44). The material and emotional losses accruing from divorce, consequently, generate stressors within a family. In turn, these stressors can cause severe life-adjustment problems or deteriorating mental health conditions that need the attention of professionals.

The increase of single-parent families, moreover, has contributed to further deterioration in child care. Although many single parents are coping with courage and success in a difficult situation, there is also ample evidence that many children are suffering (Strickland, 1985). Few adults are capable of supplying on a 24-hour-a-day basis the kind of steady, sensitive, and knowledgeable care and discipline that young children require. A second adult is needed to provide relief for those times when the primary care-giver is simply not feeling up to the demands of parenthood. But not only are children in a single-parent household denied the benefits of attention from two caring adults, in many instances they are denied the attention of even one, for single parents are usually working outside the home.

Five million American children under the age of 10 have no one to look after them when they come home from school (Strickland, 1985). It is also estimated that 500,000 children under the age of 7 are "latchkey" children. The growing absence of adult supervision of any kind places more and more of all of these children at risk of injury, abuse, and death.

Smaller family size has added implications, for example, for the care and rehabilitation of the mentally and physically handicapped. If a child is physically handicapped, the burden places additional strain upon the parent or parents, who may have no other relatives to help (Zisserman, 1981). If the handicapped person is an adult, the spouse and/or children often assume responsibility for the patient's care in the absence of other relatives. Stroke or multiple sclerosis victims often become handicapped just when their teenage children are becoming independent (Goodell, 1975).

All of these factors and pressures that are having an impact upon or taking place within families today place family members more "at risk." Living successfully as a single parent, or as an adolescent with a disabled family member, or as a child who may be alone for a few hours after school demand effective coping skills. Mental health professionals can provide opportunities to teach family members how to deal with unavoidable family changes. These professionals can also offer assistance to family members who, because of disruptive realities in family life, may be suffering varied mental health problems, that is, depression, alcohol/substance abuse, or severe anxiety.

UNDERSTANDING THE FAMILY

Although many types of family units exist, the attempts to understand this varied context of *family* has generated different theories of explaining family dynamics. A knowledge of the most widely accepted and utilized theories can lay the foundation for effective intervention by mental health counselors. Successful assistance to troubled families depends largely on how the mental health professional perceives what is going on in family life. Despite the existence of many family forms, there are three theories that provide valuable insights into family functioning. They are: role theory, developmental theory, and systems theory.

Roles in Modern Marriage

Overs and Healy (1973) believe "that increasingly the family has come to be seen as an integrated system of reciprocal roles" (p. 87). Thus, the family as a unit functions adequately or inadequately according to the degree of role perception and the interaction among the role performances of the various members. Marital success or adjustment can be defined by the degree of congruence between the husband's and wife's perceptions of their respective roles (Overs & Healy, 1973).

Parsons and Bales's (1955) theory has stimulated more research than any other role theory. They identify two main roles in marriage, the instrumental and the expressive. The instrumental role belongs to the husband. His task is getting things done, namely, earning money and maintaining the outside relationships with the economic and school systems. The wife has the expressive role; she is primarily concerned with maintaining satisfactory relationships within the family and with the expression of feelings that are a part of intimate relationships. However, these functions are not exclusive. The wife may shop for groceries and call the school about her children and the husband may settle quarrels among the children and tell his wife that he loves her. Swenson (1973) believes that this theory suggests which person assumes primary responsibility for which area. The husband is primarily concerned with instrumental functions and secondarily with expressive functions, whereas for the wife, the situation is reversed.

In role theory there are four concepts that are basic in understanding mental health and the family. They are role complementarity, role change, role conflict, and role reversal. Each of these concepts can be identified in the following case concerning a family who experienced the trauma of a young family member with leukemia.

Jennifer, age 15, was hospitalized with the diagnosis of leukemia. The illness went into remission following medication and hospital treatment care. Upon returning home, the family became aware that new, continued demands were to be made upon them, that is, frequent clinic visits and coping with their own anxiety and grief over the illness situation. The mother was particularly affected, feeling guilty that perhaps she was neglectful in the care of her child before disease onset. She became temporarily depressed, and during this time withdrew from many of her social contacts, and asked her daughter, age 14, and son, age 17, to assume many of the household chores. The husband also began to perform many more household duties, and accompanied his wife, whenever possible, to the clinic for treatment. Eventually her guilt feelings were alleviated, and through the assumption of added responsibilities in the home the family members found new strengths within one another to cope with the trauma.

Because there was a fluidity of roles among the family members—each family member should either adapt to or assume new responsibilities—the family was able to adjust to the daughter's illness. This equilibrium could not have been achieved without what is called a "complementarity of roles." Roles in the family did not exist in isolation, but were patterned to mesh with those of other family members. The mother first expressed a need to share her role responsibilities with another.

The husband and father, in addition to his role as breadwinner for the family, enlarged his role within the home by cooking for the children while the wife had to be with their daughter at the hospital. This can be referred to as a temporary role change. This change can cause role relationships within this family to become delicate. For example, as a mother changed her methods of disciplining her child or made a decision about the daughter's health care, conflicts could arise in her relationship with her husband, or she could become confused and inadequate in her role as wife, or the complementarity of roles could break down. In either instance, role conflict is generated and role complementarity is not restored until the family members become aware of the demands of the illness situation and are willing to make the effort to modify their accustomed family behavior.

One way to resolve role conflict is through role reversal. This involves looking at what is happening in the family from the other person's point of view. It requires a good understanding of what really is occurring within the family because of the disability situation.

Today roles in marriage are becoming increasingly less rigid and defined. The changes in family life reflect a high complementarity of roles. In many "modern" marriages the husband and wife are colleagues, and there is a blurring of the edges of primary responsibility with more sharing of tasks. If the husband has been performing many household tasks and has taken much responsibility, for example, for the care of the children, or if the wife has been working or feels confident to enter the work market, then the limitations on family life caused by a crisis can be minimized. Family role complementarity enables the family members to re-pattern their lives in such a way that family needs can still be met in an efficient manner.

Developmental Theory

When a mental health crisis, such as a divorce, separation, death, or illness occurs in a family, it occurs at a definite stage in the family's life cycle. The reaction of family members to the illness of a husband and father can be quite different in the earlier stages of a marriage and family life than when the couple and family have been living together for many years. For example, the factors of role expectations, intimacy, and dependency, which are strong determinants of how a family copes with a disease, will vary during different stages of family life. An illness can disrupt the balance of these factors, and the extent of the disruption depends upon the life stage of the family.

The severe cardiac patient illustrates the intermeshing of these factors and the disability. For example, when a husband has a heart attack and has been married for many years, the family's emotional system might find it very difficult to meet the patient's needs for self-esteem and competency. The patient-husband may have left all household chores and child-rearing decisions to his wife, and now, because of physical restrictions, has no other readily available role within the family. His self-esteem may be closely tied in with his ability to provide, so that the loss of this role is perceived as a loss of worth. In contrast, in addition to her role as homemaker, the wife may have to explore opportunities for a part-time job to augment the dwindling family income. The lack of a definite role for the husband and the possible added role for the wife may create conflict and disharmony for the couple. True, such conflict may occur whether the couple is newly married or has just celebrated a 25th wedding anniversary, but because the functions in the home have been so well established, the mental health counselor has a more difficult helping task. The counselor must shape a model of intervention from this particular, patterned home environment and utilize the family members in a distinctive way in order to assist in the care of the husband.

Within each stage certain family tasks emerge. These family tasks reflect the assumption that developmental tasks of individual family members have an overriding influence on or affect the nature of family life at a given time. Adequate task handling at early stages also strengthens the family's ability to handle subsequent stages effectively. Crises within a family, therefore, can be better understood within the family when each of the family stages is explored, because each stage has its own demands, responsibilities, problems, roles, and challenges. The way the family comes to terms with crisis may vary according to the respective family stage.

Two of the most frequently used systems for understanding family life stages are those containing eight life stages as described by Havighurst (1953) and Duvall (1971). Cavan (1974) has merged these two systems, and Rhodes (1977) has identified stages in the life cycle of the family in the tradition of Erik Erikson's life cycle of the individual. Much of the material on the following pages is an adaptation, interpretation, and clarification of the work of these four researchers. The names of each stage are provided by Cavan (1974), although the explanation of each stage is based primarily on the research of Duvall (1971).

Beginning Families (Married Couples without Children)

This stage is characterized by the spouses building their relationship, assuming responsibility for each other in the relationship, and negotiating differences and conflicts with one another. The partners are attempting to find mutually satisfying ways to nurture and support each other. During this time the couple often dwells on themes of mutual understanding, caring, shared interests, and enjoyment of each other's company (Duvall, 1971). In the marriage almost exclusive attention is given to personality characteristics and emotional responsibility. Usually minimal reference is made to marital roles (Rakel, 1977), although the husband is attempting to establish himself in an occupation and the wife is learning both to manage a household and perhaps to maintain her own employment responsibilities.

Extended unemployment of the principal family wage earner during this time, for example, represents a disappointment for one of the spouses, and can engender much conflict. The spouses are attempting to achieve intimacy and to discover the joys within each other. The anxiety that unemployment brings can represent a serious obstacle to developing intimacy and can inhibit the beginning of workable marital roles.

Child-Bearing Families (Oldest Child: Birth to 30 Months)

At the child-bearing time of their marriage, the spouses' ability to succor and to be available and responsive to the needs of very young children is being tapped. Their response depends on the presence of both their inner resources and a caring environment established by them (Rakel, 1977). The couple that has achieved intimacy during the first stage of married life is in a position to make the necessary adaptations to a new family member who is both helpless and demanding (Rhodes, 1977). With the arrival of children, of course, there may be a period of some disillusionment as the husband, especially, realizes that there are new demands for the wife's attention. The better integrated the marriage partners, usually, the less is the disillusionment.

The occurrence of a severe illness, for example, usually complicates the adjustment to the child. Needed treatment care, the perhaps negative emotional reaction of the adult to the disability, and the early readjustment to customary marital tasks all serve as a challenge to the couple, and the disease itself may represent a difficult hurdle for the spouses to overcome in adjusting to each other as parents. A newly disabled husband, experiencing his own loss and depression, may resent the attention given by the wife to the children. However, with many couples, one of whom is newly disabled, the presence of a child can become a source of joy and a resource for coping with the limitations imposed by a disability.

Families with Preschool Children (Oldest Child: 30 Months to 6 Years)

Most of the abilities needed by parents with small children are certainly carried over to the preschool stage. The succorance, nurturance, and availability must continue as children develop.

However, the mother may become totally involved in maintaining her home and caring for her children (Cavan, 1974). Outside opportunities may be necessary for personal replenishment. The husband and wife should spend time together in order to prevent the possibility of losing their marriage in family life.

If the presence of a significant family loss limits this opportunity, special problems can develop between the husband and wife. The aged parent of one of the spouses may move in with the family, causing a shift in family responsibilities. The adjustment to new obligations may cause frustration, anger, and tension.

Families with School Children (Oldest Child: 6 to 13 Years)

Rhodes (1977) asserted that during the school-age period families must shift the primary attention of their energies from family concerns to individual interests. She claimed that the major struggle for the partner, released from the early dependence of children, is to prepare for an identity that is not defined by that partner's roles and responsibilities within the family. The danger in this stage is when a family limits opportunities for development outside of itself. If the children feel free enough to enter into peer networks and community institutions, the parents might feel capable of developing resources for personal satisfaction outside of the home (Rhodes, 1977). If the parents are accustomed to seeking replenishment outside of the home, then the beginnings of this new identity will be facilitated. The same is true with a family crisis. If the family members have utilized community resources apart from the family, then this particular family stage will intermesh harmoniously with previous stages of the marriage. The caring responsibilities associated with a family crisis may not become as much of a burden when appropriate outlets have been established.

Families with Teenagers (Oldest Child: 13 to 20 Years)

Such factors as role models, a consistency of family life, and who is the dominant person in the home assume continued importance for the family (Duvall, 1971). At the teenager stage, separation themes surface within the family and issues emerge that may be difficult for family members to negotiate if a disabled parent has become very dependent on the children (Rhodes, 1977). The resolution of a major crisis for family members rests with their ability to develop companionship inside and outside the family. These bonds will ease the pain of loss stemming from the children who are leaving home for college or for their own living arrangements.

During this stage a new kind of parent–child relationship should be established, based on a recognition of the child's growing independence. If a severe loss strikes during this family period, and if parents have not adapted constructively to this crisis, then such a recognition will generally not be achieved. Too much attention may be continually focused on the loss. The children may feel isolated and eventually leave home abruptly (Power, 1977). Tension and fear may characterize the marital relationship.

Families as Launching Centers (First Child Gone to Last Child Leaving Home)

Seeing their children leave home may be hardest for many women who feel that their home-related competencies are no longer needed or valued. This phase of family life is usually experienced as particularly difficult for the mother and wife because there is also a renewed demand on the family's ability to foster and support individuation (Rhodes, 1977). The viability of the marital relationship is a strong determinant of how the family negotiates this stage.

When an illness, for example, has caused severe dependency and aroused conflicts or resentments among the marital partners and family members, individuation for the children may be thwarted. The attention may be focused almost exclusively on the ill family member. The children may be asked to assume a large role in treatment responsibilities, or they may often be ignored because of caring for the disabled person. The older children may feel guilty in leaving home to begin their own life. Disappointment may pervade the family scene, and the parents may not help their children make the transition from the home to a more independent life.

Families in the Middle Years (Empty Nest to Retirement)

The middle years can be particularly difficult for a couple for whom one member has experienced a severe loss. It is a time for a renegotiation of the adult–adult relationship. Rediscovery is all important because usually in the later years of marriage there is a general drop in marital satisfaction and adjustment, which can be conceived as a process of disenchantment (Rhodes, 1977). The cessation of parent functions seems to leave a vacuum and often demands major reorientation of purpose and goals. The presence of this loss, such as continued unemployment, the death of a close relative, or even a move to another geographical area, may only aggravate a loss of intimacy, especially if the loss or transition severely affects the couple's sexual life or the amount of time given to shared activities. Yet with a renewed interest in the personalities of their spouses, the husband and wife could become a source of support for each other, leading to increased satisfaction in the postparental and retirement time of their life (Duvall, 1971).

Aging Families (Retirement to Death of Both Spouses)

The retirement stage entails most of the changes related to the aging process. Rakel (1977) stated that most people in this stage who maintain a wide diversity of interests remain psychologically healthy and are satisfied with their stage of life. Although at this stage in their relationship roles may have to be redefined, based on the exchange of services, it can be a time of renewed satisfaction if the spouses have coped well with the stresses of their family and have the resources to deal with the loneliness and depression that may accompany growing old. Kin networks and community ties are necessary resources for coping with the aging process. These resources may generate alternate satisfactions and values that permit individuals to maintain a sense of personal usefulness and contentment with life (Rakel, 1977).

Many changes, such as physical infirmities, a lowered income, and loss of good friends are expected to occur to the spouses. If the couple has recaptured a needed intimacy and utilizes these kin networks and community ties, then the blows associated with the aging process can be softened. Physical and emotional closeness among family members is an important source for adaptation in stress and illness.

Systems Theory

One of the most important concepts in understanding families, as well as the framework for many approaches to assist families in crisis or continued dysfunction, is general systems theory (Foley, 1974). A basic assumption of this theory is that all parts of a family are functionally interrelated. The system of a family is not the sum of the individual personalities of the father, mother, and children, but the vital, ongoing interaction between them. Turnbull, Summers, and Brotherson (1983) identify three major elements in family systems theory: family interaction, family structure, and family functions.

Family Interaction

The family is more than a collection of individuals. Change or stress affecting one family member affects the whole family. Although mental health workers may deal with individuals one at a time, they must guard against understanding the family members while missing the family (Doherty & Baird, 1983).

Family interactions are the ways family members relate to each other on a daily basis. Family interaction, moreover, usually embraces four subsystems: The marital (husband–wife interactions), the parental (parent–child interactions), the sibling (child–child interactions), and the extra-familial-system (nuclear family interactions with external systems and individuals) (Turnbull et al., 1983). Also, the implicit rules that govern family interactions are called boundaries. Boundaries are determined by the degree of closeness or distance among family members, the family's adaptability, and family communication. Boundary rules usually define who participates and how family functions are carried out. All families develop implicit rules for daily living. They may be shown in mealtime patterns, the patterns of handling decisions, of celebrating holidays, and of relating to outside professionals such as the mental health worker. On the contrary, families may have troublesome rule-like interaction patterns, such as family members interrupting each other's conversation at any time, or singling out a particular person for blame when something goes wrong (Doherty & Baird, 1983).

The ability to adapt to change is the hallmark of healthy family functioning. Healthy families maintain a balance of cohesion, adaptability, and communication, but it does not mean that these families are always balanced. Change is an ever present challenge to families, and in times of family stress, mental health workers evaluate whether family members are supportive of one another, whether role expectations are clear and flexible, and whether family rules are clear and flexible. If boundaries are extremely rigid, or are nonexistent, or if family members are totally enmeshed in one another or disengaged (distant) from each other, then families may be unable to adapt to a particular trauma. Communication may be virtually nonexistent or so open and random as to be counterproductive.

Family Structure

Consisting of tangible features that define the family and mold its interactions, family structure includes:

1. Membership characteristics—personal attributes of members, family size, and the nature of the extra-familial system;
2. Cultural style—ethnicity, religion, socioeconomic status, and geographic location, all of which provide the family with the past and present;
3. Ideologic style—the beliefs, values, and coping styles, all of which give the family a sense of direction (Turnbull et al., 1983).

For the mental health counselor, a knowledge of family structure can provide valuable information on the family's coping styles, the way family members view a particular trauma, and the size and nature of the support system available to the family during periods of stress. Actually, family structure can be perceived as an inventory of available resources that shapes the nature of interventions (National Institute of Handicapped Research, 1984). Interventions, for example, should be consistent with a family's support system and their ideological and cultural context.

Family Functions

Such functions may be quite diverse, but the main family function should be to meet the individual family members' needs. In a time of severe loss of one of the family members, for example, these needs may take the form of increased demands on family time and resources. Intervention approaches can be designed to respond to the many family demands. Watzlawick and Weakland (1977) believed that if one phrase could be used to capture the family systems approach to understanding families, it would be the "interactional context" of human behavior and human problems. The theory emphasizes the interconnectedness of human beings in their intimate environment (Doherty & Baird, 1983). It offers a point of view rather than specific information about specific people. In examining the family system one thinks not in terms of unidirectional cause and effect, but in terms of ongoing interactions. The theory suggests to the mental health counselor that individuals' symptoms may have a function within a family. For example, if the family system goal is stability, a child's illness can be seen in the larger context of keeping the family together. The sickness may be functional in terms of stabilization for a family system because it allows the fighting parents to join around the child (Berman, Lief, & Williams, 1981).

The three theoretical approaches that have been discussed provide important insights to understanding family dynamics. They also have stimulated the development of family therapy theory, for there has been an integration of role theory and communications theory, for example, with the clinical practice of treating family problems. Helping dysfunctional families or families undergoing a transitional crisis is an object of professional attention for many mental health counselors.

APPROACHES FOR HELPING FAMILIES

Mental health counselors have been an integral part of the family therapy movement. While utilizing the family concepts found in role theory, developmental theory, or systems theory, they have provided long-term marital or family therapy and short-term counseling to alleviate different family adjustmental problems. Each direction for helping families has specific, distinguishing characteristics.

Family Therapy/Long-Term Intervention

Many family problems may require powerful therapeutic interventions. These include such problems as chronic family dysfunctional patterns; serious, acute family symptoms (e.g., child abuse, spouse abuse, and incest); chemical dependency (alcohol or other forms of substance abuse) and a family member's chronic depression and anxiety around which family interaction patterns have become rigidly stabilized (Doherty & Baird, 1983). Family therapy interventions to alleviate these serious problems that have developed have in common: (a) the assessment of the family system as a whole, (b) the focus on the process of the family's interaction (e.g., arguments over money or child-rearing practices), (c) the shaping of goals, and (d) the confronting of dysfunctional patterns. These commonalities are an essential part of any long-term family therapy approach. But within this framework mental health counselors may have different viewpoints to treating a disturbed family. These varied approaches have evolved with the growth of the family therapy movement.

History of Family Therapy

This movement, which had its origins in the early 1950s with the work of Gregory Bateson, John Weakland, Jay Haley, Don Jackson, Theodore Lidz, Stephen Fleck, Murray Bowen, Robert Dysinger, Betty Basamaria, and Warren Brady, became nationally known by the late 1950s when family researchers and clinicians in various parts of the country began to learn of each other's work (Goldenberg & Goldenberg, 1980). The main focus of interest was on studying families with a hospitalized schizophrenic member. From their research and clinical practice, such concepts as double bind, family homeostasis, and family boundaries were developed. These terms were used to describe the family process and to conceptualize the entire family system as the patient. Double bind refers to a situation in which one person issues a statement to another that contains at least two messages or demands, one of which contradicts the other. The person receiving the message is called on to make a response, but whatever response he or she makes is doomed to failure, because to respond positively to one is automatically to respond negatively to the other (Goldenberg & Goldenberg, 1980). Family homeostasis is defined as the family's attempt to maintain some kind of balance. Family boundaries are the rules governing who participates in its transactions and in what way, and they must be clear and well defined for proper family functioning.

The beginning years in family therapy were marked by an orientation to research and theory, with an emphasis on understanding the family of the schizophrenic (Okun & Rappaport, 1980). Family therapy was viewed as a new way of understanding the origins of mental disorders (Goldenberg & Goldenberg, 1980). In the 1960s and early 1970's, however, such clinicians as Jay Haley, Salvador Minuchin, Nathan Ackerman, and Virginia Satir grew to realize that more than treating individuals in a family context, the disordered family itself must be changed. Haley (1971) also indicated that the focus of treatment should be on changing the family structure and interaction patterns. Family members must learn to relate to each other in new ways and even, if appropriate, to modify their value system. An understanding of the family moved more and more toward seeing family members as interacting individuals whose behaviors influence each other and not simply as providing "crazymaking" environments in which to grow up (Goldenberg & Goldenberg, 1980).

These years, moreover, also spawned new professional publications on family therapy, new families (e.g., nonwhite minority families), and new outpatient settings (e.g., community mental health centers). Many approaches were followed, and even innovative techniques were proposed, such as multiple family therapy, multiple impact therapy, and network therapy.

Multiple family therapy is an adaptation of group therapy techniques to the treatment of whole families. Selected families meet with a counselor weekly during which they share problems with each other and help one another in the problem-solving process.

Multiple impact therapy involves an entire family in a series of continuing interactions with a multidisciplinary team of mental health professionals over, perhaps, a 2-day period. Developed by MacGregor and his associates at the University of Texas Medical Branch in Galveston, this therapy implies that a single family in crisis receives counseling full-time for 2 or more days (Goldenberg & Goldenberg, 1980).

Network therapy attempts to mobilize a number of people who are willing to come together in a crisis to be forged into a therapeutic force. Originally developed from work with schizophrenics in their homes, network therapy is based on the assumption that there is significant disturbance in the schizophrenic's communication patterns with all members of his or her social network, not just within the nuclear family (Goldenberg & Goldenberg, 1980). The goal of this network intervention is to capitalize on the strength of the assembled network to facilitate changes in the family system.

In the 1980s, no single approach to helping dysfunctional families completely dominates the family therapy field. Okun and Rappaport (1980) stated that the major theoretical approaches to family therapy today are the (a) psychodynamic approach, (b) communication approach, and (c) structural approach.

The Psychodynamic Approach

This approach applies the techniques and strategies of individual psychotherapy to family situations. The family therapist believes that behaviors and feelings of family members will change as each member gains insight about himself/herself and about other family members. Ackerman (1966), who was a psychoanalyst, explained that family therapy involves both helping a family to have a meaningful emotional exchange and assisting the family members to get in better touch with themselves. The latter is achieved through contact with the counselor, who not only helps influence the family interactional process but also withdraws as the family attempts to deal more constructively with its problems. Also, Ackerman considered the influences of social psychology and role theory as important when treating families in the psychodynamic context. In his approach to families he was always interested in how people define their roles (e.g., "What does it mean for you to be a mother?") and what they expect from other family members ("How would you like your son to react to this situation?") (Goldenberg & Goldenberg, 1980).

Communication Approach

Emphasized by such family therapists as Don Jackson, Virginia Satir, and Jay Haley, this approach assumes that one can learn about the family system by studying verbal and nonverbal communication. Communication theorists understand the family as a system, or a change in the communicative behavior of one part of the system that will change the interactions of all parts of the system. Also, within this system a dynamic equilibrium is established as the family evolves, but the balance is continually threatened by external stresses (e.g., job loss, geographic relocation, economic depression) and internal stresses (e.g., death or serious illness, birth of new children). The counselor must consider the equilibrium of the family system and the strong resistance to change that occurs when the "homeostasis" is disrupted (Okun & Rappaport, 1980).

In this perspective of communication, Don Jackson (1965) believed that the therapist's first task should be to intervene in the family's communication system. By focusing on the family's interactional system, he was able to understand the meaning of the family's dynamic equilibrium. Although he made no attempt to interpret individual behavior or to provide insight to family members, Jackson's intervention concentrated on clarifying for family members the rules that operate within the family and on helping the family establish a new homeostasis or equilibrium. For Virginia Satir, however, the counselor is a teacher of a method of communication (Beels & Ferber, 1969). Treatment is completed when the family has learned and applied her method, resulting in a deepening of their relationships. As a therapist, speaking simply and directly, she engages a family directly and authoritatively and tries to pass along her communication skills to family members. During therapy she arranges encounters between members according to the rules she has taught them (Goldenberg & Goldenberg, 1980).

As a communications theorist, Jay Haley focused on the communicative behavior within the family system, but is concerned more with the power struggle in the relationships of family members. For Haley, the goal of family therapy is behavioral change that will result in a new equilibrium or balance for the family system. Haley (1976) assumed families who come for help are also resistant to any help being offered. The result may be a power struggle, with the counselor trying to help them to improve.

The Structural Approach

Murray Bowen, David Kantor, and Salvador Minuchin are family therapists who follow structural framework variables: degree of anxiety, degree of integration, and differentiation of self (Okun & Rappaport, 1980). How a family system handles the tension that is produced by chronic anxiety determines whether members of the family system remain free from symptoms, dysfunction, or illness. Also, the family is seen as an "emotional relationship system." For Bowen, this emotional process of relating is more significant than either verbal or nonverbal language.

Salvador Minuchin, however, emphasizes in family therapy the context of family interaction and restructuring the family system through various strategies. As a therapist he joins the family as a leader, accommodating to the dysfunctional system, diagnosing, and eventually agreeing on a contract. Minuchin conceives of family pathology as resulting from the development of dysfunctional sets or reactions. These family reactions, developed in response to stress, are repeated without modification when there is conflict. As an example, a mother verbally attacks her adolescent son, the father takes the son's side, and the younger children seize the opportunity to join in and pick on their brother. All family members become involved, various coalitions develop, but the family organization remains the same, and the dysfunctional sets will be repeated in the next stressful situation. Minuchin believes restructuring is necessary. "By changing the patterns that support certain undesirable behaviors, by rearranging sequences between people, restructuring of the family can take place" (Goldenberg & Goldenberg, 1980, p. 180).

As an advocate of the structural approach to family therapy, David Kantor believes in the complexities underlying the strategies that people choose in family interaction. Because family dysfunction may motivate system members to clarify their rules, to evolve more expedient strategies for reaching their developmental goals, and to perfect their model for living, the resolution of dysfunction can become the source of new family structures and can lead to an increase in structural complexity and efficiency. During intervention Kantor explores the images, themes, and private symbols of individual family members. This exploration can facilitate more positive family interactions and a richer, more broadly sustaining, collective family identity (Okun & Rappaport, 1980).

With these three approaches, and others that have developed since 1975, but which are better understood as tactics rather than points of view (Okun & Rappaport, 1980), the mental health counselor has many theoretical resources to draw upon when planning a family therapy intervention. When assisting dysfunctional families, many counselors integrate the different viewpoints and draw from whichever perspective what appears to be most relevant to a particular family. Yet there are many family situations that really do not necessitate long-term therapy. A brief intervention may be more appropriate, and this involvement with families represents a rapidly growing area for mental health counseling efforts.

Family Counseling/Short-Term Intervention

Mental health counselors may have two roles when working with families for a brief period of time. One role consists of being primarily a family diagnostician and also helping the family with transition problems or difficulties of recent origin, such as upsetting new behaviors by a disabled child or adult, the death of a family member, an adjustment to a lifestyle change, or other acute, situational crises. Family members, for example, may be angry because the presence of an illness has interfered with their lifestyle, privacy, vacations, future plans, and possibly by the diversion of the spouse's time from other family members. The illness may represent a serious, disruptive factor to the family, or changes in customary family and occupational roles may bring unwanted stress to family members and temporarily interfere with usual family functioning. A family crisis can introduce an ever-present source of trouble or exacerbate previously existing family tensions.

Further, a family may not have made any plans for dealing with any problems associated with a disability or crisis, such as identifying other financial resources when family income has been reduced, or shifting home responsibilities in order that a family member may obtain at least a part-time job to alleviate economic hardship. Also, if the client is receiving disability-related compensation payments, this income may represent a secondary gain for the family members (Eaton, 1979). It may even provide additional recreational activities or shopping advantages that the family would not ordinarily have. Family members may then want these payments to continue and consequently block any efforts toward rehabilitation of the disabled family member.

The other role for the mental health counselor actually flows from the thesis that for effective intervention with a troubled individual, some contact with the family is essential. The mental health counselor should realize that the family may be an invaluable resource for the individual's adjustment to rehabilitation or employment. The patients' home environment can be crucial to their satisfactory coping. For example, for many patients the home becomes a moratorium, a transitional environment between the in-hospital phase of rehabilitation and more productive living. Many patients develop dependency patterns following a disability or other family crisis that may inhibit the achievement of treatment or rehabilitation objectives. But often when family members learn how to develop for the patient renewed opportunities for involvement in family life, or gain useful information about the disability, illness, or individual's crisis, they can begin to facilitate the patient's attainment of needed adjustment goals.

In the performance of either role the mental health counselor provides attention to the family. In this context of short-term intervention the family may be seen in the counselor's own office and, where privacy can also be assured, in such work settings as an employment office, a vocational rehabilitation agency, or the outpatient section of a hospital. Also, with either role mental health counselors can perform many different functions. Doherty and Baird (1983), in their discussion of primary care family counseling for family physicians and related health personnel, suggest four distinct duties: education, prevention, support, and challenge. These four duties can also be applied to mental health workers who are intervening with the family for a limited period of time.

Education

Educating families or couples can take a number of forms. To alleviate problems generated by a family transition, information can be imparted that includes a knowledge of community resources, such as peer support groups, respite care and financial aid opportunities, responding to family needs identified during family meetings, and perhaps discussing with the family the patient's emotional concerns caused by a trauma, that is, illness, accident, or unemployment. One of these concerns could be an anxiety over sexual functioning. When there are no serious underlying personal or relationship disorders, couples may respond quite well to simple teaching and encouragement by the counselor (Doherty & Baird, 1983).

Education can also supply information to the family about illness, disability, or other traumas. For example, family members may incorrectly perceive that an illness or disability causes a person to be different rather than just to act differently on occasion. They may place the patient in too dependent a role before the condition warrants it. Or, if a family only emphasizes the negative, the dreaded aspects of a disease or disability, little attention will be given to the residual capacities, the remaining strengths of the patient. Often the key to coping with a serious family crisis is the way the family views the particular crisis and whether it is perceived as continually harmful or challenging to family life (Power, 1985). When family members understand or appreciate the patient's strengths in the living, learning, and working areas of life, a family environment more conducive to the patient's adjustment efforts is created.

Moreover, upon hearing information that highlights patient assets, families begin to think more positively about the future (Power, 1977). These positive expectations contribute to family adjustment, because family members can then want the patient to continue to function as optimally as possible for as long as possible. But uncertainty about an illness, disability, or the implications of a transition, for example, divorce or unemployment, generally causes apprehension and lingering fear toward the unknown among family members. It also inhibits the establishment of family plans that focus on adjustment, because usually at the time of the family crisis onset there has been no consideration for total life planning. Information about the trauma, and how the patient can still capably perform, may already have been given by health professionals. But family members, because of their anxieties, tend not to process information very well when it is given to them by a physician or related personnel immediately after the occurrence of a crisis or during the transition itself, for example, during hospital discharge after a long hospitalization (Polinko, 1985).

Prevention

Anticipatory guidance can be of great assistance to many families who are confronted with a significant transition. Many events could cause a decline in family functioning, such as the birth of a child, a husband's first heart attack, the unexpected death of a family member, and the discharge of a family member from a mental hospital. Early in their intervention mental health counselors should explore those areas within a family that may cause adjustment problems or difficulties for a patient's readaptation to a productive life. Poor family communication patterns, a family history of alcohol abuse, an isolation of family members from each other's needs, or poor coping abilities to deal with any problems: Each could be a barrier to family adjustment. Intervention efforts can include, consequently, (a) a search for information about family dynamics, (b) assisting the family to break down problems into manageable parts that can be handled one at a time, (c) encouraging them to be optimistic about their ability to handle whatever eventualities arise, and (d) focusing on what family members can do to ward off a possible serious strain on their relationship. Preparing for stresses by discussing them in advance and normalizing them after they occur are key strategies for preventive marital intervention.

Support

When the family is undergoing changes because of a crisis, the family members are usually under emotional strain. There may be many adjustment concerns and necessary changes in family roles, leisure activities, and other aspects of home life. Also, because many chronic illnesses, disabilities, or other traumas, for example, unemployment or divorce, can facilitate continued stress, family members become very tired emotionally. The family, therefore, often needs some informal support from the mental health counselor. Support may be provided by listening to the plans, anxieties, frustrations, and questions of family members. This support can be further given by the counselor's communication to the family that help is available, when necessary, to answer phone calls when family members have questions. Frequently, this type of availability may be all that the family needs from the mental health counselor because it demonstrates that someone cares about their welfare.

Yet there is another dimension of family support. Family members frequently need to learn how to provide support to a disabled family member or a member who is experiencing a serious problem. The reality of unemployment and often the accruing loss of self-esteem, for example, can have a devastating effect. Frequently family members do not perceive the reality of the loss experienced by someone (Power, 1977). Loss of earning power or the diminution of physical capacities can be burdens borne alone by ill family members. But families can be encouraged to become aware of these losses, and the patient can learn to request support from the family. By listening to each other, and through the medium of the accepting feedback from the mental health worker, the family can gradually grow to understand itself better. They could begin to feel better about themselves and have more confidence to tackle the varied problems that occur from living with serious family crisis.

Family support also implies that the family member, despite physical or mental limitations, receives the reassurance from others that he/she would still be involved in family life. With family support and acceptance, the person's feelings of worth are partially achieved through a re-crystallization of self in terms of acceptance of the problem. As the family provides the best opportunity for growth and fulfillment, so the home is the place where individuals can best express their natural potentialities and satisfy their creative and emotional needs.

Challenge

As explained by Doherty and Baird (1983), this function involves challenging unrealistic expectations about family life, challenging family members to work together on their problems, and challenging the partners to take responsibility for solving their own problems. This "challenge" also involves alerting family members to the opportunities within the home environment for an appropriate adjustment to a serious crisis, disability, or chronic illness.

Another key for family coping with a crisis is to make living with the problem as satisfying as it can be within the framework of the family's limitations (Power, 1977). This may necessitate urging the family to build success experiences for the troubled person and themselves. For a disabled person it may mean attempting to maintain family duties and to gain the feeling of being productive. For other family members it may imply encouraging them to maintain their normal pattern and routing of activities, and seeking appropriate activities that will provide them all with a respite from caring activities and a resource for enjoyment. But frequently the family needs to be confronted with the importance of this seeking. For a disabled or ill family member to reach needed adjustment goals necessitates that the family itself survive. Survival is facilitated by having appropriate patterns of living for family members.

CONCLUSION

The family is not dying, as some have suggested (Bretto-Kelly, 1979). It is diversifying. With this diversification, and combined with the complexity of economic, technological, and social change, many families will have many more difficulties in coping with the demands of modern living. The changes in family forms and the growing incidence of family crises provide an ideal opportunity for mental health counselors. The growth of the family therapy movement has given mental health counselors added options to treat troubled families. The new attention to the family as an invaluable resource for a disabled person's adjustment provides an important expansion of mental health services.

REFERENCES

Ackerman, N. W. (1966). *Treating the troubled family.* New York: Basic Books.

American Council of Life Insurance. (1980). *Datatrack.* Washington, DC: Author

Beels, C., & Ferber, A. (1969). Family therapy: A view. *Family Process, 8*, 280–332.

Berman, E., Lief, H., & Williams, A. (1981). A model of marital interaction. In C. P. Sholeval (Ed.), *The handbook of marriage and marital therapy* (pp. 3–34). New York: Spectrum Publications.

Bretto-Kelly, C. (1979, October). *American families in the 1980's, implications for marriage and family therapy.* Paper presented at the 39th Annual Conference of the American Association for Marriage and Family Therapy, Washington, DC.

Cavan, R. S. (1974). Family life circle, United States. In R. C. Caven (Ed.), *Marriage and family in the modern world—Readings* (pp. 91–104). New York: T. Y. Crowell Co.

Conger, J. J. (1981). Families, youth, and social change. *American Psychologist, 36*, 1475–1484.

Doherty, W. J., & Baird, M. A. (1983). *Family therapy and family medicine.* New York: The Guilford Press.

Duvall, E. M. (1971). *Family development* (4th ed.). Philadelphia: J. B. Lippincott Co.

Eaton, M. (1979). Obstacles to the vocational rehabilitation of individuals receiving worker's compensation. *Journal of Rehabilitation, April/May/June,* 59–63.

Foley, V. D. (1974). *An introduction to family therapy.* New York: Grune & Stratton.

Glick, P. C. (1977). Updating the life cycle of the family. *Journal of Marriage and the Family, 39*, 5–13.

Glick, P. C. (1979). *The future of the American family* (Current Population Reports, Special Studies Series P-23, No. 78). Washington, DC: U. S. Government Printing Office.

Goldenberg, I., & Goldenberg, H. (1980). *Family therapy: An overview.* Monterey, CA: Brooks/Cole Publishing Co.

Goodell, G. E. (1975). Rehabilitation: Family involved in patient's care. *Hospitals, 49*, 96–98.

Haley, J. (1971). Approaches to family therapy. In J. Haley (Ed.), *Changing families: A family therapy reader.* New York: Grune & Stratton.

Haley, J. (1976). *Problem-solving therapy.* San Francisco: Jossey-Bass.

Havighurst, R. J. (1953). *Human development and education.* New York: Longmans, Green & Co.

Jackson, D. D. (1965). The study of the family. *Family Process, 4,* 1-20.

Melson, G. F. (1980). *Family and environment—An ecosystem perspective.* Minneapolis, MN: Burgess Publishing Co.

National Institute of Handicapped Research. (1984, September). *Disability and families: A family systems approach* (Rehab brief). Washington, DC: Author.

Okun, B. F., & Rappaport, L. J. (1980). *Working with families: An introduction to family therapy.* North Scituate, MA: Duxbury Press.

Overs, R., & Healy, J. (1973). Stroke patients: Their spouses, families and the community. In A. B. Cobb (Ed.), *Medical and psychological aspects of disability* (pp. 87-117). Springfield, IL: Charles C Thomas Publishers.

Parsons, T., & Bales, T. R. (1955). *Family: Socialization and interaction process.* New York: The Free Press.

Polinko, P. (1985). Working with the family: The acute phase. In M. Ylvisaker (Ed.), *Head injury rehabilitation* (pp. 94-101). San Diego: College-Hill Press.

Power, P. (1977). Chronic illness and the family. *International Journal of Family Counseling, 5*(1), 70-77.

Power, P. (1985). Family coping behaviors in chronic illness: A rehabilitation perspective. *Rehabilitation Literature, 46*(3/4), 78-83.

Power, P., & Dell Orto, A. E. (1980). *Role of the family in the rehabilitation of the physically disabled.* Austin, TX: Pro/Ed Press.

Rakel, R. (1977). *Principles of family medicine.* Philadelphia: W.B. Saunders Co.

Rhodes, S. (1977, May). A developmental approach to the life cycle of the family. *Social Casework,* pp. 301-312.

Robinson, S., Rotter, M., & Wilson, J. (1982). Mothers' contemporary career decisions, impact on the family. *The Personnel and Guidance Journal, 60*(9), 535-538.

Robischon, P., & Smith, J. (1977). Family assessment. In A. Rheindaide & M. Quinn (Eds.), *Current practice in family-centered community nursing* (pp. 85-100). St. Louis: C. V. Mosby Co.

Shorter, E. (1975). *The making of the modern family.* New York: Basic Books.

Strickland, C. (1985, August 11). The fading American family. *The Atlanta Journal/The Atlanta Constitution,* pp. 1C, 8C.

Swenson, C. (1973). *Introduction to interpersonal relations.* Glenview, IL: Scott, Foresman & Co.

Turnbull, A. P., Summers, J. A., Brotherson, M. J. (1983). *Working with families with disabled members: A family systems approach.* Lawrence, KS: Kansas University Affiliated Facility at Lawrence, Bureau of Child Research.

U. S. Bureau of the Census. (1979a). *Divorce, child custody, and child support* (Current Population Reports, Special Studies Series, P-23, No. 84). Washington, DC: U. S. Government Printing Office.

U. S. Bureau of the Census. (1979b). *Marital status and living arrangements: March, 1978* (Current Population Reports, Series P-20, No. 388). Washington, DC: U. S. Government Printing Office.

Watzlawick, P., & Weakland, J. (Eds.). (1977). *The interactional view: Studies at the mental research institute, 1965-1974.* New York: Norton.

Weitzman, L. (1974). Legal regulation of marriage: Tradition and changes. *California Law Review, 62,* 1169-1186.

Zisserman, L. (1981). The modern family and rehabilitation of the handicapped. A macrosociological view. *The American Journal of Occupational Therapy, 35*(1), 13-20.

9   Counseling Groups*

Mental health counseling in groups offers unique advantages for fostering clients' well-being. Individual clients' strengths are drawn out in the supportive atmosphere of group counseling. The group situation allows participants to share assets and build on each other's skills. Furthermore, group counseling enables participants to develop a social network with other group members that can serve as a base for initiating environmental change. Groups can be used to pursue the following goals:

1. *Enhancement.* Within a group situation, participants can explore their reactions to events and relationships in the group. They can then employ the new understanding they achieve to their lives, discovering greater depth in the meaning of their experiences. An example of this would be a marathon encounter group for college students.

2. *Facilitation.* Developmental transitions occurring for individuals can be facilitated through group counseling. Clients will play out their responses to the transition within the group. Group counseling offers a safe environment for both examining these responses, and determining which responses are most beneficial for the participants. The group situation also allows counselors a forum in which to present information and skills that can help participants make the transition. Methods for addressing the transitions developed in the group can be generalized to situations outside the group, particularly when group members are consistently in contact with each other outside the group. An example is a social interaction group for high school freshmen.

3. *Prevention.* Potential problems can be detected and addressed in a group environment. Skills that will prevent development of problems can be pre-

---

*This chapter was written by Michael Waldo.

sented by counselors and practiced among clients in a group. If members of the group are in contact with each other outside the group, they can assist each other in use of the skills for problem prevention, and also work together to change the environment to prevent problems. An example is a group to provide a hospital nursing staff with stress management skills.

4. *Remediation.* Identified problems can be treated in groups. The support group members who are facing a similar problem offer each other the opportunity to play out the problem and its solution within the immediate reality of relationships during the group, and the potential for members to continue to help each other outside the group. This makes group counseling a potent method of problem remediation. An example of this is a parent-effectiveness training group for abusive parents.

5. *Rehabilitation.* Group counseling also has potential for helping clients adjust to long-term disabilities. Counselors can present specific coping techniques and supervise their practice in a group. Clients can develop relationships with other clients that extend to involvement and support outside the group. Members of clients' social networks can also participate in groups where they can learn how to adjust to, and help with, clients' disabilities. Finally, clients and/or members of their social network can organize through group counseling to initiate environmental change to benefit the client. For example, after-care groups for mentally ill patients and their families are often held in community mental health centers to assist in adjustment directly following the patients' release from mental hospitals.

This chapter will offer an overview of group counseling in mental health settings. It will include a definition of group counseling and descriptions of therapeutic factors in groups; a brief history of group counseling; a description of group dynamics as they develop over time; theories of group counseling; leadership functions for group counselors; selection, preparation, and integration of group members; examples of group counseling; and professional issues related to group counseling.

DEFINITION

Group counseling has been defined by Gazda, Duncan, and Meadows (1967) as follows:

> Group counseling is a dynamic interpersonal process focusing on conscious thought and behavior and involving the therapy functions of permissiveness, orientation to reality, catharsis, and mutual trust, caring, understanding, acceptance, and support. The therapy functions are created and nurtured in a small group through the sharing of personal concerns with one's peers and the counselor(s). The group counselees are basically normal individuals with various concerns which are not debilitating to the extent requiring extensive personality

change. The group counselees may utilize the group interaction to increase understanding and acceptance of values and goals and to learn and/or unlearn certain attitudes and behaviors. (p. 305)

Another method of defining group counseling is by describing the therapeutic factors that seem to be effective in counseling groups. Yalom (1985) offered descriptions of 11 therapeutic factors that research and clinical experience indicate occur in groups. The following is a brief description of the factors as they apply to group counseling.

1. *Hope.* Members develop the belief that their problems can be overcome. This belief increases motivation and a sense of well-being. It is fostered by knowledge that the group was formed to help with members' problems, by the leaders' confidence in the group's effectiveness, and by examples of members who are successful in coping with the problems.

2. *Universality.* Group members overcome a debilitating impression that they are unique in having unacceptable problems. Hearing that others have similar concerns reduces their sense of isolation and allows validation of each member's humanness. Recognizing that others who have problems similar to their own are still worthwhile human beings allows them to view themselves as worthwhile people, in spite of their problems.

3. *Catharsis.* Interacting in the group generates feelings in group members. The group also offers a safe environment for the expression of feelings that originate both within and outside the group. Expression of feelings relieves the emotional burdens of group members: They can express their anger or fear. Releasing emotions also reduces members' needs to employ ineffective defense mechanisms such as denial, projection, and acting out.

4. *Corrective recapitulation of the primary family group (family reenactment).* The group situation allows a replay, both on conscious and unconscious levels, of experiences typical of a primary family group. The leaders are symbolic parents and other members are symbolic siblings. Joining a group constitutes a new birth and allows members an opportunity for positive development. The group can be a supportive, involved, accepting family that sets appropriate limits, unlike the real family of origin of many counseling clients. Group members can get in touch with problems they acquired from their family of origin, and correct those problems in the group.

5. *Cohesiveness.* Group membership offers participants an experience of unconditional acceptance and belonging that enables them to accept themselves more fully and be congruent in their relationships with others. Cohesiveness raises self-esteem, motivates members to remain in the group, and to behave in ways that are approved of by the group. Members may change their behavior in appropriate directions because they do not want to let the group down.

6. *Altruism.* By offering support, reassurance, suggestions, and sharing similar problems, group members can be helpful to one another. Seeing themselves as helpful to others raises members' self-esteem. Focusing on other peoples' problems turns their attention away from excessively dwelling on their own problems. Offering suggestions to others about how they can change makes it more likely that members will employ their suggestions toward dealing with their own problems.

7. *Interpersonal learning.* Interpersonal relationships define individuals' personality and adjustment. Clients have developed an interpersonal style that affects all their relationships outside of the group. They carry this style into the group. There they reconstruct relationships typical of their life outside the group within the social microcosm of the group. However, unlike typical relationships outside of the group, in the group other members let clients know what effect their style has on them. Clients have an opportunity to change the way they relate, so that they can have the effect on others that they want to have. When they are successful in changing their style so that they get the reactions from other group members that they want, it results in a corrective emotional experience for clients.

8. *Information (guidance).* The group members and leaders provide a resource of knowledge and viewpoints through which clients can learn new information or have mistaken beliefs corrected. This can include factual information or different perspectives on psychological problems.

9. *Imitation (identification).* Group members learn new behaviors by observing the behavior of the leaders and other members as models. They can imitate the behaviors they see working for others. Important components affecting learning include the status of the models, similarities between the models and observers, and rewards received by the models.

10. *Socializing techniques.* The group situation offers clients an opportunity to experiment with new behaviors. They try new responses in the group and are selectively reinforced for positive behavior. Following consistent reinforcement, positive behaviors generalize to similar situations outside the group. Negative behaviors are not reinforced, resulting in their extinction.

11. *Existential factors.* Clients usually cannot control who the other members of the group will be, or how things will go for other members in their lives outside the group. This fact puts them in touch with the reality that there are many circumstances in their own lives that they cannot control. They also face their eventual termination with the group, which represents an end of life in the group. The time-limited nature of group involvement forces the members to recognize that their lifetimes are also limited. Finally, members recognize that although they have limited control and time in the group, they still have choices in how they respond to the group situation and responsibility for their choices. This recognition generalizes to accepting responsibility for the choices they make outside the group.

The therapeutic factors described here may be seen as hallmarks of group counseling. Although they certainly would not all occur in all groups at all times, the existence of some of these factors at varying levels during the course of a group are necessary for the group to be an effective mental health counseling intervention.

HISTORY

Perhaps because of the innate therapeutic factors they offer, small groups have made important contributions to people's mental health throughout human history. Examples of such groups include nuclear and extended families, hunting bands, tribes, prayer groups, school classes, military units, guilds, and lodges.

Predecessors to current counseling groups originated from three different approaches to helping clients, all of which emerged around the beginning of the 20th century (Gazda, 1984). These approaches can be classified as educational, therapeutic, and social action/self help.

Education

In 1905, classes on tuberculosis were offered to patients suffering from the disease. It was found that the effects of these classes on patients' attitudes and adjustment were extremely positive, particularly when patients were allowed to discuss their experiences with each other. The technique of offering classes about a disease to patients suffering from it was later successfully employed with schizophrenics. Class-like group guidance procedures were also used to educate professionals and parents in the psychological development of children. Other class-like guidance procedures emerged in the early 20th century in public schools, offering students counseling in vocational, moral, and extracurricular activities. Currently, the class or structured group format is prevalent as a group counseling technique. Examples include parent effectiveness training, career guidance workshops, and stress management courses.

Therapeutic

Psychodrama was a therapeutic technique that developed at the turn of the century and was a predecessor to group counseling. Psychodrama offered individuals an opportunity to act out their concerns in groups by role-playing scenes of events that were bothering them. Psychoanalysis was another therapeutic technique that developed around the turn of the century, although it was not extensively applied in groups until the 1930s and 1940s. The economics of the depression and the crush of veterans returning from World War II who needed psychiatric help made the efficient use of professional resources particularly attractive at that time. Group counseling allowed a vast expansion of the number of clients who could be served by the same number of professionals. Currently, every major therapeutic approach is being offered in groups (Hansen, Warner, & Smith, 1980). Examples include client-centered encounter, transactional analysis groups, gestalt groups, and rational–emotive therapy groups.

Social Action/Self-help

Social action and self-help groups also emerged around the turn of the century. Groups were initially organized to help immigrants adjust to urban living in American culture. Alcoholics Anonymous started in 1935 to help problem drinkers maintain sobriety, and was followed by a number of other "anonymous"-type groups (Alanon, Narcanon, Gamblers Anonymous, Overeaters Anonymous). A major contribution to the social action and self-help group movement, and group counseling in general, was made in the late 1940s by Kurt Lewin and his associates (Bradford, Gibb, & Benne, 1964). Lewin was a social scientist who believed that a person's behavior is a function of the person in interaction with his or her environment. This perspective allowed examination of groups as an environment, and gave rise to the study of group dynamics, which will be discussed at length in the next section. Contemporary social action and self-help groups include t-groups (which grew directly out of Lewin's work), consciousness raising groups, and parents without partners.

GROUP DYNAMICS

Kurt Lewin (1951) suggested that the group is more than a collection of individuals; it is also a dynamic social environment. To understand groups we must examine not only the individuals who are members, but also the way they affect, and are affected by, each other. The sum of these ever-changing effects at any particular moment characterizes the dynamics of the group environment at that moment. Bion (1959) suggested that group dynamics may be characterized by viewing groups as responding as if they held one of three basic assumptions, in addition to the explicit or stated assumption about why the group has gathered to work together. The basic assumptions are an expression of group members' feelings, which are generated by the dynamic interaction between members in the group. The three basic assumptions are that group members must act: (a) dependent (because of their confusion and anxiety), (b) aggressive or avoidant (because of their anger and fear), or (c) intimate (because of their caring and enthusiasm). Emotions that might accompany a group's responding to its explicit work assumption would include confidence and responsibility.

Group dynamics can also be characterized as developing over time. The group, as a whole, can be seen as passing through different periods in its life, similar to the way individuals pass through periods in their lives. When a group first forms it is in childhood, then moves into adolescence, followed by young adulthood, then adulthood, and then maturity as it is about to disband. Crises occur in the group's life that are similar to crises that occur in an individual's life in each period (Erikson, 1963). Crises with which groups are faced at each period may be described as follows: childhood—trust versus mistrust; adolescence—identity versus role confusion; young adulthood—intimacy versus isolation; adulthood—generativity versus stagnation; and maturity—integrity versus despair. The group's ability to resolve the crises at each period affects its progress and functioning through future periods.

Another perspective on the development of group dynamics over time is to view groups as passing through stages (Tuckman & Jensen, 1977). Each stage carries with it a concern for members about their roles in relation to the group. Each stage also fosters members' experiences of specific therapeutic factors (Waldo, 1985). Table 9.1 lists the titles and descriptions of stages, the role concerns members have at each stage, and the therapeutic factors fostered by the stage.

TABLE 9.1. Stages in Group Dynamics

STAGE	CHARACTERISTICS
I. Forming	The group is often confused and very dependent on the leader and each other. They want structure and guidelines. They need to see examples. They are particularly open to the leader's suggestions. They appreciate help figuring out how they can fit in. Members are concerned with being a group member. Therapeutic factors include Hope and Universality.
II. Storming	Group members rebel against the leader, the structure, and each other. They want to express their opinions and feelings, and to feel they are being heard. Members are concerned with achieving a position in the group. Therapeutic factors include Catharsis and Family Re-enactment.
III. Norming	Having survived the "storm," the group is often enthusiastic, cooperative, and cohesive. They are interested in knowing each other better and becoming more intimate. Members decide on goals and ways of working together. They are concerned about their roles in caring for each other. Therapeutic factors include Cohesion and Altruism.
IV. Performing	The group takes responsibility for its tasks. It is ready to progress fairly autonomously. Members appreciate an opportunity to be productive. They are concerned about their role in the work of the group. Therapeutic factors include Interpersonal Learning, Information, Imitation, and Socializing Techniques.
V. Adjourning	The members feel sadness at saying goodbye. Also, they prepare to use what they have learned in their life after the group. They appreciate activities that offer closure and that will help them generalize their learning. They are concerned with the meaning of their roles in the group. Existential factors are therapeutic at this stage.

THEORIES

A wide array of theoretical orientations toward counseling may be successfully applied in groups (Schaffer & Galinsky, 1974). A problem with some efforts to use theories that were originally designed for individual counseling in groups has been that practitioners have failed to take into account group dynamics. This can result in a restricted understanding of what is occurring in the group and failure of the procedures that are dictated by the theory. For example, the client-centered approach of demonstrating empathic understanding of deeply felt emotional material often results in frustration for both the group leaders and members when the group is in the forming stage and is unlikely to discuss such material. However, when group dynamics are taken into account, they can serve to enhance procedures dictated by various theories (Waldo, 1985). The following are examples of how cognitive/behavioral, psychodynamic, and humanistic theories can be applied to make the best use of dynamics occurring at different stages of group development.

Cognitive-Behavioral

Cognitive-behavioral theories focus on members learning new ideas, attitudes, and behaviors that will help them adapt. Forming stage dynamics enhance group members' receptivity to new ideas and behaviors. Storming stage dynamics motivate group members to take action. Norming stage dynamics increase the reinforcement value of the group members and leaders, and increase the likelihood members will imitate the appropriate behaviors they witness in the group. Performing stage allows practice of new behaviors. Adjourning stage encourages members to internalize new behaviors and generalize them to situations outside the group. Assertion training is an example of cognitive-behavioral counseling theories applied to groups. Therapeutic factors likely to be prevalent in cognitive/behavioral groups include Hope, Information, Imitation, and Socializing Techniques.

Psychodynamic

Psychodynamic theories focus on analysis of members' unconscious dynamics that interfere with their adaptive functioning. Analytic principles applied to groups allow examination of the shared unconscious experience of group members. The shared unconscious is thought to be expressed through the topics the group addresses. Any member who is speaking at a particular moment serves as the group spokesperson at that moment. Although the shared unconscious is usually expressed through a metaphor, it always can be linked to the groups' dynamics and their association with the way members feel about their relationships with each other and the leaders (often referred to as "transference" relationships). For example, a group member who speaks extensively about a love scene in a play he or she recently attended may be metaphorically expressing the group's desire for increased intimacy rising from norming stage dynamics. The dynamics of the first three stages of groups (forming, storming, and norming) generate feelings in members that are transferred from relationships early in their psychological life (oral, anal, and phallic periods according to psychoanalytic theory). Re-experiencing these feelings in the group enables members to better understand and accept themselves. The performing stage allows interpretation of these feelings so that they can be appropriately integrated into the members' psychological make-up. The dynamics of the adjourning stage help members separate and individuate from the group. Group psychoanalysis is an example of psychodynamic theory applied in groups. Therapeutic factors likely to be prevalent in psychodynamic groups include Universality, Catharsis, and Family Reenactment.

Humanistic

Humanistic theories focus on facilitating self-actualizing tendencies within group members by offering them an environment where they experience congruence, positive regard, and empathy with others. Forming stage dynamics contribute to this process by putting members in psychological contact with each other. Storming stage dynamics allow congruent expression of deeply felt emotions. Norming stage dynamics generate positive regard among members. Performing stage dynamics enable members to work at developing full empathic understanding of each other. The adjourning stage encourages members to carry the more complete sense of themselves that they develop in the group into their relationships with others. Rogerian encounter is an example of humanistic theory applied to group counseling. Therapeutic factors likely to be prevalent in humanistic groups include Cohesion, Altruism, Interpersonal Learning, and Existential factors.

Each of these theories suggests goals and procedures for group leaders. Although these (and many other theories) can, and often are, adhered to exclusively in running groups, research indicates that effective group leaders employ an eclectic approach that integrates leader functions associated with each of the theories. A factor analytic study of a variety of groups (Lieberman, Yalom, & Miles, 1973) indicated that regardless of the leaders' theoretical orientations or group format, leader functions could be characterized by the following four categories.

1. *Executive function.* The group leaders determine the purpose, procedures, time, and place of the group. They recruit clients and screen out people who would be inappropriate for the group. They educate clients about the group and what behaviors will be expected of them in order to prepare them for group membership. They set limits and suggest or set rules. They suggest

goals and directions of movement. They manage time by sequencing, pacing, stopping, blocking, and interceding. They suggest procedures for the group or a person. They direct the content of group discussion toward topics that are of concern to members, but do not explore in depth any one member's personal experiences, or feelings between members. The content of group interaction encouraged by a leader in the executive function is extrapersonal, addressing an issue in the abstract ("it") rather than through how members directly experience the issue. For example, a leader in executive function would encourage discussion of the principles of assertive behavior and how *it* can be learned.

2. *Emotional stimulation.* The leaders stimulate emotional reactions in participants by asking them to reveal feelings, personal values, attitudes, and beliefs. They ask provocative questions and provide an unsettlingly ambiguous atmosphere in the group. They often are not explicit about their intentions. They use challenge, confrontation, and exhortation. They frequently participate as members in the group, drawing attention to themselves and disclosing their reactions to group members. They direct the content of the group's discussion toward the intrapersonal experience of group members. Members are encouraged to talk about "I" rather than "it." For example, a group member who is discussing the difficulty some people have finding a middle ground between passive and aggressive behaviors might be asked instead to express his/her own passive and aggressive emotions in the group.

3. *Caring.* The group leaders provide support and warmth. They demonstrate caring by offering friendship, love, and affection. They frequently invite members to seek and offer feedback, support, praise, and encouragement. They focus on how members feel about each other, directing the content of discussion toward interpersonal relationships between members in the group. Members are encouraged to talk about "we" rather than "I" or "it." For example, a member who was describing anxiety about being assertive with a person outside the group would be encouraged to instead talk with another member in the group about his or her feelings when trying to assert him- or herself with that member.

4. *Meaning attribution.* The group leaders provide members with concepts for understanding their experiences, both in and outside the group. They offer members new insight, awareness, and knowledge by interpreting, explaining, clarifying, and providing frameworks for how to change. This function involves directing the content of interaction so that it integrates extrapersonal topics, intrapersonal experience, and interpersonal relations. It combines "it," "I," and "we." For example, group members might be encouraged to use principles of assertion to offer a balanced expression of their angry and passive emotions in relation to each other in the group.

All of the leadership functions described here are employed by eclectic group leaders. Some functions are likely to be stressed more when leaders are using certain theoretical orientations or are at certain stages in the development of the group, and each function tends to generate specific therapeutic factors (Waldo, 1985). Executive function employs cognitive – behavioral theories, fits the dynamics of the forming stage, and generates the therapeutic factors of Hope and Universality. Emotional stimulation employs psychodynamic theories, fits the storming stage, and generates Catharsis and Family Reenactment. Caring employs humanistic theories, fits the norming stage and generates Cohesion and Altruism. Meaning attribution employs cognitive – behavioral, psychodynamic, and humanistic theories, fits the performing stage, and generates Interpersonal Learning, Information, Imitation and Socializing Techniques. Executive function also fits the adjourning stage, generating Existential Factors.

MEMBERSHIP

Because the majority of the benefits clients receive through participation in a group are the result of their relating to other group members, the selection, preparation, and integration of members in a group are critical to effective group counseling (Corey & Corey, 1982). Each of these areas will be examined in this section.

Selection

A primary consideration in selection is that there be similarities between the client and other members of the group. Most important is the nature of the client's concern. If it is similar to those of the other clients, it will serve as a working bond between members. If it is vastly different (such as an individual struggling with active alcoholism entering a single parents' group), the client is likely to become discouraged and alienated from the group, and other members are likely to feel helpless and uninvolved with the client. In addition to similarity of concern, other areas of similarity help build relationships between members. These include gender, age, stage of psychosocial development, race, socioeconomic status, educational background, severity of problem, and level of commitment to getting help. Although it is neither possible nor desirable to have groups be homogeneous in all these areas, similarity in at least one of these areas with at least one other group member is critical for a client to feel comfortable in a group.

Other things to consider when selecting participants for group counseling include the following.

1. *Sources of stress in the client's life.* A recent death of a loved one; impending academic dismissal; financial crisis; serious health problems; or difficulties with the expense, schedule, or location of the group may interfere with a client's benefiting from or continuing with group counseling.

2. *Sources of support in the client's life.* Family, friends, roommates, or roman-

tic relationships can help clients benefit from groups by offering them support as they learn new things about themselves and how they relate to others in the group. If they do not have relationships outside the group, clients may be particularly vulnerable to negative experiences in the group. If their outside relationships are not supportive of their involvement in the group, they may be influenced to terminate membership.

3. *Past or present experiences with counseling.* People who have been in counseling or psychotherapy may have had positive or negative experiences that will affect how they view group counseling. Persons who are currently in counseling should discuss being in a group with their counselor and get their agreement before joining.

4. *Past and present experiences in groups.* People who have always disliked being in groups are likely to have more problems in group counseling than those who have always enjoyed being in groups.

Information in each of these areas should be gathered on potential group participants prior to their joining the group. To save time, information can be gathered through telephone interviews, written applications, or in large pregroup meetings. Problems in any of these areas do not preclude a person participating in a group. If there are problems, it is worthwhile for the leader to discuss them with a potential member so that they can be resolved in a way that will allow the member to benefit from group counseling (for example, alleviating mistaken fears about groups, or a member consulting with their counselor about participating).

Preparation

Clients who have been selected to participate in a group need to be prepared for the experience. Members who know what they want, and have realistic goals, are likely to achieve their goals in a group. On the other hand, members who are unclear about their goals or have unrealistic expectations are likely to end their involvement with a group feeling confused and/or disappointed. This can be avoided by offering clients proper preparation for group participation. Carefully addressing the following points will prepare clients for optimum participation in groups:

1. Value of group counseling — (history of group counseling, therapeutic factors in groups, development of social contacts, research evidence).
2. Explanation of group's goals and theoretical orientation.
3. Exploration of match between group's and client's goals.
4. Description of necessary client behaviors (listening, self-disclosure, impression sharing).
5. Exploration of potential problems in participation (client's misperceptions about group, prior negative group experiences, withholding important concerns).

6. Detailed description of group's methods and procedures (possibly including a role play or demonstration).
7. Description of other group members (age, sex, race, concerns).
8. Discussion of ground rules necessary for a productive group, including:
    (a) Confidentiality—expected but not guaranteed with regard to members; legal, research, and supervision constraints for the counselor.
    (b) Attendance—punctual, consistent, drug free, right of exit, counselor responsibility to determine membership.
    (c) Participation—expectation of involvement, right to temporarily decline involvement, counselor responsibilities to guide involvement.
9. Check for understanding and agreement on these points.

Member Integration

Following selection and preparation, the integration of clients into meaningful involvement with other group members is a critical and ongoing process that is essential for productive group counseling. A variety of methods may be used to integrate group members. The methods may be adjusted in relation to the developmental stage of the group and pursued through a variety of leader functions (see Table 9.2).

Another method of influencing member integration is to analyze the role each member plays in the group (such as initiator, opinion seeker, evaluator, etc.). If a member seems to consistently take a negative role (blocker, cynic) steps can be taken, with the member and/or the group, to change that mem-

TABLE 9.2. Methods for Group Member Integration at Different Stages of Group Development

GROUP STAGE	LEADER FUNCTION	METHOD
Forming	Executive	Have members pair up and exchange nonthreatening personal information. Then have each member introduce their partner to the group.
Storming	Emotional stimulation	Have members draw pictures of themselves and their families, of themselves and the group, and of how they would like to be in the future. Have members describe their feelings about the pictures to each other.
Norming	Caring	Demonstrate understanding and respect for the positive feelings members have for each other.
Performing	Meaning attribution	Point out an unexpressed conflict between members, interpret its meaning, and suggest they give each other direct feedback.
Adjourning	Emotional stimulation	Ask members to identify an important impact another member had on them over the course of the group.

ber's role to one that makes a constructive contribution to the group.

A final method of member integration to be suggested here is to assess and act upon the immediate interaction occurring in the group. This can be done through the following steps:

1. Select a particular member and attend to his or her verbal and nonverbal behavior.
2. Using the information from Step 1 and background information on the member (personal history, concerns, previous behavior in the group), make an empathic judgment about what the member is currently experiencing, and what he/she wants from other group members.
3. Attend to the verbal and nonverbal responses of other members in response to the selected member.
4. Similar to Step 2, make an empathic judgment about what other members are experiencing and want in response to the selected member.
5. Determine in what ways the relationship between the selected member and other members can be modified, within the context of their experience in the group, so that they will be more effective at fulfilling what they want with each other.
6. Intervene by acknowledging the experience of the members and suggest how they might work together more productively.

For example, a member who constantly gives advice to other members may be nervous about his or her role in the group and want to be helpful to others. If other members are ignoring this person's comments, they may be frustrated with the constant advice, wanting this member just to listen and understand. By actively listening and demonstrating understanding, the member could satisfy his or her desire to be helpful and other members' desire to be understood. The following intervention could be made, directed primarily to the selected member.

> You work hard to give suggestions to others to solve their problems. Among other things I think that shows you care. I'm worried though that sometimes others miss the caring message because it is buried under the advice. I know that I, and I think others too, would appreciate knowing that you understand our problems and that you are concerned. Rather than advice, I'd like for you to tell us what feelings you hear people having about their problems.

EXAMPLES OF GROUPS

This section will offer specific examples of the practice of group counseling in mental health. Examples will be offered in the areas of enhancement, facilitation, prevention, remediation, and rehabilitation. A different setting will be offered for each example and the theory, leadership function, and therapeutic factors that are characteristic of the example will be suggested. Although the groups and settings that will be presented are typical of enhancement, facilitation, and so on it should be remembered that they are by no means exclusionary. For example, assertion training is a typical form of prevention in a community mental health center, but it also is used for remediation in psychiatric hospitals and for rehabilitation in drug treatment centers.

Enhancement

Marriage encounter groups are offered by religious congregations to enhance the quality of marriages. Although often open to the public at large, the groups are primarily attended by members of a congregation. They are held in churches or in retreat settings. Based on a humanistic premise, they involve marital partners taking time to address together issues that are pertinent to their marriages. There is time allotted for all participants to share what they are learning within their marriage with other couples. The leaders primarily take an executive function, establishing the time and place for the meetings and offering a structure for couples' discussions. Therapeutic factors include Interpersonal Learning and Socializing Techniques within a couple, and Cohesion and Universality between couples. Marriage encounter builds on individual marital partners' assets and also causes environmental change, in that it strengthens marriages and builds stronger social networks within a congregation.

Facilitation

Quality circle discussions in industry offer an example of group facilitation. In such groups, members of a working unit discuss how to increase their mutual effectiveness to achieve higher productivity and satisfaction. The goals may be seen as humanistic, that is, the fulfillment of individual and group potential. Leaders function in a caring capacity, offering members support as they examine conflicts and detriments to efficient co-worker relations and explore solutions. Predominant therapeutic factors include Cohesion, Altruism, Interpersonal Learning, Information, and Imitation. Quality circles build on individuals' strengths, increasing their career clarity and commitment, and strengthen relations between co-workers and management. Discussions often result in changes in the environment of the work place.

Prevention

Groups for foreign-born spouses of military personnel offer an example of prevention-oriented groups. Foreign-born spouses face a dramatic transition when the military person is reassigned back to the United States. The spouse faces loss of extended family and the task of assimilating into American culture. In an effort to prevent adjustment problems that could affect the spouse and the military member, many military bases provide groups for these spouses. Based on cognitive–behavioral models, the groups provide training in spoken English, shopping, cooking, and familiarization with American customs. The groups also allow participants the opportunity to discuss their feelings about their transition into the American culture. Leaders primarily serve a meaning attribution function. Benefits to members include Hope, Universality, Cohesion, Information, Imitation, Socializing Techniques, and Existential Factors. In addition to preventing adjustment problems through development of skills and confidence in dealing with American culture, potential problems for spouses may also be forestalled by the social network that develops among members. These groups also often take an advocacy role on military bases, influencing that environment to be more supportive of foreign-born spouses.

Remediation

Psychoanalytic therapy groups are often held in outpatient community mental health centers to help patients overcome depression. The groups encourage members to discuss the development of their symptoms and usually involve careful examination of members' childhood experiences. Based on the psychodynamic model, the groups seek to discover the subconscious causes of depression by uncovering the emotional balance the clients established in response to their early childhood relationships. The leaders function as sources of emotional stimulation by calling on participants to examine their feelings, as well as serving as symbolic parent figures. The leaders also offer meaning attribution to help participants understand and overcome their depression. Therapeutic factors include Hope, Universality, Catharsis, and Corrective Recapitulation of the Primary Family Group.

Rehabilitation

Assertion training in groups is often offered to recovering alcoholics. Participants learn how to be more direct in asking for what they want, and how to refuse unwanted requests or pressure from others. Assertion skills are seen as important for recovering alcoholics because they need to refuse offers of alcohol if they are to maintain sobriety. Also, assertion skills help alcoholics get more of what they want in life directly from people, rather than turning to alcohol to fulfill unmet needs or to express aggression in a passive fashion. Cognitive–behavioral theories are used to guide leaders' behaviors, which usually are predominantly executive functions. Therapeutic factors in such groups include Information, Imitation, and Socializing Techniques. Catharsis also plays a major role as participants get in touch with their true feelings about situations in preparation to practice asserting themselves. Concurrent meetings of the members of the alcoholics' families are often held in which family members learn assertion skills they need to help with the alcoholic's recovery. Meetings with family members also have a preventive effect because the social support that participants experience helps them deal with the stresses associated with being related to a alcoholic.

PROFESSIONAL ISSUES

Research evaluating the processes and outcomes of group counseling is an important responsibility for mental health professionals involved in group work. Through research, the complex interaction of variables that affect group process and outcomes may be examined. These variables include (but certainly are not limited to): purpose of the group; personalities of leaders; theories guiding groups; group activities; duration of meetings; setting; the nature of members' problems; and composition of groups with regard to members' ages, gender, personality, development, and so on. Research on group work has been extensive (Zimpfer, 1984). However, because groups are so complex, there are many methodological problems associated with group research (Bednar & Kaul, 1978). Also, because each group is unique, there is danger in generalizing findings from one study to another. Extensive programmatic research efforts are needed to advance understanding of group counseling.

Because group counseling is a powerful and complex form of mental health intervention, the American Association of Counseling and Development (AACD) includes a division devoted to professional issues related to group work, the Association for Specialists in Group Work (ASGW). The ASGW serves as a network for maintaining contact between counselors involved in group work. It arranges presentations at national and regional AACD conventions, and publishes a newsletter, along with the *Journal of Specialists in Group Work*, which reports research and innovative practice with groups. In addition to these activities, the association has generated "Standards for Group Counseling," which focus on core competencies and necessary training experiences for group counselors, and "Ethical Guidelines for Group Leaders," which addresses ethical issues specifically as they apply to group counseling (reprinted in Gazda, 1984).

CONCLUSION

This chapter has presented an introduction to group counseling, an efficient and potent form of mental health counseling. An attempt has been made to acquaint the reader with a variety of applications of group work and the theories, functions, and methods typically employed by group counselors; as well as to provide a description of the professional structure of group counseling. For more detailed exposure to the area of mental health counseling in groups, readers are encouraged to examine the references for this chapter, in particular the introductory texts (Corey & Corey, 1982; Gazda, 1984; Hansen, Warner, & Smith, 1980; Shaffer & Galinsky, 1974; Yalom, 1985), and a bibliography that offers extensive references on specific uses of groups (Zimpfer, 1984).

REFERENCES

Association for Specialists in Group Work Executive Board (1980). *Ethical guidelines for group leaders.* Alexandria, VA: Association for Specialists in Group Work.

Bednar, R. L., & Kaul, K. J. (1978). Experiential group research: Current perspectives. In S. L. Garfield & A. E. Bergin (Eds.), *Handbook of psychotherapy and behavioral change: An empirical analysis* (pp. 769–817). New York: Wiley.

Bion, V. R. (1959). *Experiences in group.* New York: Basic Books.

Bradford, L. P., Gibb, J. R., & Benne, K. D. (1964). *T-group theory and laboratory method: Innovation in re-education.* New York: Wiley.

Corey, G., & Corey, M. S. (1982). *Groups: Process and practice* (2nd ed.). Belmont, CA: Wadsworth.

Erikson, E. H. (1963). *Childhood and society* (2nd ed.). New York: Norton.

Gazda, G. (1984). *Group counseling: A developmental approach* (3rd ed.). Boston: Allyn & Bacon.

Gazda, G. M., Duncan, J. A. & Meadows, M. E. (1967). Group counseling and group procedures. Report of a survey. *Counselor Education and Supervision, 6,* 305–310.

Hansen, V. C., Warner, R. W., & Smith, E. J. (1980). *Group counseling: Theory and process* (2nd ed.). Chicago: Rand McNally.

Lewin, K. (1951). *Field theory and social science.* New York: Harper & Row.

Lieberman, M. A., Yalom, I. D., & Miles, M. B.. (1973). *Encounter groups: First facts.* New York: Basic Books.

Shaffer, J. B. P., & Galinsky, M. D. (1974). *Models of group therapy and sensitivity training.* Englewood Cliffs, NJ: Prentice-Hall.

Tuckman, B. W., & Jensen, M. A. (1977). Stages of small group development revisited. *Group and Organizational Studies, 2,* 419–427.

Waldo, M. (1985). Curative factor framework for conceptualizing group counseling. *Journal of Counseling and Development, 64*(1), 52–58.

Yalom, I. D. (1985). *The theory and practice of group psychotherapy* (3rd ed.). New York: Basic Books.

Zimpfer, D. (1984). *Group work in the helping professions: A bibliography* (2nd ed.). Muncie, IN: Accelerated Development.

10 Counseling with Communities

Earlier chapters in this book have indicated from available statistics that many Americans are in "serious need" of mental health services. With the large consumption of tranquilizers and the realization that millions of people are addicted to barbiturates, heroin, cocaine, methadone, and alcohol, it is no wonder that mental health problems are endemic. In searching for answers to the problems of mental health, one tends to forget that they often have roots in the particular conditions of our society (Gordon, 1977).

"Man lives in a double environment, an outer layer of climate and terrain and natural resources, and an inner layer of culture that mediates between man and the world about him" (Paul, 1955, p. 467). Culture includes the society, the community in which one lives, and conditions in that community. Such conditions as poverty, fragmenting societal structures, pressured and alienating working conditions, the lack of employment opportunities, and a narrow societal vision can predispose people to a wide variety of mental health problems. Depression, alcoholism and other drug abuse, and even schizophrenia could be promoted by particular factors in one's community (Gordon, 1977).

This chapter will focus on community, and will identify in the following section an understanding of the concept of community. It will also discuss how the mental health counselor can act within the community to foster mental health planning. Importantly, moreover, this chapter will include an explanation of how the community can be utilized as a therapeutic resource. Although the community may facilitate mental health problems, it can also foster "wellness" and the development of positive life adjustment behaviors.

THE CONCEPT OF COMMUNITY

According to Sanders (1966):

A community is a territorially organized system coextensive with a settlement pattern in which (1) an effective communication network operates, (2) people share common facilities and services distributed within this settlement pattern, and (3) people develop a psychological identification with the locality symbol (the name). (p. 26)

Warren (1972) defined the community, however, as a combination of social units and systems that perform the major social functions having locality relevance. Warren (1972) identified these functions as: (a) the local participation in the process of producing, distributing, and consuming those goods and services that are a part of daily living and access to which is desirable in the locality; (b) socialization or the process by which the community transmits prevailing knowledge, social values, and behavior patterns to its individual members; (c) social control, or the process through which a group influences its members to behave in conformity with its norms; (d) social participation, or the opportunities provided by religious organizations, other voluntary organizations, the business community, the family, extended kinship relationships, and other, less formal, associations; and (e) mutual support, namely, that support provided in time of need by family and friends as well as by institutionalized governmental public-welfare and social service mechanisms. This conceptualization of community implies that the community serves to provide the means of satisfying both individual and societal needs (Sanders, 1966; Warren, 1972).

Bloom (1977), when referring to Bernard (1973), provided a useful distinction between the term *community* and the term *the community*. Bernard (1973) suggests that the major component of the concept of the community is locale, whereas the major components of the concept of community are common ties and social interaction. This concept of community involves personal intimacy, emotional ties, moral commitment, social cohesion, and continuity in time (Bernard, 1973).

As advanced by Bernard (1973), Bloom (1977), Sanders (1966), and Warren (1972), community has a multidimensional character, and there are a variety of ways to understand community. Community can be perceived, for example, as a place to live; and therefore the counselor, in studying community, would explore the kinds of people who live in the area, the employment opportunities, the shopping facilities, the opportunities for recreation, the housing patterns, and the prevailing community attitudes and sentiments. Community can also be viewed in demographic or spatial terms. In this approach, the social scientist studies the spatial distribution of people and of occupations as well as defines neighborhood characteristics and the interrelationships of these characteristics. Another way to understand community is to view community as a way of life. Though this perspective may be highly subjective and requires a high level of participation in community life, insights are developed into the total culture that can be useful to anthropologists. A fourth viewpoint of perceiving community is by concentrating on its social relationships—the patterns of interactions through which daily activities are carried out. This approach involves considering the community as a social system (Bloom, 1977).

The word *community* has also been used to refer to a "therapeutic community." Though this term seems to mean different things to different people, the concept grew out of the highly regulated hierarchical system of British military hospitals during World War II (Wilmer, 1981). It is a form of milieu therapy, in which role status and authority are used in the direction of a democratic social organization, each client has a particular function to perform and has a clear idea of how this function is applied, and the staff community is intimately aware of the roles of the other team members. There are other elements in the therapeutic community, but the principal revolution in this intervention was the change in the role of staff vis-à-vis their clients. For example, more informal relationships with clients could be developed (Wilmer, 1981).

The term *community* has come to be used, consequently, very loosely in the mental health field, is prone to multiple connotative meanings, and so can be easily misunderstood (Bachrach, 1980). An attempt was made to give the word *community* a solid operational definition in the guidelines for federal catchment areas, but the effort did not succeed in correcting imprecision (Kirk & Thierren, 1975).

For the mental health counselor, these different viewpoints of community can be confusing, but when one understands the community as client, then the meaning of community for mental health intervention is brought into clearer focus. The understanding of community as client supposes the interaction of relationships within this community and the factors of social cohesion and emotional ties among community members. This particular perspective suggests that the community is a strong influence in the development of "wellness," that the community can shape both the different life adjustment patterns of individuals and the parameters of mental health care, and that it has strengths and weaknesses that must be considered when planning varied approaches to mental health intervention. In other words, community itself contains both resources for the generation of positive mental health patterns in the life of its people and conditions that represent obstacles to satisfactory client adjustment.

Both the definition of community and the different perspectives for understanding this term provide a beginning realization of what, theoretically, the idea of community is all about. For effective mental health intervention, however, the counselor must go beyond this understanding to an identification of the needs, goals, pattern of life, and the living environment of the community members, as well as to a knowledge of how these members interact with one another. Approaches to this identification and knowledge will now be discussed.

SPECIFIC APPROACHES TO UNDERSTANDING THE COMMUNITY

One of the most effective ways to explore how mental health counseling intervention can be relevant to a particular community is through a needs assessment. A needs assessment approach is discussed in chapter 12, "The Evaluation of Services." But there are modifications to that method needed when one is considering the community and mental health intervention. In 1964, federal regulations called upon each state seeking federal funds for the development of community mental health programs to spell out the specific steps through which it has assessed a community's mental health needs. Included in these regulations were the following steps:

1. Geographic catchment areas must be identified with populations between 75,000 and 200,000 people;
2. Need is to be assessed on the basis of prevalence of mental illness and emotional disorders, both in terms of rate and absolute number of persons affected;
3. Poverty, social pathology, and population subgroups with special needs were to be used as three specific indices as being related to need for mental health services.

Schulberg and Wechsler (1974), however, in reviewing these regulations explained that (a) National Institute of Mental Health insistence that planned catchment areas not exceed a population of 200,000 forced an arbitrary exclusion or division of towns and neighborhoods that traditionally have worked together to form the community base upon which comprehensive programs could be established; (b) planning for community mental health centers on the basis of admission rates to current mental hospitals or to other existing programs may perpetuate current patterns, that is, an area having low rates of hospitalization or other treatment would be viewed as having low need, but quite the opposite may be true; (c) accurate prevalence statistics on the number of people, for example, in the subgroups with special needs are not generally available for all communities in a state.

Consequently, reservations about those federal regulations for assessing community need have been reported. An expanded array of environmental factors, which together with individual-oriented indices help to define the need for service is perhaps a better design for evaluating community needs (Schulberg & Wechsler, 1974).

In contrast to these federal guidelines, Lemkau (1967) has identified three general strategies for developing community needs. The first is to compare the services offered by one community with those offered by others and to "relate those of a community that we presume is excellently served to the needs of the population under study" (Lemkau, 1967, p. 65). A second strategy is to collect and interpret service statistics or data on patients in treatment. This has been a practice used since the early 1800s, but there are many objections to it, such as, the act of hospitalization for a psychiatric disorder is less an indication of psychopathology on the part of the patient than it is an indication of society's reaction to what it labels deviant behavior, and, using patient-care data as a measure of psychiatric disability in a population promotes the danger of systematic underestimation (Bloom, 1977). The third strategy is to survey the general population or a sample of that population. Yet such surveys are expensive and have severe problems of reliability and validity (Bloom, 1977).

All of the strategies have as their focus the exploration of the need for mental health services for those who could be mentally ill. Apart from the fact that from the many population surveys conducted since 1950 there is an indication that the reported prevalence rates of identifiable mental disorders was from less than 1% to over 60%, a range that defies credibility (Bloom, 1977), the attention has not been given to "wellness" patterns in a community. Also, there has not been a focus on the need for other types of services arising from the community that mental health counselors can provide, such as mid-life transition counseling, family counseling, or life adjustment services for the disabled and elderly. Further, there should be an identification of community views on mental health problems and service priorities (Hargreaves, Attkisson, Siegal, & McIntyre, 1974).

Although it was earlier stated that a needs assessment approach is discussed in this book (chapter 12), Neuber, Atkins, Jacobson, and Reuterman (1980) have developed an approach that also responds effectively to the demands of a more comprehensive type of needs assessment. It is called the "Community Needs Assessment Model," and its purpose is to collect data from three discrete and interrelated sources for purposes of comparison and utilization in program planning and evaluation. It collects data from three sources: demographic/statistical profiles, designated key informants, and individual interviews with randomly selected consumers and potential consumers.

Concerning demographic statistical profiles, information pertaining to areas of public concern can be collected from public records that are available through local and state resources. Key informants are defined as persons having direct contact with individuals experiencing problems in living; and random samples may be drawn from such people as clergy, law enforcement personnel, lawyers, medical doctors, nurses, and so on. These informants are asked to provide information on how professionals perceive community problems and needs from their vantage point as front-line human service providers (Neuber et al., 1980). Finally, one of the greatest advantages of the community-oriented approach is the involvement of consumers in the needs assessment process. As Neuber et al. (1980) explained, "A representative sample of the general public is given the opportunity to impact directly on the future service delivery of mental health and other human services in the community" (p. 18).

The primary goal of needs assessment is to generate usable information. The primary goal of community-oriented needs assessment is to facilitate community input into human service delivery. Another way to understand the community, moreover, is to assess the environment in which the person's thought and behavior occur. The concept of environment may be defined by the norms, attitudes, and habits of the specific groups with which an individual interacts directly, for example, at home or at school. Environment can also be viewed as the physical surroundings, that is, buildings, parks, lakes, homes, and streets. Environment can be perceived, consequently, as it is, independent of the interpretations made by the individuals responding to it (Walsh & Betz, 1985).

Craik (1971) identified five different approaches to environmental assessment. One approach focuses on the physical, spatial properties of places and how they tend to influence behavior. A second approach is concerned with the organization of material artifacts in places. Gough (1974), for example, developed a brief objective inventory for assessing social–economic factors in home and family environments. A third approach involves evaluating the traits of environments or situations by means of human observers. Adjective checklists, bipolar rating scales, and cue-sort decks are being developed to permit observers to record their impressions of environments in rather rapid, comparable, and comprehensive ways. A fourth approach, according to Craik (1971), focuses on assessing the behavioral attributes of environments or behavior settings. An analysis of behavior patterns can yield a comparison of environments on the basis of the relative frequency and duration of types of behaviors within these environments or behavior settings (Walsh & Betz, 1985). The fifth approach directs an assessment to the institutional attributes of environments. Attributes include such properties as satisfaction, beauty, and social climate, all of which tend to have an evaluative as well as a descriptive component. The focus in this approach is on how different groups of people (staff, residents, participants, observers, personnel people, patients, students, faculty, administrators) tend to perceive the environment and how these perceptions tend to influence their behavior (Walsh & Betz, 1985).

Moos (1974, 1976) has developed a series of nine social climate scales applicable in a variety of different environments. The scales are designed in such a way that they solicit information from people about their patterns of behavior in certain environments. Moos (1974) believes that the consensus of individuals characterizing their environment constitutes an assessment of the environment or social climate. Moos and his colleagues (Moos & Lemke, 1979) have also developed the Multiphasic Environmental Assessment Procedure in order to assess, measure, and describe sheltered-care settings, such as skilled nursing facilities and senior citizen housing facilities. From such information, it is possible to review the quality of the environment, to assess the impact of specific features on programs, and to explore the interaction between resident and environmental characteristics (Lemke, Moos, Mehren, & Bauvain, 1979).

In environmental assessment the physical and social environments are described and evaluated, but, in addition, how the individual's perceptions of the environment tend to influence the way he or she behaves in that environment are understood (Walsh & Betz, 1985). An individual is influenced, therefore, by situations in which he or she interacts, and also affects and changes situations in which he or she is interacting. Both of these general approaches, namely, needs assessment and environmental assessment, help the mental health counselor to understand different patterns of client thinking, the attitudes toward mental health intervention, and how the individual has been affected by past interventions in such settings as a community mental health center, or a family or employment agency. These assessments may also target areas within the community where primary prevention efforts are needed. The approaches may further indicate what is necessary when developing an intervention program for a specific community. Program development builds on a comprehensive needs assessment and a knowledge of the environment that has an impact on clients, as will be discussed in the next section.

PROGRAM DEVELOPMENT: A COMPREHENSIVE APPROACH

Program development is a comprehensive term that can apply both to individuals and to organizations within the community. Individual program development could comprise the formulation of plans to assist a client to better life functioning. If the goal of psychiatric rehabilitation, for example, is to restore to clients their capacity to function in the community, then specific plans may be developed to assist these persons to progress from their present level of functioning to their needed level of functioning (Anthony, Pierce, Mehren, & Cohen, 1979). Agency or organizational program development utilizes, on the other hand, a broader range of information and usually involves many more steps in the planning stage. For the busy and harassed mental health counselor, program planning may appear to be a dull or luxurious pastime. But the planning generally involves systematic action and the formulation of realistic and vital goals. Goals are the starting point in program planning. They chart the course and provide the destination for all that follows (Aubrey, 1982). This section will focus both on program development for agencies within the community, and for the formulation of plans that mental health counselors will generate for their individual clients. Most mental health counselors engage in private practice, and program planning can facilitate their own efforts. Two approaches will be explained.

The comprehensive approach encompasses the components of planning, developing, and implementing, all of which are basic steps or phases in program development.

Planning

This phase involves determining what the staff and perhaps the consumers/clients want to accomplish and integrating this with system or institutional needs. This is largely a data-gathering phase and uses information collected from needs or environment assessments. The key to good foundation building for a program is identifying the important needs of that program's consumers. This phase also implies that the agency has articulated its philosophy, has determined how an existing program is functioning, and then based on these data, formulates needs statements and establishes a workable set of program goals. In other words, desired outcomes are identified and the current status of program resources, allocation of resources, and the current status of program consumers are evaluated. With all of this collected information, then, program goals are developed. Though initially these program goals may be formulated as global, abstract statements, it is important that as program plans continue to evolve these goals become more specific. Generalized goal statements often fail to indicate exactly what the program consumers should be able to do within the particular program.

An example of this planning phase is a mental health agency that seeks to start a program to prepare clients to live productive lives after retirement from their employment or profession. The staff who wish to begin this intervention will review the literature on the issue of post-retirement life. Then they will target the intended population within a specified community and develop an approach to ascertain future client needs. Interviews with people about to retire or questionnaires may be utilized to collect data from future consumers. The staff may also wish to talk with mental health personnel who have been involved in delivering services to the older population. Whatever the approach chosen for identifying client needs, the format should best suit the purposes of the staff and the abilities of the consumer to respond to the requested information. After these data are collected, a generalized goal for the program will be formulated, such as to help post-retirement persons increase their productivity.

Developing

In this phase, three steps are usually involved: (a) specifying immediate program participants and objectives; (b) investigating, selecting, and structuring program procedures, and (c) communicating and evaluating program structuring decisions and activities. The first step implies that the target population may have to be narrowed down further because staff and other resource availability, that is, financial or space, may necessitate a reduction in original program participants. Examining demographic data is one way to obtain more precise estimates of the target population. A crucial part of this step is to identify the specific goals that the program participants are to achieve. If possible, these goals should be measurable and priorities should be established among these objectives. The second step focuses on identifying those particular events or activities that will be developed and used to achieve the planned objectives. The third step involves promoting the program itself within the community and evaluating through outcome measurement as to whether or not the program objectives have been attained.

To apply these steps to the designated example, the first demand for the staff might be to review again whether agency resources are sufficient to meet the identified needs of the target population. Though this was initially done in the planning phase, added information from the needs assessment may demand a re-examination of who in the target population can actually be served. Also, more specific program objectives will be developed that might include vocational, educational, personal–social, health, and leisure goals. As an example of educational goals, behaviors in this area might involve exploring and pursuing educational opportunities independent of, or not immediately having, vocational concomitants. In the second step activities will be selected and structured in the vocational, educational, personal–social, health, and leisure areas. This will demand, of course, that the staff develop these activities in harmony with information collected from the needs assessment and the recognized capabilities of the program participants. Finally, once these activities have been planned, they are advertised among the intended target population. As the program begins, moreover, an evaluation approach can be designed that will assess the achievement of the program's activities. Suggested approaches are found in chapter 12.

Implementing

In this phase the activities are begun and program participants have an understanding of the program objectives. Prior to the implementation, program staff will have to be selected and perhaps staff development activities will also be initiated. Before all the activities are implemented, however, a mental health agency may wish to field test or "pilot" a particular activity in order to evaluate participant involvement and the feasibility of the design of the activity. When initiating the program for the recent retirees, the agency may want to begin with a personal–social activity in order to assess (a) whether it will appeal to the population, even though the needs assessment emphasized the activity, and (b) whether the way in which the staff has designed the personal–social activity, that is, time selected, or type of activity, really is capable of helping the post-retirees to meet the stated objectives.

The three phases of planning, development, and implementation explained here comprise one, systematic approach to program development. It is based on comprehensive data, and each of the phases involves many individual tasks for the program staff. The systematic nature of the program development does not remove the need for hard work. Another approach has been developed, however, that is even more systematic in its program development. It is a model that is relevant not only to organizational needs, but also to the mental health counselor working with an individual client. One of the assumptions of this approach is that if the client is to function productively in the community, then he or she will usually have to be taught appropriate, needed skills (Anthony, et al., 1979).

A MENTAL HEALTH PROGRAMMING MODEL

The material that will be used to explain this approach is taken from Anthony et al. (1979), and then modified for mental health counselors. These authors believe that although it is most important to diagnose client needs, behaviors, strengths, and deficits, another skill is required to enable clients to act on those diagnosed strengths and deficits. Thus, to identify community needs is essential for program planning; to act upon these identified needs necessitates an orderly, very systematic approach. In other words, if the diagnostic process is to assist clients to develop insights into their problems, then program planning is to help to develop client action. The stages and skills of this programming model are as follows:

1. Exploring the client's/organization's unique programming needs
   (a) Establish priorities for the client's/organization's mental health goals
   (b) Develop the overall program plan
2. Understanding the specific program steps
3. Implementing the specific program steps

Exploring the Client's/Organization's Unique Programming Needs

Establish Priorities for the Client's/Organization's Mental Health Goals

The process of assigning priorities involves assessing mental health from three perspectives: (a) mental health urgency; (b) client and organization motivation; and (c) client level of skill functioning or organizational level of resource availability. Mental health urgency refers to deficits or needs that, if not overcome or met, will limit the client's ability to survive and the organization's capability to grow. Client motivation refers to the client's desire to either overcome or ignore specific skill deficits; organization motivation implies that the agency wants to expand to meet the widening demands of the population. Client level of skill functioning differentiates between the skill areas where the client is functioning poorly and the skill areas where the client is functioning relatively well. Organizational level of resource availability is concerned with, for example, an identification of adequate resources, namely, staff, financial, or space, and what is needed to function in a manner that better serves the particular goal.

Develop the Overall Program Plan

The goal of this step is to describe the responsibilities of the person(s) who will be held accountable for the program. Usually the person who develops the program is the person responsible for writing and sequencing the necessary program steps. In some cases, however, a number of people may be involved in the development, implementation, and monitoring process. This is particularly true when a mental health agency is developing a program that will have an impact on the community. One of the key components in this development, however, is the monitoring process. Often, well-designed programs go awry because no one maintains responsibility for determining on a periodic basis whether the program is being implemented. Also, on an individual client basis, the person who monitors the program assures when possible that differential reinforcement occurs as a result of the client's successful or unsuccessful program performance. Another important component of the plan is the determination of when the plan will begin and end, because there should always be a target date for each part of the program.

With individual clients, the mental health counselor might wish to specify on the plan the specific client behaviors that should be changed, or what skills should be acquired or enhanced if the client is to achieve productive living. Anthony et al. (1979) emphasized that the goal specified on the client's plan should be observable. For example, after evaluating the client's problem the counselor might believe that the client's physical, emotional, and intellectual functioning will have to improve if the client is going to make a suitable adjustment. The main problem might be a continued state of anxiety that is preventing the client from making necessary decisions in his/her life.

For example, a client reports that she feels badly about being overweight and this covers a feeling of inferiority and loss of confidence in herself. Yet as a single mother of three children, she must make continued decisions about the home and school issues and about problems that occur with her position as an accountant. Because she unnecessarily delays making these decisions, she believes she is living in a constant state of anxiety. To alleviate this anxiety, the client might have to feel better about herself physically, begin to utilize her intellectual capabilities, and perform activities that, mentally, will help her to have peace of mind. Each area — physical, emotional, and intellectual — would have to be identified in the plan for improvement. An example of an observable goal in the physical area might be, "In 4 weeks, the client will lose 5 pounds."

A modification of a sample program planning chart as devised by Anthony et al. (1979) for this client is illustrated in Figure 10.1.

FIGURE 10.1. Program Planning Chart

Goal: To reduce client's anxiety and increase client's decision-making skills in the home-making and employment areas:

AREA	PROGRAM DEVELOPER	PROGRAM MONITOR	DATE OF IMPLEMENTATION	DATE OF COMPLETION
Physical To lose 5 lbs. in 4 weeks	Counselor	Counselor	As soon as possible	4 weeks from beginning of plan
Emotional				
Intellectual				

Understanding the Specific Program Steps

Within this second stage, the counselor would develop the major program steps. On an organizational level, once a programming goal has been identified (for example, implementing a primary prevention program for substance abuse among adolescents), this might involve using brainstorming sessions with the agency staff to identify how a program can be promoted and then initiated in the community, defining the current prevention efforts in the specific community, and finding the "ideal" prevention strategies. The steps to promote and implement the program would be created, and each step would be written, if possible, in behavioral terms. On the client level the development of the major program steps would include: (a) defining the client's present and needed skill functioning in observable terms, such as in the physical area, the needed weight loss; (b) involving the client in the program development; (c) using brainstorming questions to identify the steps that will advance the client from where he/she is to where he/she needs to be; (d) listing the steps as they are created; and (e) writing the steps in behavioral terms.

For the client who is having decision-making problems because of his/her overwhelming anxiety, once the counselor has identified weight loss as one approach to alleviate the problem, then the counselor will explore with the client the ways to lose this weight. Exercise and diet can both be discussed, and once a method is agreed upon, then the specific steps to pursue regular exercise or to change eating habits will be noted. Engaging in regular exercise might involve the specific steps of (a) identifying what kind of exercise is the most feasible; (b) deciding where this exercise could be performed; and (c) establishing a schedule to do the exercise.

Implementing the Specific Program Steps

This third stage includes, according to Anthony et al. (1979), the setting of time lines for program implementation; creating reinforcement steps; implementing, when necessary, the teaching steps; and then monitoring client performance. The setting of time lines is a valuable component in program development because these guidelines give clients or organizations a target for which to aim and a structure to keep them on the program's schedule. Time lines also serve as the criteria by which client performance can be evaluated, and are set for the completion of each major step. For example, if the mental health counselor is to recommend weight loss as one approach to alleviating the client's severe anxiety, then the client's self-expectation might be enhanced with the guidelines of a time framework. This framework might even increase the client's motivation to lose weight.

Another dimension of this stage that is quite helpful for programming efforts is the development of reinforcement steps. Although perhaps not as applicable to organizations as to clients, reinforcements can act as motivators and rewards for acquiring new skills. These reinforcers should come from the client's frame of reference, namely, the client must perceive the reinforcer as actually reinforcing. The counselor's perception of a certain behavior as reinforcing may not necessarily be what the client considers reinforcing (Anthony et al., 1979). Even the counselor can be a potent reinforcer to clients, and this is particularly true of counselors who have demonstrated a high level of interpersonal skills with their clients. Yet the unique things and activities that each client finds to be reinforcing can be learned by observing the client, by questioning the client, and/or by soliciting the observations of significant others.

Both of the approaches to program development discussed here—the comprehensive model and the mental health programming model—use systematic methods in their planning efforts. The effectiveness of planning for human services is not only dependent upon the involvement and cooperation of the target community and the participation of agency staff and clients in the planning process, but also relies upon the skills of the program developers to focus on specific strategies that can prevent or remediate particular problems. When planners are faced with many attractive alternatives to alleviate community problems, there is the temptation to run off simultaneously in all directions. If a counselor in a mental health agency wants to develop, for example, a program to prevent adolescent substance abuse, there are many options to pursue. A systematic approach to planning provides guidelines for the selection of options. Furthermore, the planner must distinguish between the short- and long-term objectives, because they may be antithetical, for example, providing remedies to those young people who are already using drugs can be of immediate benefit to these people, but it may reduce the community's support for the more fundamental and long-range changes needed to alter the substance abuse cycle. There are many issues to consider, consequently, when conducting program development. Effective program development can make a difference in how the community influences the client's own attainment of life adjustment goals. The community itself can also become a therapeutic resource for clients. A discussion of how this has been accomplished is in the next section.

THE COMMUNITY AS A CHANGE AGENT

As discussed earlier in this chapter, the concept of community includes many meanings, several of which evolve from the term *environment*. The community is viewed as an environment in which people live, learn, work, and pursue related activities. For the mental health counselor, community can be understood as an environment that is the object of intervention efforts, or as an environment in which people who have serious mental health problems can get better. When the counselor perceives the community as a possible resource for intervention approaches, then the reality of de-institutionalization is introduced. A discussion of community either as an environment, a setting, or the interaction between persons must include an overview of de-institutionalization. Some mental health counselors' focus for understanding community is developed from the appreciation that the community can provide appropriate alternatives for intervention, education, and rehabilitation of the mentally disabled who do not need to be in institutions.

Deinstitutionalization

Chafetz, Goldman, and Taube (1983) explained that after the United States Congress passed, in 1963, the Community Mental Health Centers (CMHC) Act and instituted the first national policy of community care for the mentally disabled, the goals of community care became ambitious, going far beyond the notion of hospital reform. These goals included not merely the relocation of the mentally disabled into more humane settings, but the rehabilitation of institutionalized psychiatric clients and their reinsertion into society. The goals also emphasized prevention of the behaviors associated with long-term hospitalization and, through this, eventual elimination of the need for large, custodial-type facilities.

A pluralistic, community-based system was developed after the passage of the CMHC Act, and the many activities and goals comprising this system fall under the umbrella of "deinstitutionalization." Bachrach (1977) defined de-institutionalization as (a) the prevention of inappropriate mental hospital admissions through the provision of community alternatives for treatment, (b) the release to the community of all institutionalized patients who have been given adequate preparation for such a change, and (c) the establishment and maintenance of community support systems for non-institutionalized people receiving mental health services in the community. A U.S. General Accounting Office report (1977) on deinstitutionalization added that it is a process of finding and developing appropriate alternatives in the community for housing, treatment, training, education, and rehabilitation of the mentally disabled who do not need to be in institutions, and a process for improving conditions, care, and treatment for those who need institutional care. This approach is based on the principle that mentally disabled persons are entitled to live in the least restrictive environment and lead their lives as normally and independently as they can.

Although the term *deinstitutionalization* only came into popular use in the mid-1970s, its core ideal—the phasing out of state mental hospitals—has been the subject of continuous policy debates since the early 1950s (Morrissey, 1982). Morrissey (1982) explained,

> These debates were sustained by two essentially antagonistic ideologies, one rooted in institutional psychiatry and the other in community mental health. The first called for a regeneration of state mental hospitals as the hub of the mental health services network, while the second called instead for the early demise of state hospitals and their replacement by a new community-based and community-controlled mental health services delivery system. (p. 150)

During the 1950s and 1960s, state government policymakers encouraged both models of care.

The philosophical basis for deinstitutionalization in the United States is derived from values deeply rooted in American history and culture (Bachrach, 1978). Individual rights and human perfectibility are values that have always influenced American thought. The moral treatment and mental hygiene movements emphasized environmental approaches to treatment and rehabilitation (Bockoven, 1963; Caplan, 1969; Rothman, 1980). Bachrach (1978) also believed that in some respects deinstitutionalization is a protest movement, colored by current beliefs about social action. One of these was the belief in federal action to achieve social justice and distribution of services. Linked to increased federal involvement was a parallel "professionalism of social reform" (Moynihan, 1969). During the post–World War II years, federal expenditures for behavioral science increased steadily, enabling universities "to produce cadres of technical experts in disciplines related to social problems and policy" (Chafetz et al., 1983, p. 50). Social action also became increasingly associated with behavioral research and social theory. Consequently, the movement for community alternatives to the hospital was grounded in the clinical and social research of the period.

The process of deinstitutionalization is both varied and comprehensive. Bachrach (1978) described this process as a dynamic and continuing series of adjustments involving all parts of the mental health system. There were regional variations, as some states moved more rapidly than others. Community services and hospital alternatives were available in some states, but not in others. Chafetz et al. (1983) believed that the primary adjustment in many respects occurred within the former "monolithic system of public hospitals" (p. 52). Though at one time they were the major providers of inpatient services, these hospitals became the treatment centers of last resort. One statistic indicates a 75% drop in resident population between 1955 and 1980 (Goldman, Adams, & Taube, 1983).

New admissions policies, moreover, altered "input" to the public hospital system. Adults faced stringent admission criteria that excluded all but the most severely impaired. The impaired elderly were rerouted to nursing homes in the community. Admissions to mental hospitals were characterized more by the younger and more acutely disturbed clients, and an emphasis was placed on brief treatment and early discharge (Chafetz et al., 1983). Public mental hospitals became major providers of short-term care for chronic patients, the majority (80%) of whom were destined for release within 3 months of admission (Goldman et al., 1983).

"Output" from these institutions included transfers to nursing homes that offered intermediate- and extended-care settings (Goldman et al., 1983). But to a larger extent, hospital releases involved "revolving-door" patients who required episodic treatment but were under community care for the better part of a year (Chafetz et al., 1983). The presence of this group in the community, in combination with those patients excluded from public hospital care, gave rise to the development of a series of accommodations at other levels of the mental health system.

Goldman et al. (1983) explained that services for the acutely ill in local settings rapidly increased. Federally assisted community mental health centers were created. Veterans Administration facilities and general hospitals more than doubled their volume, and the community-based emergency unit adjusted to a considerable expansion in services (Bassuk & Gerson, 1979). There was a significant increase in ambulatory care between 1955 and 1975, with resources serving those with less severe problems. Yet, as Chafetz et al. (1983) stated, "The new system was sometimes inadequate for meeting the needs of the mentally disabled who apparently required more social support than that provided through traditional outpatient therapy" (p. 54).

However, a number of innovative programs were developed that offered creative, life adjustment opportunities for the chronic population. Fountain House (Beard, Malamud, & Rossman, 1978), the Fairweather Lodge (Fairweather, 1980), Thresholds (Dincin & Selleck, 1980), and the PACT programs (Paul & Lenz, 1977) are examples of resources that attempted to demonstrate the feasibility of community care. With this agency development, moreover, deinstitutionalization policy has produced a number of major changes in the mental health service system. Chafetz et al. (1983) identified them as the following:

1. Public hospital residency has declined dramatically.
2. Nursing homes have supplanted the psychiatric institution as the major source of long-term custodial care in the United States.
3. Brief hospital treatment predominates over long-term care. This pattern is seen in the increased number of brief admissions to state and county facilities each year.
4. The most urgent needs of the community-based populations are for fundamental social services. Many of the mentally disabled may live independently; others return to families, but a large segment of the chronically mentally disabled depends on public services to maintain a minimal living standard (Minkoff, 1979). Approximately 300,000 to 400,000 of the chronically mentally disabled rely on residential placements in which the functions of custody and asylum are assumed by the private sector through public financing (Mellody, 1979). An unknown but substantial number are in need of support to meet their most fundamental material requirements: meals, hygiene, shelter. They form one of the most vulnerable segments of the poor in the United States (Talbott, 1981).
5. Outpatient care now handles 70% of all psychiatric episodes in the United States. Outpatient visits have expanded twelvefold between 1955 and 1977. A community-based network has evolved to provide these visits.

Deinstitutionalization policies, therefore, have facilitated a greater and more varied volume of mental health services than ever before. But there are major obstacles to addressing the problems of deinstitutionalization. Outcomes of deinstitutionalization have been controversial (Keisler et al., 1983). The policies leading to the dramatic reductions in state mental hospital censuses in the 1970s can be seen as a rapid acceleration of a trend to transfer financial responsibility for the chronically mentally disabled client from the state mental health departments to the social welfare system (Gruenberg, 1974). Gruenberg (1974) believed

> . . . that the present crisis of abandonment of the seriously mentally disabled has arisen because no similar transfer of responsibility for their care and treatment has taken place. . . . While these disabled are a visible problem causing much concern, and espousing their cause has become a very gratifying role, the tendency has been to advocate solutions that are someone else's responsibility to execute. (p. 701)

Another obstacle to deinstitutionalization has been a failure by mental health professionals to recognize that there are many different kinds of long-term patients and that they vary greatly in the degree to which they can be rehabilitated (Lamb, 1981). Lamb (1981) explained that "patients vary widely in their ability to cope with stress without decompensating and developing psychotic symptoms, and they differ in the kinds of stress and pressure they can handle" (p. 106). Long-term clients also vary in their motivation to change. What may appear to be, at first glance, a homogeneous group, turns out to vary from people who can tolerate almost no stress at all to people who can, with some assistance, cope with life's demands (Lamb, 1981). Long-term psychiatric clients are almost by definition a marginal population; and for a significant majority of these clients, rehabilitation in terms of competitive employment, high levels of social functioning, and return to the mainstream may not be a realistic goal. Perhaps a great step forward would be if "only" the quality of life for these patients was improved and they became comfortable living relatively undemanding but satisfying lives in a nonhospital environment (Lamb, 1981).

Bachrach (1977) described a number of problems in the process of deinstitutionalization that impede its effective implementation, such as:

1. Discharged patients have not been adequately prepared to learn the practical skills needed to function in the community.
2. Some programs are irrelevant to the needs of the clients, especially disadvantaged minority groups.
3. The range of treatment services available to ex-patients has been inadequate, except for the provision of medication.
4. Services available have not been well-organized and often not easily accessible.
5. The general public continues to stigmatize mental patients and continues to maintain perceptions of ex-patients as potentially dangerous.
6. Fiscal responsibility for care of clients is often not clearly laid out among federal, state, and local groups.
7. Deinstitutionalization often occurred in haste and without adequate preparation.

The community mental health centers have grown up, moreover, largely as a separate delivery system without formal linkages to state hospitals (Morrissey, 1982). Also, rather than "deinstitutionalization," a process of "trans-institutionalization" has occurred for many clients over the past two decades (Morrissey, 1982). Thousands of former patients are now living in nursing homes, board and care homes, adult homes, and other institutional settings in the community (Shadish & Bootzin, 1981). These mainly private, profit-making concerns now serve the custody, asylum, and treatment functions for the mentally disabled that were once performed almost exclusively by state mental hospitals.

All in all, as Morrissey (1982) believed, the rapid expansion of mental health and other protective services in the United States since 1955 has diminished but not supplanted the role of state mental hospitals. The mental health system has expanded and become much more diversified, both in terms of the mix of inpatient-outpatient services and the mix of public-private providers. Persons suffering from the milder and more acute forms of mental disorders have been the primary beneficiaries of these changes in the organization and locus of mental health care. Many of these persons are now able to receive appropriate care in general hospitals and outpatient settings. Those who suffer from more chronic conditions, the violent and more disturbing, as well as those who are socially incapacitated, still reside in state hospitals or alternative institutional settings in the community (Morrissey, 1982).

An important issue related to the deinstitutionalization movement is the rights of clients to receive adequate care and treatment. Of particular significance are the cases of *Wyatt v. Stickney* (1972), which was the first case to recognize that mental patients have a constitutional right to receive adequate care and treatment, and of *O'Connor v. Donaldson* (1975), which indicated that a person cannot be confined in a mental hospital if adequate treatment is not provided. *Brewster v. Dukakis* (1978) established the principle that a person with mental health problems is entitled to adequate treatment in the least restrictive environment, that is, in the community. *Rennie v. Klein* and *Rogers v. Okin*, two 1979 cases, indicated that patients have the legal right to refuse treatment (in both cases, antipsychotic medication). For a detailed discussion of these cases and their implications, see Herr, Arias, and Wallace (1983).

Although these cases were generally concerned with clear-cut issues (for example, Donaldson was kept locked for long periods in a large room with 60 other patients and denied any access to professional staff) and they did establish legal principles, it must be recalled that it is not always clear as to how far and in what situation each of these principles apply. For example, how does one determine what constitutes "adequate treatment," even though it is not hard to pick out grossly inadequate treatment? The principle of "least restrictive environment," which became a justification for much of the deinstitutionalization movement, clearly presents its own set of problems for the mental health professional. Turnbull, Ellis, Boggs, Brooks, and Biklen (1981) listed the following issues as problematic: (a) quantity of choices offered to the client (too many or too few); (b) quality of choices (too important or too trivial, too complex or too simple); (c) individualizing the choices offered on the basis of the client's needs and capacities; and (d) the role of the professional in shaping the choices as determinants of the client's behavior (for example, by only allowing the client choices at which the client can succeed, the client may incorrectly come to believe that failure is impossible). In essence, one must ask if the "least restrictive" environment (that is, total freedom) is necessarily the most beneficial for every client. Is freedom to freeze to death while sleeping on a city street an acceptable option?

Although certainly the deinstitutionalization movement has been the forerunner in the utilization of the community for mental health services, there are other alternative services that have important usefulness for the mental health counselor. Drop-in centers, free clinics, runaway houses, group foster homes for the mentally retarded, shelters for battered women, and hotlines were developed in direct response to the needs of disaffected people. They are nonprofessional alternatives to mental health facilities and social service agencies, which these people had found threatening, demeaning, and inadequate (Gordon, 1977). Gordon believed that these alternative services share certain assumptions, attitudes, and practices that make them particularly useful, and he identified particularly the following 12 assumptions:

1. These alternative resources respond to peoples' problems as those problems are experienced. A teenager, for example, who leaves home is seen, housed, and fed as a runaway and is not diagnosed as an "acting-out disorder."
2. They provide services that are immediately accessible, with a minimum of waiting and bureaucratic restriction. They are usually open 24 hours a day to anyone who calls or comes in off the street.
3. They emphasize the strengths of those who seek help and their capacity for self-help.
4. They reach out to help the individual change the social situation—job, family, school, work place—in which he or she is feeling distressed. This could mean helping an adolescent boy talk to his parents, or guiding a disabled adult through the maze of the rehabilitation process.
5. They are willing to change, to expand their services as the community's needs dictate and their increasing skills permit. Gordon (1977) cited an example of phone aides who became aware that young people would not go to traditional mental health facilities and so they expanded their hotline services from information and referral to phone counseling and crisis intervention.
6. They are actively involved in educating the larger community about individual needs and in helping that community to participate in meeting these needs. Staff members give frequent talks at local schools, churches, and civic groups.
7. They actively encourage those they have helped to become helpers and reduce feelings of loneliness and uselessness by doing useful work with others.
8. They rely to a large degree on nonprofessional workers. Gordon (1977) believed that in many alternative services, more than half the paid staff are nonprofessionals.
9. They are committed to using volunteers from their own community. Some programs use nonprofessional volunteers as an important adjunct to paid staff.
10. They generally operate under some form of participatory democracy or consensus decision-making.
11. They function as minicommunities or extended families. In other words, staff are provided with a sense of warmth and security and they grow and change to meet personal as well as work-related needs.

12. They are far more economical than traditional mental health facilities. When one compares the price for staying 1 day at a runaway house to the cost of that of a general hospital psychiatric ward, the former is about one eighth to one fifth the latter (Gordon, 1977).

These alternative resources may not offer crisis intervention or residential services, but they provide persons experiencing difficulties with the opportunities, such as expertise, advocacy, and education, to help them deal with their own problems. Individual counseling is available, but clients are helped to develop a capacity to analyze their social situations and needs and thus be better able to use a network of helpers both within and outside the centers.

Another illustration of alternative services has been described by O'Donnell and Sullivan (1974) as the neighborhood center. The settings of these centers are as diversified as the programs they offer and the people they serve. They could be located in a variety of places, including public housing projects, settlement houses, neighborhood stores, and shopping centers. They may provide social services as well as employment, economic, housing, family, and health assistance. They are usually located in low-income areas and, by virtue of their physical locations, are at least more accessible than traditional agencies.

CONCLUSION

The concept of community as client is a broad one and it implies that the community itself, whether in the form of a foster home, a mental health agency, or a related alternative service, can influence a client's functioning. In turn, the community can be the focus of attention of intervention efforts. This is frequently done in primary prevention programs. When the mental health counselor, moreover, has a more comprehensive perspective about assisting a client to attain appropriate life functioning, then substantial emphasis is usually given to mobilizing the client's environments—including family, work, and leisure settings. An appreciation of community dynamics often makes a difference as to how effectively client outcomes are achieved.

REFERENCES

Anthony, W. A., Pierce, R. H., Mehren, R., & Cohen, M. (1979). *The skills of diagnostic planning* (Psychiatric Rehabilitation Practice Series: Book 1). Amherst, MA: Carkhuff Institute of Human Technology.

Aubrey, R. C. (1982). Program planning and evaluation: Road map for the 80's. *Elementary School Guidance Counseling, 17,* 51–57.

Bachrach, L. (1977). *Deinstitutionalization: An analytical review and sociological perspective.* Rockville, MD: National Institute of Mental Health, Division of Biometry and Epidemiology.

Bachrach, L. (1978). A conceptual approach to deinstitutionalization. *Hospital and Community Psychiatry, 29,* 573.

Bachrach, L. (1980). Overview: Model programs for chronic mental patients. *American Journal of Psychiatry, 137,* 1023–1031.

Bassuk, E. L., & Gerson, S. (1979). Into the breach: Emergency psychiatry in the general hospital. *General Hospital Psychiatry, 1,* 31.

Beard, J. H., Malamud, T. J., & Rossman, E. (1978). Psychiatric rehabilitation and long-term rehospitalization rates: The findings of two research studies. *Schizophrenia Bulletin, 4,* 622.

Bernard, J. (1973). *The sociology of community.* Glenview, IL: Scott, Foresman.

Bloom, B. L. (1977). *Community mental health.* Monterey, CA: Brooks/Cole Publishing Co.

Bockoven, J. S. (1963). *Moral treatment in American psychiatry.* New York: Springer.

Brewster v. Dukakis, 76-4423 F. (D. Mass., December 6, 1978).

Caplan, R. B. (1969). *Psychiatry and community in nineteenth century America.* New York: Basic Books.

Chafetz, L., Goldman, H. H., & Taube, C. (1983). Deinstitutionalization in the United States. *International Journal of Mental Health, 11,* 48–63.

Craik, K. H. (1971). The assessment of places. In P. McReynolds (Ed.), *Advances in psychological assessment (Vol. II, pp. 40–62). Palo Alto, CA: Science and Behavior Books.*

Dincin, J., & Selleck, V. (1980). Implementing the rehabilitation approach in a community residential setting. *Rehabilitation Counseling Bulletin, 24,* 72–83.

Fairweather, G. W. (1980). The Fairweather Lodge: A twenty-five year retrospective. In G. Fairweather (Ed.), *New directions for mental health services* (Vol. 7, pp. 89–101). San Francisco: Jossey-Bass.

General Accounting Office (1977). *Returning the mentally disabled to the community: Government needs to do more.* Washington, DC: U. S. Government Printing Office.

Goldman, H. H., Adams, N. H., & Taube, C. A. (1983). Deinstitutionalization: Data demythologized. *Hospital and Community Psychiatry, 34,* 129–134.

Gordon, J. S. (1977, February 13). Community approaches to mental health. *The Washington Post,* pp. C1, C4.

Gough, H. G. (1974). *Manual for the home index.* Berkeley, CA: Institute of Personality Assessment and Research.

Gruenberg, E. (1974). The social breakdown syndrome and its prevention. In S. Arieti (Ed.), *American handbook of psychiatry* (Vol. 2, pp. 697–711). New York: Basic Books.

Hargreaves, W. A., Attkisson, C. C., Siegal, L. M., & McIntyre, M. H. (Eds.). (1974). *Resource materials for community mental health program evaluation. Part II. Needs assessment and planning.* San Francisco: National Institute of Mental Health.

Herr, S. S., Arias, S., & Wallace, R. E., Jr. (1983). *Legal rights and mental health care.* Lexington, MA: D. C. Heath.

Keisler, C., McGuere, T., Mechanic, D., Mosher, L., Nelson, S., Newman, F., Rech, R., & Schulberg, H. C. (1983). Federal mental health policy: Making an assessment of deinstitutionalization. *American Psychologist, 38,* 1292–1297.

Kirk, S. A., & Thierren, M. E. (1975). Community mental health myths and the fate of former hospitalized patients. *Psychiatry, 38,* p. 209.

Lamb, H. R. (1981). What did we really expect from deinstitutionalization? *Hospital and Community Psychiatry, 32,* 105–109.

Lemkau, P. V. (1967). Assessing a community's need for mental health services. *Hospital and Community Psychiatry, 18,* 65–70.

Lemke, S., Moos, R. H., Mehren, B., & Bauvain, M. (1979). *Multiphasic Environmental Assessment Procedure (MEAP) hand scoring booklet.* Palo Alto, CA: Sheltered Care Project of the Social Ecology Laboratory.

Mellody, J. (1979). *Delivery assessment of boarding homes: Technical report, Region 3.* Philadelphia: Department of Health and Human Services.

Minkoff, K. (1979). A map of chronic mental patients. In J. A. Talbott (Ed.), *The chronic mental patient* (pp. 11–37). Washington, DC: American Psychiatric Association.

Moos, R. H. (1974). *The Social Climate Scale: An overview.* Palo Alto, CA: Consulting Psychologists Press.

Moos, R. H. (1976). *The human context.* New York: Wiley.

Moos, R. H., & Lemke, S. (1979). *Multiphasic Environmental Assessment Procedure (MEAP) preliminary manual.* Palo Alto, CA: Sheltered Care Project of the Social Ecology Laboratory.

Morrissey, J. P. (1982). Deinstitutionalizing the mentally ill: Process, outcomes, and new directions. In W. Gore (Ed.), *Deviance and mental illness. Sage Annual Review of Studies of Deviance* (Vol. 6, pp. 147–176). Beverly Hills, CA: Sage Publications.

Moynihan, D. P. (1969). *Maximum feasible misunderstanding* (pp. 21–37). New York: The Free Press.

Neuber, K. A., Atkins, W. T., Jacobson, J. A., & Reuterman, N. A. (1980). *Needs assessment: A model for community planning.* Beverly Hills, CA: Sage Publications.

O'Connor v. Donaldson, 422 U.S. 563, 569 (1975).

O'Donnell, E. J., & Sullivan, M. M. (1974). Service delivery and social action through the neighborhood center: A review of research. In H. W. Demone & D. Harshbarger (Eds.), *A handbook of human service organization* (pp. 133–158). New York: Behavioral Publications.

Paul, B. D. (Ed.). (1955). *Health, culture and community.* New York: Russell Sage Foundation.

Paul, G. L., & Lenz, R. J. (1977). *Psychosocial treatment of chronic mental patients.* Cambridge, MA: Harvard University Press.

Rennie v. Klein, 653 F. 2d 836 (3rd CIR 1981).

Rogers v. Okin, 634 F. 2d 650 (1st CIR 1980).

Rothman, D. J. (1980). *Conscience and convenience: The asylum and its alternatives in progressive America.* Boston: Little, Brown.

Sanders, I. T. (1966). *The community: An introduction to a social system* (2nd ed.). New York: Ronald Press.

Schulberg, H. C., & Wechsler, H. (1974). The uses and misuses of data in assessing mental health needs (pp. 430–441). In H. W. Demone & D. Harshbarger (Eds.), *A handbook of human service organizations.* New York: Behavioral Publications.

Shadish, W., & Bootzin, R. (1981). Nursing homes and chronic mental patients. *Schizophrenia Bulletin, 7,* 488–498.

Talbott, J. A. (1981). The national plan for the chronic mentally ill: A programmatic analysis. *Hospital and Community Psychiatry, 32,* 699.

Turnbull, H. R., III, Ellis, J. W., Boggs, E. M., Brooks, P. O., & Biklen, D. P. (1981). *The least restrictive alternative: Principles and practices.* Washington, DC: American Association on Mental Deficiency.

Walsh, W., & Betz, N. (1985). *Tests and assessment.* Englewood Cliffs, NJ: Prentice-Hall.

Warren, R. L. (1972). *The community in America* (2nd ed.). Chicago: Rand McNally.

Wilmer, H. A. (1981). Defining and understanding the therapeutic community. *Hospital and Community Psychiatry, 32,* 95–99.

Wyatt v. Stickney, 325 F. Supp. 781, 785 (M. D. Ala. 1971); 344 F. Supp. 373, 379–386 (M. D. Ala. 1972).

IV ADDITIONAL COUNSELOR FUNCTIONS

11 Other Counselor Roles and Functions

Two events are having an impact on professional practice and on services to clients. One is the growing technical culture surrounding social services and professional practice (Meyer, 1985). Mental health counselors are often tied to the strict accountability measures of public funding sources. There are increasing controls or guidelines in almost every field of practice. With accountability in mind, many counselors, moreover, have become comfortable with planned short-term, task-centered, action-oriented approaches, and there is increased evidence that these approaches are more effective in helping clients with their life problems than are the older open-ended models whose purposes are different (Meyer, 1985).

The second event is the changing nature of the human services job market. During the 1970s the human services profession experienced an era of unparalleled growth and development. Yet Randolph, Lassiter, and Newell (1986) have explained that the 1980s have been characterized by inflation, declining tax revenues, and reductions in public funding for human services. These changes have caused a consolidation of many activities in community mental health centers. A mental health counselor must now perform many varied functions. Both the diversity and variety highlight the many roles that counselors may enact when bringing services to clients. Some of the roles have been utilized in mental health practice for many years; others are relatively new. This chapter will identify and discuss four more traditional roles, namely, prevention, advocacy, consultation, and education; and two emerging roles: mediation and mentoring. The explanation of each role, however, assumes that the underlying premises of the helping process are that the mental health counselor assists the client in a joint exploration of the problem, the client is given the responsibility for drawing conclusions and making decisions, and the counselor makes a joint exploration of alternative solutions. This helping process orientation has been espoused in this book, and this important perspective provides a basic structure to understand the six roles and functions to be discussed in this chapter.

PREVENTION

Prevention is the inverse side of crisis coping (Barclay, 1984). It is a recognition of factors involved in optimum human development and is particularly tied to the development process of the individual. The topic of prevention has received a great deal of attention in the literature (McMurty, 1985), though the present mental health system may be said to be directed toward tertiary programs, namely, those that attempt to avert further consequences of a problem already manifested. Tertiary prevention involves efforts to keep the problem from getting worse and to rehabilitate the client.

But prevention of mental disorder and the promotion of mental health are among the distinguishing themes of the community mental health movement and are conventionally grouped under one rubic, "primary prevention" (Matus & Nuehring, 1979). Adapted from public health models, primary prevention refers to strengthening the resistance of populations and groups and the offsetting of harmful influences in advance of their impact (Caplan, 1964). DeWild (1981) believed, however, that "the burst of enthusiasm for primary prevention in the sixties has been followed by a series of articles in the seventies trying to explain why the dream of primary prevention has not become a reality" (p. 306). With all the discussion on primary prevention, which will be discussed later in this section, what has been lost in the shuffle is secondary prevention.

Secondary prevention is illustrated by programs that try to identify individuals at risk, for example, for heart disease, and then prescribe remedial activities (such as dieting or reduction of smoking) to avert the onset of the disease (McMurty, 1985). Directions for this approach have been frequently addressed to the problem of child abuse and neglect. Early case finding, predictive screening, and appropriate interventions are important components of this secondary approach. According to McMurty (1985), a significant issue for secondary prevention is whether sufficient information is available to proceed with broader implementation of these prevention programs and, if so, what form these programs should assume.

Though many approaches to prevention still remain largely in the realm of exhortation rather than practice, and much of intervention is still focused on tertiary prevention—preventing further recurrence of an illness—the challenge for the effective delivery of services resides in the primary prevention area. The role of the mental health counselor should be largely focused on the identification of individuals at risk and intervention before illness occurs.

Many primary prevention techniques are new, and newer still is its acceptance as a legitimate and necessary part of any balanced human services program (Shaw & Goodyear, 1984). Mental health programs have traditionally emphasized remediation and therapy over prevention. People with existing problems tend to command the attention of the mental health counselor more than do people who manifest no apparent problems. Yet if counselors can prevent people from developing problems, there should ultimately be, of course, fewer problems to which mental health personnel must attend (Shaw & Goodyear, 1984). Another difficulty faced by primary prevention is demonstrating that an event did not occur because of the intervention, rather than that it would have occurred on its own.

Primary prevention includes efforts aimed at improving the coping skills of groups such as expectant parents and pre-retirees, community planning and development to improve the quality of social conditions and resources, developing programs like genetic counseling and preschool screening for disabilities and disturbances, beginning crisis intervention such as divorce counseling, and the training of other care-givers to sharpen their skills in detection and intervention (Matus & Nuehring, 1979). It now also comprises a broadening range of interventions, including new skills of collaboration, network building, and a new emphasis on alliances with the new manpower sources of informal care-givers and consumer citizens themselves.

Yet while acknowledging the many activities that comprise primary prevention, there is an important practical distinction between the primary level and the secondary and tertiary levels. Gilbert (1982) stated that this involves the dimension of time. Primary prevention takes place before the problem has struck, or at least at some beginning stage at which its symptoms are barely discernible. The main objective of secondary and tertiary prevention is to treat the existing problem, not to deal with its potential aftermath.

Activities labeled as "primary prevention" aim to anticipate life crises, to offset their impact, and to change damaging aspects of the broader social networks that shape human behavior. Matus and Nuehring (1979) identified six categories of activities that constitute primary prevention: (a) program consultation; (b) public information (the agencies' activities); (c) public information (mental health in general); (d) training community care-givers; (e) growth and education groups; and (f) community planning and development.

In other words, prevention has come to be defined as the promotion of mental health in the community. Prevention and primary prevention have become synonymous among many mental health professionals. Cowen (1984) elaborated on an understanding of primary prevention by explaining that:

primary prevention's overarching goal (i.e., to enhance adjustment) can be pursued along two complementary pathways: (a) providing people with skills, competencies, and conditions that facilitate effective adaptation and ward off psychological problems before they occur; and (b) developing interventions designed to short-circuit negative psychological sequelae for those who have experienced risk-augmenting life situations or stressful life events. (p. 485)

An illustration of one program that develops competency-building services is the Human Service Center of Peoria, Illinois. The center's consultation and education department is oriented toward sharing mental health–related skills with the community at large (Lewis & Lewis, 1984). The primary method used is the delivery of educational programs offered to community members or to specific organizations. Workshops address such topics as alcoholism and addiction, child abuse, communication, crisis intervention, coping with chronic illness, leisure education, stress management, suicide, sexuality, parenting, changing roles, aging, depression, and child development.

It is apparent, consequently, that primary prevention can take many forms. It is more group than individually oriented, and it must have a before-the-fact quality, that is, be targeted to groups not yet experiencing significant maladjustment. Primary prevention must also be intentional, that is, rest on a solid knowledge base suggesting that the program holds potential either for improving psychological health or maladaptation (Shaw & Goodyear, 1984).

With an understanding of the meaning of prevention for mental health, the question may be asked, "How would the counselor conduct primary prevention?" Considering Bolman and Westman's (1967) three major categories of preventive services, namely, person-centered programs, family-centered programs, and society-centered programs, what would be the steps that one would take to achieve prevention goals in these areas? Cowen (1984) has identified a number of steps, with each step tapping different tasks and skills, and each presenting its own special set of issues and problems. These steps are:

1. *Developing a generative base.* This implies learning about the types of interventions that may hold promise for a particular population and positive (primary prevention) payoff. This development is shaped by a knowledge of related issues that may feed into the problem, and can include areas of education, sociology, economics, family relations, and social ecology. This knowledge base or primary prevention is much broader than the mental health fields as classically defined (Cowen, 1984), and accessing this comprehensive information calls for communication between mental health professionals and members of other disciplines. For example, if the mental health counselor is considering primary preventive efforts in the area of family-centered programs, such issues as job loss, housing, and health care opportunities can have a serious effect on the family's adjustment.

2. *Developing a program concept.* Once a knowledge base is established, then a need develops for specific primary prevention interventions. Questions will be asked, such as: "Which specific competencies should the program convey?" and "Which program elements can forestall such negative outcomes?" Other important questions remain to be answered concerning the particular people

and skills on which to focus. In a family-centered program, for example, it might be more worthwhile to target the program to very young children on the rational ground that skills acquired so early would have maximal potential for doing good (Cowen, 1984). But as Cowen (1984) emphasized, a generative knowledge base helps both to identify needed types of primary prevention programs and to frame an early guiding concept of program goals and mechanisms.

3. *Developing a workable program technology.* This step implies that from the knowledge of the targeted population, and an understanding of related issues that may influence the adjustment of this population, a program is developed that is in harmony with the target population's needs, interest patterns, motivational systems, and natural styles. Cowen (1984) believed that in order to make the transition from the generative knowledge base and program concept to a specific program strategy requires: (a) a knowledge of the defining characteristics of the population to be served; (b) use of people who have close, everyday contacts with the target group as sounding boards and devil's advocates about specific program components; and (c) piloting of specific program elements.

4. *Conducting the program.* At this step the goal is to be sure that the planned program is in fact well-implemented. Initial program guidelines may have to be modified when initial feedback about the program is provided. If the primary prevention program is conducted in a group format, there may be problems of group management and dynamics theoretically extraneous to the program's purposes and scope (Cowen, 1984). For example, a children's group may be disrupted by one child's flagrant acting-out or attention-seeking behaviors. Such structural programs detract from the transmission of intended program substance and make for significant departures from a program's ideal scenario. In other words, programs must allow for needed corrections and unanticipated discoveries. Mechanisms must be built for identifying problems when they occur. Training meetings, regular observations of the program in action, consultation, periodic progress reports of program events, and regular program review meetings involving supervisors and those in line program training—all are potentially helpful mechanisms for identifying and resolving practical problems (Cowen, 1984).

5. *Evaluating the program.* In order for the primary prevention program to be useful to others, there should be evidence of effectiveness through careful program evaluation. Yet there are special problems involved in evaluating primary prevention programs, which include subject attrition, conditions that shift during the study, and associated problems of research in the community milieu (Bloom, 1977). Suggestions on how to conduct the program evaluation itself are discussed in chapter 12.

In conducting a primary prevention effort, it is apparent that, as mentioned earlier, many skills are necessary for the mental health counselor. But the potential for preventive intervention is almost boundless, and in the words of Adolf Meyer, written more than 50 years ago:

> Communities have to learn what they produce in the way of mental problems and waste of human opportunities, and with such knowledge they will rise from mere charity and mere mending, or hasty propaganda, to well-balanced early care, prevention and general gain of health. (cited in Brand, 1968, p. 69)

ADVOCACY

Effective primary prevention efforts focus on environmental factors in mental health and attempt to bring about positive change. The social environment can be health-promoting or illness-provoking, but a major concern in mental health is that many people feel powerless over their own lives (Lewis & Lewis, 1984). To alleviate these feelings, counselors should recognize the importance of attempting to change the environments that influence potential clients. In other words, mental health professionals should attempt to alter reality. One way to facilitate this change is by advocacy functions.

Although many counselors may have a strong professional identification with advocacy, the literature on the activity is sparse and scattered. There was a surge of articles in the late 1960s and early 1970s, but only occasional comments have appeared since that time (Sosin & Caulum, 1983). Relatively little is known about advocacy styles and strategies, and almost nothing is known about what methods are most effective (Sosin & Caulum, 1983).

Advocacy involves directed activity on behalf of individuals or organizations in relation to mandated or proposed services; it is ultimately designed to assist in the protection of rights. Generically, advocacy means to plead the cause of another individual and to follow through with action in support of that cause (Tesolowski, Rosenberg, & Stein, 1983). Consequently, a mental health counselor-advocate is one who is the client's supporter, the advisor, the champion, and, if need be, the client's representative in dealings with the court, the police, the social agency, and other organizations that affect one's well-being. Sosin and Caulum (1983) believed that the focus of an advocacy definition should be on the activities involved in advocacy, and not on the overall role. Therefore, the advocate is simply defined as one who, at a given moment in time, is carrying out an advocacy attempt. Sosin and Caulum (1983) described advocacy as:

> An attempt, having a greater than zero probability of success, by an individual or group to influence another individual or group to make a decision that would not have been made otherwise and that concerns the welfare or interests of a third party who is in a less powerful status than the decision maker. (p. 13)

This definition, although implying that the advocacy activity is not necessarily appropriate for all situations in which a specific decision or problem is being considered, includes everything from political advocacy to child advocacy. Advocacy is an attempt, in other words, to influence a decision maker using such techniques as persuasion or coercion.

During the past 20 years, several categories of advocates have been identified. Some of these categories have been referred to as surrogate parents, professional advocates, citizen advocates, ethical review boards, and intracommunity action networks (Tesolowski, et al., 1983). Each advocacy category has its own functions and goals, and utilizes its own methods to accomplish its objectives.

Surrogate parents, for example, might include those persons who, when parents or guardians are unavailable, are appointed by a local education agency or a court to represent personally a handicapped child in the educational process through proper identification, evaluation, and placement. Professional advocates usually focus upon the protection of client rights and generally work in a direct-care human service profession. Citizen advocates are volunteers who may be matched with such a population as handicapped persons. The ethical review board has been established as a safeguard against inhumane treatment and the violation of human and civil rights of individuals (Tesolowski et al., 1983). This review board can operate as a screening mechanism at two levels: (a) for the review and modification of all proposed individual and general service programs, and (b) for consideration of institutional policies. Finally, intracommunity action network is a resource through which local government services and private sector merchants are integrated to assist a specific, needy population.

Similar forms of advocacy have been identified as case advocacy or policy advocacy. In the former, the mental health counselor is an advocate for the client and his or her welfare. In the latter, the counselor works as an advocate of societal change or changes in agency policy. Nulman (1983) maintained that in policy advocacy the professional plays essentially a disruptive role. The task is to remedy, to change, whereas institutions generally operate to minimize change. To accomplish this change the counselor has to work to shape, to select, and to influence policy. Many claim that case advocacy is the best technique (Sosin & Caulum, 1983).

Another important issue concerning advocacy is the appropriate level of intervention. Advocacy can occur at the individual level, the administrative level, or the policy level. Each level of advocacy represents an attempt to influence a different type of decision (Sosin & Caulum, 1983). At the individual level, advocacy focuses on the manner in which a specific client or group is dealt with in a single, concrete situation. A question concerning the acceptance of a client for services is an example of advocacy at the individual level. Administrative-level advocacy attempts to convince decision makers to change agency regulations — such as the verification procedures used in public welfare. Policy-level advocacy attempts to convince decision makers to alter basic rules or laws, such as the overall nature of the criteria relating to national social welfare eligibility (Sosin & Caulum, 1983).

The issue of the appropriate strategy is a significant one in advocacy. Gamson (1968) identified three strategies: coercive, utilitarian, and normative. Coercive strategies rely on conflict, dissension, and complaint. Utilitarian strategies rely on bargaining and negotiation. Normative strategies rely on moral arguments and the mobilization of common values. Sosin and Caulum (1983) believed that normative strategies are best used in an alliance situation, namely, the two parties share a basic understanding about advocacy and perhaps about the needs of clients. The role of the advocate is "thus to mobilize these widely shared, normative sentiments" (Sosin & Caulum, 1983, p. 16). An adversarial context often calls for coercive strategies. In the absence of the willingness to listen or shared understandings, it might be difficult to use normal procedures to get the attention of the decision maker.

If a mental health counselor is to utilize advocacy skills, how should they be implemented, and what are the components of these skills? These are many and include:

1. *Timing.* The helping process, for example, can be a difficult one beset with an incredible number of stumbling blocks, hurdles, and pitfalls. The counselor should be aware when a decision maker is most attuned to listen to an advocacy position. On a legislative level to introduce legislation to change policy, it has been suggested that introducing a bill early in a governmental session increases the chances of favorable consideration (Dear & Patti, 1981).

2. *Support.* It is advisable for the mental health counselor to gather as much support as possible. The value of multiple support tends to be enhanced even further when at least one of the supportive people has a distinct position of authority or credibility on the particular issue. A mental health counselor, for example, who may be advocating for services for a particular child will enhance one's efforts when support is gained from such professionals as a school psychologist, when it is warranted, and the child's teacher. Multiple supports are likely to make the advocacy more visible, and they multiply the power that can be applied to push the issue past crucial obstacles. On a policy level, the advocate of social legislation should seek to obtain the support or sponsorship of the majority party.

3. *Knowledge.* If an advocate is to be successful, an understanding both of the appropriate laws or policy and how the human delivery system works is essential. Many advocacy attempts have failed because the mental health counselor has not taken the time to become familiar with the intricacies of the "system," and who the influential people within that system are who make the important decisions. Included in the knowledge is an awareness of the vital interests of the decision maker. When an issue touches on the keen concerns of decision makers, support for the steps to change can more readily follow.

4. *Compromise.* When appropriate, successful advocacy is based on compromise, gaining support, and nullifying opposition (Dear & Patti, 1981). When advocating for a particular issue, negotiations may have to be made. In other words, without serious harm to the client, a mental health counselor may have to modify somewhat one's position in order to gain needed support. This is especially true on the legislative level. There is "probably nothing more axiomatic in the legislative process than the notion that successful action requires an accommodation to diverse and sometimes conflicting interests" (Dear & Patti, 1981, p. 294).

5. *Communication.* The ability to listen, to present one's position cogently, to understand the needs of the other person, and to confront in a facilitative manner are not only counseling skills, but also advocacy skills. These counseling skills help to establish a better relationship with the other party. They engender more receptivity for one's position.

These skills, as well as the advocacy process itself, can be illustrated in the advocacy for those with mental health problems. Mental health professionals have always held that (a) their primary duty is to help the client, and (b) no one is usually more qualified than they to know what assistance the client needs (Willetts, 1980). For years, moreover, the plight of mental patients was ignored. The perceptions of the outside world combined with the atmosphere of the hospital or institution tend to make the patient feel dependent and to take away initiative. Clients need advocates to speak for them if abuses occur. The client is often poor, uninformed about the human service delivery process, and intimidated by what is going on either in the institution, agency, or with the helping professional.

A basic issue regarding advocacy for clients with mental health problems is who the advocate should be. Lawyers are expensive, for example, and it is debatable whether social resources should be used to pay lawyers for case advocacy (Willetts, 1980). Many complaints of clients can be satisfactorily resolved simply by talking things over among all parties. In the selection of the advocate, attention should be given to whether an inhouse advocate is more effective than one from outside the institution or agency. The problem of conflict of interest arises, and perhaps one way to lessen the possibility of conflicts of interest is for the advocate to be an employee of a separate but related mental health program, such as a state employee working in a locally funded program (Willetts, 1980).

Once the issue over who is the advocate for the client is resolved, then advocacy steps might include investigating complaints, talking with the client, showing a commitment for the client's rights through an interest to learn about the client's needs and how the "situation" could be better, writing a report or presenting verbally the issue to relevant parties, and following up on any decisions that are made. The communication of the relevant issues for the client imply timing, the gaining of needed support, a knowledge of the policies and "system," and the ability to compromise, when necessary, while still respond· ing to the basic complaint.

State-mandated advocacy programs are spreading throughout the United States (Willetts, 1980). Although each state may design its own program, the responsibility for representing the rights of clients often falls on the mental health counselor. With more formally institutionalized persons, for example, living in the community and receiving outpatient care, the need for counselors as advocates will increase. While advocacy requires a sustained immersion in social equality endeavors (Tesolowski, et al., 1983), human service programs must facilitate the development of their professionals as advocates.

CONSULTATION

Since passage of the Community Mental Health Act in 1963, consultation has become recognized as a more broadly defined helping process (Kurpius, 1978). This act specifically stated that consultation services were to become an "essential" part of the community mental health programs of the future. Kurpius (1978) explained that "the intent of this early legislation was to urge the helping professions to move from individual and small group remedial activities as the primary caregiving intervention toward more developmental and preventive approaches" (p. 320).

There is no one universally agreed upon definition of consultation (Kurpius & Robinson, 1978), but a number of diverse definitions delineate its key components. Ohlsen (1983) defined it as "an activity in which a professional helps another person in regard to a third. . . . " (p. 347). Kurpius (1978) agreed and stated "by definition the process . . . tends to be triadic (consultant, consultee, and client or client system)" (p. 335). The ethical code of the American Association for Counseling and Development goes one step further and defines consultation as "A voluntary relationship between a professional helper and help-needing individual, group or social units in which the consultant is providing help to the client(s) in defining and solving a work-related problem or potential problem with a client or client system." Finally, Caplan (1970) explained that mental health consultation has been defined as:

> A process of interaction between two professional persons—the consultant, who is a specialist, and the consultee, who invokes the consultant's help in regard to a current work problem with which he is having some difficulty and which he has decided is within the other's area of specialized competence. (p. 19)

Bloom (1977) believed that it is important to distinguish consultation from other mental health activities with which it is sometimes confused. He stated that it can be differentiated from supervision on the grounds that (a) the consultant may not be of the same professional specialty as the consultee, (b) the consultant has no administrative responsibility for the work of the consultee, (c) consultation may be irregular in character rather than continuous, and (d) the consultant is not in a position of power with respect to the consultee. Bloom (1977) added that consultation can be distinguished from education on the basis of (a) the relative freedom of the consultee to accept or reject the ideas of the consultant, (b) the lack of a planned curriculum on the part of the consultant, and (c) the absence of any evaluation or assessment of the consultee's progress by the consultant. Bloom (1977) further mentioned that consultation is different from counseling because in the latter there is a clear contractual relationship between an individual designated as a client and another individual designated as a counselor. Also, the goal of consultation is improved work performance rather than improved personal adjustment. Consultation is different, moreover, from collaboration, because in the case of the former there is no implication that the consultant will participate with the consultee in the implementation of any plans. The task of the consultant is to assist the consultee in meeting his or her work responsibilities more effectively.

In its earliest stage of development during the late 1940s and early 1950s, consultation was viewed as a direct service to clients or to client systems (Kurpius, 1978). As more experience was gained with this direct service approach, it was recognized that it would be beneficial to include the consultee in the problem-solving process. By the end of the 1950s, consequently, a major breakthrough in mental health consultation resulted—the consultee became active in the consultation process. During this time Gerald Caplan's work became decisive in formulating a direction for consultation. Among his contributions was the innovative concept of "theme interference," defined by Caplan (1964) as "a symbolic inhibition of free perception and communication between consultee and client and a concomitant disorder of objectivity" (p. 223). Theme interferences reduce the consultee's effectiveness in working with clients, and the technique of theme-interference reduction employed by the mental health consultant is designed to modify the line of reasoning being followed by the consultee as well as the consultee's feelings (Bloom, 1977).

In the 1960s the consultant was established as a trainer. With the assumption that the consultant had expert knowledge and skills for problem solving, organizations hired consultants to educate their members in areas of need. Kurpius and Robinson (1978) explained that this area of need could have been defined by either the consultees or the consultant. When the consultant had the responsibility of defining the problem, the purpose of the consultation was to get a diagnosis or critical evaluation of the problem. Although the practice continues, at the present time there is a rapid movement toward an even more generic purpose of consultation in which the consultant facilitates the consultee's use of one's own skills and knowledge to resolve difficulties (Berkowitz, 1973; Brokes, 1975).

The process of consultation is molded by the goals of the consultant. The typical steps in the process, as stated by Kurpius and Robinson (1978), are: (a) building a working relationship, (b) gathering information, (c) identifying the problem, (d) exploring possible solutions, (e) implementing an intervention, and (f) evaluating the effectiveness of the intervention.

Although this process has many steps, consultation models have been developed that articulate a philosophy on how to conduct these basic steps. Four of these models are identified by Kurpius and Brubaker (1976):

1. *Provision.* In this type of consultation, the consultant provides a direct service to consultees who do not have the time, inclination, or perceived skills to deal with a particular problem area. Historically, this mode of consultation was the first to develop (Kurpius & Robinson, 1978) and was used extensively in the 1940s and early 1950s. The advantage of the model is that experts can handle difficult problems and thus leave consultees free to manage their other duties without work conflicts. Schein (1978) referred to this form of consultation as the expert model because of the role the consultant plays.

2. *Prescription.* This form of consultation does not require the consultant to bring about a change or "cure" as in the provision model. Instead, the consultant advises the consultee about what is wrong with the targeted third party and what should be done about it. A good way to conceptualize this method is to draw an analogy with the traditional medical model, where a patient's problem is diagnosed and a prescription to rectify the situation is given (Schein, 1978).

3. *Mediation.* In this model, consultants act as "coordinators." Their main function is to help unify the services of a variety of people who are trying to solve a problem. They accomplish this goal in one of two ways: (a) they either coordinate the services already being provided, or (b) they create an alternative plan of services that represents a mutually acceptable synthesis of several solutions.

An example of a situation where a consultant would function in this role is in a community mental health agency where a client with both mental retardation and mental health problems is receiving a variety of services that are confusing to the client. Through mediation, services are offered in a more systematic way and the client, consequently, appears less disrupted.

4. *Collaboration.* Consultants who operate from this position are facilitators of the problem-solving process. Their main task is to get their consultees actively involved in finding solutions to the present difficulties they have with clients. Thus, consultees must define their problems clearly, analyze them thoroughly, design workable solutions, and then implement and evaluate their own plan of action. Setting up an atmosphere in which this process can happen is a major task for collaboration consultants. It requires the use of a number of interpersonal conseling skills, as, for example, empathy, active listening, and structuring. In addition, to make the process work, consultants must be highly intelligent and analytical thinkers, who are able to generate enthusi-

asm, optimism, and self-confidence in others. They must be able to integrate affective, behavioral, and cognitive dimensions of problem solving and know how to use each appropriately.

Bloom (1977) explained another perspective on the different types or "models" of consultation. He used the four varieties of consultation suggested by Caplan (1963), which are:

1. Client-centered case consultation: In this variety of consultation the primary goal is to help the consultee deal with the presented case. To accomplish this goal, the consultant uses his or her specialized skills and knowledge to assist the consultee in making an assessment of the client's problem and to recommend how best to deal with the problem (Bloom, 1977).
2. Consultee-centered case consultation: The consultant attempts to identify the consultee's difficulties in handling the case and to remedy these difficulties, whether they stem from insufficient skill, knowledge, self-confidence, or objectivity.
3. Program-centered administrative consultation: The consultant's primary goal is to suggest some actions the consultee might take in order to effect the development, expansion, or modification of a clinical or agency program. The consultant draws not only on general mental health skills, but also on his or her understanding of the functioning of social systems and of the principles of mental health program administration (Bloom, 1977).
4. Consultee-centered administrative consultation: In this instance, the consultant attempts to identify difficulties within the consultee that appear to be limiting his or her effectiveness in instituting program change.

Within these varied models there is one particular approach that has many applications for mental health counselors. Called *behavioral consultation*, the counselor uses social learning theory to understand and treat the client's problematic behavior but also to examine the consultee's behavior and conduct the consultation process. Guided by learning principles, the consultant reviews the interrelationships between both the client and the consultee as well as those between the consultee and the consultant (Russell, 1978). Russell (1978) stated that more than likely the most frequently used consultation technique for increasing or maintaining new consultee behaviors is positive reinforcement, such as verbal praise or encouragement when the consultee attains specific objectives. Another technique used to establish a new consultee behavior is role-play, in which the consultee practices the new behaviors and the consultant assumes the role of the client. As in modeling, role-play offers the consultee the opportunity to discriminate significant antecedent events, perform the new behaviors, react to typical client behaviors, and experience the consequences associated with the proposed behaviors (Russell, 1978).

As the models and approaches to consultation can be diverse, so are the roles that consultants can assume. The consultant may function as a provider of direct services so that the consultant, assuming direct responsibility for a "cure" for the problem, becomes the problem solver. Often a person called a consultant is hired as a trainer or educator (Kurpius & Robinson, 1978). Within an agency setting, for example, the consultant may serve as an educator by teaching the staff the most newly developed techniques in counseling interventions. Also, the function of negotiation is sometimes filled by a consultant who helps a client deal with the questions of who does what, how, and with whom? (Kurpius & Robinson, 1978).

Schein (1978) provided a somewhat different perspective by discussing the persistent dilemma that faces many consultants, namely, how to be helpful in a situation in which there is a choice between telling others what to do, being a content expert, or facilitating through various interventions a better problem-solving process that permits those same others to solve the problem for themselves. If the consultant were to function in the expert model of consultation, one would be hired as the resource of specific information or expertise, or one would be hired into an organization to do a diagnosis and suggest various remedies for whatever ailments are found (Schein, 1978). In the process consultation model the consultant does not know the solution but has skills in helping a client to figure out his or her solution, or, the consultant may have ideas and possible solutions of one's own but for various reasons decides that a better solution will result if one withholds his or her content suggestions and, instead, consciously concentrates on helping the group or client system to solve their own problem (Schein, 1978).

With these varied roles that a consultant may enact, there are specific skills that override the different approaches to doing consultation. Havelock (1973) and Kurpius and Brubaker (1976) identified many skills, such as being a skilled relationship builder, utilizing basic counseling skills of listening, attending, reflecting accurately, and probing objectively. These authors also believed that the skill to perform problem assessments is vital, because unless the problem is correctly assessed and defined, the consultation process will be ineffective in that resulting change will often treat the symptom, not the problem. Also, the skill of being able to bargain and negotiate is often necessary.

Kurpius and Robinson (1978) added that when the consultant functions as a trainer, the ability "to discern significant content details of the related problem situation and characteristics of the audience or client system members proves helpful in planning and implementing training strategies" (p. 322). Also, skills in areas such as conflict resolution, team building, or behavior modification enhance a consultant's effectiveness. "Observing accurately, pinpointing problem areas, and exploring alternatives and consequences are all necessary facets in planning effective behavior change programs" (Kurpius & Robinson, 1978, p. 322).

Bloom (1977) suggested that an effective consultant needs to have both substantial competence in the areas that are of concern to the consultee and certain general personality traits. He explained that "these traits should include the capacity to be permissive and accepting, the ability to share ideas constructively, the ability to relate effectively to other people, personal warmth, and an awareness of the subtleties of interpersonal relationships" (p. 123). Bloom (1977) also reported on a study by Robins, Spencer, and Frank (1970) which examined these factors influencing the outcome of consultation. These authors were able to show that the more prepared the consultants, the better the outcome; the more interested the consultant was in the project, the better the outcome; the more supportive the consultant was, the better the outcome; the more familiar the consultees were with the consultants prior to the consultation, the better the outcome; and the higher the agreement among the participants on the purposes of the consultation, the better the outcome. Yet Bloom (1977) believes that studies are still needed that attempt to determine whether personal attributes of the consultant allow the consultation to be effective even if the consultant has little or no competence in the substantive area of consultation.

There are many skills, consequently, that the consultant should possess. All of these skills are utilized when actually performing the work of consultation. Dustin and Ehly (1984) suggested a five-stage model of consultation along with counselor techniques and behaviors that go with each. Though the model assumes that the consultant is working in a school setting with either a parent or a teacher, it has usefulness outside of that particular environment.

Stage 1 of this model is *phasing in*. It centers on relationship building. The consultant at this juncture in the process uses such skills as active listening, self-disclosure, and empathy. A basis of trust is thus promoted.

Stage 2 consists of *problem identification*. At this time, consultants use focusing skills to determine whether a suspected third party problem really exists. They may also employ other counseling techniques such as paraphrasing, restatement, genuineness, and goal setting.

Stage 3 is *implementation*. Strategies are defined and a time frame is set. Feedback is an important part of this process. Flexibility, dealing with resistance and negative feelings, and patience are other counselor skills involved.

Stage 4 is *follow-up and evaluation*. It merges with Stage 3 at times. The focus of the stage, however, is distinct and it concentrates on the results gained from the consultation process, especially if the consultee is satisfied with the outcome of changes. Counselor skills involved in this stage are risk taking, openness, and persistence. These skills are especially important if it appears the consultee is dissatisfied or frustrated.

Stage 5 is *termination*. In this stage the consultant helps bring closure to previous activities. Some relationship skills, such as empathy and genuineness, are again employed. Giving and asking for feedback at this time are also important. It is vital that the consultant and consultee evaluate what was most profitable for each and what aspects of the procedure were less effective.

These steps can be cogently illustrated when consultation is performed with community mental health agencies. Werner (1978) identified three factors that contribute to a rationale for doing consultation with community agencies. The first factor pertains to issues in providing clinical treatment. Werner (1978) believes that many persons seeking clinical treatment at a particular community mental health center have many problems that are not strictly psychological—many of these problems require the resources of a number of other community agencies, who may be the real experts in dealing with the environmental and social realities of daily living. Consequently, the exclusive focusing on remediation for one and all clients who come to the community agency may not be feasible. The agency may not be able to allocate economic resources for costly clinical treatment, and it simply may be more cost effective to purchase, when needed, consultation services. A second factor concerns the reality that many persons seeking help at a community agency are for various reasons cut off from their natural emotional support system and require immediate and large amounts of basic survival and emotional support assistance (Werner, 1978). But due to the lack of funding and training resources available to these community agencies, many of the front-line workers possess little formal training. There is an immense amount of emotional stress on these workers, and consultation opportunities could alleviate this problem.

The third factor relates to the possibility that mental health consultants can build helping relationships with existing community agencies and develop their trust and confidence to a point of mutual enhancement and strength (Werner, 1978). With this development a better opportunity exists for marshaling the community resources for solving difficult community problems. Haller and Monahan (1972) stated this concept when they described mental health consultation as an approach to community change through the improvement of existing social agencies.

Mental health consultation is defined, consequently, by Werner (1978) as

> an interaction between two or more people—the consultants who are mental health specialists, and the consultees who are involved in some aspect of the comunity's social service network and who require the consultant's help in regard to a current agency or community problem that is relevant to enhancing the delivery of social services or identification and development of needed social services contributing to the mental health of agency recipients or community members. (p. 365)

This definition of consultation implies that ultimate responsibility of the identifed problem remains with the consultee. The major goals of the consultation efforts is to enable the consultee or community to handle a similar problem in the future (Werner, 1978).

Werner (1978) explained the different levels of consultation intervention within community mental health agencies, such as client-centered case consultation, consultee-centered case consultation (the consultant collaboratively identifies consultee problems in dealing with the client), program-centered administration consultation, consultee-centered administrative consultation, and community-centered ad hoc consultation. Each of these levels of consultation can be applied to primary, secondary, or tertiary prevention areas. Yet Werner (1978) believed that primary prevention is where the levels are most efficiently employed.

Currently a large amount of professional time is allocated to consultation. Although the potential of consultation remains high, there is still little documentation on its effectiveness as a strategy for preventing mental health problems. But consultation has a secure place in the mental health movement because it has a measurable positive impact on consultees. Although the problems inherent in identifying the positive effects on this population are great, consultation programs have resulted in increased job satisfaction, increased productivity, and decreased turnover in the consultee group (Bloom, 1977).

MEDIATION

One of the increasing roles for mental health counselors in the United States is that of a mediator. Conciliation courts in many states now offer mediation as a court-related service for people in divorce. In 1978, the Law Enforcement Action Agency (LEAA) funded Neighborhood Justice Centers in Atlanta, Kansas City, and Los Angeles. Individuals with domestic, business, landlord/tenant, neighborhood, and legal conflicts can walk into one of these centers and resolve their disputes with a mediator instead of taking them to court (Kessler, 1979). Mediation has also been extended to educational institutions. Counseling centers at many universities have offered mediation as a free service to students and employees where conflict can be safely worked through.

Mediation has been defined by Witty (1980) as the "facilitation of an agreement between two or more disputing parties by an agreed upon third party" (p. 4). Each party agrees to utilize the services of a mediator, but the outcome is an agreement made by the disputants themselves. Mediation uses a cooperative rather than competitive conflict resolution. Its focus is "where do we go from here" rather than finding fault. Its ingredients are self-disclosure rather than deception, empathy rather than intimidation, self-imposed rather than other-imposed decisions, and creative alternatives rather than win/lose positions (Kessler, 1979; Koopman, 1985).

Mediation, like another social process, may be analyzed along both instrumental and expressive dimensions (Kolb, 1985). From the instrumental perspective, actions taken by the mediator are understood in terms of their immediate goal—a settlement. In this view, tactics that mediators use to learn about the issues and the players, or to gauge priorities and foster movement on the disputed issues, may be analyzed for the substantive contribution the tactics make toward these goals. Expressive behavior concerns the symbolic messages mediators convey about themselves (Kolb, 1985). Such behavior is meant to impress the parties with the practitioner's ability and skill. Kolb (1985) believed that in a context where formal power is lacking and behavioral skills are paramount, "it is impossible to understand fully how mediators contribute to dispute settlement without also considering both the explicit and tacit ways expressive features of the process are managed" (p. 12).

In explaining mediation, Chandler (1985) described several principles on which mediation is based. They are:

1. Mediation seems to be most successful when there is some ongoing personal connection or personal interaction between the disputants. Because the process is voluntary and noncoercive, disputants who come to mediation must be willing to discuss their concerns.
2. Mediation is most effective when both parties are willing to express personal wants and needs. Mediation could provide a valuable mechanism for allowing people to communicate with each other.
3. The mediation process stresses mutual agreements in which both sides win. In mediation the counselor works to emphasize the bonds between the participants and encourages broad discussion of the issues so that all viewpoints are expressed. As Chandler (1985) stated, "A conflict-resolving system for persons interested in maintaining and enhancing their relationship may also function to prevent future conflict, stress, and disputes" (p. 347).
4. Mediation is believed to be most successful when there is a relatively egalitarian relationship between the disputants.
5. People are more likely to adhere to agreements they understand and have an integral part in making than in agreements that are externally imposed. The mediation process documents the areas of agreement between the parties. The agreement is written in the participant's own words and accurately states the items to which they have agreed.
6. Mediation is a process of joint advocacy, which, as Chandler (1985) believed, "empowers people and enhances their sense of dignity and self-worth while preserving the responsible aspects of self-determination" (p. 348).

From an understanding of both the meaning and identified principles of mediation, one can surmise that the task of the mediator is a difficult one. A mediator is still an outsider to a dispute and really has no power to compel the involved parties to resolve their differences. Kolb (1985) explained that what direct and indirect influence mediators have emanates from their person, their reputation and skill, and the parties' ongoing assessment of them during the case. Also, it is generally acknowledged by practitioners and observers that the ability to make a contribution in the dispute depends on how the mediator is viewed by the parties involved (Kolb, 1985). In other words, if mediators are to influence parties into rethinking their positions and into modifying these positions in order to achieve some form of compromise agreement, then practitioners must be seen as competent and credible.

To express this competency and credibility, it is helpful if the mediator follows certain steps in the mediation process. Mediation itself is usually a short-term (one to three sessions), structured, decision-making process (Kessler, 1979). The steps that a mediator may follow are:

Step 1. The structuring of the process is done in this first step, and at this beginning stage the mediator (a) establishes a cooperative tone, (b) sets the rules, (c) obtains a commitment to the process, and (d) foreshadows what is to come (Kessler, 1979). During the first meeting the mediator will introduce oneself, explain one's credentials and agency, discuss the mediator's function, and announce something of one's intentions for how the process will be run—informally—and the kind of cooperation one expects from the parties (Kolb, 1985). Kessler (1979) believed that "a good rule of thumb in mediation is the greater the mistrust of the two parties, the clearer the rules of the process need to be" (p. 195). In divorce mediation, for example, Kessler (1979) explained that these rules should be initially negotiated and written out. Some of these rules might include issues of confidentiality, whether the sessions will be taped, whether the individuals will disclose fully any information pertinent to the conflict, and the necessity of putting anger aside and dealing with the concerns in a fair and equitable fashion.

It is important during this step for the mediator to build confidence in oneself. Such confidence can be facilitated by discussing one's job and one's intimate knowledge about the mediation process. During this step, moreover, which Chandler (1985) calls the "forum phase," the mediator explores the issues and gauges the appropriateness of the conflict or mediation. If mediation is appropriate, the mediator explains the process and secures an agreement for his or her involvement from the participants. Then the mediator can begin the information-gathering activities, which could include both face-to-face interactions with all parties or individuals and confidential caucuses with one party at a time (Chandler, 1985).

Step 2. Identified by Chandler (1985) as the "strategic-planning phase," the mediator examines all the information gathered, reviews the history of the conflict, and assesses the issues, positions, and interests involved. This step first demands learning the issues and the background of the conflict, and questioning the parties about the facts of their dispute. The problem is viewed as one of facts, but these facts are analyzed and, if necessary, the mediator may reconvene the parties if some issues remain unclear or the mediator feels that an issue has not been fully explored. But the mediator wants to create the impression, through the interchange of information, that these "facts" matter and what may be resolved will more than likely be shaped by the "facts" surrounding any proposed agreement. Toward the end of this phase, moreover, after the information has been evaluated, then the mediator begins to develop a design or specific plan of action and asks the disputants to become active in the process.

   Step 3. Identified by Chandler (1985) as the "problem-solving phase," the mediator works with all parties to define the potential solutions to the problem. The counselor may use either negotiation, creative problem solving, joint meetings, and private caucuses, all directed toward the goal of helping the parties come to specific agreements. The agreements themselves are written solutions that the disputants develop themselves. The determination of the content of these agreements remains with the disputants, according to Chandler (1985). During this step the role of the mediator is to create a climate of agreement in which the parties ready themselves to negotiate a solution to the conflict.

   Though following these steps insures some structure to the mediation process, mediation does not function equally well with all types of cases. Studies of programs that handle a wide variety of disputes found that the likelihood of mediation and the stability of agreements vary among different types of cases (Cook, Roehl, & Sheppard, 1980; Davis, Tichane, & Grayson, 1980). Certain cases, such as more serious, ongoing disputes between persons with a continuing relationship, are likely to be mediated but are also prone to agreement breakdowns and to further problems between the parties after the mediation hearing (Roehl & Cook, 1985). On the contrary, disputes over money and/or property are concrete, and they may lack room for compromise when compared to the promises made in agreements in interpersonal disputes. Roehl and Cook (1985) believe that agreements may be difficult to formulate when positions in money disputes are entrenched. But once made, such concrete agreements are easier to keep, and the disputants are apt to have infrequent contact, making future problems unlikely.

   In different settings, however, under different sponsors and philosophies, mediation programs have consistently shown that a high proportion of mediated cases end in agreements satisfactory to the parties involved and are upheld by both (Davis et al., 1980; Roehl & Cook, 1985; Schwartzkoff & Morgan, 1982). Research indicates that disputing parties typically hold positive views of mediation: They feel satisfied with the process and would return if a dispute arose in the future (Roehl & Cook, 1985). Speed is another measure of the effectiveness of mediation. Mediation hearings are typically held within a week or two of intake, considerably faster than the usual time required for final court disposition (Roehl & Cook, 1985). In summary, the evidence consistently shows that, across the criteria of major importance, the basic mechanism of mediation can be effective in resolving a wide variety of disputes in a lasting manner and to the satisfaction of disputants. It appears to be an increasingly attractive alternative to either court processing or avoiding disputes (Roehl & Cook, 1985).

MENTORING

A role that is emerging for counselors is one of mentoring. Mentoring itself is not new. It may date back to the Neolithic Age or earlier (Gerstein, 1985). What is new, according to Gerstein (1985), is that this common human practice is being recognized and accepted by major business corporations; colleges, universities, and schools; and various agencies, foundations, and associations as a formal component of overall career and human resource development.

Mentoring is defined as the process by which a trusted and experienced supervisor or advisor takes a personal and direct interest in the development and education of younger or less experienced individuals (Krupp, 1982). The research demonstrates that a mentoring relationship helps the mentor, the less experienced person, and the organization involved (Lester & Johnson, 1981; Lynch, 1980; Vaillant, 1977). Alleman, Cochran, Doverspike, and Newman (1984) found mentoring to be a behavioral phenomenon not dependent on personal traits. Gerstein (1985) reported that mentoring relationships can be established or enriched by learning or encouraging mentor-like behavior rather than by selecting certain types of people to serve as mentors. Moreover, Farren, Gray, and Kaye (1984) looked at mentoring as a process that brings added power to organizational drive, and they focused more on the formal programs of mentoring. Though these programs must be monitored carefully because of such problems as poor chemistry between mentor and mentee, expectations that are too high because of program visibility, and perpetuation of the myth that people must have mentors to succeed, the benefits of a program can be exceptional for all the involved parties (Gerstein, 1985).

Mentoring has often been performed within programs that emphasize career development. In this career perspective, Farren et al. (1984) have formulated several principles that can serve as helpful guidelines when organizations are interested in developing formal mentor relationships. These principles are:

1. Ensure the voluntary participation of mentors. Such factors as time commitment and a review of past problems should be discussed.
2. Minimize rules and maximize the mentor's personal freedom.
3. Create networking possibilities for mentees.
4. Share and negotiate expectations between mentors and mentees.
5. Reward mentors and increase their visibility.

With these principles, there are further guidelines that Rawlins and Rawlins (1983) suggested for the development of any mentoring relationship. These include such factors as: (a) mentors have skills, knowledge, or power that mentees lack and need; (b) although mentors may be the same age as or younger than mentees, typically they are 8 to 15 years older; (c) as mentees develop competencies, mature professionally, and assume their own responsibilities, the mentoring relationships can often realign themselves as peer relationships, and (d) helping professionals in search of mentoring can look to experienced colleagues with qualities such as a history of scholarly publications, involvement in professional organizations, willingness to give time, recognized expertise, and compatible value systems (Rawlins & Rawlins, 1985).

For many mental health professionals, finding a mentor, especially as one begins a new employment position, can enhance job performance and even provide a boost on one's professional ladder. A mentor can begin to facilitate a network of available community resources for a beginning mental health counselor. Mentors, in turn, can also benefit in the mentoring process by having help with work and perhaps gaining satisfaction from developing new talent. All in all, mentoring can help to develop for all involved parties a broad base for professional support and effective career building.

EDUCATION

As explained in many sections of this book, mental health counselors have varied job functions. Within one agency they could wear several hats, such as counselor, evaluator, advocate, and mediator. In other words, the helping process has different facets, but underlying this helping process is the basic assumption that mental health counselors are both assisting people to a more personally capable life, and, when possible, promoting change within communities and organizations. To achieve these goals often demands that the mental health counselor play the role of educator. The process of helping someone to lead a more productive life is often called a learning process. Mental health intervention has been referred to as the remediation of a skill's deficit, in which skills training becomes an integral part of an individual's transition from disablement to more effective functioning (Anthony, 1979). In this remediation, education is a vital component.

Education is a thread that weaves its way through the pattern of the delivery of mental health services. Intervention approaches have been devised that have as their foundation a psycho-educational approach. A variety of educational techniques can be used to assist clients and their families to more productive functioning. The increased understanding of a particular trauma, the reduction of stress, the enhancement of social networks, and the diminution of long-term issues contributing to client or family stress may all be at least partially achieved by a helping approach that includes education.

Education plays an important part, moreover, in many mental health counselor functions. When primary prevention was discussed earlier in this chapter, the assumption for this intervention was education of individuals, communities, and organizations. People need information if primary prevention is to be attained. Mental health counselors should be a major resource for information pertaining to the prevention of a particular problem. Primary prevention for a target population becomes, then, a planned learning experience in which the counselor uses a combination of methods, such as teaching, counseling, and perhaps behavior modification techniques to influence the individual's knowledge and mental health behavior.

When the helping process is conceptualized as a learning process, this focus implies that the mental health counselor will teach either clients or organizations certain necessary skills. For those clients who are undergoing the transition from the institution to an urban community, it may be the teaching of community living skills; for those clients who are experiencing a career change, the development of skills to adjust to a new school or job environment may be important. Many community mental health organizations, who wish to change their goals to correspond with new, emerging client needs, may need input to learn just how this change may be accomplished. Such organizations may call on the services of a consultant, and as a consultant, the counselor teaches others preferred ways to implement a change.

Consequently, education for the mental health counselor can assume many forms. The educative function may include direct service practice in a complex, hierarchical mental health agency where the counselor teaches life adjustment skills to needy clients; it may embrace an outreach neighborhood practice, where a large group of existing and potential consumers of mental health services face difficulties in gaining access to services, dissatisfaction with the location and quality of services, or a lack of knowledge about where to obtain services (Dinerman, Schlesinger, & Wood, 1980); it may further comprise planning efforts for mental health care. To function effectively, therefore, mental health counselors must operate from a framework that allows them to use educational approaches.

A counselor may be called upon to testify or to submit reports as an expert witness in a law case. In this role, counselors may be called upon, in some states, to testify as to the competency of a person being considered for legal commitment to a mental hospital, as to the suitability of individuals as parents in custody or adoption hearings, as to the effects of emotional problems on a person's capacity to work in disability determinations, as to a client's risk to society during sentencing procedures following a criminal conviction, or on any of a wide number of other matters brought before the legal system. In these instances, it is essential that the counselor become familiar with the legal issues involved in the case and relate the mental health considerations to them. Generally, the activities involved in being an expert witness are so complex and so atypical of counselors' training and experience that counselors take special courses to prepare themselves to function in this role. The reader is referred to books by the following authors for a discussion of the role of the mental health professional as an expert witness: Gross and Weinberger, 1982; Van Hoose and Kottler, 1985.

CONCLUSION

The many roles and functions for the mental health counselor that are described in this chapter illustrate the variety of ways that persons in need of services can be helped. The inherent complexity of mental health is mirrored in the variety of roles and functions for the mental health counselor. Also, mental health counseling in America is responding to numerous changes in society. Changes will continue, and they will necessitate a re-examination of the roles and functions of mental health counselors. New roles and functions may evolve commensurately with the emergence of social phenomena.

REFERENCES

Alleman, E., Cochran, J., Doverspike, J., & Newman, I. (1984). Enriching mentoring relationships. *The Personnel and Guidance Journal, 62,* 329–332.

Anthony, W. A. (1979). *Principles of psychiatric rehabilitation.* Amherst, MA: Human Resource Development Press.

Barclay, J. R. (1984, April). Primary prevention and assessment. *The Personnel and Guidance Journal,* pp. 475–478.

Berkowitz, G. (1973). A collaborative approach to mental health consultation in school settings. In W. C. Claiborn & R. Cohen (Eds.), *School intervention* (pp. 53–64). New York: Behavioral Publications.

Bloom, B. L. (1977). *Community mental health: A general introduction.* Monterey, CA: Brooks/Cole.

Bolman, W. M., & Westman, J. C. (1967). Prevention of mental disorder: An overview of current programs. *American Journal of Psychiatry, 123,* 1058–1068.

Brand, J. L. (1968). The United States: An historical perspective. In R. H. Williams & L. D. Ozarin (Eds.), *Community mental health: An international perspective.* San Francisco, Jossey-Bass.

Brokes, A. A. (1975). Process model of consultation. In C. A. Parker (Ed.), *Psychological consultation: Helping teachers meet special needs.* Minneapolis, MN: Leadership Training Institute.

Caplan, G. (1963). Types of mental health consultation. *American Journal of Orthopsychiatry, 33,* 470–481.

Caplan, G. (1964). *Principles of preventive psychiatry.* New York: Basic Books.

Caplan, G. (1970). *The theory and practice of mental health consultation.* New York: Basic Books.

Chandler, S. M. (1985, July–August). Mediation: Conjoint problem solving. *Social Work,* pp. 346–349.

Cook, R. F., Roehl, J. A., & Sheppard, D. (1980). *Neighborhood justice centers field test: Final evaluation report* (Institute for Social Analysis). Washington, DC: U. S. Government Printing Office.

Cowen, E. L. (1984, April). A general structural model for primary prevention program development in mental health. *The Personnel and Guidance Journal, 62,* 485–490.

Davis, R., Tichane, M., & Grayson, D. (1980). *Mediation and arbitration as alternatives to prosecution in felony arrest cases: An evaluation of the Brooklyn Dispute Resolution Center.* New York: Vera Institute of Justice.

Dear, R. B., & Patti, R. J. (1981). Legislative advocacy: Seven effective tactics. *Social Work, 26,* 289–296.

DeWild, D. W. (1981). Toward a clarification of primary prevention. *Community Mental Health Journal, 16,* 306–315.

Dinerman, M., Schlesinger, E. G., & Wood, K. M. (1980, April). Social work in health care: An educational framework. *Health and Social Work,* pp. 13–20.

Dustin, D., Ehly, S. (1984). Skills for effective consultation. *The School Counselor, 31,* 23–29.

Farren, C., Gray, J. D., & Kaye, B. C. (1984). Mentoring: A boon to career development. *The Personnel and Guidance Journal, 61,* 20–24.

Gamson, W. (1968). *Power and discontent.* Homewood, IL: Dorsey Press.

Gerstein, M. (1985). Mentoring: An age old practice in a knowledge-based society. *Journal of Counseling and Development, 64,* 156–157.

Gilbert, N. (1982, July). Policy issues in primary prevention. *Social Work,* pp. 293–296.

Gross, B. H., & Weinberger, L. E. (Eds.). (1982). *The mental health professional and the legal system.* San Francisco: Jossey-Bass.

Haller, K., & Monahan, J. (1972). *Psychology and community change.* Homewood, IL: Dorsey Press.

Havelock, R. G. (1973). *The change agent's guide to intervention in education.* Englewood Cliffs, NJ: Educational Technology.

Kessler, S. (1979, November). Counselor as mediator. *The Personnel and Guidance Journal,* pp. 194–197.

Kolb, D. M. (1985). To be a mediator: Expressive tactics in mediation. *Journal of Social Issues, 41,* 11–26.

Koopman, E. J. (1985). The education and training of mediators. In S. Grebs (Ed.), *Divorce and family mediation.* Rockville, MD: Aspen Systems Corporation.

Krupp, J. (1982). *Mentoring as a means to personal growth and improved school climate: A research report.* Colchester, CT: Project Rise.

Kurpius, D. (1978). Consultation theory and process: An integrated model. *The Personnel and Guidance Journal, 56,* 335–378.

Kurpius, D. J., & Brubaker, J. C. (1976). *Psycho-educational consultation: Definitions–functions–preparation.* Bloomington, IN: Indiana University Press.

Kurpius, D., & Robinson, S. E. (1978). An overview of consultation. *The Personnel and Guidance Journal, 56,* 321–323.

Lester, V., & Johnson, C. (1981). *Mentoring.* Unpublished manuscript.

Lewis, J. A., & Lewis, M. D. (1984, May). Preventive programs in action. *The Personnel and Guidance Journal,* pp. 550–553.

Lynch, S. (1980). The mentor link: Bridging education and employment. *Journal of College Placement, 40,* 44–47.

Matus, R., & Nuehring, E. M. (1979). Social workers in primary prevention: Action and ideology in mental health. *Community Mental Health Journal, 15,* 33–38.

McMurty, S. C. (1985, January–February). Secondary prevention of child maltreatment: A review. *Social Work*, pp. 42–46.

Meyer, C. H. (1985). Occupational social work and the public services: Gains and losses. *Social Work, 30,* 387.

Nulman, E. (1983, January–February). Family therapy and advocacy: Directions for the future. *Social Work*, pp. 19–23.

Ohlsen, M. M. (1983). *Introduction to counseling.* Itasca, IL: F. E. Peacock Publishers.

Randolph, D. L., Lassiter, P. S., Newell, K. G. (1986). Agency staffing needs for the mid- and late-1980s. *American Mental Health Counselors Association Journal, 8,* 27–34.

Rawlins, M. E., & Rawlins, C. (1985, October). Mentoring and networking for helping professionals. *The Personnel and Guidance Journal*, pp. 445–448.

Robins, P. R., Spencer, E. C., & Frank, D. A. (1970). Some factors influencing the outcome of consultation. *American Journal of Public Health, 60,* 524–534.

Roehl, J. A., & Cook, R. F. (1985). Issues in mediation: Theoretic and reality revisited. *Journal of Social Issues, 41,* 161–178.

Russell, M. C. (1978). Behavioral consultation: Theory and process. *The Personnel and Guidance Journal, 56,* 346–350.

Schein, E. H. (1978). The role of the consultant: Content expert of process facilitator? *The Personnel and Guidance Journal, 56,* 339–343.

Schwartzkoff, J., & Morgan, J. (1982). *Community justice centers: A report on the New South Wales pilot project (1979–1981).* Sydney, Australia: The Law Foundation of New South Wales.

Shaw, M. C., & Goodyear, R. K. (1984, April). Introduction to the special issues on primary prevention. *The Personnel and Guidance Journal*, pp. 444–445.

Sosin, M., & Caulum, S. (1983, January–February). Advocacy: A conceptualization for social work practice. *Social Work*, pp. 12–17.

Tesolowski, D. G., Rosenberg, H., & Stein, R. J. (1983, July, August, September). Advocacy intervention: A responsibility of human service professionals. *Journal of Rehabilitation*, pp. 35–39.

Vaillant, G. E. (1977). *Adaptation to life.* Boston: Little, Brown.

Van Hoose, W. H., & Kottler, J. A. (1985). *Ethical and legal issues on counseling and psychotherapy: A comprehensive guide* (2nd Ed.). San Francisco: Jossey-Bass.

Werner, J. L. (1978). Community mental health consultation with agencies. *The Personnel and Guidance Journal, 56,* 364–368.

Willetts, R. (1980, September). Advocacy and the mentally ill. *Social Work*, pp. 372–377.

Witty, C. (1980). *Mediation and society: Conflict management in Lebanon.* New York: Academic.

12 Evaluation of Services

Mental health counselors are now involved in a variety of innovative roles and functions. Social programs at all levels are expanding enormously, and with this expansion demands for services are increasing. These new roles and growing programs are positive signs of a strong growth in the mental health field. But this increase brings about closer scrutiny and accountability from such a variety of sources as legislative and regulatory bodies, agency administration, service consumers, and the general public (Wheeler & Loesch, 1981). Increasing popular distrust of government and the concern about fraud, waste, and abuse in publicly funded programs also contribute to the pressure for more accountability (Keppler-Seid, Windle, & Woy, 1980). Evidence of the benefits obtained from public and private expenditures is being sought from program administrators.

The credibility of the mental health profession is a continuing issue for both consumers and legislators. The evaluation of services provided by community mental health centers has emerged as an important topic since 1980 (Lebow, 1982). Wheeler (1980) stated, "Backed by recent judicial decisions establishing standards of clinical care, fostered by the disillusionment of the general public, and mandated by legislative action, mental health evaluation has become a critical component of program operations" (p. 88). Though the spring 1984 issue of the *Community Mental Health Journal* was devoted to a description of selected, statewide outcome evaluations in the mental health field, outcome evaluation is still not flourishing on a statewide level (Berren, 1984). Most human service organizations evaluate policies and programs only periodically, if at all (Schulberg, 1981).

Another factor that has contributed to the creation of an evaluation climate within the mental health profession is the Community Mental Health Center Amendments of 1975 (P.L. 94-63). This legislation requires mental health centers to establish ongoing quality assurance programs and provides an emphasis on research with local application. Administrators must think in terms of evaluating the techniques and programs used in their centers (Anderson, 1981).

This chapter will discuss the different aspects of program evaluation. It will not only explain the varied meanings of evaluation and its history, but will also highlight such important considerations as the settings and roles of the mental health counselor when performing program evaluation activities and the difference between evaluation and research. Further, the different "types" of program evaluation, and characteristics of good evaluations, will be identified.

DEFINITION, PURPOSES, AND HISTORY
OF PROGRAM EVALUATION

Unfortunately, the term *program evaluation* does not have a standardized and commonly accepted meaning. Though a popular term, *evaluation* is an elastic word and does not only imply measurement and data collection. An evaluation can cover processes ranging from simple score-card tallies to elaborate number crunching systems (Burgrabbe & Swift, 1984). It can be based on facts or on unfounded assumptions, or express a label that is applied loosely to a number of methods for gathering and analyzing data. Program evaluation is a key concern of management, and its distinctive feature is that it is concerned with the program. It addresses questions about both the implementation of the program's activities and their resulting outcomes (Rutman & Mowbray, 1983). It is a way to compare program components, activities, or outcomes to standards of desirability and a way to see how closely a mental health program meets its goals and objectives.

Consequently, there are widely different interpretations of the term *program evaluation*, but one accepted meaning is the process of identifying the decision areas of concern, selecting appropriate information, and collecting and analyzing information in order to report summary data useful to decision makers in selecting among alternatives (Franklin & Thrasher, 1976). It is a systematic effort to describe, understand, and judge the status of an organization and the effects of its operations and to recommend and implement suggestions for enhancing progress toward and achievement of the goals of the particular program. This definition implies that an evaluation make specific statements for actions that should be taken by decision makers. With its emphases both on decision-making functions and the determination of program effectiveness, program evaluation is seen as an aid to policy analysis. It explores such possible program characteristics as the efficient acquisition of resources, the transformation of program inputs into outputs, and the extent to which a program achieves its goals or produces certain effects.

In summary, the main purposes of program evaluation include: (a) determining effectiveness of programs, (b) determining success in achieving objectives, (c) placing a value on objectives, (d) valuing effectiveness, (e) assessing desirable and undesirable outcomes, (f) acting as a tool of management, (g) focusing on decision making, (h) structuring feedback of evaluation results, (i) judging evaluations, and (j) recommending alternatives to decision makers.

There is another perspective, however, for understanding the purposes of program evaluation. Rossi, Freeman, and Wright (1979) explained that there are four sets of questions with which one is concerned in doing evaluation.

1. Program planning questions
   (a) What is the extent and distribution, for example, of the mental health population?
   (b) Is the program developed in harmony with its intended goals?
2. Program monitoring questions
   (a) Is the program reaching the persons, community, or other target units to which it is addressed?
   (b) Is the program providing the services or other benefits that were intended in the project design?
3. Impact assessment questions
   (a) Is the program effective in achieving its intended goals?
   (b) Can the results of the program be explained by some alternative process that does not include the program?
4. Economic efficiency questions
   (a) What are the costs to deliver services and benefits to program participants?
   (b) Is the program an efficient use of resources compared with alternative uses of the resources?

Although the basic purposes of evaluation are to provide objective estimates of achievement and to provide guidance for the conduct of program activities, achieving these purposes can generate many evaluation activities. Neigher and Schulberg (1982) pinpoint four such activities.

Generating Better Information for Decision Makers

Frequently, the evaluation process begins after the decision has been made to implement an education, training, or social-action program. But a needs assessment, or estimates of cost and operational feasibility, or projections of demand and support, are all important precursors to decisions about whether to actually start a program. It is important to determine if there is a need for a program before one seriously considers installing it. A program, for example, requiring large financial expenditures may be developed in a mental health clinic before an assessment is made whether a particular population will use the service. Or, training programs for mental health workers may be offered without determining whether organizational barriers will make it possible for the trainees to apply their newly acquired skills.

Information further extends to seeking facts about program objectives, namely, whether the objectives are valid and useful for attacking the needs the program is designed to serve, and, is the content relevant to the program objectives and does it cover those objectives adequately? If either the objectives or the content are not relevant, then evaluation can contribute to decisions about program modification.

Determining Accountability

Accountability can take many forms, and includes public data disclosure and citizen participation in the evaluation process. A funding source may want to know whether a program has been effective to meet specific population needs. Effectiveness may be judged in comparison with the performance of another group or with earlier performance by the same group. Also, effectiveness may be viewed as either short- or long-term, and this depends on the nature of the program and the needs it serves. Moreover, assessment of actual costs can fall under the term *accountability*, and this assessment can be related to the effects or benefits the program appeared to achieve: "Have we spent $5.00 on a 50-cent program?" Much of the discussion of accountability in the mental health field assumes as an underlying premise that improved information and delivery structure can contribute to the productivity and efficiency of resource use. In other words, can greater benefits or effects be obtained at the same cost?

Performing Advocacy

This considers program evaluation as a strategy used by organizations to advance their interest when vying for resources. This activity has many implications for policy makers. Frequently, a program needs support in order that it may continue. For example, evaluation in the areas of community mental health may indicate that recidivism rates have been reduced, or, in contrast to institutionalized care, services delivered in a community setting are 50% more cost-effective. When this information is communicated to those responsible for making decisions, then the program or particular service may be viewed in a much more favorable light.

Conducting Evaluation Research

This activity applies scientific methods to establish causal linkages between intervention and their outcomes. These linkages can be explored either by isolating dependent variables and manipulating independent ones, or by maximizing the influence of independent variables while minimizing sources of variance. Yet, Neigher and Schulberg (1982) indicated that key requirements of the evaluation research model often cannot be met in evaluating human service programs. "It is seldom possible to randomly assign subjects among experimental and control groups; intervention technique anticipated outcome may have only tenuous theoretic linkages, and many programs simultaneously employ multiple interventions" (p. 735). Mental health programs are not like laboratory experiments. They seldom start and end at specific predetermined points. Baselines and final measurements cannot be clear-cut.

HISTORY

The definitions and purposes of program evaluation show a wide array of activities. It has not always been so. In fact, until the mid-1960s there were relatively few attempts to evaluate the delivery of human services, especially mental health programs. The history of program evaluation is unfortunately brief, and most writers agree that as a specialized function it is largely a post–World War II emergence (Franklin & Thrasher, 1976).

Rossi et al. (1979) explained that the immediate post–World War II period saw massive inputs of resources to remedy unattended problems and unmet needs for urban development and housing, technological and cultural education, occupational training, and preventive health activities. They further state that this was the initial period of major commitments to international programs of family planning, health and nutrition, and rural community development. Resource expenditures were huge, and these commitments were accompanied by continual cries for "knowledge of results."

Despite these needs, however, prior to the mid-1950s there were few reported studies of program evaluation in human service agencies. In 1939, the Cambridge–Somerville Youth study was begun to evaluate the effectiveness of therapeutic interventions. It explored the efficacy of using "big brother" counseling to reduce antisocial behavior among teenage pre-delinquent males (Rutman & Mowbray, 1983). It was completed and published in 1951. In the mid-1950s an experiment was designed to test the effectiveness of a preventive social work service to schoolgirls defined as potentially delinquent (Meyer, Borgatta, & Jones, 1965). About the same time, a study entitled "the Chemung County Evaluation of Casework Service to Multi-Problem Families" was reported (Rutman & Mowbray, 1983). The focus of this study was on the effectiveness of intensive case work with multiproblem families.

By the 1960s, during the "Period of the Great Society" a program transition occurred from one of expansion to one of accountability. Evaluations of penal rehabilitation projects, public housing programs, delinquency prevention programs, and psychotherapeutic and psychopharmacological treatments were being undertaken in the United States. Knowledge of the methods of social research, including the art of the social survey and the technology of computer-assisted statistical analysis, became widespread (Rossi et al., 1979). Yet, initially, accountability entailed little more than documenting the program efforts that were expended, that is, the numbers of clients receiving various types of services. More objective evidence on program effectiveness was being requested by funding bodies, legislators, and the general public. This account-ability change must also be viewed within the context of reforms that were taking place in public administration, such as zero-base budgeting, manage-ment by objectives, and cost-benefit analysis.

The growth of publications, national and international conferences, and spe-cial sessions on evaluation studies at the meetings of academic and practitioner groups are testimony to the recent development of the field. Today, there are also expanded organizational arrangements for the conduct of evaluation research. Program evaluation is currently more than the application of meth-ods. It is a political and managerial activity, an "input into the complex mosaic from which emerge policy decisions and allocations for the planning, design, implementation, and continuance of programs to better the human condition" (Rossi et al., 1979, p. 27).

EVALUATION OPPORTUNITIES FOR THE MENTAL HEALTH COUNSELOR

Though evaluation is a major tool of management, as well as an aid to policy analysis (Spaniol, 1975), evaluators generally come out of the academic research tradition (Weiss, 1972). There has been an academic orientation to program evaluation in which the activities have mainly comprised conducting studies and analyzing the data. Yet academic researchers usually have been hesitant to make practical recommendations based upon the data analysis. Because they often are unfamiliar with agency politics and internal manage-ment issues, academicians have not taken the responsibility for translating and interpreting evaluation results. But if program evaluation is to have any rele-vance for agency decision making, recommendations must be made and actions taken that are in harmony with an agency's philosophy. Such relevance demands participation both in the implementation of the evaluation results and the research process itself.

This participation is what Kurt Lewin called "action research" (Weiss, 1972). It involves self-study procedures and requires that an evaluator identify agency difficulties, collect information, help make necessary changes, and after the changes have been effected, evaluate their effectiveness. All of these activities are, with training, within the capabilities of the mental health coun-selor. Although mental health counselors usually wear many hats in the perfor-mance of their varied tasks, there are many evaluation opportunities that can be understood easily and can be carried out by persons of modest expertise and experience. When these tasks are accomplished, then mental health workers have a better understanding, not only of whether their job activities are in harmony with agency goals, but also of how to improve work performance and how much impact their work efforts have had on positive client outcome.

Another opportunity for mental health counselors to perform evaluation activities is when they act as a consultants for agencies. A consultant role has many dimensions and, frequently, the role implies that the consultant advises an agency on what is wrong with the delivery of services or becomes actively involved in finding solutions to an agency's current difficulties when they occur with clients. Agency consultation itself came about as a result of the passage of the Community Mental Health Act in 1963 (Werner, 1978). Prevention was emphasized, with special attention to primary prevention, namely, a reduction in the incidences of mental disorders. Werner (1978) suggests that one example of assisting an agency in its primary prevention efforts is to help an agency deal more effectively with specific parts of a mental health program.

In order for the mental health counselor to implement the role of a program evaluator, specific knowledge and skills are required. These are many and include:

1. A knowledge of the different operations of an agency, as well as an understanding of its goals and the needs of the population that the agency is attempting to meet.
2. An understanding of the different ways to collect reliable information or data that are related to the purpose of the evaluation.
3. A knowledge of how to utilize available resources for statistical analysis.
4. Interpersonal skills to communicate with the different managers or supervisors of an agency. An evaluator can face considerable problems of rapport and resistance both to evaluation procedures and, later, to changes in a program that may be suggested by evaluation results.
5. The skill to determine among the many issues or problems of an agency what particular issue is evaluable.
6. The skill to organize evaluation activities.
7. Advocacy skills to promote evaluation results.
8. A knowledge of the different methods of program evaluation, methods that have been developed to respond to varied evaluation needs of an agency.

With an awareness of the purposes, activities, and history of program evaluation, as well as a knowledge of selected opportunities for performing evaluation, an understanding is needed both of whether a program is evaluable and of the differences between research and evaluation. Much confusion over the differences of the two terms has been generated. Though research and evaluation may overlap, there are decided differences. Whereas basic research puts the emphasis on the production of knowledge and leaves its use to the natural processes of dissemination and application, program evaluation starts out with use in mind (Weiss, 1972). Evaluation also usually takes place in an action setting, where the most important thing that is going on is the program. A research activity has relevance to the extent that it relates to one hypothesis or theory. Research methods are limited and emphasize "hard" data obtained through tightly controlled experimental procedures. But program evaluation methods may include a full range of activities, and utilizes both "hard" and "soft" data (Wheeler & Loesch, 1981).

Table 12.1 illustrates the further differences between program evaluation and basic research. However, as Weiss (1972) indicated, there are important similarities between evaluation and other brands of research. She explained that like other research, "Evaluation attempts to describe, to understand the relationships between variables, and to trace out the causal sequel" (p. 8). Also, program evaluators use a broad array of research methods to collect information—interviews, questionnaires, tests of knowledge and skill, attitude inventories, observation, content analyses of documents, records, and examination of physical evidence.

Though there are more differences than similarities between basic research and program evaluation, an important ingredient for an effective evaluation is when an agency has clearly defined goals or objectives. Such clarity facilitates "evaluability" of a program. Many "opportunity-type" programs, namely, those activities that attempt to increase an agency's capabilities or opportunities to bring about a positive change in a client's capacity to earn or to adjust to life circumstances, have often been elusive and difficult to sort out and measure. Most of the innovative antipoverty and other programs of the 1960s were designed to provide "opportunities" for people and their goals were vaguely formulated.

TABLE 12.1. Differences between Program Evaluation and Basic Research

PROGRAM EVALUATION	RESEARCH
Basic management function	Not a basic management function
Broad concept—includes "hard" research as one of its potential components	More narrow concept
Broad approach to "ways" of knowing	Necessary adherence to experimental standard
Management decision focus	Focus on new knowledge or causes
Emphasis on applicability to agency concerns and priorities	Emphasis on more general concerns and priorities that may not have immediate applicability
Concerned with understanding relationship of events to established goals and objectives	Concerned with explaining and predicting
Frequent use of personal judgment	Least use of personal judgment
Descriptive, intuitive, qualitative, and quantitative	Tends more toward quantitative
Least generalizability "scientifically"	Most generalizability "scientifically"

designed to provide "opportunities" for people and their goals were vaguely formulated.

There are many criteria to determine whether a program is evaluable. The main ones are: A well-defined program, plausible causal linkages, and purpose.

A Well-Defined Program

One of the essential ingredients of a well-defined program is clearly specified goals and effects. Goals are the end results that programs claim to pursue and for which they can be held accountable. If an evaluator is to provide feedback for improving a program, then information should be obtained linking the program's activities to goal attainment. When goals are clearly specified, moreover, the question can then be answered: "Is the program adequately meeting the purposes for which it was funded?"

Frequently, a program is simply a statement on paper of what the planners in an agency hoped to accomplish (Hyman & Wright, 1971). It may never have been fully translated into action by the field staff. Consequently, a program is often merely a sketch that has to be completed.

Unfortunately, program goals are often vaguely stated. Examples of nebulous goals are "attain individual adjustment," "fulfill individual capacities," or "improve the quality of life." Though it may be necessary to tolerate a certain amount of vagueness for funding or legislative purposes, clear goals should be specified that are in harmony with the mission of an agency. A community mental health center, for example, which seeks to reduce the recidivism rate of de-institutionalized patients, should specify, upon implementation of a program for this purpose, what is meant by "reducing the recidivism rate." When there is a clear specification of program outcomes, this can serve as the basis for an effective evaluation exercise.

Plausible Causal Linkages

For program evaluations to be effective, it means that the program being examined has a realistic chance of reaching its specified goals and effects. In other words, cause and effect relationships between program activities and the effects should be identified. If a job-finding program, for example, has been developed and implemented in an agency working with the mentally disabled, then the relationship must be explored between this program and such effects as increased awareness of employment opportunities, interviewing skills, and the actual attainment of a job. Yet often the causal assumptions linking a program to some of its goals or effects are weak. Many "counseling interventions" are illustrative of these weak linkages. Such interventions are developed with the assumption that with proper counseling more people will find jobs or will lead satisfying lives. This could be true, but a more definite link between "counseling" and a "more satisfying life" should be established.

Purpose

This is an important factor because the purpose for conducting a program evaluation can also establish the criteria used to judge the value of a particular evaluative activity. An evaluation could be used as an attempt to justify a weak or bad program by deliberately selecting only those aspects that "look good" on the surface. If that is the purpose, then the standard for a good evaluation might be simply the number of people who request services from a particular agency, and not the quality of services that are delivered. Or, an evaluation might be done to "whitewash" a program, namely, cover up a program's failure by utilizing a subjective approach in the evaluation. In other words, an evaluator may be asked by agency administrators to overlook "hard data" or statistics identifying a large number of "unsuccessful" cases in preference for information generated from the impressions of staff on what the agency should be accomplishing.

Although there may be additional realities that could be considered when planning a useful evaluation, such as methodology, cost, and the implementation of the program evaluation design, the factors of a well-defined program, plausible causal linkages, and the purpose must be initially explored when developing a plan for a program evaluation. An appreciation of these issues establishes a basis, therefore, for understanding the different types of program evaluations. Once a determination is made that a program is evaluable, then the next decision can be considered: "What kind of an evaluation should be conducted?"

APPROACHES AND MODELS OF PROGRAM EVALUATION

The many approaches to performing program evaluation studies reflect different agency needs. One agency may be looking for information to establish a program relevant to a specific population. Another may be seeking an answer to whether their programs are really making a difference in the lives of the consumers of services. Still another agency may be asking how to improve existing services. Whatever the agency's need, there are a variety of ways that correspond to the many agency needs for program evaluation. There is no one theory of evaluation per se. Most of the approaches for program assessment are outgrowths of established bodies of knowledge (Franklin & Thrasher, 1976).

Burck and Peterson (1975) identified six common evaluation strategies, but explain them with a tinge of tongue-in-cheek cynicism. They feel they also exemplify common ills in program evaluation. The approaches are:

1. *The Sample-of-One method.* The evaluator uses a restricted sampling of opinion, often discussing a program with one or two others and then offering an opinion as if a comprehensive survey had been taken.

2. *Brand A versus Brand X method.* Many evaluators feel that a valid program evaluation effort must include a comparison group. In the attempt to compare the outcomes of one program, perhaps an experimental one, to a traditional program, the outcomes of nonequivalent groups are often compared because of practical limitations. The results are consequently inconclusive, if not misleading.

3. *The Sunshine method.* This method assumes that elaborate program exposure is evidence of a good program. Administrators may judge programs, for example, on how they appear, and questions of quality and impact are seldom raised.

4. *The Goodness-to-Fit method.* The credibility of a program is sometimes judged by the degree to which it can fit into established procedures. But a service program requiring special scheduling or temporary adjustments in staffing assignments may be considered frivolous and a nuisance. Seldom does anyone raise the issue of whether clients may benefit from the program (Burck & Peterson, 1975).

5. *The Committee method.* This approach implies that to evaluate effectiveness, simply bring together a group of congenial people who have been associated with the program and who are willing to discuss its effectiveness. After the group process runs its predictable course, a committee arrives at a seemingly spontaneous consensus.

6. *The Shot-in-the-Dark method.* This method of evaluation is used when well-intended program activities are conducted without a clearly established set of program objectives. Because there is no clear direction or standard, an evaluation randomly searches for any outcome measure that demonstrates the fact that the program has made an impact (Burck & Peterson, 1975).

Lebow (1982) has identified five models or approaches to program evaluation of mental health services, which comprise:

1. *The Organizational model.* This approach evaluates the appropriateness and viability of the organizational structures, the scope of the operation, the efficiency of management, the quantity of services provided, and the relation of services to community need and demand. This model examines the quantity of services offered; the productivity of staff, programs, and facilities; and the movement patterns of clients within the care system. The information generated from this evaluation describes only quantity, not quality, and how the agency's structure is conducive to offering good treatment and not how treatment is offered.

2. *The Care-Process model.* In this approach the quality of service is compared with some standard of practice. As Lebow (1982) stated, "This model focuses on appropriate assignment of clients to services and the effectiveness of service delivery" (p. 101). It evaluates the actual behavior of the agency staff, for the "quality" of a facility can be measured by the services offered by the practitioners.

3. *The Consumer-Evaluation model.* This model focuses on the consumer's opinion about services offered. These consumers may either be clients who assess services they have received, or residents of the community who evaluate the service system as a whole.

4. *The Efficacy model.* This approach evaluates the community mental health center's (CMHC's) performance in changing clients and consultees. Questionnaires may be used to collect information, and data may be gathered from clients, the counselor, and significant others, that is, family members or close friends. Outcomes are the goals in this model, but many factors that affect outcome may be well beyond the control of the counselor (Lebow, 1982).

5. *The Community-Impact model.* This model assesses the CMHC's influence on the community as a whole. Measures of community impact include the community's knowledge of services and the mental health of the community. But the community's mental health is even harder to measure than that of clients.

According to Lebow (1982), each model has a distinct focus and intent, and a place in community mental health center evaluation. Each approach offers unique and valuable data. The best approach to CMHC assessment will combine information from several models.

Underlying the preceding specific models for conducting program evaluation within agencies are more comprehensive approaches to agency assessment. The evaluator should be familiar, however, with these approaches, and when guided by this knowledge is then able to make a timely decision about what particular evaluation would be the most feasible. For example, many evaluations are conducted around the question: "Is our program effective?" when a more appropriate evaluation might focus on how the program was developed and whether or not program activities are in harmony with an agency's mission. Each evaluation direction demands a specific methodology. In this chapter, four kinds of program evaluations will be discussed. They represent the most frequently used approaches for program assessment.

NEEDS ASSESSMENT

The assessment of needs is perhaps the most important part of planning or evaluating any new program. Needs assessment has become an important concept in community mental health (Stewart, 1979). It is absolutely fundamental to evaluation, because there is no way to do a complete evaluation without knowing what clients need. Traditionally, needs assessment has been defined as a determination of the difference between what is and what ought to be, or between the actual and the ideal. Yet Scriven and Roth (1978) explained that the principal weakness in this approach is that it appears to require that one know what the ideal state is in order to determine a need.

These authors suggest another, purportedly more meaningful definition, that is, "A need is the gap between actual and satisfactory" (p. 1).

There is an accepted definition of needs assessment (Stewart, 1979). The word *need* can be both a noun and a verb, or it can describe a condition of lack, a want, or anything that is felt to be needed. Stewart (1979) proposed the following definition: "A comprehensive needs assessment is an activity through which one identifies community problems and resources to meet the problems, develops priorities concerning problems and services, and is part of program planning and development of new or altered services" (p. 294).

Regardless of this definition, the term *need* has still been used frequently in confusing ways. Actually, needs assessment should be operationalized in terms of the several ways it has normally been done. Assessment of need in community mental health centers has usually been related to the assessment of the deficit, or social problems involved; the desire for new services or consumer demand analysis; and the solution needed to solve the problems or priority list of desired services (Stewart, 1979).

Needs assessment programs vary in comprehensiveness, complexity, cost, length of time to be conducted, information received, and relative effectiveness. Within these programs there can be many approaches, such as key informant, community forum, rates-under-treatment, social indicators, and field survey. An explanation for each approach is as follows:

1. *Key informant.* This is an activity based on information secured from those in the area who are in a position to know the community's needs and utilization patterns. The kinds of persons normally sought as key informants include: public officials; administrative and program personnel in the health and welfare organizations of the community; health purveyors from both the public and private sectors, including physicians and public health nurses; the program clinical staff of agencies such as community mental health centers, vocational rehabilitation organizations, guidance clinics, and others engaged in either the delivery of primary care or the administration of health programs.

2. *Community forum.* This approach relies on individuals who are asked to assess the needs and service patterns of those in the community. Though similar to the key informant's approach, the circle of respondents is widened to include persons from within the general population. A forum study is designed around a series of public meetings to which all residents are invited and asked to express their beliefs about the needs and services of the community.

3. *Rates-under-treatment.* This activity is based on a descriptive enumeration of persons who have utilized the services of the health and welfare agencies of a community. The underlying assumption is that the needs of the population in the community can be estimated from a sample of persons who have received care or treatment.

4. *Social indicators approach.* This activity utilizes inferences of need drawn

from descriptive statistics found in public records and reports. The underlying assumption of this approach is that it is possible to make useful estimates of the needs and social well-being of those in a community by analyzing statistics or factors found to be highly correlated with persons in need. These statistics are regarded as indicators of need.

5. *Survey approach.* This approach uses data from a sample or entire population of a community. This activity begins by conceptualizing and operationalizing the methods by which valid information can be obtained most practically and economically.

The methods employed to gather information about client or community needs are varied, and include the interview, questionnaires, tests, group interviews, performance review, and records and reports study. Although the interview affords the maximum opportunity for free expression of opinion, it is time-consuming and usually can reach relatively few people. But the questionnaire can reach many people in a short time, is relatively inexpensive, and gives an opportunity of expression without fear or embarrassment. This method, however, may be difficult to construct and has limited effectiveness in getting at causes of problems. Tests are useful as diagnostic tools to identify specific areas or deficiencies, but often their validation for many specific situations are not available. The group interview, moreover, can stimulate the giving of suggestions and promote general understanding and agreement, but it is also time-consuming and initially expensive. Performance reviews as a method for collecting information is also time-consuming, but it can produce precise information about a job or someone's performance. Finally, records and reports studies are able to provide objective evidence of results of problems as well as suggest clues to trouble spots. But they do not show causes of problems or possible solutions, and may not reflect the current situation or recent changes.

All of these methods are used in the many needs assessment approaches, with perhaps the interview, the questionnaire, and the examination of reports and records as being the most frequently used. Also, any one specific needs assessment approach may use a variety of these methods to gather information. This can be illustrated in the following example.

As a mental health counselor, you wish to develop a program within your community mental health center to treat and reduce cocaine use among adults in your geographic or catchment area. To explore "what is" the usage situation, you could specify the target population of police officials, administrators of outpatient clinics within hospitals, and perhaps, if one has access to them, selected users of the drug. You would be following a key informant and community forum approach in needs assessment, with, when available, the rate-under-treatment technique, supposing that you can have access to those users who have utilized the services of a health agency in the community. When contacting the target population, you may utilize an interview or questionnaire method. Their use would depend on your available time and your knowledge of how to construct a questionnaire or to conduct an interview. But these methods would be ways to find out as much as possible about the characteristics of the population using cocaine, for example, age, sex, frequency, how drugs are obtained, and specific client needs.

After collecting the information about cocaine and the relevant factors, you would then analyze the data from the interviews or questionnaires to determine "what should be," or, in the Scriven and Roth (1978) framework, what your program should have without which it could be viewed as unsatisfactory. This determination could also include meeting with other program directors in the region or state and obtaining their ideas on the critical needs of these cocaine users, and also to discover what treatment modalities have worked, if any. Talking with other individuals engaged in similar activities helps you to develop a program that is built on their successes and failures.

Needs assessment, consequently, is comprehensive and develops information that is essential for program planning. Needs assessment is also an area in program evaluation that should always be considered when conducting any type of program evaluation activity. Many programs or agencies are begun without determining the needs of the target population. Frequently, an evaluator is requested to assess the effectiveness of a program, when the relevant question would be: "Was the program developed in harmony with the intended client need?" Many programs are ineffective because of this initial planning deficit.

FORMATIVE EVALUATION

Often agency or program administrators want to know how a program can be improved, or how it can become more efficient or effective. The appropriate label for this kind of evaluation is "formative evaluation," and it encompasses the 1,001 jobs connected with helping the staff to get the program running smoothly (Fink & Kosecoff, 1978). In order to improve a program, it will be necessary to understand how well the program is moving toward its objectives so that changes can be made in the program's components. It is a time-consuming form of evaluation because it requires becoming familiar with multiple aspects of a program and then providing personnel with information and insights to help improve it (Morris & Fitz-Gibbon, 1978). But before beginning a formative evaluation, the evaluator should make sure that there actually is a chance of making changes for improvement. Consequently, such questions will be asked as:

1. What problems are there and how can they be solved?

2. What are the program's most important characteristics—materials, activities, administrative arrangements?
3. How are the program activities supposed to lead to attainment of the objectives?
4. Are the program's important characteristics being implemented?
5. Are they leading to achievement of the objectives?

As a result of the formative evaluation, revisions are made in the materials, activities, and organization of the program. These adjustments are made throughout the formative evaluation period. Morris and Fitz-Gibbon (1978) identified steps that should be followed in conducting a formative evaluation.

1. Find out as much as one can about the program. Written documents describing the program should be read, and people should be asked what the program is supposed to be and do.
2. Estimate how much the evaluation will cost.
3. Focus the evaluation. Visualize what components of the program appear to provide the key to whether it succeeds or fails: Where is the program too poorly planned to merit success, and what effects might the program have that its planners have not anticipated?
4. Negotiate one's own role as an evaluator. The evaluator and the program staff should agree about the basic outline of the evaluation, which includes the approaches to measure program implementation. It also means coming to an agreement about services and responsibilities.
5. A program statement is prepared, which entails holding a meeting with agency/program administrators to specify the program's goals, and developing and examining a program rationale, namely, why each activity, for example, is expected to lead directly or indirectly to the achievement of the program objectives.
6. Write the program statement. This is an inhouse report describing what the evaluator has learned about the major goals of the program as well as why and when the implemented program is expected to achieve them.
7. Monitoring program implementation and the achievement of program objectives. This step involves making sure one is asking the right questions, identifying what courses of action will result from the information that the evaluator provides, and designing a monitoring system that could include the construction or purchasing of instruments. If instruments are to be administered, a design for their implementation and most effective use will have to be developed. Following their administration, the data will be analyzed with an eye toward program improvement.
8. Report and confer with planner and staff. This is the last step, and includes deciding what the evaluator wants to say and choosing a method of presentation. Presenting the report is an important aspect of evaluation, for priorities for program improvement must be carefully considered, and changes that are more likely to be implemented could be suggested.

The varied steps in the formative evaluation process can be illustrated by briefly examining a transitional care services program in a community mental health center. Developed for chronically and severely disabled patients, the treatment was built upon behavioral theory. Though strongly supported by staff, it does not seem to be doing an efficient and effective job. The administration is exploring and replacing this approach with a treatment based upon psychoanalytic and therapeutic milieu principles, but this exploration is becoming controversial. A change of programs could be seen as a direct criticism of the staff's theoretical orientation.

In approaching this evaluation task, the evaluator would want to find out as much as possible about the behavioral program and the possible new approach. After talking with people, including clients served by the existing program, the evaluator would begin to identify one's own evaluation role and come to an agreement about services and responsibilities. A meeting would then be held to specify the program's goals and a program statement would be developed which would include the outcome objectives, the persons responsible for program implementation, the specific activities, the materials used, the duration of the activities, and the progress expected. A plan would be developed to monitor the program implementation and the achievement of the program's objectives. This may include the use of measuring instruments, such as paper and pencil tests. When the monitoring time is completed, the data will be analyzed to assess whether the program is meeting the designated objectives, and if not, why.

SUMMATIVE EVALUATION

This is the most popular approach in conducting a program evaluation. It answers such questions as: "How effective is Program Y?" "Is it worth continuing or expanding?" The goal of this evaluation is to collect and present information needed for summary statements and judgments of the program and its value. An evaluator, when attempting this kind of assessment, should provide a basis against which to compare the program's accomplishments. It is a good idea to contrast the program's effects and costs with those produced by an alternative program that aims toward the same goals. Summative evaluations, moreover, result in recommendations to continue or discontinue the program and to expand or cut it back.

There are five distinct phases of a summative evaluation according to Morris and Fitz-Gibbon (1978). They are:

Phase 1. Focusing the evaluation. This phase includes deciding what needs to be known, and by whom. It comprises finding out as much as one can about the program, identifying a similar program and describing precisely these programs.

Phase 2. Selecting appropriate measures. After deciding what should be measured, one's evaluation concerns would be consolidated into a few instruments, data analysis should be planned, and a sampling strategy for administering the instruments will be chosen.

Phase 3. The collection of data. This will include establishing the evaluation design, such as, for example, a control group design with a pretest, administering the instruments, scoring them, and recording the data.

Phase 4. Analyzing the data.

Phase 5. Preparing an evaluation report.

These phases provide more understanding when an example is identified. As an illustration, a youth-service bureau that provides services to youths age 8 to 18 who are having personal, family, and legal problems wants to determine if their program is effective. The agency is funded by the state juvenile services administration, and matching funds are provided by the county. Additional funding consists of individual and corporate donations. The services offered include individual, family, and group counseling; information and referral; crisis intervention; and informal and drop-in counseling. Services that are considered optional include tutoring, education, and youth advocacy. The goal of the agency is to deter youth who have been identified by the juvenile justice system from further delinquent activity. Voluntary referrals are accepted from other social service agencies, police, courts, families, schools, and the state's juvenile services administration.

In beginning the evaluation, one would consult with program administrators for the meaning of "effective" and to learn as much as possible about the agency. Let us state that the staff responded by explaining, "significantly reducing the number of youth who have been referred to us for delinquent acts from any further contact with the juvenile services administration." Of particular importance in this evaluation is determining also what the state juvenile services administration means by "effective." Following an understanding of the agency and its objectives, the evaluator would then locate another, similar agency, perhaps in a different county of the same state, with similar activities that promote a reduction of further delinquent activity. The evaluator may then decide that a brief questionnaire, to be given to all the recipients of services of both agencies, would be the most appropriate instrument to collect needed information. The questionnaire is then sent to the "consumer," and necessary steps are followed to insure the maximum return rate. Also, a form of the questionnaire should be sent to the juvenile services administration to solicit feedback on information from their records on any delinquent activity by the consumers that received attention from the agency. Questionnaire results are then analyzed. Finally, a report would be prepared that described the evaluation, identifies its results, and makes recommendation on whether the program was "effective."

THE SYSTEMS APPROACH

In contrast to the summative model of evaluation, which is concerned with the degree of success in reaching a specific objective, the systems model establishes the degree to which an organization realizes its goals under a given set of conditions (Schulberg & Baker, 1971). It is concerned with establishing a working model of an organization that is capable of achieving a goal. This approach is appropriate to a large community mental health center which has many functions or activities. The systems model would then focus upon the effective coordination of the agency's many activities, the acquisition and maintenance of necessary resources, and the adaptation of the organization to the environment and to its own internal demands. This approach will ask the question, for example, "How close does the organizational allocation of resources approach an optimum distribution?" (Etzioni, 1960).

This model of evaluation is a more demanding and expensive one for the evaluator (Schulberg & Baker, 1971). It requires that one determines what is the highly effective allocation of means. This demands considerable knowledge of the way in which an organization functions. Yet one advantage of this approach is that the evaluator can include in the data collection much more information than is possible in classical research design. For example, if an evaluator is assessing the effectiveness of an agency that has a transitional program that assists ex-mental patients to find and maintain paid employment, one might discover that the success rate is very low. The evaluation results could suggest that the program be dropped. Yet if the evaluator shifts to a system model of evaluation and considered the data within the context of all the functions of the agency, which might include, for example, the promotion of better attitudes toward hiring the mentally disabled, the development of everyday living skills, and the enhancement of the client's low self-concept, then the objective of hiring the mentally handicapped would be viewed within the context of other, but related functions. From this perspective, the evaluator would be able both to develop many hypotheses explaining the failure of the job finding effort and to suggest possible concrete avenues for bringing about future change.

Schulberg and Baker (1971) have done extensive work in utilizing the systems approach for evaluating the mental hospital. They view the hospital as an open system exchanging inputs and outputs with its environment. They examined the intra-organizational processes of the hospital, the exchanges and transactions between the hospital and its environment, and the processes and structures through which parts of the environment are related to one another. A change in community attitudes toward the function of the mental hospital, for example, could influence the types of hospital activities that prepare the patient for a return to the community. A system evaluation approach, consequently, would examine the many linkages, and recommendations would be suggested that offer different options for program improvement.

These four approaches to conducting a program evaluation within mental health settings respond to different questions or demands that agencies generate when delivering services. As an example, for some mental health centers it may be important to appraise their overall impact and the consistency with which they produce certain outcomes. Requested usually by the program's sponsors or by legislators, several types of evaluation information would be collected. A summative evaluation, and occasionally a systems approach, will then be used for evaluating the program's impact. However, other mental health programs may be more concerned with identifying the changing needs of a specific, client population in order to develop new activities or improve existing agency objectives. A needs assessment approach may then be utilized.

Whatever the approach, the evaluation itself may be done well or poorly. But good evaluations have certain characteristics that can be used as guidelines to determine whether a specific program evaluation will be credible or not. These characteristics are:

1. *Conceptual clarity.* This refers to whether the evaluator shows a clear understanding of the particular evaluation one is proposing. Is an effectiveness evaluation being planned, or will the evaluation be directed to improve the program?

2. *Precise information needs and sources.* Good evaluations cannot depend on randomly collecting information, gathering "a little here, a little there." An adequate evaluation plan specifies at the onset the information to be collected. If the evaluation is a needs assessment, the evaluation plan will specify what information is important to obtain in order to identify needs of the client population.

3. *Description of the object of evaluation.* No evaluation is complete unless it includes a thorough, detailed description of the program or system being evaluated. If a mental health center has been modifying a well-known treatment approach because of its own client needs, then the approach and its modifications need to be described accurately. Otherwise, judgments may be made about an activity that doesn't really exist.

4. *Representation of legitimate audiences.* An evaluation is adequate only if it includes input from all the legitimate audiences for the evaluation. An evaluation of a community mental health center that answers only the questions of the center's staff and ignores questions of clients and community groups is a bad evaluation. Obviously, some audiences will be more important than others and some weighting of their input may be necessary.

5. *Technical adequacy.* Good evaluations are dependent on construction or selection of adequate instruments, the development of adequate sampling plans, and the correct choice and application of techniques for data reduction and analysis.

6. *Consideration of costs.* Costs are not irrelevant, and it is important for the evaluator to know how much a certain program will accomplish and at what cost. This is particularly important when the evaluator is examining, when

writing an evaluation report, other alternatives that range in both cost and effectiveness.

7. *Explicit standards/criteria.* Criteria or standards used to determine whether objectives have been met, or if a program was a success or a failure, should be identified when performing a program evaluation. The information taken in an evaluation cannot be translated into judgments of worth without the application of standards or criteria.

8. *Recommendations.* An evaluator's responsibility does not end with the collection, analysis, and reporting of data. Recommendations must be provided that imply, for example, whether a program or agency is effective or ineffective. These recommendations must also be tailored to the audience for whom the evaluation was contracted.

9. *Sensitivity to political problems in evaluation.* Evaluation itself has a political stance (Weiss, 1973). The evaluator needs to recognize that different value systems are operating in any evaluation scheme. The evaluator should consider the values of the agency under evaluation, the sponsoring authority, the subjects of the evaluation, and the evaluator's own values. Because evaluation is usually undertaken to recommend stability/survival and growth/change, its results enter the political area. These results often suggest such political issues as the problematic nature of some programs and the unchallengeability of others (Weiss, 1973).

The programs with which an evaluator deals in mental health have developed from the conflict of political opposition, support, and bargaining. Attached to these political realities are the reputations of legislative sponsors, the careers of administrators, and the jobs of program staff. As Weiss (1973) states, social programs are the creatures of legislative and bureaucratic politics. The evaluator is faced with the tasks of understanding these issues, for being aware of political sensitivities helps the evaluator formulate an evaluation design that will be both effective and appropriate to the realistic needs of the agency. Often, for example, inflated promises are made in the guise of program goals. As an illustration, an agency that provides independent living skills for deinstitutionalized patients may also promise the procurement of employment for these clients. The goals of independent living may be real; the employment goals may be the program's "window dressing." The evaluator must sift the real from the unreal, the important from the unimportant. The program evaluation itself is most likely to affect decisions when the evaluator considers the values, assumptions, and even the covert goals that may set the direction of a program.

CONCLUSION

The Community Mental Health Center Amendment of 1975 requires community mental health centers to establish ongoing quality assurance programs (Anderson, 1981). Techniques and programs used in these centers should be evaluated for their effectiveness and possibility of improvement. There are now a wide range of opportunities for acceptable approaches in program evaluation. The number of mental health counselors who are concerned about evaluation is growing.

At the same time, many mental health counselors perceive themselves as not being adequately prepared in program evaluation methods and skills (Wheeler, 1980). Though the majority of mental health counselors may be well versed in basic scientific research and statistical procedures, there is a lack of training in the specific methods of program evaluation. The increased public and private expenditures of the past decade may have improved the social order, but new problems with the mentally ill, drug abusers, and unemployed have emerged. Social change efforts will necessarily continue and grow. Program evaluation, emphasizing the adequate assessment of existing and innovative programs, can have a major impact on social problems.

Systematic evaluations of social programs are a relatively recent development (Rossi et al., 1979). Program evaluation is an important area of activity devoted to collecting, analyzing, and interpreting information on the need, implementation, and impact of intervention efforts to improve social conditions and community life. The ability to conduct meaningful program evaluation is rapidly becoming a survival skill for counselors as they become increasingly dependent on external sources of funding for programs (Wheeler, 1980). Accountability demands have intensified and this trend is likely to continue. This chapter is intended to help the reader to conceptualize and to understand the purposes of evaluation and the methods by which it obtains information and generates conclusions.

REFERENCES

Anderson, W. (1981, April). How to do research in community mental health agencies. *Personnel and Guidance Journal, 59,* pp. 517–522.

Berren, M. (1984). Statewide outcome evaluation: An introduction to the special issue. *Community Mental Health Journal, 20,* 4–13.

Burck, H. D., & Peterson, G. (1975). Needed: More evaluation, not research. *Personnel and Guidance Journal, 53,* 563–569.

Burgrabbe, J., & Swift, J. (1984, March/April). Evaluating your EAP: A practical approach. *EAP Digest,* pp. 12–34.

Etzioni, A. (1960). Two approaches to organizational analysis: A critique and a suggestion. *Administration Science Quarterly, 5,* 257–278.

Fink, A., & Kosecoff, J. (1978). *An evaluation primer.* Beverly Hills, CA: Sage Publications.

Franklin, J., & Thrasher, J. (1976). *An introduction to program evaluation.* New York: John Wiley.

Hyman, H., & Wright, C. (1971). Evaluating social action programs. In F. Caro (Ed.), *Readings in evaluation research.* New York: Russell Sage.

Keppler-Seid, H., Windle, C., & Woy, J. (1980). Performance measures for mental health programs. *Community Mental Health Journal, 16,* 217-234.

Lebow, J. (1982). Models for evaluating services at community mental health centers. *Hospital and Community Psychiatry, 33,* 1010–1014.

Meyer, H., Borgatta, E., & Jones, W. (1965). *Girls at vocational high.* New York: Russell Sage.

Morris, L., & Fitz-Gibbon, C. (1978). *Evaluator's handbook,* Beverly Hills, CA: Sage.

Neigher, W., & Schulberg, H. (1982). Evaluating the outcomes of human service programs. *Evaluation Review, 6,* 731–752.

Peterson, G., & Burck, H. (1982). A competency approach to accountability in human service programs. *Personnel and Guidance Journal, 60,* 491–495.

Rossi, P., Freeman, H., & Wright, S. (1979). *Evaluation: A systematic approach.* Beverly Hills, CA: Sage.

Rutman, V., & Mowbray, G. (1983). *Understanding program evaluation.* Beverly Hills, CA: Sage.

Schulberg, H. C. (1981). Outcome evaluations in the mental health fields. *Community Mental Health Journal, 17,* 132–143.

Schulberg, H. C., & Baker, F. (1971). Program evaluation models and the implementation of research findings. In F. Cara (Ed.), *Readings in evaluation research.* New York: Russell Sage.

Scriven, M., & Roth, J. (1978, Spring). Needs assessment: Concept and practice. *New Directions for Program Evaluation, 1.*

Spaniol, L. (1975). *A model for program evaluation in rehabilitation.* Madison, WI: University of Wisconsin, Regional Rehabilitation Research Institute (Monograph XIX, Series 3).

Stewart, R. (1979). The nature of needs assessment in community mental health. *Community Mental Health Journal, 15,* 287–295.

Weiss, C. H. (1972). *Evaluating action programs.* Boston: Allyn & Bacon.

Weiss, C. H. (1973). Where politics and evaluation research meet. *Evaluation, 1,* 4–13.

Werner, J. (1978). Community mental health consultation with Agenus. *Personnel and Guidance Journal, 56,* 364–368.

Wheeler, P. T. (1980). Mental health practitioners' perceptions of their preparation in program evaluation. *American Mental Health Counselors Association Journal, 2,* 88–96.

Wheeler, P. T., & Loesch, L. (1981, May). Program evaluation and counseling: Yesterday, today, and tomorrow. *Personnel and Guidance Journal, 59,* 573–581.

V RESOURCES

13 Practice Settings

The mental health counseling profession has grown rapidly since 1975. With this growth there has been a parallel increase in the number of settings where counselors respond to the needs of clients. The history of the counseling profession suggests that counseling programs have been initiated in response to the needs of major segments of the population for assistance that could not be or was not being provided through traditional institutions (Gibson, Mitchell, & Higgins, 1983). For example, the steadily increasing proportion of divorces, and spouse and child abuse has led to a greater expansion of marriage, family, and crisis counseling throughout the United States. Counseling services are growing to meet the rising incidence of adolescent suicides and substance abuse.

Gibson et al. (1983) believe that the increased development of mental health settings is not only due to the proliferation of counseling programs for new target populations. More likely, it is the outgrowth of a mental health evolution that began decades ago that is associated with the broad interest in the psychological well-being of all age groups from the children through the elderly, the emergence of counseling services in a wide range of institutional and agency settings, and the development of new professional specialists to serve the needs of unique populations. Mental health counseling assistance is now being made available in or pertaining to virtually every type of community agency or institution. Chapter 11 identified the many roles and functions of the mental health counselor. These responsibilities are being carried out in an ever-expanding range of agencies.

With this growth of mental health settings, there has been the awareness of specific characteristics of community and other mental health organizations. Gibson et al. (1983) identified such factors as: (a) mental health agencies and institutions are human service organizations designed to enhance the mental well-being of individuals; (b) these resources are usually tax-supported public service agencies that tend to assume certain bureaucratic characteristics associated with large governmental and industrial complexes; and (c) community mental health agencies tend to have interdisciplinary staffs representing such fields as medicine, psychology, and social work. Because of these characteristics, mental health settings are frequently more vulnerable and susceptible to public pressures. Also, as Goodstein (1978) explained, because many organizations in the public sector are ordinarily not task-oriented, but rather are bureaucratic, doing things properly is often more important than getting things done.

This chapter will both identify and discuss a number of settings where mental health counselors are serving a diverse group of clients. Each setting will be explained in the framework of its history, philosophy, services provided, the professionals involved in the setting, the role of mental health counselors in the agency or program, and the current status and future perspectives of the setting. These selected institutional or agency settings and alternative services represent a wide range of approaches for delivering the services of the mental health profession to individuals in the community.

COMMUNITY MENTAL HEALTH CENTERS

Community mental health agencies are one of the most popular sources of employment for counselors. On December 31, 1960, the Joint Commission on Mental Illness and Health, funded by Congress to analyze the human and economic problems caused by mental illness, submitted its final report to Congress, "Action for Mental Health" (Bloom, 1977). Based on this report, Congress passed, and President John F. Kennedy signed into law, the Community Mental Health Centers (CMHCs) Act of 1963 (Title II, Public Law 88-164). This act authorized funds for federal assistance to states in the construction of community mental health centers, which were defined in the act as "providing services for the prevention or diagnosis of mental illness, or the care and treatment of mentally ill patients, or rehabilitation of such persons . . . residing in a particular community or communities in or near where the facility is situated" (Title IV, Sec. 401 [c], Public Law 88-164). The regulations accompanying Title II specified that to qualify for funds, states had to develop a state plan for comprehensive mental health services that included:

1. Inpatient services;
2. Outpatient services;
3. Partial hospitalization services, such as day care, night care, weekend care;
4. Emergency services 24 hours per day must be available within at least one of the first three services listed above;
5. Consultation and education services available to community agencies and professional personnel;
6. Diagnostic services;

7. Rehabilitative services, including vocational and educational programs;
8. Pre- and after-care services in the community, including foster home placement, home visiting, and halfway houses;
9. Training; and
10. Research and evaluation (Sec. 54.203).

Subsequent laws relevant to this one: (a) authorized funding of start-up costs for staffing these community mental health centers (Public law 889-105, 1965); (b) continued support for the earlier acts (Public Law 90-31, 1967); (c) specified the addition of preventive and treatment services for alcoholism and narcotics addiction (Public Law 90-574, 1968); (d) specified that child mental health services be provided (Public Law 91-211, 1970); (e) expanded the category of narcotics addiction to include all drug abuse or dependency problems (Public Law 91-513, 1970); and (f) extended the earlier acts (Public Laws 93-45, 1973 and 94-63, 1975, in both cases opposed by the president and in the latter case passed by Congress over a presidential veto). President Jimmy Carter, in large part because of his wife's interest in mental health, revived presidential support for mental health services. Soon after his inauguration in 1977, he created the President's Commission on Mental Health to determine the current and projected needs for service and research and to suggest the role of the federal government and other agencies in meeting those needs. The commission's report was completed in 1978, the same year that P.L. 95-622 was signed, extending support for the CMHCs until September 1980.

Suggestions made in the commission's report for a network of coordinated community-oriented services led to the immediate development of a number of new programs, including the community support programs initiated and supported by the National Institute of Mental Health (Turner & TenHoor, 1978). In October 1980, PL 96-398 was signed into law by President Carter This act authorized continued support for community mental health services created under earlier laws and added a number of provisions suggested by the presidential commission report of 1978. A month later, however, President Carter was defeated for re-election by Ronald Reagan, who instead of implementing this act, instituted a program of block grants to the states. Mental health, drug, and alcohol-abuse programs were allocated a certain amount of funding within a larger health services block grant, with broad latitude given to each state to decide how to apportion these funds. Under this policy, there was less money in toto and even less assurance that the available money would be used for mental health.

One of the objectives for the development of CMHCs was to focus attention on the opportunity for federal funds to change rapidly the balance of community versus mental hospital resources (Gruenberg, 1972). Since the legislation was enacted in 1963, more than 760 catchment areas have received federal support for the development of a local, population-based, prevention-oriented system of services that was intended to be accessible and available to all who needed it irrespective of their ability to pay (Pardes, 1982). The federal commitment to community mental health, fueled by the steady infusion of millions of dollars of federal funds, was reaffirmed regularly for almost two decades (Winslow, 1982).

Since their inception, these centers have attempted to maintain an emphasis on:

1. Primary prevention, namely, a service designed to assist groups of individuals identified as high risks for the development of behavior disorders (Gibson et al., 1983).
2. Crisis intervention, a major service of most community mental health agencies.
3. Consultation, an indirect service that may take the form of consulting with other institutions or agencies, such as schools, welfare agencies, law enforcement personnel, substance abuse centers, and hospitals.
4. Remediation and rehabilitation services, including the diagnosis and treatment of mental disorders. The clients of mental health centers may range in severity from those who require intensive psychiatric–medical treatment to those who need what can be simply labeled routine adjustment counseling. The treatment approaches might include a broad spectrum from intensive, long-term psychotherapy to a skill orientation in which the individual is helped to acquire the social and other skills that are necessary for adjustment to everyday-life tasks and roles.
5. Educational programs, which include programs concerning the nature of mental health and those that encourage community involvement in planning and evaluating services.

Also, many community mental health agencies might offer advocacy services on behalf of individual clients, assistance in organizing the local community to bring about needed environmental change, and linkage resources with support systems and helping network (Lewis & Lewis, 1977). Further, partial hospitalization and home services have been offered by many centers, but these opportunities have decreased as federal funds have been reduced (Okin, 1984). Community mental health centers (CMHCs), moreover, have played a significant role in the education and training of mental health professionals (Winslow, 1982).

Though the main target population in the CMHC was intended to be the severely and chronically mentally ill, during the period from 1971 to 1975 there was a significant decrease in the percentage of new patients diagnosed as having a depressive disorder or schizophrenia, and an increase in the percentage classified as socially maladjusted, no mental disorder, deferred diagnosis, or nonspecific condition (DHEW, 1978). Over the years, centers have been widely criticized for inadequate attention to this population, for evidence is cited demonstrating that patients with schizophrenia and affective illness constituted only 16% and 18%, respectively, of total admissions in 1971 and declined further to 10% and 13% in 1978 (Goldman, Regier, & Taub, 1980; Langeley, 1980). Considering this information, the reader should note two factors of particular importance: the inability of hospital-affiliated centers to gain access to general and private hospital inpatient beds for their acutely disturbed patients; and the fact that the entire financing and reimbursement system appears to conspire against the noninstitutional care of the chronically ill client (Talbott, 1978). But there is evidence that the block grant mechanism, which will be discussed later in this section, has resulted in greater attention to the chronically mentally disabled population (Okin, 1984).

The staffing patterns have changed significantly since the initial development of CMHCs. A shift is continuing to occur between core mental health 1982). There has been a decline in psychiatrists, and administratively the percentage of centers directed by psychiatrists decreased from more than 60% in 1971 to 16.4% in 1980 (Winslow, 1982). Large gains have been made, however, by psychologists and social workers, whose positions in the average center increased by 55% and 32%, respectively, between 1973 and 1979 (Okin, 1984). The involvement of registered nurses has also grown considerably in CMHCs. CMHC leadership has been increasingly entrusted to nondoctoral level professionals. More centers are being directed by master's and bachelor's level staff who often are not mental health professionals but who have a wide variety of human service-related skills.

In 1979 Randolph directed a study to explore CMHC employers' perceptions of desirable skills and characteristics of master's level psychologists/counselors. Using a 76-item questionnaire, and with 117 completed instruments that were returned to the author, Randolph (1979) reported that some high ranking areas were as follows: good oral and written communication skills; knowledge of community referral sources; training in assessment; basic individual, group counseling, and consultation skills; and a basic psychology course-work foundation.

A central piece of legislation that has affected the continued growth of the CMHC was the Omnibus Budget Reconciliation Act of 1981, known as the block grant legislation. The central features of this legislation were the amalgamation of the funds for alcohol, drug abuse, and mental health into a single block grant, and the transfer of authority for planning, priority-setting, and administration, distribution, and monitoring of the block grant funds from the federal government to the states (Okin, 1984). With the reduction in other federal programs on which the mentally disabled depend, many CMHCs have had to decrease their overall level of services and staffing when, at the same time, they are experiencing increased demands for services. A new population of young, adult, chronically mentally disabled clients who have spent relatively little time in mental hospitals is emerging in the community (Green & Koprowski, 1981). In order to serve this population, and at the same time survive in an era of increasing budget cuts, CMHCs must begin, according to Winslow (1982), "To develop closer relationships with community health centers, clinics, hospitals, and medical centers" (p. 276). The real question for the future of CMHCs may not be whether they will survive, but in what form, responding to which funding sources, caring for which patients, with what manpower, and through what services (Okin, 1984).

HEALTH MAINTENANCE ORGANIZATIONS

A major change toward prepaid group health practices is occurring today in the United States. Skyrocketing medical costs and increasing inflation since 1975 have made necessary the search for innovative, more cost-effective ways of providing health care to consumers (Forrest & Affemann, 1986). This trend is best exemplified by a 10% annual growth rate of health maintenance organizations (HMOs) with a projected membership of 50 million Americans by 1993 (Mayer & Mayer, 1985).

Although HMOs have been in existence since the turn of the century, their real period of growth has been since the passage of the Health Maintenance Organization Act of 1973 (P.L. 93-222), which provided a mechanism to qualify HMOs federally. Currently, all employers offering health benefits with more than 25 employees are required to offer their employees access to a federally qualified HMO (Deleon, Vyeda, & Welch, 1985).

The philosophy underlying HMOs is essentially prevention or primary care, and this philosophy is expressed through a contractual arrangement to promise a range of specified health services to subscribers in return for prepaid enrollment. The incentive, therefore, from the HMO standpoint is to maintain health by providing programs or strategies that contribute to healthy behaviors or to increased personal control over medical conditions.

The attractiveness of HMOs comes from their documented cost-effectiveness relative to fee-for-service health care systems. The emphasis on prevention also reduces the long-term, lifetime costs associated with unhealthy behaviors: financial, physical, and emotional. Yet HMOs have also been criticized as impersonal and lacking in "quality" care because the user purchases services from a system rather than from an individual.

When considering practice settings, it is important to understand that HMOs are essentially controlled by medical systems and service providers. This is always the case, despite the fact that they do not ostensibly espouse the traditional medical model of remediation. There are three typical HMO models with various service plan emphases:

1. The individual practice association (IPA) model, which most nearly approximates the traditional medical care model. Under this model, fee-for-ser-

vice practitioners function as separate legal entities and submit claims to HMOs for services provided to members of that HMO. The IPA model is the one most frequently used by HMOs, particularly ones that have been established since the 1973 Health Maintenance Organization Act.

2. The group practice model, in which professional staff are salaried employees of the HMO.

3. A combination of the IPA and staff models, in which a group of providers who are separately incorporated receive payments of services on a per member/per month basis.

Mental health services must be offered by federally qualified HMOs. Forrest and Affemann (1986) have identified several reasons for including a mental health department in HMOs. For example, the HMO's stress on secondary (developmental problems) and tertiary (crisis issues) necessitates the use of varied counseling approaches, and this utilization can assist primary physicians in evaluating the contribution of psychological and social factors to the development, course, and outcome of physical and psychiatric disorders. Also, clients would receive counseling in settings with which they were already familiar and comfortable and that often were near their work places. Moreover, financial barriers would be kept at a minimum and follow-up could be encouraged because clients would maintain an affiliation with the plan (Forrest & Affemann, 1986).

The patterns of mental health services offered by HMOs have been documented by Chafetz and Salloway (1984). Services include short-term (up to 20) outpatient visits for evaluation and crisis intervention and "as needed" inpatient services. The prevention focus and nature of intervention strategies provided by HMOs are consistent with current mental health counseling philosophies, particularly the "counseling ecology" of Conyne (1985), developmental models of Egan (1982), and the orientation of this book.

The types of services utilized by enrollees of federally qualified HMOs in the survey of Chafetz and Salloway (1984) were in descending order of frequency: diagnostic interviews, individual psychotherapy, group psychotherapy, marital therapy, behavior therapy/modification, alcoholism and drug abuse programs, school problem counseling, psychological testing, biofeedback, psychiatric day-hospital, and vocational counseling. Additional health education approaches utilized include weight control, stress adaptation, and smoking control programs.

Among the workers employed by HMOs are psychiatrists, psychologists, psychiatric nurses, counselors, and social workers. Sank and Shapiro (1979) identified the various roles that mental health workers have performed in HMOs, including:

1. Organizational consultant to the unit on an as-needed basis;

2. Administrator or liaison between full-time administrative staff and clini-

cal providers, particularly when the well-being of patients must be weighted against the limited availability of services and funds;

3. Patient ombudsman, particularly with chronic patients whose needs may be beyond the scope of routine treatment;
4. Clinical consultant as a resource to health care providers in dealing with behavioral and emotional problems of patients;
5. Teacher to outside groups, such as medical students;
6. Supervisor as part of internship programs at the HMO.

These roles are familiar to most mental health counselors. Furthermore, Resnick (1982) stressed the importance of developmental theory and life-span work as part of the preventive philosophy of HMOs. Forrest and Affemann (1986) stated that "According to Resnick (1982), the largest, most prevalent, and most appropriate role for mental health providers in HMOs is offering short-term counseling" (p. 67). The provision of short-term intervention severely limits, of course, the opportunity to deliver consultation, education, and other primary preventive services (Forrest & Affemann, 1986).

The role of the mental health counselor within HMOs is still being determined. Although the HMO approach is wholly consistent with that currently offered by mental health counselors in private practice and other service settings, recurring issues of professional "turf" must be resolved. Also, a terminal degree in a mental health discipline (e.g., a master's or doctoral degree) is not as important as licensure or certification status (Chafetz & Salloway, 1984). Also, there appears to be a tendency for larger HMOs to employ master's level practitioners for the provision of mental health services, although these practitioners are usually nurses or social workers. It would seem, therefore, that employment possibilities in HMOs will become more frequently available for mental health counselors as they obtain certification and licensure status, and focus on gaining and maintaining skills in the most medically acceptable but nonmedical treatment procedures (i.e., relaxation training, cognitive restructuring, and biofeedback for stress-related physical problems). Mental health counselors have expertise to offer and a useful contribution to make to HMOs.

SCHOOLS

Schools provide a major setting for preventive mental health programs. There are several reasons for this focus. First of all, schools are educationally and developmentally oriented and embrace the philosophy of a sound mind in a sound body. Second, affective life adjustment education is usually considered part of a school's mission, despite recent attempts by some groups to limit schools' responsibilities strictly to cognitive growth (e.g., the "back to basics" movement). Third, educational philosophies recognize the importance of building upon existing strengths, the contribution of self-esteem to motivation and achievement, and the necessity of working with the whole person to effect that individual's optimal development. Obviously, the best time to prevent the onset of mental dysfunction and to promote healthy coping strategies is early in a person's life, before the manifestation of major problems.

The school's role in prevention has become pivotal because of the breakdown of other societal support systems that promote healthy attitudes and behaviors. The disappearance of extended families, the anonymity of many neighborhoods and communities, divorce, single-parent families, and other societal trends noted elsewhere in this book mean that, for many children, the school remains the major conduit for the transmission of values and the source of a sense of personal connectedness and strength.

The consequences of reduced societal support systems can be seen in the recent media focus upon problems of youth: endemic pregnancy rates; increased drug and alcohol abuse; and a much increased incidence of suicide, homicide, crime, and high school dropout rates. The demands placed on schools to cope with these problems and meet a myriad of other needs that were formerly assumed by parents, friends, or religious organizations suggest an increased role for mental health professionals in the schools.

An additional burden has been placed on the educational system with the passage of P.L. 94-142 (Education for All Children Act, 1975). This legislation mandates the "least restrictive environment" or, maximum "mainstreaming" for physically and mentally disabled children and the preparation of individualized education plans (IEPs) to reach appropriate goals for these children. Most school personnel, including school counselors, are not prepared educationally or experientially to cope with the unique and special needs of these children.

Mental health counselors may provide services to educational institutions in two major ways. The first way is through working within the school system as a member of the professional staff. Because of restrictive hiring practices that usually do not provide for mental health counselors within school systems, this role is rare except in larger more innovative school systems that can provide for differential staffing patterns. A more obvious role for the mental health counselor is as a consultant to school systems on special issues.

As a consultant, the mental health counselor can provide group in-service training as well as individual consultation with staff regarding issues confronting the system or regarding students and their families. Services can be informative and educational on such topical areas as substance abuse, prevention of sexual assault, helping children deal with the loss of a parent through death or divorce, and teaching behavioral awareness in groups. Because among the most pressing problems in elementary schools today is the high incidence of disruptive behavior (Safran & Safran, 1985), consultation dealing with brief family interventions in a school setting (Golden, 1983) and with adolescent suicide are also helpful. Currently, suicide is possibly the most common cause of death among adolescents and youth (Matter & Matter, 1984).

Moreover, with the school counselor's own emerging role as consultant in primary prevention programs (Dinkmeyer & Dinkmeyer, 1984), the need exists to provide information to these counselors on varied prevention approaches. In their developing consultative roles, the school counselors' expertise focuses on an understanding of the entire school administrative process, as well as how the learning process of students can be influenced by indirect services to administrators, teachers, and parents (Dinkmeyer & Dinkmeyer, 1984). The mental health counselor can provide assistance not only on the understanding and application of theories of human behavior that comprehend both cognitive and affective factors, but also on the impact of beliefs, feelings, goals, and attitudes on the educational process.

Another type of consultation would be case-centered, in which the mental health counselor would emphasize with the professional staff both educational programming and intervention strategies for individual students. Bonebrake and Borgers (1984) reported that in their survey of counselors and principals from schools designated as upper-elementary, middle, or junior high, these participants agreed that individual counseling with students is the main task for school counselors. A variety of problems are raised by young people, from those created by environmental disasters (Crabbs, 1982) to academic issues. The mental health counselor has the opportunity to give valuable input concerning effective interventions.

Wilson and Rotter (1985) believe that although school counselors of the future will likely retain the same basic roles, priorities will shift as society presses the school system for optimal relevance and value. These authors explain that some possible trends that are likely to be part of tomorrow's school counseling include: a focus on families, greater community involvement, increased public relations work, increased peer counseling, and a focus on special populations and stress management. Emphasis in these areas invites the mental health counselor to utilize his/her expertise as a consultant.

COLLEGES

For many years the college environment has been a setting where young people received crisis intervention services and other forms of counseling assistance. Counseling centers on many university campuses, for example, provide individual counseling and psychotherapy in areas of personal, educational, vocational, marital, family, and social problems; group counseling and therapy to help clients establish satisfying personal relationships and to become more effective in areas such as interpersonal processes, communication skills, decision making concerning personal and educational–vocational matters, and the establishment of personal values; administration and use of psychological tests and other assessment techniques, when appropriate, to foster client self-understanding and decision making; outreach efforts to address developmental concerns of students who otherwise would be unlikely to request counseling services; and full and active use of referral sources within the institution and the local community (Garni et al., 1982). Consequently, these centers have developmental, preventive, and remedial functions or roles, with the preventive role focusing on the identification of those skills presently needed by individuals or those that may be needed in the future and to provide a means for their acquisition. Also, career counseling has become one of the few forms of mental health services the public seeks without fear of social stigma (Welfel, 1982).

College counseling centers are staffed by professionals from disciplines such as counseling and clinical psychology, counseling and personnel services, psychiatry, social work, and others with appropriate training and experience, such as mental health counselors. Because college counseling centers and related resources (i.e., health service, hotline network, residence hall counseling), on university campuses offer multiple counseling opportunities for crisis intervention, educational help, and decision-making assistance, professionals come from a variety of human service backgrounds. Garni et al. (1982) emphasize that college counseling resources should take advantage of the services of specialists for assistance with case management, program development, and evaluation. These specialists would include not only occupational information and reading-learning personnel, but also mental health counselors who have particular expertise in crisis interventions and counseling techniques with special populations. Nugent (1983) reported that the presenting problems of college students center around vocational/educational, personal, and social decisions that can cause self-doubt or confusion. Upon entering college, many minority students (i.e., ethnic or physically disabled), find it particularly difficult to respond to the new academic environment. Self-doubt and confusion may be nagging problems; and mental health counselors who work with these client populations on a consultant basis frequently have a particularly valuable contribution to make.

MILITARY SETTINGS

Within the military environment, mental health counselors work in a variety of settings, such as family service centers, hospitals, outpatient clinics, and educational programs. These counselors encourage the delivery of meaningful guidance, counseling, and educational programs for all members of the armed services, their dependents, veterans, and civilian employees of the armed services. Educational counseling represents a large part of the counseling services offered in the military, because personnel and manpower policies of the military are moving education to a more central role (Cox, 1985). These policies are taking the form of increased opportunities and new programs for men and women in uniform. Every major military installation in the United States and overseas has an on-base education program.

An interesting dimension to mental health delivery for the military are the increasing number of family service centers for those in the armed forces overseas. Usually staffed by psychologists, social workers, family counselors, or related professional personnel whose main job function is prevention and remediation, these centers are responding to a growing mental health need. Willis and Power (1985) reported that mobility (families in the military are usually moved every 2 to 3 years, causing a disruption in family life), separation from the extended family, cross-cultural parentage, a fortress mentality (in which families reside, work, and attend school in a tightly organized, closely observant community that demands conformity to conservative and relatively inflexible behavioral demands), the single-parent military family caused by extended temporary duty, and cross-cultural divorce are all problems for military personnel and their dependents while living overseas. These concerns often cause severe life adjustment problems, and the military, beginning to recognize these difficulties, is establishing resources to assist in their prevention and remediation. Whether located in a family service/support center of the outpatient department of a military clinic or hospital, human service providers, namely social workers, psychologists, and/or mental health counselors act as consultants to on-base elementary and secondary schools, and provide individual and group counseling and psychotherapy. Importantly, with a stronger emphasis on the family of military personnel, prevention is being highlighted in many mental health programs on overseas bases. Within the armed forces, the role of consultant to different military units in order to address potential problems is becoming a large part of the counselor's job duties.

EMPLOYEE ASSISTANCE PROGRAMS

Employee Assistance Programs (EAPs) are providing an increasing number of employment opportunities for mental health counselors. Associated with business and industry, these programs are intended both to assist employees who either have job performance problems or are likely to as a result of personal problems, and to help alcoholic people. Twenty percent of United States employees have problems that adversely affect their jobs and personal lives (Myers, 1984). Causes include alcoholism, marital discord, legal and financial difficulties, and excessive stress.

Employee assistance programs are mushrooming across corporate America. They represent a set of company policies and procedures for identifying (or responding to self-identified) employees experiencing personal or emotional problems that may interfere, directly or indirectly, with acceptable job performance (Walsh, 1982). Yet within those guidelines there remains wide scope for variation from one program to another. Policies and procedures may vary widely in their specific content, and the identification process of employee problems differs from program to program. Also, EAPs respond to problems, but vary in the functional units of the company to which they report (medical, personnel,industrial relations), and in the specific arrangements they make with outside referral resources for diagnostic, treatment, and follow-up services (Walsh, 1982).

It is out of the background of occupational alcoholism efforts that the basic ideas on which the EAP concept is based were conceived (Wrich, 1980). In the early 1940s, Alcoholics Anonymous (AA) was beginning to gain recognition as an effective means of helping people to recover from alcoholism and live successful lives without the use of alcohol. A few companies allowed alcoholic employees to return to work after having been terminated when they were able to demonstrate they could maintain sobriety with the help of AA. The idea emerged that perhaps employers could be effective as a resource for alleviating the alcoholism problem (Wrich, 1980). In addition to helping in the recovery process by employing recovering alcoholics, perhaps they could participate in the identification process by recognizing employees' problems and then encouraging them to get help before poor job performance resulted in termination. Wrich (1980) explained that "As this concept evolved, the idea emerged that supervisors could be trained in alcoholism symptomatology enabling them to look for these symptoms among subordinates" (p. 11).

In the 1960s, however, programs began to shift their focus from symptomatology of alcoholism to impaired job performance caused by alcoholism. Contributing to this change were such factors as: (a) it would be less stigmatizing to focus on job performance rather than alcoholism symptoms, and (b) supervisors simply were not very good diagnosticians (Wrich, 1980).

Consequently, the underlying theory behind the development of EAPs has been that business and private industry can benefit from providing mental health and related support services to employees and their families. Talagrand (1982) estimated that the behavioral and medical problems of employees represent an annual expense of $1,500 to $4,000 per worker in terms of reduced productivity and absenteeism. These programs are normally designed to provide a range of early intervention services to troubled employees and their families in order to improve the employee's on-the-job performance and productivity. EAPs operate on the premise that both employees and employers can benefit from early detection and treatment of a wide range of employee problems (NCCMH, 1984).

Many EAPs provide: (a) supervisor training in the identification and referral of troubled employees, (b) employee education and orientation to the program, (c) personnel policy development, (d) short-term counseling or referral for all of the previously described problems, and (e) periodic program evaluations. In addition, programs may offer a variety of other services, such as 24-hour emergency treatment, one or more telephone hotlines, on-site workshops, and extensive consultation services for management. When an EAP includes the availability of direct treatment to employees and their families, the service setting may be at the work location or the offices of the community mental health facility.

The traditional EAP is designed as a "top down" program. McClellen (1982) explained that

> It starts with top management support and utilizes a pyramid-shaped, supervisory structure to identify and confront employees with impaired work performance. It works best when superiors are dealing with subordinates; there are clear lines of authority, and there are job descriptions with specific, measurable work performance criteria. (p. 25)

Yet many modern professional and technical work settings are not structured with pyramid-shaped lines of authority. Work teams sometimes replace authoritarian supervisory structures, and when such an organization does exist, it often has little practical application for many white-collar workers (McClellan, 1982). Also, the nature of a professional's work makes it difficult to document impaired work performance objectively. Consequently, because the pyramid model does not appear to function well for professional, technical, managerial, and clerical workers, other EAP models have developed, such as: (a) the peer group confrontation model as a means of motivating fellow company members into appropriate treatment; or (b) the EAP Service Center model, namely, contracting with an outside agent for EAP services. McClellan (1982) believes that professional and technical workers are even more willing than other workers to use EAP services that are located off work premises than to use services located at their place of work. External programs also have the advantage that they can simultaneously use supervisory, personnel department, peer group, family, and voluntary referral systems, whereas an internal program is severely limited in how it can link to peer groups, family members, and self-awareness models as methods of helping the impaired professional.

The backgrounds of service providers and internal EAPs vary. To explore the backgrounds of EAP staff, questionnaires were mailed to member centers of the National Council of Community Mental Health Centers. Of the 614 centers that were mailed the survey questions, a response rate of 74% was obtained. The EAPs reported that social workers and counselors comprised 47% and 36%, respectively, of the staff, and psychologists were 38%.

The EAP staff have many duties, which include the assessment of each client's presenting problem; referral, when necessary, to selected community resources most capable of addressing the situation; following the intervention plan, developed in conjunction with the community resource; serving as consultant to physicians, insurance companies, worker's compensation resources, unions and management, and others concerned with the client's well-being; providing professional supervision of employees who volunteer to provide peer support and follow-up services; conducting short-term counseling with referred clients; performing related administrative duties such as budget; and maintaining timely, accurate, and concise case records.

Cost control is a major goal of EAPs, but there is insufficient evidence of their effectiveness in achieving it (Myers, 1984). Yet EAPs are responding to a definite need in the corporate business community, and companies attuned to health and cost savings concerns will continue to develop or expand their EAPs. Moreover, there is a continued interest in employee assistance programs by community mental health centers (NCCMHC, 1984).

PRISONS AND CORRECTIONAL AGENCIES

Many prisons serve to help rehabilitate criminals and to control and isolate persons viewed as hazards to the general public. Though programs to rehabilitate offenders through prison counseling and vocational education classes have recently been de-emphasized (Geis, 1983), these efforts have resulted in counselors performing multiple roles such as assessment, treatment, training, consultation, and research (Whiteley & Hosford, 1983). Yet the need for counseling services in prisons and jails is substantial (Scott, 1985). Widespread prison overcrowding and the process of incarceration induce high levels of stress (Masuda, Cutler, Hein, & Holmes, 1978).

Scott (1985) explained that "Because of the diversity and magnitude of problems encountered in prison environments, counselors often function in interrelated roles, assessing and treating prisoners, training prison staff, and serving as human relations or research consultants to prison administrators" (p. 272). Such role diversity, however, may lead to ethical and therapeutic dilemmas (Scott, 1985). Counselors who function in a prison and who attempt to maintain awareness of their professional values or ethical codes that emphasize the value, worth, and dignity of the individual, often find themselves enmeshed in at least two roles—individual counselor and environmental consultant or potential environmental change agent. These two roles and their competing ethical responsibilities may pose serious ethical dilemmas (Scott, 1985).

Though many public offenders—those who have broken the law and who have problems living within the confines of society—are located in prisons or jails, these persons can also be found in corrections facilities, divisions of youth services, rehabilitation settings, schools, mental health setting, and private practice settings (Page, 1985). Mental health counselors who have an interest in this client population may be employed, consequently, in a variety of settings, including probation/parole agencies and local/state governments. Similar to counselors in prisons, however, the role of counselors in correctional agencies can be a conflictive one. Though they perform assessment, consultation, and short-term counseling functions, it is difficult to form effective relationships with clients (Page, 1985). The counselor is often expected to act as a custodial officer, namely, to police the deviant behavior of clients and to punish clients, when necessary (Page, 1985).

The role of the mental health counselor working in correctional settings is, therefore, a challenging one. The future for programs to assist in the vocational education and life adjustment of public offenders is uncertain. Ethical dilemmas are ever present, and a pervasive problem related to the fact that the average citizen of the United States probably has, as Page (1985) stated,

> a great deal of ambivalence about whether or not public offenders should receive counseling. The average American often thinks that public offenders have broken the law, are manipulators, and should be punished for what they have done. The hardening of people's attitudes in society and within the criminal justice system toward criminals has been a problem for the Public Offender Counselor Association because there has been a tendency within the criminal justice system to eliminate rehabilitation programs. (p. 455)

SUBSTANCE ABUSE CENTERS

Since 1978 there has been a substantial increase in what are labeled nontraditional or specialized counseling centers. Among the more popular of these have been those catering to alcohol and drug abuse (Gibson et al., 1983). Many of these centers are located in large metropolitan areas and medium-sized communities. They tend to provide three categories of services: (a) educational/prevention, (b) treatment and rehabilitation, and (c) consultation. Some of the programs have residential treatment centers, and staffing is often comparable to other community mental health agencies.

Client assessment is an important function for mental health counselors in these facilities, for most substance abuse centers do extensive "work-ups" on their clients. Family, education, and career information is gathered, as well as the history of substance abuse and personal traits. From this assessment an intervention plan is developed. Gibson et al. (1983) explained that in the formulation of this plan, the staff should be aware of the legal guidelines and implications in the treatment of drug use and of federal regulations governing client records and information exchange.

Other job duties for mental health counselors in these agencies are short-term individual and group counseling; family counseling, when necessary; and liaison with the community. Many substance abuse centers also assume a prevention role in the community. Early detection and intervention of youthful abusers is a particularly essential element of a preventive program.

These centers may be located in hospitals as part of the outpatient services, in a community mental health setting, or as a separate agency not attached to a larger institution. Within these resources various intervention approaches may be followed. Many agencies assist the client by utilizing a medical model approach, whereas others, once the substance abuse is under control, follow more a psycho-educational model that emphasizes the client's development of needed skills to function effectively in the community.

With the incidence of substance abuse increasing in the United States, communities are reaffirming the need to respond to this growing problem. Substance abuse centers are a vital part of the delivery of mental health counseling services. For a mental health counselor to work effectively in these settings, however, not only requires special training, but within this training is emphasis both on the inherent dynamics of substance abuse and the need to use direct, tough, and often radical approaches to break through the client's gamesmanship (Forman, 1979).

MARRIAGE AND FAMILY COUNSELING CENTERS

The ever-increasing divorce rate, children living in single-parent households, and the stress often created by dual-career marriages: All of these factors have led to a significant increase in marriage and family counseling. Much of this increase is reflected in the case loads of the mental health counseling professionals in private practice or working out of the traditional community mental health and university counseling centers. But additionally, private and tax-supported marriage and family counseling centers have been growing in large metropolitan areas (Gibson et al., 1983).

Different counseling approaches are used in these settings. They include:

1. Conjoint marital counseling, perhaps the most popular approach among marital counselors today, which emphasizes the counseling of both spouses together during all the therapeutic sessions (Gibson et al., 1983);
2. Concurrent marital counseling, when both partners undergo concurrent but separate counseling directed at providing each partner with insights that may lead ultimately to change;
3. Family counseling, which involves the whole family;
4. Group counseling, which consists of groups comprised of marital couples seeking assistance;
5. Enrichment groups, or programs that focus on enhancement of the marital and family relationship by emphasizing, for example, educational skill-building techniques in the areas of communication, cooperation, and problem-solving; and
6. Sex therapy or counseling.

Mental health counselors employed in these settings usually meet the licensure standards of the American Association of Marriage and Family Therapists. Besides providing counseling to troubled couples and families, these counselors also perform assessment and community education functions. An accurate diagnosis of marital and family problems is essential if intervention is to be successful. Community education may take the form of developing programs that alert families to existing resources for help.

MENTAL HEALTH SETTINGS FOR THE ELDERLY

The number of persons over 60 years of age continues to grow rapidly, concomitant with social and economic problems inherent to their age group. Shanks (1983) reported there is a pressing demand, therefore, to expand mental health counseling services to the elderly. The very nature of the aging process strongly implies a need for intensified and additional support.

Yet older people are underserved by all forms of mental health service (Redick & Taube, 1980). Myers (1983) reported "that it has been well established that although over 12% of the nation's population is elderly, only 2% to 4% of persons seen in outpatient mental health clinics are in the over-60 age group" (p.69). Well over half of all nursing home patients have symptoms of mental health problems, yet mental health services for this group are, in general, nonexistent (Edinberg, 1985). Puterski (1982) stated that programs that successfully reach the elderly are usually ones that bring in the least amount of fees, are costly in terms of outreach and coordination, and are therefore the first to be cut back when budgets become tight. As a result, however, of a trend in the late 1960s to "return" older schizophrenics and persons with senile dementia to their communities, which often meant a nursing home ill-prepared to cope with behavioral problems presented by these persons, custodial care of the elderly has risen proportionately. Older persons have left or never entered the formal mental health system, and settings such as nursing homes have frequently become the agencies to provide mental health care (Kahn, 1975). Edinberg (1985) also asserted that agencies that fall under the auspices of the Older Americans Act of 1965, including meal programs, certain social service programs, and programs funded by discretionary grants do not, as a rule, have close working relationships with mental health system services.

Even with all of these realities that represent obstacles for effectively serving the elderly, community agencies to serve this population have increased since 1978, and many employ mental health counselors. The delivery of services to the elderly usually takes place within organizations. These organizations are of two general types, namely, institutions and community settings. Ordinarily, institutional facilities include nursing homes and mental hospitals, both of which are designed to care for persons from a few weeks to an indefinite period of time. The number of elderly patients in public facilities, however, has been decreasing substantially, suggesting that in the future, nursing homes and community services will need to provide better follow-up and active treatment for the growing number of older persons with diagnosed and identified chronic mental health problems (Edinberg, 1985). At any moment in time, moreover, 5% of the elderly population is institutionalized, primarily in nursing homes (Butler & Lewis, 1982).

Concerning community settings, a wide variety of agencies providing mental health services may be available to the elderly in a given community. These include community mental health centers; adult day care; and geriatric day hospitals, one of the most rapidly growing services for the elderly (Edinberg, 1985). Agencies generally fall under two types: a medical-rehabilitative model and a psychosocial model. The former emphasizes recovery and rehabilitation from strokes or surgery; the later emphasizes adaptation and coping with losses, including cognitive impairment (Weiler & Rathbone-McCuen, 1978). These agencies also comprise senior centers, which emphasize recreation and leisure activities, though some have active and ongoing programs for health, legal or housing benefits, and mental health intervention. These senior centers are located in a variety of settings, ranging from newly built senior centers in the middle of towns to church basements, and with adult day care provide excellent opportunities for the delivery of mental health services (Edinberg, 1985). There are private, nonprofit social service agencies that offer such programs as home health aides, outreach, family support groups, and counseling; congregate meal sites established in churches, housing for the elderly, senior centers, and so on. Although social services and outreach are supposed to be provided in each of these settings, the meals and transportation are usually a higher priority. There are also state and municipal programs, developed to provide mental health assistance, and hospitals and visiting nurse associations.

Mental health counselors working in these different settings may perform a variety of functions, such as short-term counseling, crisis intervention, consultation, program development, and education. The principal duties, of course, will depend on the main goals of the agency and its particular intervention approach, namely, a medical model or a psychosocial model. Importantly, there are several trends in mental health services to the elderly that can be considered extensions of traditional direct service and comprise outreach, peer counseling, and working with support systems (Edinberg, 1985). *Outreach services* locate older persons and inform them of available services (Harbert & Ginsberg, 1979), and Edinberg (1985) believes that "the major mental health service offered through outreach is creating a trusting relationship that becomes the basis for other services" (p. 273). *Peer counselors* are older individuals who are trained by professionals and offer counseling to their peers under the auspices of a service agency (Bratter & Tuvman, 1980). *Working with support systems* usually refers to family, friends, or neighbors who help maintain the older person in his or her home. The family is usually the focus of most professional interest, though other, unrelated older persons can be utilized as volunteers for the source of support.

From their research to identify the essential goals and appropriate roles of counselors engaged in assisting older persons, Johnson and Riker (1982) reported that a preventive, developmental, positive growth approach to counseling older persons is preferred among gerontological counselors. Instead of a reactive, or crisis-oriented approach, counselors recognized the need for both preventive and remedial services for older persons. Yet the concerns of older persons are multidimensional and thus demand mental health counseling services that are equally comprehensive in scope (Johnson & Riker, 1982).

There is a vast array of opportunities for mental health counselors who choose to work with the elderly, and for whom there is a job slot in a particular agency. Barry (1980) reported that the counselor who deals with aging clients must be aware that health needs and financial support are likely to be among their most prevalent and pressing problems. These problems interact with other psychological problems that the aging client may bring to the mental health counselor. Other important problems may include loneliness, low self-esteem, a lack of independence, feelings of uselessness, and dissatisfaction (Barry, 1980).

Mental health counselors, along with other helping groups, are becoming more and more interested in understanding the aging and their needs. This commitment, along with demographic changes and the increased appreciation of nontraditional approaches, strongly suggest that the professional community may change its focus to better serve the elderly. This change should also bring a continued, though slow, growth in settings to assist this population.

MENTAL HEALTH COUNSELORS IN PRIVATE PRACTICE

Weikel (1985) reported that the majority of mental health counselors (22%) are now working in private practice. There has been a significant increase in the number of counselors who are active in the private, profit-making sector. Much of this development is due to the growing number of states that have passed counselor licensure laws. Licensure requirements for counselors vary from state to state, but they have generally facilitated opportunities for mental health counselors to deliver services with the intent of making a financial gain.

The reasons for referral to these counselors include a wide range of problems, such as emotional, marital, family, job-related, and alcohol. The intervention approaches vary, of course, according to the philosophy of the counselor and the specific problem. But the process of helping usually involves an initial interview, an information analysis, assessment, the development of counseling objectives, and the implementation of the counseling plan. This implementation may embrace such approaches as individual short-term or long-term counseling, group counseling, and marriage and family counseling.

Most private practice settings are in an office-like environment. The business is usually developed by referrals, which are generally created by contacts made in the community by the mental health counselor. Networking is most important for a continuous flow of referrals.

An interesting phenomenon in the private practice sector is the increased number of mental health counselors who are receiving referrals from insurance companies to assist their work-related injured employees. Of the approximately 4,150 professionals who are employed in the private sector (Workman, 1983), many are mental health counselors. A large number of these have clients who have back injuries, with other physically disabling conditions, (i.e., knee, hand, head, neck, and leg injuries) comprising the rest of this disabled population. The development of vocational objectives is essential to the assistance of those industrially injured clients, and often the referral source expects job development exploration and job placement. Workman (1983) reported that a strong emphasis is placed upon the processes of (a) job analysis, (b) labor market surveys, and (c) job placement. Because of the many aspects or needed steps to the rehabilitation of these clients, and the special training that is required for job development and job placement, the mental health counselor may only perform the assessment and counseling phases with the industrially injured.

Essential to the credibility of the mental health counselor in private practice is the achievement of certification and, where necessary, licensure. As indicated earlier, all states have somewhat differing licensure requirements. Also, however, once licensure is gained in one state, other states may allow reciprocity.

DOMESTIC VIOLENCE AND CHILD ABUSE SHELTERS

Domestic violence and child abuse is rampant in the United States and the personal, social, and economic costs are inestimable. Abramson reported in 1977 that one third of all married people engage in spouse assault. The National Center on Child Abuse and Neglect estimates that every year approximately 1 million children are maltreated by their parents; of these, 100,000 to 200,000 are physically abused, 60,000 to 100,000 are sexually abused, and the remainder are neglected (Barnett, Pittman, Ragan, & Salus, 1980). To respond to these serious problems, agencies and programs have been established to assist helping professionals, including mental health counselors, to aid these victimized individuals.

Safe houses, refuges, or shelters have become the cornerstone of treatment for battered women who do not wish to return home (Walker, 1979). Erin Pizzey founded the first known refuge in England in 1971; and since then, approximately 400 have been established in the United States (Alessi & Hearn, 1984). These shelters may provide medical help, vocational training, counseling, and rehousing, as well as impart information on women's legal rights, welfare, and court advocacy. Many shelters also offer a self-development program for the women that will encourage their self-determination, facilitate increased public awareness of the problem of household violence and the need for the support of the public and private sector, and attempt to induce change within the existing public agencies that are in a position to respond effectively to the victims of household violence (Roberts, 1984). Many shelters further provide a 24-hour crisis telephone line.

Most of the differences between the varied shelters is with the degree of community established among members. They all provide a community support system that nurtures these women and children, which did not exist for them in their original communities or families. Some shelters operate on the premise that everyone is expected to be responsible for herself and for others' welfare (Walker, 1979). Decisions are made by consensus and everyone has an equal stake in running the house. Whatever the approach that is adopted by a particular resource, the importance of the shelter movement is that it provides a sense of community and a support system. The amount of time that women spend in a shelter varies. Most shelters in this country find between 4 and 6 weeks to be the optimum stay (Walker, 1979).

A new treatment population has recently emerged within the area of domestic violence. This population is the children who find themselves in shelters for victims of domestic violence (Alessi & Hearn, 1984). They are usually in crisis and are experiencing acute feelings of separation and loss (experienced as anger, fear, and emotional pain), and they have difficulty coping with these feelings in a healthy fashion (Fleming, 1979). A crisis model and educational components have been developed within the shelters to alleviate these problems (Alessi & Hearn, 1984).

Programs for abused and neglected children may include day care, foster care, physical health care, mental health services, companion advocacy, or group residential treatment. There are very few settings that deal exclusively with the delivery of mental health services for abused children, because assistance opportunities can be found in community mental health centers and many marriage and family counseling resources. Many programs have been initiated, however, for abusive parents, and they are frequently offered by municipal and county governments (Benjamin & Walz, 1983). Community-based volunteer groups have also been successful in providing multidisciplinary consultation for developing a comprehensive management plan in cases of child abuse and neglect (LeBlang, 1979). Also, primary prevention programs are vitally important to remedy this widespread problem, and they are offered in school, family counseling, and community centers.

The predominant staffing pattern for the shelters of battered women includes paraprofessionals and volunteer workers (Roberts, 1984). Almost half of existing programs report having a former battered woman on staff, and self-help or peer counseling groups are generally an important component of programs for abused women (Roberts, 1984). Roberts (1984) has also explained that survey research conducted in 1980 among shelters for abused women indicated that 44% of the reporting agencies had professional counselors, social workers, and/or psychologists on staff. To function effectively in these shelters, mental health counselors need an extensive background not only in crisis, short-term, and group counseling approaches, but also in marriage and family dynamics. Mental health counselors may also act as consultants for these shelters. In this capacity they conduct training for paraprofessionals, and/or assist the staff in improving their group counseling techniques, intervention approaches with the abusive partner, and methods of influencing local community agencies (i.e., police, courts), about the necessity for early identification of family violence. Roberts (1984) believes, moreover, "that battered women's programs should recruit counselors with advanced training who, in addition, possess the following attributes: nonjudgmental attitude; good listening ability, supportive and caring attitude; and an overriding concern for the welfare of the client" (p. 74).

Because many differing kinds of mental health agencies deliver services to the abused children and their families, the job functions of the mental health counselor will vary. Depending upon the orientation of the agency or program, mental health counselors may be consultants for early identification and prevention programs or provide direct intervention services to the abusing family. In the latter capacity, they may also work with the courts.

OTHER SETTINGS

The growing number of mental health counselors offer an expanding variety of services. Of course, mental health counselors have worked for years in large institutional settings, such as hospitals that offer services to the chronically mentally disabled and/or crisis intervention or short-term care for the "acutely disturbed." Counselors are also working in outpatient clinics associated with hospitals that, among their services, also provide help for individuals and families with mental health problems. The responsibilities of the mental health counselors include diagnostic interviewing, assessment of the presenting problem, the development of an intervention plan, and counseling. Consultation services may also be provided within these settings, with remediation of client problems usually the primary focus of assistance.

There are two settings, moreover, that have not yet been identified in this chapter but that will be discussed because of the presence of mental health counselors. One is psychosocial centers and the other is career counseling and vocational rehabilitation as performed by the Veterans Administration.

Over the past three decades, models of psychosocial rehabilitation have evolved in the community. Leitner (1986) explained that throughout the 1950s and 1960s, several agencies emerged providing community psychosocial rehabilitation services. Following accumulation of 25 years of community experience, the International Association of Psychosocial Rehabilitation Services (IAPSRS) was established in 1975, based on the belief that psychosocial rehabilitation is the core of community support programs. The organization suggested a comprehensive definition of psychosocial rehabilitation:

> A goal oriented program for the mentally ill which provides coping experiences toward improved living in the community. The program emphasizes common sense and practical needs and usually includes services of vocational, residential, social, educational and personal adjustment, and the prevention of unnecessary hospitalization. The psychosocial rehabilitation setting is purposely informal to reduce the psychological distance between staff and members and consciously engages the member as an active participant in program planning, development, policy making, implementation and evaluation. (Tanaka, 1983, p. 7)

Lanoil (1982) summarized the common elements and goals of many psychosocial centers. These centers provide a type of rehabilitation that emphasizes social, vocational, educational, residential, and evaluation services. In addition, they play an advocacy role in the community while providing emotional support through fostering warm relationships between staff and clients. Clients are called members and are highly involved in the daily running of the "clubhouse." Basic guidelines include: (a) profound respect for individual differences; (b) belief in mutual self-help; (c) no time limits on participation; (d) basic acceptance of members; (e) emphasis on short-range, realistic goals; (f) social climate of warmth and action; and (g) active participation of members working toward obtaining optimal level of functioning in the community.

Smith, Brown, Gibbs, Sanders, and Cramer (1984) discussed key ingredients that facilitate implementing these principles: an open and clear structure, supportive staff who provide clear limits while fostering client responsibility, and an informal agency atmosphere. These elements encourage clients to make their own plans as well as gain a sense of belonging and pride that contribute to improving functional abilities. "Significant client involvement makes empowerment of clients possible. Client empowerment means a better mental health system for consumers, families and friends, and that, in turn, means a better community" (Smith et al., 1984, p. 42).

Around the country, many individual programs exist. Each has its unique features resulting from its specific target population and cultural, environmental setting. The initiator of each innovative program takes the responsibility not only to implement the specific program, but also to evaluate it, report outcome measures, and seek improvements (Leitner, 1986).

Mental health counselors working in these psychosocial centers not only should have an understanding of mental disability and varied counseling approaches, but should also possess diagnostic planning skills. These include extensive interviewing and assessment skills in order to explore the client's strengths and deficits and how they affect one's abilities to function in a particular environment; programming skills, namely, the ability to teach new skills through systematic programming and outlining a series of behavioral goals; career counseling skills; career placement skills; and community coordinating skills, namely, the ability to develop and implement an appropriate program and aid in overcoming client and/or environmental barriers in using available resources (Anthony, Cohen, & Cohen, 1983). Mental health professionals can also serve as consultants, especially in the training of paraprofessionals, who are frequently utilized in psychosocial centers.

When considering the field of career counseling and rehabilitation, the vocational rehabilitation of veterans warrants special attention. Lemons and Sweeney (1979) explained that various legislative and administrative provisions underlying the Veterans Administration (VA) vocational rehabilitation program serve "to create a distinct, but heterogeneous, client population and a unique configuration of rehabilitation services" (p. 295). An eligible veteran applying for vocational rehabilitation is provided with comprehensive counseling to determine the need for rehabilitation and to develop an individually tailored training plan, if need is established.

Extensive information is collected about the veteran and following psychological testing or other assessment methods, and counseling, an exploration is conducted of available educational or training opportunities. A suitable rehabilitation objective, which must be expected to restore employability upon attainment, is identified. The achievement of the objective may require training, and it becomes the responsibility of the vocational rehabilitation specialist to further develop the training program, induct the veteran into training, and supervise the veteran during training. Follow-up is also conducted for 6 months after the completion of training, in case further assistance is needed.

This type of veteran's assistance is available at 58 regional offices, additional decentralized VA locations, and at VA-contracted guidance centers. The professional counselors have at least a master's degree in counseling or a related field. Outreach services to identify veterans in need of assistance are also found in many counseling locations.

CONCLUSION

Mental health counselors work in a vast array of agencies and programs. Each agency or program may have distinctive expectations for how their services will be delivered. With these expectations are the needs of major segments of the population for assistance. The mental health counseling field has demonstrated a flexibility in the way these needs receive attention. This flexibility, as well as the variety of agencies offering services, will increase because mental health counselors are responsive to the changing environment and are open to the development of new intervention approaches.

REFERENCES

Abramson, C. (1977). *Spouse abuse—An annotated bibliography.* Washington, DC: Center for Women's Policy Studies.

Alessi, J. J., & Hearn, K. (1984). Group treatment of children in shelters for battered women. In A. R. Roberts, (Ed.), *Battered women and their families* (pp. 49–61). New York: Springer.

Anthony, W., Cohen, M. R., & Cohen, B. F. (1983). Philosophy, treatment process, and principles of the psychiatric rehabilitation approach. *New Directions in Mental Health, 17,* 67–69.

Barnett, E. R., Pittman, C. B., Ragan, C. K., & Salus, M. K. (1980). *Family violence: Intervention strategies.* Washington, DC: U.S. Department of Health and Human Services, Office of Human Development Services, U.S. Government Printing Office.

Barry, J. R. (1980). Counseling the aging. *Personnel and Guidance Journal, 57,* 122–124.

Benjamin, L., & Walz, G. R. (1983). *Violence in the family: Child and spouse abuse.* Ann Arbor: University of Michigan.

Bloom, B. L. (1977). *Community mental health. A general introduction.* Monterey, CA.: Brooks/Cole.

Bonebrake, C. R., & Borgers, S. B. (1984). Counselor role as perceived by counselor and principals. *Elementary School Guidance Counseling, 18,* 194–200.

Bratter, B., & Tuvman, E. (1980). A peer counseling program in action. In S. S. Sargent (Ed.), *Nontraditional therapy and counseling with the aging.* New York: Springer.

Butler, R. N., & Lewis, M. I. (1982). *Aging and mental health: Positive psychosocial approaches* (3rd ed.). St. Louis: C.V. Mosby.

Chafetz, D. I., & Salloway, J. C. (1984). Patterns of mental health services provided by HMOs. *American Psychologist, 39,* 495–502.

Cox, W. E. (1985). Military education and counselor association. *Journal of Counseling and Development, 63,* 461–463.

Conyne, R. K. (1985). The counseling ecologist: helping people and environments. *Counseling and Human Development, 18,* 1–12.

Crabbs, M. A. (1982). Children and environmental disasters: The counselor's responsibility. *Elementary School Guidance Counseling, 16,* 228–234.

Deleon, P. H., Vyeda, M. K., & Welch, B. L. (1985). Psychology and HMOs: New partnership or new adversary? *American Psychologist, 40,* 1122–1124.

Department of Health, Education, and Welfare. (1978). *The president's commission on mental health. Report to the president* (Vol. 1). Washington, DC: U.S. Government Printing Office.

Dinkmeyer, D., Jr., & Dinkmeyer, D., Sr. (1984).School counselors as consultants in primary prevention programs. *Personnel and Guidance Journal, 62,* 194–200.

Edinberg, M. A. (1985). *Mental health practice with the elderly.* Englewood Cliffs, NJ: Prentice-Hall.

Egan, G. (1982). *The skilled helper: Model, skills, and methods for effective helping.* Monterey, CA: Brooks/Cole.

Fleming, J. B. (1979). *Stopping wife abuse.* New York: Anchor Press.

Forman, S. I. (1979). Pitfalls in counseling alcoholic clients. *Personnel and Guidance Journal, 57,* 546.

Forrest, D. V., & Affemann, M. (1986, April). The future for mental health counselors in health maintenance organizations. *American Mental Health Counselors Association Journal, 8,* 65–72.

Garni, K. F., Gelwick, B. P., Lamb, D. H., McKinley, D. L., Schoenberg, B. M., Simono, R. B., Smith, J. E., Wierson, P. W., & Wrenn, R. L. (1982). Accreditation guidelines for university and college counseling services. *Personnel and Guidance Journal, 61,* 116–121.

Gatz, M., Smyer, M. A., & Lawton, M. P. (1980). The mental health system and the older adult. In L. W. Poon (Ed.), *Aging in the 1980s: Psychological issues* (pp. 5-18). Washington, DC: American Psychological Association.

Geis, G. (1983). Criminal justice and adult offenders: An overview. *The Counseling Psychologist, 11,* 11-16.

Gibson, R. L., Mitchell, M. H., & Higgins, R. E. (1983). *Development and management of counseling programs and guidance services.* New York: Macmillan.

Golden, L. (1983). Brief family interventions in a school setting. *Elementary School Guidance & Counseling, 17,* 288-294.

Goldman, H., Regier, D., & Taub, C. (1980). Community mental health centers and the treatment of severe mental disorders. *American Journal of Psychiatry, 137,* 83-86.

Goodstein, L. D. (1978). *Consulting with human service systems.* Reading, MA: Addison-Wesley.

Green, R. S., & Koprowski, P. F. (1981). The chronic patient with a nonpsychotic diagnosis. *Hospital and Community Psychiatry, 32,* 479-481.

Gruenberg, E. M. (1972). Obstacles to optimal psychiatric service delivery systems. *Psychiatric Quarterly, 46,* 483-496.

Harbert, A. S., & Ginsberg, L. H. (1979). *Human services for older adults: Concepts and skills.* Belmont, CA: Wadsworth.

Johnson, R. P., & Riker, H. C. (1982). Counselor's goals and roles in assisting older persons. *American Mental Health Counselors Association Journal, 4,* 30-37.

Kahn, R. L. (1975). The mental health system and the future aged. *The Gerontologist, 15,* 24-31.

Langeley, D. G. (1980). The community mental health center: Does it treat patients? *Hospital and Community Psychiatry, 31,* 815-819.

Lanoil, J. C. (1982). An analysis of the psychiatric psychosocial rehabilitation. *Psychosocial Rehabilitation Journal, 5,* 55-59.

LeBang, T. R. (1979). The family stress consultation team: An Illinois approach to protective services. *Child Welfare, 58,* 597-604.

Leitner, R. (1986). *Deinstitutionalization and community alternatives for the chronically mentally ill.* A seminar paper submitted for the completion of the MEd degree, University of Maryland, College Park, MD.

Lemons, S. L., & Sweeney, P. C. (1979). Veterans vocational rehabilitation: a program in transition. *Personnel and Guidance Journal, 58,* 295-297.

Lewis, M. D., & Lewis, J. A. (1977). The counselor's impact on community environments. *Personnel & Guidance Journal, 55,* 356-358.

Masuda, M., Cutler, D. L., Hein, L., & Holmes, T. H. (1978). Life events and prisoners. *Archives of General Psychiatry, 35,* 197-203.

Matter, D. E., & Matter, R. M. (1984). Suicide among elementary school children: a serious concern for counselors. *Elementary School Guidance Counseling, 18,* 260-268.

Mayer, T. R., & Mayer, G. G. (1985). HMO's: origins and development. *The New England Journal of Medicine, 312,* 594.

McClellan, K. (1982, September/October). Changing EAP services. *EAP Digest,* pp.25-29.

Myers, D. W. (1984, March/April). Measuring EAP cost effectiveness: results and recommendations. *EAP Digest,* pp. 22-25, 44.

Myers, J. E. (1983). A national survey of geriatric mental health services. *American Mental Health Counselors Association Journal, 5,* 69-74.

National Council of Community Mental Health Centers. (1984). *Community-based employee assistance programs: A providers' overview.* Rockville, MD: Author.

Nugent, F. A. (1983). *Professional counseling: An overview.* Monterey, CA: Brooks/Cole.

Okin, R. L. (1984). How community mental health centers are coping. *Hospital and Community Psychiatry, 35,* 1118–1125.

Page, R. C. (1985). The unique role of the public offender counselor association. *Journal of Counseling and Development, 63,* 455–456.

Pardes, H. C. (1982). Budget, policy changes: NIMH in transition. *Hospital and Community Psychiatry, 33,* 525–526.

Puterski, D. (1982, August). The role of the community mental health center: A case study. In M. Edinberg (Chair), *Aging and mental health: A continuum of care?* Symposium at the annual meeting of the American Psychological Association, Washington, DC.

Randolph, D. L. (1979, July). CMHC requisites for employment at master's level psychologists/counselors. *American Mental Health Counselors Association Journal,* pp. 64–68.

Redick, R. W., & Taube, C. A. (1980). Demography and mental health care of the aged. In J. E. Birren & R. B. Sloane (Eds.), *Handbook of mental health and aging.* Englewood Cliffs, NJ: Prentice-Hall.

Resnick, H. (1982). The counseling psychologist in community mental health centers and health maintenance organizations—Do we belong? *Counseling Psychologist, 10,* 53–59.

Roberts, A. R. (1984). *Battered women and their families* (Vol. 1, Springer Series on Social Work). New York: Springer.

Safran, J. S., & Safran, S. P. (1985). Teaching behavioral awareness in groups. *Elementary School Guidance and Counseling, 20,* 91–97.

Sank, L. I., & Shapiro, J. R. (1979). Case examples of the broadened role of psychology in health maintenance organizations. *Professional Psychology, 10,* 402–406.

Scott, N. A. (1985). Counseling prisoners: Ethical issues, dilemmas, and cautions. *Journal of Counseling and Development, 64,* 272–273.

Shanks, J. L. (1983). Expanding treatment for the elderly: Counseling in a private medical practice. *Personnel and Guidance Journal, 61,* 553–555.

Smith, M., Brown, D., Gibbs, L., Sanders, H., & Cramer, K. (1984). Client involvement in psychosocial rehabilitation. *Psychosocial Rehabilitation Journal, 8,* 35–42.

Talagrand, P. C. (1982, March/April). Implementation of an employee assistance program in a local government setting. *EAP Digest,* pp. 12–25.

Talbott, J. A. (Ed.). (1978). *The chronic mental patient: Problems, solutions and recommendations for a public policy.* Washington, DC: American Psychiatric Association.

Tanaka, H. (1983). Psychosocial rehabilitation: future trends and directions. *Psychosocial Rehabilitation Journal, 6,* 7–12.

Turner, J. C., & TenHoor, W. J. (1978). The NIMH community support program: pilot approach to a needed social reform. *Schizophrenia Bulletin, 4,* 319–344.

Walker, L. E. (1979). *The battered woman.* New York: Harper & Row.

Walsh, D. C. (1982). Employee assistance programs and untested assumptions. *Milbank Memorial Fund Quarterly/Health and Society, 60,* 493–517.

Weikel, W. J. (1985). The American Mental Health Counselors Association. *Journal of Counseling and Development, 63,* 457–460.

Weiler, P. E., & Rathbone-McCuen, E. (1978). *Adult day care: Community work with the elderly.* New York: Springer.

Welfel, E. R. (1982). The development of reflective judgment: Implications for career counseling of college students. *Personnel and Guidance Journal, 61,* 17–21.

Whiteley, S. M., & Hosford, R. E. (1983). Counseling in prisons. *The Counseling Psychologist, 11,* 27–34.

Willis, B., & Power, P. W. (1985). Counselors as a resource for teachers in overseas schools. *Elementary School Guidance and Counseling, 19,* 291–299.

Wilson, N. H., & Rotter, J. C. (1985). School counseling: A look into the future. *Personnel and Guidance Journal, 60,* 353–357.

Winslow, W. W. (1982). Changing trends in CMHCs: Keys to survival in the eighties. *Hospital and Community Psychiatry, 33,* 273–277.

Workman, E. L. (1983). Vocational rehabilitation in the private, profit-making sector. In E. L. Pan, T. E. Banker, & C. L. Vash (Eds.), *Annual review of rehabilitation* (Vol. 3). New York: Springer.

Wrich, J. T. (1980). *The employee assistance program.* Center City, MN: The Hazelden Foundation, Inc.

14 Co-professionals and Co-helpers

Mental health counselors clearly do not function in a realm that is devoid of other persons who simultaneously are seeking to help their clients. Many professions seek to assist individuals encountering problems of living. Some of these professions work exclusively with such clients; other of these professions serve a particular need (e.g., job placement) of individuals with problems of living along with other client groups having the same need (e.g., the mentally retarded or the physically handicapped); and still other categories of helpers serve a clientele based on some characteristic other than their mental health status (e.g., homeless persons or legal offenders) but that tends to include a significant number of individuals with mental health difficulties. Because of this multiplicity of fields, there is a good deal of complementarity; that is, one profession serving a particular need for a range of clients, while another profession serves a different need of the same client groups. There is, however, also inevitably a certain amount of overlap or even duplication of function across professions; and it is at these points that interprofessional frictions arise (particularly in times or places in which the supply of professionals exceeds the demand for their services). To function to the benefit of the client, a mental health counselor must be familiar with these other, related professions, what specialized services their practitioners can offer to his/her client, and how to interact with these co-professionals. Moreover, when referring a client to a practitioner of one of these professions for a specific service, the mental health counselor is obligated to evaluate that practitioner's performance of that service, so as to know whether to refer other clients to that practitioner for that service in the future.

In this chapter, we shall introduce these co-professions of mental health counseling, starting with those professions that are most closely related to mental health counseling in primary mission, that is, those that directly focus on assisting persons with problems of living to overcome those problems.

Much of the information concerning the occupations discussed in this chapter was obtained from the *Occupational Outlook Handbook*, a publication of the U.S. Department of Labor (1982), which describes the preparation, duties, and employment opportunities in many fields of work and is regularly used by counselors doing career counseling. Additional information was provided by national professional organizations in a number of professions discussed.

CORE PROVIDERS

Under various federally legislated programs (for example, Medicare, for the elderly; and Medicaid, for the poor), there are four so-called "core provider" professions designated as qualified to receive reimbursement for providing mental health services. These professions are psychiatry, clinical psychology, psychiatric social work, and psychiatric nursing. Attempts are currently being made within Congress to add mental health counseling to this group of "core providers." These professions all state their mission as assisting individuals to overcome or to prevent mental health difficulties.

Psychiatrists

Psychiatry is the medical specialty that seeks to study, diagnose, and treat "mental illness." As a branch of medicine, it is only natural that psychiatry would conceptualize problems of living as a category of "illness," because the role of physicians is to treat illnesses. However, some psychiatrists (e.g., Laing, 1967; Szasz, 1961) have questioned the appropriateness of the illness model for mental health problems, suggesting that the term *illness* serves the sociopolitical needs of the profession and/or its host society more than the therapeutic needs of the patient (the medical term for client). Psychiatrists receive extensive education: 3 to 4 years of college premedical program, 4 years of medical school, a year of internship in a hospital, followed by a residency of 3 or 4 years in length. Of this education, however, only the residency period is exclusively focused on working with mental health/mental illness problems. During the rest of the psychiatrist's training, "mental illness" is treated as only one of the many medical conditions studied. Among the core providers, psychiatrists are uniquely qualified to prescribe psychotropic medication (tranquilizers, antidepressants, etc.), and all other mental health fields must turn to physicians (generally, but not necessarily, psychiatrists) if such medication is needed by their clients. As was just implied, although any licensed physician is legally able to prescribe these medications, psychiatrists are generally more knowledgeable about the effects, side effects, indications, and contraindications of psychotropic medicines. Also, psychiatrists are uniquely qualified to prescribe and administer various physical treatments for mental health problems, such as electroconvulsive shock, a treatment the efficacy of which has been hotly debated. In the main, however, most psychiatrists spend most of their working hours either in office private practice or in outpatient clinics, doing verbal psychotherapy; or in psychiatric hospital treatment and/or administration. Some psychiatrists pursue research into the neurological, physiological, or biochemical basis of mental illness. Until recently, psychiatrists were the only mental health professionals who could hospitalize a patient, but in the past few years, some mental health inpatient facilities in some locations have also allowed one or more nonphysician service providers (clinical psychologists, psychiatric nurses, etc.) to hospitalize clients and treat them in that inpatient setting (sometimes independently, sometimes only under medical supervision).

A subgroup of psychiatrists are psychoanalysts. These psychiatrists choose to undergo several additional years of specialized training and supervision, as well as a personal psychoanalysis, to qualify themselves to practice psychoanalysis (that is, the therapeutic technique developed by Sigmund Freud and his disciples). It is of interest that in the United States, the psychiatrists have insisted that only persons with prior medical and psychiatric training may be allowed into psychoanalytic training, even though Sigmund Freud (the founder of psychoanalysis and himself a physician) wrote:

> I have assumed . . . that psycho-analysis is not a specialized branch of medicine. I cannot see how it is possible to dispute this. Psycho-analysis falls under the head of psychology; not of medical psychology in the old sense, nor of the psychology of morbid processes, but simply of psychology. It is certainly not the whole of psychology, but its substructure and perhaps even its entire foundation. The possibility of its application to medical purposes must not lead us astray. Electricity and radiology also have their medical application, but the science to which they both belong is none the less physics. (Freud, 1957, p. 207)

Thus, although elsewhere in the world one may become a psychoanalyst without first having been a psychiatrist and although some of the greatest contributors to psychoanalytic theory have not been physicians (for example, Erik Erikson, who was an art teacher before receiving psychoanalytic training in Europe; or Erich Fromm, who studied psychology and sociology and earned a PhD degree), American-trained psychoanalysts (that is, most of those practicing in the United States) will have been physicians and psychiatrists first.

In the fall of 1985, there were 16,548 board-certified psychiatrists in the United States, 2,828 of whom were psychoanalysts.

Finally, it should be noted that not all physicians who practice psychiatry have necessarily undergone the special training or passed the medical specialty board in psychiatry. In the United States, any physician licensed to practice medicine can choose to limit his/her practice to a particular type of illness. Thus, a physician with just an internship in general medicine may hang out a shingle stating "practice limited to psychiatry." Consequently, mental health counselors should familiarize themselves with the credentials of the psychiatrists to whom they refer clients for medication, physical treatments, or hospitalization. Generally, board-certified psychiatrists are more likely to possess the greatest knowledge of the field.

Clinical Psychologists

In 1896, Lightner Witmer founded the first psychological clinic at the University of Pennsylvania, as a setting in which to apply the then-existing academic–experimental psychology to the study and treatment of children with physical problems or mental retardation that might interfere with their progress in school. In 1907, he coined the term "clinical psychology" for this activity. The diagnosis of children's learning problems remained the principal focus of the field until the 1930s, when its role expanded to include the diagnosis of adult personality and mental health status. It was not, however, until World War II that clinical psychologists became involved in treatment as well as diagnosis of mental health problems. Just after that war, the Veterans Administration provided a tremendous impetus to the growth of clinical psychology in seeking to meet its need for therapists for veterans of the war. As a direct result of this growth spurt, today just about half of all doctoral-level psychologists are clinical psychologists, equaling in number all experimental, social, educational, industrial, and other psychological specialties combined. Goldenberg (1973) has suggested that recently the role of clinical psychologists has expanded even further to include community consultation, along with diagnosis, psychotherapy, and clinical research. Although all the "core provider" professions practice psychotherapy, clinical psychologists are generally seen as having particular expertise in diagnostic testing and clinical research.

Clinical psychologists are trained in graduate programs in university departments of psychology or in independent schools of professional psychology (few in number). In most cases, those trained in universities are awarded the PhD degree, while independent schools give the PsyD degree. Doctoral training generally involves at least 4 years of graduate school, including a 1-year internship and the research and writing of a doctoral dissertation. There are also some graduate schools that offer 1- or 2-year-long master's degree programs in clinical psychology, but almost all states now require a PhD for licensure or registration as a psychologist doing independent practice. Although all graduate programs in clinical psychology, doctoral or master's, require an undergraduate degree for admission, not all programs require that the undergraduate degree include a major in psychology. Some states require graduation from a doctoral program in clinical psychology that is approved by the American Psychological Association for licensure as a clinical psychologist. In most states, however, any PhD in psychology (experimental, developmental, industrial, etc.) can become licensed by passing the required examinations. Thus, just as not all physicians practicing psychiatry are board-certified or

specialty educated, so, in many states, not all PhD licensed psychologists practicing clinical psychology have gone through a clinical psychology academic
program. The best indication of a clinical psychologist's professional competence is if he or she is a diplomate of the American Board of Professional Psychology in clinical psychology. This is the equivalent of specialty boards in
psychiatry as an indication of expertise in one's profession.

Because PhD programs require a considerable amount of study of statistics
and research methodology and require that the student designs and carries out
an original research project for the doctoral dissertation, clinical psychologists
are generally perceived as the most competent in research among the core providers. In reality, however, most clinical psychologists do very little research
following graduation (the average number of research publications during the
professional career being less than three) but devote themselves to direct service. A relatively small number of clinical psychologists are primarily involved
in clinical research and account for a disproportionate amount of the research
generated in this field. Most PsyD programs place less emphasis on research
training than do PhD programs. Graduate education in clinical psychology
does involve more intensive study of psychodiagnostic testing than is taught to
other core providers. Therefore, most diagnostic work-ups that involve testing
(objective and/or projective tests) are performed by clinical psychologists.
These work-ups may be necessary in order to determine if a particular behavior has an organic basis, such as brain damage, or whether it is symptomatic of
a problem of living. Such determinations are necessary in order to decide what
mixture of physical treatments, medication, and/or counseling is called for.

As with psychiatrists, clinical psychologists may work in mental health clinics, hospitals, or private practice. Some are employed in teaching and/or
research in clinical psychology graduate training programs. In 1983, there
were approximately 23,500 clinical psychologists in the United States, of
whom approximately 2,200 were diplomates of the American Board of Professional Psychology in clinical psychology.

Of the four core provider professions, the two discussed so far, psychiatry
and clinical psychology, require professional education through a 4-year graduate program (leading to the doctoral degree of MD or PhD/PsyD, respectively). The other two core provider professions that will be discussed next,
psychiatric social work and psychiatric nursing, require a 2-year graduate program leading to a master's degree. These two groups, therefore, possess the
same level of graduate education as is required of mental health counselors.

Psychiatric Social Workers

Social workers are traditionally trained in three approaches: casework (providing social services and counseling to individuals and families with medical, legal, economic, or social problems); group work (working with youth

groups, senior citizen groups, minority groups, etc., in community or institutional settings, to assist these groups to formulate and achieve their goals); and community organization (working with civic, religious, political, or industrial groups to develop community-wide programs to address particular social problems that exist in that community). Social workers frequently work in family and children's service centers, child welfare and adoption agencies, hospitals and nursing homes, and correctional institutions. Psychiatric social workers (generally using casework approaches) assist psychiatric patients and their families to cope with the social and economic problems associated with illness, hospitalization, and return to home and the community. They may work in mental hospitals, mental health clinics, community mental health centers, halfway houses, or community-based programs. In the course of their work, psychiatric social workers engage in verbal psychotherapy with persons experiencing problems of living, just as do the other core provider professions. Their unique expertise is their knowledge and utilization of the community welfare resources available to the client and the client's family.

It may be noted that although the fully trained social worker possesses a master's (generally, master's in social work) degree, over the recent past, a large number of undergraduate degree programs in social work have been started. Graduates of these programs generally serve as technicians, performing routine agency tasks. The fully qualified professional social worker can be recognized by having the master's degree and the professional certification ACSW (Academy of Certified Social Workers). Many states also require licensure of social workers, which is frequently designated by the initials CSW (certified social worker) or LSW (licensed social worker). In the spring of 1985, there were 97,000 members in the National Association of Social Workers (Cunninghamn, 1985).

Psychiatric Nurses

Psychiatric nurses possess a master's degree (generally, master of science in nursing), obtained following the completion of an undergraduate degree in nursing and passing the examinations to qualify as a registered nurse (RN). In their graduate work, psychiatric nurses undergo specialized training in the care of mental patients. Generally, psychiatric nurses work in mental hospitals or clinics or in visiting nurse programs. Some are in private practice as nurse practitioners. In hospitals, psychiatric nurses supervise patient treatment regimens and administer wards. In outpatient settings, they are more involved in supervising treatment regimens and in performing individual therapy.

In 1980, there were 9,888 master's or doctoral degree level psychiatric nurses in the United States (American Nurses' Association, personal communication, 1985).

It should be pointed out that although the practitioner's degree in psychiatric social work and in psychiatric nursing is the master's degree, one may go on for further education and obtain a doctorate in both these fields if one wishes to qualify for academic, research, or some administrative positions.

Mental Health Counseling and the Core Providers

From the viewpoint of the mental health counselor, there are two important things to know about these four core-provider groups: the professional qualifications and unique expertise of each group, and their own professional interrelations. The first of these is necessary for mental health counselors seeking to obtain appropriate services for their clients. The second is necessary for mental health counseling to be aware of in seeking to establish its own position among these fields. To summarize the former: Psychiatrists should be board-certified in psychiatry and can assist mental health counselors in the prescription of psychotropic medication, in the use of physically based therapeutic interventions, and in hospitalizing clients who are in need of that environment. Clinical psychologists should hold the American Board of Professional Psychology (ABPP) diploma in clinical psychology; they can assist mental health counselors by doing psychodiagnostic work-ups of clients, in designing clinical research studies, and (if they are trained as behaviorists) in constructing behaviorally based treatment programs for particular clients. Social workers should hold the certified social worker (CSW) certificate; they can assist mental health counselors in locating and obtaining welfare and social services for clients and the families of clients. Psychiatric nurses should hold a master's degree in psychiatric nursing; they can assist in developing ways of keeping clients on treatment regimens. All four of these groups also offer verbal psychotherapy, just as mental health counselors offer verbal counseling.

Clearly, the four core-provider groups and mental health counselors have some functions (e.g., verbally based interventions) that overlap, as well as each having their unique approaches and areas of expertise. It should not be surprising that interprofessional frictions exist, particularly in areas that all the groups have in common. Psychiatry is, historically, the senior of these professions, with its medical roots going back to the ancient Greeks. During the period of their development as professions in the mid-19th to early 20th centuries, nursing and social work were fields that primarily attracted women. Prior to the raising of women's consciousness in mid-20th century, these fields were willing to assume a subordinate role to the male-dominated medical specialty of psychiatry. Therefore, psychiatry had the greatest problem with the challenge presented by clinical psychology when it moved into the treatment realm following World War II. Clinical psychologists were more likely to be males and to be more aggressively self-assertive and more actively in competition with psychiatrists for third-party payment for independent private practice. Psychiatry, however, finally more or less came to accept clinical psychology's claim to practice therapy, particularly because there were, at the time, more patients and more funds for treatment than could be absorbed by the existing numbers of psychiatrists. Thus, psychiatry did not then face a serious economic threat. Having come to terms with clinical psychology, its most assertive rival for independent practice, the field of psychiatry clearly was not going to seek to deny recognition to its two former handmaidens, psychiatric nursing and social work. These fields, however, were changing as to their composition, attracting more men and more self-assertive, feminist women to their ranks. Over the past few years, funds to pay for mental health treatment have become less available, and so psychiatry has begun once more to seek to erode the rights of the other core provider groups to recognition and payment for engaging in independent practice. Ironically, in their extensive study of psychiatrists, psychoanalysts, clinical psychologists, and psychiatric social workers, Henry, Sims, and Spray (1971) found that the four professions had much more in common than they had separating them in their professional practice. Indeed, taken together, they constituted the "fifth profession" of psychotherapists, rather than four distinct entities.

As mental health counseling has stepped into this economically constricting arena, it is psychology and social work that have been most opposed to its acceptance as a peer profession. Once again, the grounds appear to be economic, in that mental health counselors most directly compete with these two groups in the nature of services they offer (Asher, 1979). No one disputes the fact that the need for mental health services in the United States far exceeds the capacities of all five groups combined, from psychiatrists to mental health counselors. The issue stems from the fact that there are not sufficient funds committed to mental health to pay everyone capable of meeting the public's needs in this area of practice. Therefore, psychiatry once more is trying to drive clinical psychology off the independent practice field, while clinical psychology and social work are trying to keep mental health counseling from entering the field. In both of these attempts at exclusion, the economic self-interest of the group attempting to do the excluding is in conflict with the rights and needs of clients. This is highlighted in the case of clinical psychology and social work, which are in the compromising position of trying to do to mental health counseling exactly what they are simultaneously complaining that psychiatry is trying to do to them. Because all of these attempts at exclusion of other professions serve to deprive the public of their freedom of choice of services and serve to cut even further into the already inadequate numbers of mental health workers, it is safe to assume that all these ill-advised, self-serving activities will be rejected by the public and by its legislative bodies. Legislation is already under consideration by Congress to include mental health counselors as core providers of mental health services under the Medicare and Medicaid programs.

OTHER MENTAL HEALTH WORKERS

In addition to the four professional core provider groups, there are a number of mental health paraprofessionals and volunteers with whom the mental health counselor will come into contact in the course of professional counseling practice.

Mental Health Technicians

These paraprofessionals generally are educated in 2- or 4-year undergraduate college programs, majoring in such fields as social work, human services, rehabilitation services, psychology, or sociology. They perform routine tasks, such as taking family histories or contacting referrals. They are employed in hospitals, clinics, or community mental health centers, thereby freeing the time of the fully qualified professionals to serve more clients with their specialized skills. Utilizing a somewhat different model, Magoon, Golann, and Freeman (1969) reported on a group of eight mature women, all of whom held college or graduate degrees, who were trained in counseling skills in an in-service program over a 2-year period. These women proved to be effective practitioners of many counseling skills. Mental health technicians may also operate halfway houses or other residential programs for discharged, formerly hospitalized individuals.

Mental Health Aides and Indigenous Mental Health Workers

These positions require, at most, a high school education. These workers receive in-service training to perform less-skilled tasks than are required of mental health technicians. In some instances, however, these tasks are no less vital just because they are technically less skilled. For example, an indigenous worker may be accepted by a client belonging to the same cultural group of which the worker is a member, whereas a white, Anglo, middle class professional may face suspicion or resistance. Aides and indigenous workers may serve in such capacities as case-finding, getting clients to clinic appointments, gathering data about the community, and talking to clients' relatives about the clients' behavior.

It is possible to work one's way up a career ladder in the field of mental health, starting as an aide after high school, moving up to a technician while completing an undergraduate college degree program, and then going on to complete professional training as a mental health counselor or social worker (2 years of graduate school) or as a clinical psychologist (at least 4 years of graduate school). Finally, master's degree level mental health counselors or social workers may seek a doctoral degree, if their career goals involve teaching, research, or certain administrative jobs. Thus, there are career steps from high school through doctoral education for mental health workers. One may enter and/or stay at any step, or one may seek to move up the career ladder. Similar career ladders are available in psychiatric nursing (nurse's aide, nursing student, RN, and then completion of master's degree in psychiatric nursing).

Volunteers

Another essential group of persons involved in mental health work should be mentioned along with paraprofessionals. These individuals generally are not paid for their work, but act out of personal concern with the mental health needs of their community. Volunteer workers may assist with administrative tasks at mental health agencies, serve to meet the public at agencies, work at establishing relationships with individual clients to assist them to reenter the community, serve on agency boards or committees, speak on behalf of mental health issues or particular mental health agencies in their community, or work on fund-raising campaigns. In essence, volunteers may assist with almost any and all aspects of mental health programs. It is incumbent on mental health counselors to show respect for the work of volunteers and to learn how to assess and to utilize the talents of individual volunteers most effectively, so that the volunteer feels fulfilled by services donated and the agency benefits from the volunteer's efforts. It might be pointed out that the nature of volunteers has been changing, now that more middle and upper-middle class women are seeking paid employment. These traditional volunteer groups are being replaced by retirees seeking a fulfilling activity and by young people involved in exploring possible career choices. Therefore, professionals have to develop innovative approaches to utilize volunteers that will capitalize on the assets and the needs of these new groups of volunteers.

GROUPS NOT SPECIFIC TO MENTAL HEALTH BUT WITH FREQUENT CONTACT

Despite the wide range of occupations devoted exclusively to working with mental health problems reviewed so far in this chapter, the fact remains that most individuals experiencing problems of living do not seek out one of these professionals. Instead, most people seek help from their family physician, their family or friends, or their clergyperson (Mechanic, 1980, pp. 6–7). Some of this pattern stems from lack of knowledge about available mental health services; some from the stigma attached in our society to acknowledging that one has mental health problems. By avoiding going to a mental health professional, one may deny the existence of a problem in this area and so seek to avoid the stigma attached both to having problems of living and seeking professional help for them. Nonetheless, because they are so frequently turned to, physicians and clergy must be prepared to counsel or to refer individuals in need of mental health services.

Physicians

Some physicians may attempt to treat problems in this area by prescribing psychotropic medication, which, as licensed physicians, they can do. In many instances, physicians take this approach only if the patient resists referral to a mental health professional but is nonetheless experiencing debilitating emotional discomfort.

Clergy and Pastoral Counselors

Some clergy are trained in pastoral counseling, and some houses of worship have one or more pastoral counselors, other than the clergy, on their staff. Although most clergy and pastoral counselors are trained to recognize serious emotional problems, not all are trained to work with individuals experiencing such problems. Those who are not should, however, know when to refer their clients for more intensive help from a mental health professional.

Family, Friends, and Co-workers

Undoubtedly, no group is turned to for help by persons experiencing problems of living as much as are family members, friends, and co-workers. Unfortunately, these groups are also the least systematically trained to assist persons having problems to deal with them. A major role for mental health professionals, including mental health counselors, is to assist families and friends to cope with the demands placed upon them. Feelings of anger at being required to give help, frustration at the apparent failure of their efforts, and fatigue from trying to help the person in need while meeting the demands placed on them by their own work and family responsibilities are common. Thus, self-help groups for the families and friends of individuals with mental health problems have become prevalent. At these groups, often organized on a community basis, friends and relatives of those with mental health problems gather on a regular basis to share their experiences and feelings, learn new ways of coping for themselves and of being helpful to the person experiencing problems, and gain comfort from the awareness that they are not alone in facing this set of circumstances and the feelings it evokes in them. The topic of the role of the family is discussed in detail in chapter 8.

Welfare Workers

Finally, welfare workers constitute another group that comes into very frequent contact with individuals experiencing problems of living despite the fact that working with such people is not their stated mission. Particularly since the thrust toward deinstitutionalization has put many of those formerly in mental hospitals into the category of homeless persons, the contacts welfare workers have with persons experiencing mental health problems have come to account for almost half of their case loads. From July 1982, to March 1985, 47% of the 461,800 Social Security disability awards were to those with conditions classified as "mental disorders" (Social Security Administration, Office of Disability, personal communication, 1985). Even without this new population, it is not uncommon for those with mental health problems to sink to the bottom of the income scale and, conversely, for those at the bottom of the income scale to experience more severe mental health problems with greater frequency (Hollingshead & Redlich, 1958). Given this association between mental health problems and poverty, welfare workers, whose job involves providing economic assistance to low income persons, would inevitably have a large proportion of clients with mental health problems, even before the homeless ex-mental patients were added to their case loads.

Mental health counselors must be prepared to assist physicians, clergy, pastoral counselors, welfare workers, and other professionals who are turned to by large numbers of persons with mental health problems, even though these professions do not present themselves to the public as specialists in treating mental health problems. Indeed, physicians (other than psychiatrists) present themselves to the public as offering treatment for physical problems; clergy, for spiritual matters; and welfare workers, for economic need. Conversely, these professions must recognize when to consult or to refer clients to mental health professionals who are trained to assist with problems of mental health. It is, therefore, incumbent on mental health professionals to educate these other professions about when, how, and to whom to refer persons in need of mental health services.

Similarly, mental health professionals (including mental health counselors) must make their presence and availability known to the families, friends, and co-workers of those experiencing mental health problems. Mental health professionals must assist these groups to help their relative, friend, or co-worker in need of help and to maintain their own health and stability while being of help to the person in need. Community education programs, public service announcements in the print and broadcast media, and direct contact with local support groups can all be used to inform family, friends, and co-workers of the availability of mental health professionals who are ready and able to help.

Conversely, it is necessary for the mental health counselor to know what services these groups can offer the client, to assist in the recovery process. Thus, a mental health counselor will refer clients to a physician to check that there is no physical basis for emotional symptoms, to treat co-existing physical illness that can debilitate a client and exacerbate mental health problems, and to prescribe psychotropic medication if no board-certified psychiatrist is available. Mental health counselors should refer those clients expressing religious concerns to clergy or pastoral counselors, for assistance in meeting the clients' spiritual needs. Such help may greatly assist some clients in dealing with their problems of living. Counselors should refer clients in economic need to welfare services. Just as it is important for counselors to make sure that these other professionals know when and how to contact them, so counselors must also know when and how to enlist the services of a physician, member of the clergy, or welfare worker to benefit their client, as well as knowing which physician, cleric, or welfare worker has what particular expertise and will work well with a given client. Finally, mental health counselors must know how to enlist the help of family, friends, and/or co-workers in their client's treatment, so that the client's environment facilitates, rather than impedes, the client's adjustment.

OTHER PROFESSIONS THAT WORK WITH SOME MENTAL HEALTH CLIENTS

In addition to the frequent contact groups just discussed, there are a number of other human service professions that offer services used by some mental health clients. Once again, it is important for the mental health counselor to know what services each of these professions can offer to clients and when and how to enlist these services. Again, as with nonpsychiatrist physicians, clergy, and welfare workers, none of these professions view their primary mission as treating those with mental health problems, per se. Rather, they see their mission as helping persons to work on some other specific problem or set of problems encountered by a broad range of persons, including some persons with mental health problems as well. In referring a client to a member of one of these professions, it is important for the mental health counselor to ascertain that the particular professional is not only competent in her/his own profession, but is also skilled in and sympathetic to working with individuals experiencing mental health problems. Some of the most widely called upon among these occupations are discussed in the following paragraphs.

School Psychologists

School psychologists should either possess a 60-credit master's degree from a university program approved by the National Association of School Psychologists or a doctoral degree (PhD, EdD, or PsyD) in school psychology from a program approved by the American Psychological Association and, optimally, hold the diploma in school psychology from the American Board of Professional Psychology. Doctoral degree holders are more frequently found in supervisory positions or in private practice. School psychologists assess children for school readiness, grade placement, learning difficulties, and behavior problems. They consult with teachers, parents, and school administrators as to how to help the child cope with the problem. Occasionally, they offer direct treatment, such as play therapy with younger children; but usually, the demand for diagnostic work-ups does not leave much time for the school psychologist to do therapy. Mental health counselors may seek work-ups from school psychologists for younger clients who are still in school, and mental health counselors may seek to enlist the school psychologist to help a student whose parent or other family member is experiencing mental health problems. The school psychologist can consult with teachers, school counselors, and administrators as to how they can facilitate the child's coping with the mental health problem at home and its effects on the child's schoolwork.

Counseling Psychologists

Counseling psychologists should possess a doctoral degree from a program in counseling psychology approved by the American Psychological Association and should hold a diploma in counseling psychology from the American Board of Professional Psychology. The stated mission of counseling psychologists is to work with persons in the normal range of emotional adjustment, offering counseling on problems of daily living in the personal, interpersonal, and career areas. They also have knowledge of research methodology as applied to the counseling process. Counseling psychology is one of the options most frequently chosen by mental health counselors who decide to go on for doctoral training, because there is a good deal of content in common between the two fields. As its name implies, counseling psychology has been essentially a bridge field, drawing its theory and knowledge bases both from counseling and from psychology. The boundary between counseling psychology and clinical psychology remains vague, at best. Counseling psychologists generally are conceived of as emphasizing work with essentially mentally healthy persons and as having particular expertise in vocational behavior, whereas clinical psychologists are seen as tending to work with those facing more severe mental health difficulties and as having greater expertise in the diagnosis and treatment of psychopathology. In actual practice, however, the degree of overlap in function is greater than any difference between these two specialties (Watkins, 1985). Even the theoretical differences between the two have begun to blur, as counseling psychologists have come to work with clients having more severe emotional problems and as clinical psychologists have placed greater emphasis on identifying clients' assets (traditionally the orientation of counseling and of counseling psychology) as well as their pathology. Counseling psychologists are probably of greatest use to mental health counselors as consultants on research, given the counseling psychologists' familiarity with both counseling procedures and research methodology.

Marriage and Family Therapists

Marriage and family therapists possess either a master's or a doctoral degree and are certified by the American Association for Marriage and Family Therapy. Their area of expertise is in resolving marital or family discord, working with the family unit as a system. Although their function may overlap with the practice of some mental health counselors, other mental health counselors refer their clients to marriage and family therapists for help in resolving problems in that sphere of living.

Counselors

Mental health counselors belong to the group of occupations that identify themselves as professional counselors. These occupations also include the following six, which are of direct relevance to the present discussion: school counseling, college student personnel work, career counseling, rehabilitation counseling, correctional counseling, and employment counseling. All of these counseling fields are represented by divisions of the American Association for Counseling and Development, which is also the parent organization of the American Mental Health Counselors Association. All of these occupations apply the principles and practices of professional counseling to different client groups, just as mental health counselors apply these principles and practices to individuals experiencing problems of daily living.

School Counselors

School counselors work in elementary or secondary schools, helping school children with their emotional, social, and behavioral adjustment to the school environment, the learning process, and their post-school plans. Elementary school counselors work particularly on the learning and the behavioral problems of school children at this level of education, whereas secondary school counselors are more involved with the academic program and career and college planning of high school students. School counselors at both levels also consult with parents, teachers, and school administrators to enlist their cooperation in working with the student to resolve the problem. In some states, one can only be hired as a school counselor if one has several years of prior teaching experience. School counselors are generally trained at the master's degree level, although some states permit teachers with fewer graduate credits in counseling to become counselors. A fully qualified school counselor should be a regular member or be eligible for regular membership in the American School Counselor Association, which is a division of the American Association for Counseling and Development. Mental health counselors may work with school counselors in connection with their work with a family, one of whose members is in school and one or more of whose other members are seeing a mental health counselor. There may also be referrals of clients by school counselors to mental health counselors, at the time these clients graduate from or leave school (and so are no longer eligible to be seen by the school counselor).

College Counselors and Student Personnel Workers

Individuals with master's or doctoral degrees in counseling or in college student personnel work are employed in colleges and other higher educational institutions, both as counselors in college counseling centers and as administrators of co-curricular student development programs and services, such as orientation, campus activities, financial aid, career placement, and so on. College counseling centers vary as to the depth and extent of counseling they offer, some limiting themselves to a few counseling sessions per student and referring any students in need of more extensive services off campus. Other college counseling services offer a complete range of services, including intensive counseling for as long as the student is enrolled. Those counseling centers with limited service may refer students in need of more extensive counseling to mental health counselors in the surrounding community, and mental health counselors may enlist student development services to assist their clients who are attending the college. These services can be particularly helpful to adults who are entering or returning to the role of college students in mid-life, and so are out of touch with what to expect from college.

Career Counselors

Career counselors assist individuals from mid-teens to old age to explore, choose among, and implement career plans. They also work to develop career awareness in younger persons, so that they will not come to the point of entering the world of work ignorant of their options and what further training and experience may be necessary to achieve their career goal. Career counselors help mid-career workers and older workers with career problems and transitions, including the handling of retirement. Career counselors are expert in the use of aptitude, abilities, and interest measures and in the use of printed and computerized career information, as well as in the application of counseling to career issues. Although many mental health counselors know a good deal about career development and career counseling, there are counselors who specialize in these issues to whom mental health clients are often referred for service in this area. A fully qualified career counselor has a master's or doctoral degree in counseling and has passed the examination required to obtain the designation of Nationally Certified Career Counselor (NCCC), which is a specialty within the National Board for Certified Counselors. It may be noted that career counseling is the oldest organized professional counseling field in the United States; the National Vocational Guidance Association (recently renamed as the National Career Development Association) was founded in 1913.

Rehabilitation Counselors

Rehabilitation counselors are employed in state, private nonprofit, and private for-profit agencies to assist individuals with physical, mental, emotional, or social disabilities to attain productive employment and/or independent living. Rehabilitation counselors seek to help clients obtain these goals through the use of counseling and of coordination of medical, social, vocational, and educational services necessary for the client's restoration or development of working and living skills. Under a national program, every state and territory has a rehabilitation agency cooperatively funded by both state and federal levels of government to provide counseling and to purchase services for those in need of rehabilitation. Rehabilitation counselors also work in hospitals, rehabilitation centers, sheltered workshops, and (in some states) schools to assist persons with disabilities to enter or to reenter vocational and personal sufficiency. Finally, rehabilitation counselors may work in industry or for insurance companies, assisting disabled workers to return to work, rather than to remain on disability payments. Rehabilitation counselors work with mental health clients, as well as the physically disabled and the mentally retarded. Mental health rehabilitation is a well-established area of practice, and it is incumbent on mental health counselors to be familiar with these techniques and to know when and how to refer their clients to a mental health rehabilitation counselor for specialized services. The principles and techniques of mental health rehabilitation are discussed in greater detail in chapter 7. A fully qualified rehabilitation counselor can be recognized by the designation Certified Rehabilitation Counselor (CRC), awarded based on a combination of graduate education and supervised experience in rehabilitation counseling and passing an examination covering the principles, laws, and practices related to rehabilitation in particular and counseling in general. Professional rehabilitation counselors generally belong to the American Rehabilitation Counseling Association, a division of the American Association for Counseling and Development, and/or to the National Rehabilitation Counseling Association, a division of the National Rehabilitation Association.

Correctional Counselors

A certain number of master's or doctoral level educated professional counselors work in prisons, juvenile detention centers, work release programs, and parole. They generally focus on helping the client cope with the prison experience and prepare for life following return to the community. If the client of a mental health counselor runs afoul of the law and is incarcerated, that client may receive counseling from a correctional counselor while under legal supervision. If so, the mental health counselor should consult with and coordinate treatment plans with the correctional counselor, so that there will be no conflict between pre- and post-prison counseling and the counseling received while in prison. A fully trained correctional counselor should qualify for regular membership in the Public Offender Counselor Association, a division of the American Association for Counseling and Development.

Employment Counselors

Finally, there are counselors who work in public and private employment agencies and in company personnel offices, evaluating applicants' skills, interests, and work experiences, and matching them with available jobs. Mental health counselors frequently refer clients to such agencies in the course of their clients' search for jobs. The mental health counselor should work with the employment counselor to locate the most appropriate option for the client, given both the employment and the mental health considerations. It may be noted that although employment counselors and rehabilitation counselors are regularly concerned with job finding, job development, and job placement for their clients (specifically for clients with disabilities, in the case of rehabilitation counselors), career counselors rarely engage in job placement, although they may help a client assess possible options open to the client. Professional employment counselors are those who qualify for regular membership in the National Employment Counselors Association, a division of the American Association for Counseling and Development.

Addiction Counselors

In addition to these professional counseling specialities, there are several fields that use the term *counseling* in their title but do not require any graduate education in counseling or any other field. These careers often attract individuals who formerly had the problem in question and overcame it. In some instances, these "counselors" are quite effective in working with individuals with the specific problem. Some, however, enter these careers more to help themselves than to help their fellow-sufferers; and in a conflict situation, they may not clearly see or act in the client's best interests. The same risk, of course, exists with professional counselors; but because of the graduate professional education and certification process they undergo, there is a greater opportunity for quality control with regard to such issues. Among the groups of helpers using the word *counselor* in their title but not requiring graduate education in counseling are:

1. *Alcoholism counselors*, who work with persons having drinking problems. There is a credential for those working in this field, Certified Alcoholism Counselor (CAC), but it does not require graduate education in counseling.
2. *Substance abuse counselors*, who work with drug-dependent persons. Again, no formal training is necessarily required, but a personal history of having overcome addiction is frequently either required or preferred.

There are occasions in which a mental health counselor may wish to refer a client with an addiction problem to one of these types of counselors; but given their lack of formal training, such referrals should only be made to practitioners whose competence is personally known to the mental health counselor.

There are a number of other professional specialists whose work involves, among others, mental health clients. These include specialized therapists, evaluators, and law officers.

Occupational Therapists

Occupational therapists are trained at either the undergraduate baccalaureate level or in master's degree programs. Graduates of either type of program must pass the occupational therapy registration examination, which earns them the designation OTR. Occupational therapy paraprofessionals are trained in 2-year junior college or vocational school programs and must pass an examination to obtain the designation of certified occupational therapy assistant (COTA). Occupational therapists apply activities to diagnose and help correct musculoskeletal, neurological, and psychiatric problems. Some occupational therapists specialize in working with persons with mental health problems, using activities to promote socialization, feelings of competence, and release of anger or tension. Some occupational therapists specialize in the diagnosis and treatment of learning disorders, using activities to promote neurologic integration. Others work with the upper extremity physically disabled, to help them overcome or compensate for arm or hand dysfunction. (Generally, physical therapists work with lower limb and mobility problems.) If one's clients are hospitalized, they may well receive occupational therapy services; so it is important for the mental health counselor to be aware of and to monitor the client's progress as reflected in those activities.

Recreational Therapists

Individuals are trained in academic programs in therapeutic recreation at the junior college, college, and master's degree levels. Recreational therapists are generally required to hold a state license or professional registration if they are to be employed in hospitals or nursing homes. In these settings, they utilize recreational activities to promote therapeutic change. The boundary between occupational therapy and therapeutic recreation remains unclear, and there are unresolved disputes between the two fields as to professional domain. As with occupational therapists, some recreational therapists work in mental hospitals or inpatient units. As such, mental health counselors should consult with them about the progress of any of their clients who are hospitalized and receiving recreational therapy.

Vocational Evaluators

Vocational evaluators are trained at the baccalaureate or the master's degree level to assess an individual's current capacity for work and what sorts of changes must be induced to prepare that person for entry into a work role. These changes may involve learning work habits (neatness, promptness, reliability), job skills, or social skills (relating to co-workers and bosses); or they may involve unlearning behaviors that will prevent the person from getting or keeping a job. Many work evaluators specialize in working with mental health clients. Work evaluators are employed in sheltered workshops, work evaluation programs, job training and placement agencies, and rehabilitation programs. They should be certified by the Vocational Evaluation and Work Adjustment Association, a division of the National Rehabilitation Association. Mental health counselors should refer clients to work evaluation programs to determine how ready these clients are for a given level of employment (sheltered, transitional, or competitive) and what they will need to do to prepare themselves to enter or return to work at any specified level. Clients may have to go through work adjustment programs in order to attain needed skills, or they may be able to overcome some deficits as part of their counseling "homework."

Disability Examiners

The various state, regional, and federal social security offices employ disability examiners whose job is to review medical, psychological, work history, and other relevant records to determine if a claimant qualifies for social security disability payments. Mental health counselors should familiarize themselves with the regulations as to what constitutes disability status and the application procedures, so that they can advise their clients as to when it is appropriate to seek these benefits and how to apply for them.

Police, Corrections, and Parole Officers

Law officers come into frequent contact with certain categories of mental health clients (particularly the poor, those who act out either via criminal behavior or as public nuisances, and those with drug or alcohol problems).

Generally, police officers are involved in arrests, corrections officers in imprisonment, and parole officers in post-release supervision. Mental health counselors must work on the client's behalf with all three groups, depending on the current state of the client's involvement with the criminal justice system. Also, as noted earlier, there may be a professional correctional counselor assigned to the client, with whom the mental health counselor should coordinate services to the client. In dealing with law officers, the mental health counselor must temper the advocacy role to the reality of the client's offense. Strident advocacy, regardless of the client's offense or state of mind, may harm, rather than help the client's treatment. On the other hand, the mental health counselor does have an important role in seeing to it that any relevant problems that the client has are considered and taken into account throughout the client's contact with the criminal justice system.

OTHER PROFESSIONS WHOSE WORK AFFECTS MENTAL HEALTH CLIENTS

Other professions with which mental health counselors should be familiar because of services they could render to clients include the following. Unlike those discussed earlier, a relatively small proportion of the clients seen by these professionals have mental health problems. Nonetheless, these professionals can be of great assistance to mental health clients, if their cooperation is enlisted.

Personnel Managers

Mental health counselors may interact with personnel managers at a client's place of employment to help create working conditions that will facilitate the client's adjustment to the job. This same function may alternatively be performed by contacting the *human resources development officer* in corporate settings where such line positions exist.

Nurses and Other Allied Health Professionals

These include speech pathologists, who work on speech and language communications problems; audiologists, who assist persons with hearing difficulties; physical therapists, who assist persons with mobility and muscular problems; nurse practitioners in various nursing specialties; and other similar professions. Clearly, problems with physical health, speech and hearing communication, and/or mobility have an impact on a person's mental health; and resolving such problems can materially contribute to an improvement in a client's mental health status.

Lawyers

Clients may encounter lawyers both in protecting their rights and interests and in bringing actions against them. Lawyers may be involved in protecting clients' employment and insurance rights, in divorce and child custody cases, and in criminal proceedings against clients. Where appropriate, the mental health counselor should advocate with lawyers on behalf of the client. Also, mental health counselors may be called upon to testify concerning their clients in legal proceedings, sometimes by friendly lawyers and sometimes by opposing ones. Counselors must be aware of the laws concerning privileged communication with clients, so that they will know how to act on the witness stand. This is discussed in greater detail in chapter 11.

Environmental Planners

Urban land-use and social planners have an indirect but definite impact on clients' mental health. Inasmuch as the environment affects client behavior and adjustment, the planner who designs that environment influences the course and outcome of treatment for better or for worse. Planners have been involved in designing mental hospitals and wards, as well as community facilities (e.g., parks and recreation centers) so as to facilitate mental health. The interaction between mental health counselors and planners is, however, less frequent than it should be if environments that truly engender mental health are to be designed and constructed and if pathogenic environmental conditions are to be prevented.

Politicians

Politicians are vital in establishing and in funding mental health services, in determining which professions gain licensure and third-party payment, and in establishing legal rights for certain conditions of professional practice (for example, confidentiality of communication). Mental health counselors should work actively with their elected representatives to introduce and/or support legislation that will benefit mental health clients and the mental health counseling profession. Other, longer established mental health professions (psychiatry, clinical psychology, social work) learned this lesson many years ago, and they have been very effective in advancing their own interests and those of their clients through the political process. If it is to achieve its full measure of recognition, mental health counseling must learn from and emulate its peer professions in using the political–legislative process at the local, state, and federal levels.

THE TEAM CONCEPT

A wide variety of professions concerned with the treatment of individuals experiencing mental health problems has been reviewed. Some of these professions overlap in some functions (for example, the core providers, occupational therapy and therapeutic recreation, clinical and counseling psychology, career and rehabilitation counseling, etc.), yet each one has at least some degree of unique expertise and focus. The team approach has been evolved to bring to bear these specialized aspects of treatment in a single setting, in order to benefit the client through their coordinated, summative effects. Thus, a treatment team may include a psychiatrist (to provide medical supervision and to prescribe needed medication), a clinical psychologist (to do diagnostic workups), a social worker (to work with the client's family), a mental health counselor (to provide individual and/or group counseling for clients), an occupational therapist (to use planned activities to facilitate the client's treatment), and a career counselor (to assist the client with career entry, change, or reentry). The team meets regularly, to assess the client's progress and, based on that, to plan future treatment strategy and the roles of each of the team members in implementing that strategy. It is common practice for teams to assign one member the role of leader for work with a particular client. By rotating that role among the team members from client to client, the team can avoid the problem of interprofessional rivalries. These rivalries can easily develop among different professionals who work in such close interrelationship that individual professional identities sometimes become blurred and/or conflicts between professions are played out in microcosm.

The team concept is also implicit in multiservice community counseling agencies, where a range of professional resources are located in one place, so that clients do not get lost going from service to service. Frequently, clients become discouraged and leave treatment out of the frustration of trying to locate and to schedule services at different agencies in different locations. By having a range of services under one roof, the client can have access to all of the more typically called for treatment modalities without being required to go to unfamiliar and sometimes hostile territory (e.g., in a neighborhood that is populated by citizens who are known to be prejudiced against persons of the client's race). In some multiservice clinics, the team approach is used. In others, however, the main impetus for interprofessional consultation is the presence of all of the treating personnel in one location, where they cannot help but run into each other. The latter, of course, is less effective than a coordinated team effort; but is still superior to situations in which several professionals are seeing the same client with little or no contact with each other. Obviously, in settings that do not structure it, it is incumbent on the mental health counselor to keep in regular contact with other professionals who are working with the same client.

CONCLUSION

Throughout this book the fact has been emphasized that an individual functions within an environmental context, and that this context may facilitate or may hinder effective coping. This principle is as true for counselors as it is for clients. The counselor does not practice the profession of mental health counseling in a vacuum, even if she/he is engaged in a one-person, full-time private practice. One cannot exist as a mental health counselor, let alone assist one's clients, without frequent interactions with many of the categories of co-professionals and co-helpers discussed in this chapter. Just as the counselor must assist the client to identify, develop, and apply personal skills to changing the environment so that it will be supportive, so the counselor must develop and apply professional skills to making the client's environment of co-professionals and co-helpers as facilitative for the client as possible. Thus, interacting with these groups of persons on the client's behalf (either directly or through the client) is as much a part of the counselor's professional duties as is sitting alone with the client in an office counseling session. Therefore, it is as important for the mental health counselor to know in what ways these other persons or groups can help the client and to know how good a job they can do in their area of competence as it is to know the different techniques of individual counseling and when to use each one. It is as important for the counselor to know how to refer a client and how to maintain contact with the co-helper so as to maximize the help needed by the client as it is to know how to establish a counseling relationship with a client. Neither individuals nor professions exist in isolation; and so the knowledge and skills to mobilize co-helpers are a necessary part of mental health counseling.

REFERENCES

Asher, J. K. (1979). The coming exclusion of counselors from the mental health care system. *AMHCA Journal, 1,* 53–60.

Cunningham, S. (1985, April). NASW. *APA Monitor, 16*(4), 8.

Freud, S. (1957). Postscript to a discussion on lay analysis. In J. Strachey (Ed.), *Collected Papers.* (Vol. V, pp. 205–214). New York: Basic Books. (Original work published in 1927)

Goldenberg, H. (1973). *Contemporary clinical psychology.* Monterey, CA: Brooks/Cole.

Henry, W. E., Sims, J. H., & Spray, S. L. (1971). *The fifth profession.* San Francisco: Jossey-Bass.

Hollingshead, A. B., & Redlich, F. C. (1958). *Social class and mental illness: A community study.* New York: Wiley.

Laing, R. D. (1967). *The politics of experience.* New York: Ballantine Books.

Magoon, T. M., Golann, S. E., & Freeman, R. W. (1969). *Mental health counselors at work.* New York: Pergamon.

Mechanic, D. (1980). *Mental health and social policy* (2nd ed.). Englewood Cliffs, NJ: Prentice-Hall.

Szasz, T. (1961). *The myth of mental illness.* New York: Paul B. Hoeber.

U.S. Department of Labor, Bureau of Labor Statistics. (1982). *Occupational outlook handbook. 1982–83 Edition.* Washington, DC: U.S. Government Printing Office.

Watkins, C. E., Jr. (1985). Counseling psychology, clinical psychology, and human services psychology: Where the twain shall meet? *American Psychologist, 40,* 1054–1056.

15 Coordination of Resources

The role of the mental health counselor involves more than just meeting with a client (individual, family, or group) in the isolation of an office setting. The mental health counselor, by virtue of the philosophy of the profession, must also assist the client in bringing to bear those environmental resources that can facilitate the client's coping with his/her problem. In order to perform this function, the counselor must possess a specialized set of knowledge and skills that are different from those involved in counseling. This specialized area may be termed coordination of resources and involves: (a) knowledge about existing resources; (b) knowledge about where to find information about such resources; and (c) skills in coordination, including accessing, referral, linking, networking, and evaluating resources. This chapter will first discuss these skills, and then review some of the categories of resources to which these skills are applied, including those related to work, living arrangements, finances, and health.

COORDINATING SKILLS

Accessing

Accessing is the skill of obtaining information about and entry into the resource that can best meet one's client's need. For this purpose, many counselors maintain indices or card files of agencies and contact persons on the intake staff of those agencies with whom they have had prior contact. These files indicate (or are classified by) the particular services rendered by the agency; and where possible, some indication of the quality of performance of the agency in delivering each of those services. This evaluation would be based first and foremost on the counselor's personal experience with other clients referred to the agency in the past. Some agencies may do a better job of providing the same service to some clients than to others, based on client characteristics (age, sex, race, religion, socioeconomic status, primary language, personality traits). Likewise, some of the staff members at one agency may work better with some clients than with others, based on client characteristics. Knowing this, the counselor can direct a client to the agency and even to the staff member at that agency who has the strongest proven record of success with similar clients needing the same service.

In many communities, the local council of social service agencies publishes a directory of agencies, including a list of the particular services offered by the agency and the key persons to contact. In some communities, this is called "the social service blue book," or some similar name (frequently reflecting the color of its cover). The counselor should obtain and regularly use one of these directories (making sure that it is the most up-to-date edition; they are frequently loose-leaf). This should supplement but not replace the counselor's personal file of resources. In communities in which no such directory exists, the mental health counselor may use the telephone directory "yellow pages" to locate the names of possible resources to be looked into.

Referral and Linking

Having accessed the most appropriate agency, the counselor must next connect the client with that agency. Some writers (for example, Lewis & Lewis, 1983) distinguish between referral (turning a client over to another agency and surrendering any further regular contact with the client) and linking (sending a client to one or more other agencies for particular services, while maintaining regular contacts with the client on one's own case load). Others, however, use the term *referral* to indicate surrendering responsibility for only one specific service to be given to a client. Agencies and individual counselors also differ as to whether they require feedback from agencies referred to and/ or from the clients who are referred. Some counselors require feedback in order to evaluate the agency for future possible referrals. Other counselors view such follow-up as a responsibility owed to the client who was referred.

Linkage, by its very nature, requires greater coordination between agencies to prevent duplication of services, work at cross-purposes, conflicting messages to the client, or vital areas that go unattended because each party to the linkage thinks that the other is dealing with the matter.

Thus, the referral/linkage process may be seen as having several dimensions including: (a) the range of services the second agency is asked to provide to the client, (b) the responsibility taken for a client after the client is put into contact with the second agency, and (c) the feedback expected from the second agency and/or from the client. Clearly, the needs of the client should be the primary factor in determining what point along each of these dimensions is to be sought.

Another consideration in making a referral or linkage is how it is presented to the client. It must be made clear that it is not intended as a rejection of the client as a person, but as an action taken to provide the client with the best service available to meet the client's need.

Networking

The referral/linking process focuses on client needs; the networking process focuses on agency capabilities. Networking involves the coordination of agencies to share resources, to divide responsibilities on a systematic basis, or to integrate their functions. Networking may involve getting a number of agencies to work on different problems of a single client or getting each of several agencies to assume responsibility for working on one designated problem presented by a number of different clients. The intent of networking may be economic efficiency or the fostering of specialized expertise not presently available within a community. In order to promote networking, the counselor must possess both negotiating and leadership skills (such as persuasiveness). Backer and Trotter (1986) recently summarized the five basic rules of effective networking as: (a) keep a clear, specific focus to the network; avoid dispersion of goals; (b) keep in touch regularly with the others in the network; (c) keep the network small (many small, focused networks work better than one large one); (d) keep it simple and inexpensive; and (e) reciprocate, if you wish the network to stay together.

Agencies tend to guard jealously their prerogatives and territories, and it takes great skill to convince them to share power or to limit their range of action. Many agencies will only agree to joining a network if the consequences of failing to do so are made clear to them, and those consequences outweigh the risks of "going it alone." Schwartz (1986) has also demonstrated how networks can be used to help mental health counselors expand their own professional skills and power base.

Evaluating

Counselors must engage in a continuous process of evaluation of agencies and of particular staff members at those agencies. Decisions about referral, linking, and networking are based on who does the best job of providing each particular service. This information comes from evaluations, insofar as possible based on objective criteria. See chapter 12 for a full discussion of the evaluation process.

Now that we have briefly overviewed the skills the counselor must use in coordinating resources on behalf of a client, we may look at some of the major categories of resources to which those skills are to be applied. In addition to having the skills necessary to perform the functions we have just discussed, the mental health counselor must know the major types of resources available and as many local examples of each of those types as is possible. The counselor must also be familiar with examples of effective resources not locally available in order to work with the community to establish such a resource locally, so clients can use it. To accomplish this, the counselor will need other skills, such as those involved in advocacy, in community organization, and in using the political process.

RESOURCES

Resources Discussed Elsewhere in This Book

It is difficult to separate resources distinctly from some of the topics dealt with in other parts of this book. For example, the most significant resource is often the client's *family*, a topic discussed in chapter 8. The family may be the client's greatest source of support, difficulty, or both of these simultaneously. In any case, where a family is significantly involved in the client's environment, the counselor must work with them to maximize their helpfulness to the client and to minimize their contribution to the client's problem.

Physicians, including those who specialize in psychiatry, are another frequently used resource, in their role as prescribers of psychoactive medication and in the general maintenance of the client's physical health, a factor that directly affects mental health. Psychiatrists and other physicians were discussed in chapter 14.

Religious institutions are another resource that can serve as a powerful source of support for many clients. The relevant personnel in these institutions, clergy and pastoral counselors, were also discussed in chapter 14.

Social service agencies provide a wide range of resources, in terms of both direct services and money to purchase other services (and even, in some instances, for economic support while services are being rendered). The professional staff of these agencies include the welfare workers, social workers, career and rehabilitation counselors, and many of the other groups described in chapter 14. The number and variety of these groups represented at any one agency will depend on the mission of the agency.

Educational institutions are resources for teaching clients new skills. The mental health counselor will, in the case of clients enrolled in educational institutions, frequently be in contact with the school or college counselors, also described in chapter 14.

Given sufficient ingenuity, a mental health counselor may employ almost any community service or facility as a resource on behalf of some client. Although the number of such resources is almost infinite, we shall limit the rest of this discussion to four categories of resources: (a) those related to working, (b) those related to living arrangements, (c) financial resources, and

(d) health-related resources.

It should be noted that we have differentiated the types of agencies discussed here under the topic of resources from those listed as practice settings in chapter 13 on the bases that resources: (a) do not primarily employ mental health counselors as staff members; (b) serve a wide range of clientele, not all of whom have mental health needs; and (c) focus their interventions on providing services other than remediation. Naturally, however, if a counselor is engaged in referring a client to another agency of a type discussed in chapter 13, then that agency becomes a resource for the purpose of referral. Thus, any practice setting may be a resource and, conversely, any resource that employs a mental health counselor may be a practice setting.

Resources Related to Work

Work is a phenomenon that has been an aspect of the human condition since time immemorial. At different times, this phenomenon has been viewed with greater or lesser pleasure. Thus, to the writers of the Bible, work was a curse imposed on humanity as a result of Adam and Eve's disobedience to God in the Garden of Eden. In the Reformation, conversely, work became associated with gaining eternal salvation for one's soul. As technology has changed the nature of work—such as the development of agriculture, the Industrial Revolution, or robotics—the meaning of and attitudes toward work have correspondingly changed. For a fascinating discussion of the changes in the meaning of work throughout history, see Tilgher (1930).

Inevitably, as a major life activity, work has become intertwined with mental health. Work has been seen as an index of mental health, a way of promoting or restoring mental health, and a cause of poor mental health. Frequently, mental health professionals have held all three of these views of work at the same time. Slocum (1974) listed the functions of work in modern industrial society as providing: (a) a source of subsistence (income), (b) regulated activity (work time/free time), (c) patterns of association (co-workers, unions, professional groups), (d) an identity or label by which to define oneself, and (e) meaningful life experiences (successes, failures, topics of conversation).

Given these multiple major functions, it is small wonder that work has been considered to be tied to mental health. Generally, either too little work ("lazy," "dependent," "passive," etc.) or too much work ("workaholic") are viewed as symptomatic of poor mental health. At the same time, work can be either destructive (e.g., job stress, role conflicts, etc.) or restorative (work therapy) of mental health.

Be it for good or for ill, work is a necessary major life activity for most persons, consuming the largest single block of their waking hours. Neff (1977) proposed a taxonomy of seven types of maladaptive work behaviors, including being: (a) fearful of persons or things at work; (b) dependent, unable to initiate a task on one's own; (c) impulsive, unable to stick to a task and complete it; (d) socially naive or behaving inappropriately in the work setting; (e) apathetic or withdrawn; (f) self-deprecatory; and (g) hostile, negativistic, hypercritical. Neff indicated that the last two of these categories were particularly true of individuals who had been recently discharged from mental hospitals. On this point, Simmons (1965) suggested that institutionalization has definite detrimental effects on a person's patterns of work behavior.

From the point of view of the mental health counselor, work may be classified as competitive or sheltered. Competitive work is that which exists on the open labor market. Sheltered work—in workshops or training programs—may be either transitional (short-term, in preparation for movement into competitive employment as the goal) or long-term (where there is little hope of successful placement in competitive jobs). Depending on the client, any of these settings—including long-term sheltered work—can be stressful or a source of satisfaction. It is up to the mental health counselor to work with the client to create a situation and a frame of mind in which work is a positive aspect of the client's life.

Recently, an increasing number of companies have come to realize that workers who have mental health problems are less productive, have significantly greater absenteeism, and can serve to disrupt company operations. Therefore, companies have been establishing or contracting for "employee assistance programs" (EAPs), which are frequently staffed by mental health counselors. These programs vary in scope from some that deal only with substance abuse problems to others that are concerned with any aspect of worker mental health (retirement planning, family life, career change, handling stress, etc.). Because EAPs meet our definition of practice settings, they are discussed in detail in chapter 13. It should also be noted that labor unions are also assuming greater concern and responsibility for their members' mental health.

A mental health counselor may, with a client's permission, work with the EAP counselor or job supervisor at the client's place of employment to make the client's work situation more positive. Thereby, work may become a setting in which a client attains success, improves self-confidence, and develops life skills that are applicable both at and away from work. In some sheltered work settings, such goals can be the primary focus for the client's experience. In competitive employment, of course, the employer must be concerned with productivity above all other considerations. Nonetheless, with appropriate structuring, the mental health counselor can use almost any type of work setting as a positive resource. McLean (1970) has suggested many of the issues to be considered in seeking to make work settings more conducive to positive mental health.

In addition to work itself as a resource, the mental health counselor should be aware of resources that prepare clients for work. Among these are the vocational training obtainable through the state divisions or bureaus of vocational rehabilitation (for any person judged to have a physical or mental condition that interferes with employment and that could be expected to be ameliorated by intervention), through the Veterans Administration (for veterans of military service), and in many locales through voluntary agencies. Some of the state and/or federally funded programs provide not only training but even the tools necessary to pursue the line of work for which the person was trained. Training may involve the development of pre-vocational skills (such as promptness, neatness, reliability, appropriate socialization in the work setting, etc.) in a sheltered workshop or vocational skill training in a training or apprenticeship program or a school.

Finally, the mental health counselor may use employment services as a resource to assist a client. These services may be either state or private. In the latter, the fee may be paid by either the client or the employer. Placement may be open or selective, that is, in a job uniquely structured to meet the client's needs and capacities. Where possible, the mental health counselor should have the client try to work through a professional employment counselor, as described in chapter 14. It must, of course, be pointed out that getting a job is only half the battle; the other half is keeping the job. Thus, a mental health counselor should not treat a client's work life as a totally resolved issue once a job has been found. The counselor must also work with the client to develop job maintenance skills if the client does not already have them.

Resources Related to Living

The clearest consequence of the movement toward de-institutionalization has been the need to consider ways to provide living accommodations for the persons who were formerly maintained in mental institutions. Relatively few of the long-term residents who were released have family or friends who are willing or able to take them in. To date, few bright spots have emerged on this issue. This is not surprising, given the lack of enthusiasm and of preparation by communities to accept these persons and the speed with which the policy of de-institutionalization was pursued. Bachrach (1980) has forcefully pointed out that the rallying cry of providing the "least restrictive environment" (see discussion of the evolution of this term in chapter 10) is frequently counterproductive, because what is really required is the "most therapeutic environment." As an example, Bachrach cited the case of 10 patients moved from the confines of a large mental hospital into "less restrictive facilities"—a foster home in which they all burned to death in a house fire. Bachrach (1980) argued that whereas "least restrictive" focuses on the physical environment, "most therapeutic" focuses on the needs of the individual client; and this is where the focus really should be.

Given the validity of Bachrach's argument, one must still deal with the fact that these formerly institutionalized persons are now out on the streets and in immediate need of living arrangements. As some of these persons become clients of mental health counselors, it will become more necessary for these counselors to concern themselves with resources for living for clients.

The term *independent living center* has come into current use to categorize facilities that provide at least the following services: housing assistance, attendant care, peer or professional counseling, financial and legal advocacy, and community awareness and barrier-removal programs (Frieden, 1980). Such centers may be residential or nonresidential (e.g., storefront service centers); may provide services themselves or may refer clients to collaborating agencies; may be run largely by the residents, largely by the professional staff, or largely by a board of directors; and may seek to provide transitional or permanent living arrangements. The needs of the client should determine which sort of center is most appropriate. Another consideration in choosing a center is who is to pay for the client's use of the facility—a public agency or the client (out of earnings or savings). Usually, the most important decision factor is whether the facility is transitional or ongoing. Transitional facilities (often called halfway houses or some variant of that term, such as "quarter-way houses" for clients needing a more structured environment) serve to prepare clients to live on their own, just as transitional sheltered workshops prepare clients for competitive employment.

It may be noted that other clients than those recently discharged from institutions may benefit from independent living facilities. Clients needing to establish their independence, battered spouses, elderly and physically handicapped clients, among others, may be referred to independent living resources.

The final category of resources for living to be mentioned is shelters for homeless persons. The presence of increased numbers of homeless persons living on city sidewalks, sleeping on heating grates in order to try (not always successfully) to keep from freezing to death, and wandering aimlessly during daylight hours is finally receiving a measure of public attention. In the last 4 months of 1985, for example, major articles on the plight of the homeless appeared in the newsletter of the American Association for Counseling and Development (Harold, in the September 5, 1985 issue), *Time* magazine (Krauthammer, December 2, 1985 issue), and the *Washington Post* (Aiken & Mechanic, December 18, 1985 issue). All of these articles noted that a large proportion of the homeless have serious mental health problems. Many were formerly in mental hospitals or other total care institutions and were de-institutionalized just at the time that funds for transitional care facilities were being cut. As funds for social services were cut, many agencies sought to avoid taking on new classes of clients, in order to preserve their dwindling resources to serve their traditional clientele. The result has been a chaotic pattern of attempting to avoid or shift responsibility for this population, rather than to serve them in an effective, coordinated way. The net effect of this is that the same problems, at equal or greater costs, appear elsewhere. Thus Basler, in the December 8, 1985 *New York Times*, reported that while New York State mental hospitals have accepted 25% fewer patients in the last 3 years, the number of persons with mental health problems treated at New York's municipal (general) hospitals has doubled over the same period. Moreover, the municipal hospitals are banned by law from providing the long-term care or follow-up services needed by this population.

Clearly, all the homeless need shelter, and those with mental health problems need treatment, as well. So far, few professionals have championed this cause, and it has been left to volunteers. A cynical explanation for this would be that the homeless do not carry insurance that pays for mental health services. Equally true, however, is the rejection by the homeless of the sorts of help professionals offer. This, however, does not free professionals from the obligation of trying to bridge the gap and provide appropriate, effective, attractive resources for this potential client group. Mental health counseling, as the only mental health profession not yet tied to third-party payment practices, may take the lead in developing effective service delivery systems for this most needy group. These services must begin with the establishment of resources for living.

Financial Resources

Mental health counselors must be familiar with financial resources available or possibly applicable to their clients. These generally include a number of government programs and private insurance plans. The principal government programs are tied to workers' compensation laws, vocational rehabilitation, and the social security system. For a detailed review of these programs, see Erlanger and Roth (1985).

Lesser (1967) pointed out that during the 1960s, workers' compensation laws came to be construed by the courts as no longer requiring the worker to prove a causal relationship between employment and the disability, as long as it could be shown that the disability occurred on the job. Thus, in a number of cases compensation has been awarded to workers for mental health problems that they claimed were the result of a physical injury or of stress suffered in the course of doing one's job. A client may be entitled to long-term financial support if her/his emotional problems can be shown to be work-related. It must, however, be pointed out that this can be a two-edged sword: Receiving workers' compensation payments may act as a disincentive to recovery, because the person who recovers may have to work hard to attain the same level of income now provided by remaining mentally incapacitated.

Workers' compensation is paid for out of insurance funds that employers are legally required to carry. Depending on the state law, this insurance may be from either a private insurer or a state fund. The cost of insurance to the employer depends on the number of persons employed, the hazards involved in their work, and the past record of claims upheld against the company. The process of adjudicating workers' compensation claims is generally a quasi-legal one, involving awards by a board with legal appeal of their decisions to the courts possible. Because workers' compensation laws are written at the state level, there is wide variation from state to state as to procedures and benefits.

Although workers' compensation laws go back to 1911 and the legal precedents for them go back much further, it was not until 1918 (for disabled veterans) to 1920 (for civilians) that the United States government undertook a program of vocational rehabilitation for the physically disabled (Berkowitz, 1979). The impetus for the original vocational rehabilitation law was World War I, but it was not until the time of World War II, in 1943, that the law was expanded to include persons with mental health problems. It should be noted that workers' compensation laws, as their name implies, provided compensation for injuries sustained while one was working. Vocational rehabilitation, however, did not require that one's disability resulted from prior employment; rather, this law was aimed at assisting persons with disabilities that stood in the way of their employment (even if the disability was there from birth) to attain the training and medical help that would allow them to become employed. Thus, the tests for qualifying for vocational rehabilitation services are: (a) the presence of a documented disabling condition, (b) evidence that this condition interferes with one's ability to be employed, and (c) an evaluation that providing services will be likely to make the person employable. No prior work history is necessary. The program is administered in each state by a state agency (generally called the division or bureau of vocational rehabilitation), with funds coming primarily from the federal government. The funding to each state depends on the size of the state's population and its record of successfully rehabilitated cases during the prior year. The state division of vocational rehabilitation offices are staffed by rehabilitation counselors (discussed in chapter 14), and the mental health counselor would refer a client to such a co-professional.

Under the vocational rehabilitation program, a client would first be evaluated for eligibility for service and, if deemed eligible according to the three criteria just noted, would then be evaluated as to what services would be needed to make the client employable. These services could involve the purchase of medical and dental treatments, prosthetic devices, prevocational and vocational training, further formal education, related transportation, the purchase of tools of a trade, and/or the provision of counseling services. Naturally, only those services actually required by the client would be provided in each case. The rehabilitation counselor and the client would then agree on a written plan (the Individualized Written Rehabilitation Plan or IWRP), signed by both of them, which outlines the services, time-lines, and goals of the rehabilitation program for that client.

The next group of financial resources with which the mental health counselor should be familiar are those connected with the federal Social Security program. Social Security Disability Insurance (SSDI) provides a worker whose disability—including mental health problems—is expected to prevent him/her from engaging in substantial employment for a period of at least 12 months with payments equal to his/her Social Security retirement benefits, including dependents' allowances. To qualify for SSDI, the person must have worked and been covered by Social Security in 20 of the 40 quarters prior to the onset of the disability period. Benefits under SSDI may be offset by other benefits (e.g., workers' compensation benefits) and may be terminated if the recipient earns more than a specified amount.

Another benefit possibly available to one's clients under the Social Security program is Supplemental Security Income (SSI), which provides a minimum income to elderly and disabled persons, including those with mental health problems. Unlike SSDI, no prior record of Social Security contributions or employment is required; however, also unlike SSDI, a client must pass a "means test" (that is, demonstrate financial need) in order to qualify for SSI benefits.

Associated with these two Social Security programs are two sets of benefits to help recipients defray the costs of health care. Medicare provides partial coverage for the costs of hospital and outpatient treatment for persons below the age of 65 who have qualified for SSDI coverage for 24 months, as well as for all persons over age 65 who qualify for Social Security retirement benefits. Medicaid provides partial coverage of health care costs for those whose income falls below a certain level. All persons who either receive or qualify for SSI meet this "means test." Medicare is an insurance program, paid for out of the deductions from one's salary made for Social Security. Medicaid, however, is an assistance program, funded by the federal and state governments out of general tax revenues, rather than by contributions of the participants. States vary in their approach to Medicaid, some states providing supplementary funds to recipients; but Medicare is a uniform program nationally. Some mental health care services are covered under both Medicare and Medicaid. To qualify for coverage, these services must have been provided by a member of one of the "core provider" professions, that is, a psychiatrist, clinical psychologist, psychiatric social worker, or psychiatric nurse. Legislation is now pending in the United States Congress to add mental health counselors to this list of "core providers."

Applications for SSDI, SSI, and Medicare are made through the client's local Social Security Administration office. Applications for Medicaid are made through the local office of the state department of social services. The regulations governing all of these programs are quite complex. A good overview of them is provided by Webster and Perry (1983).

The National Council on the Handicapped (1986) has recently catalogued 45 different federal programs concerned with persons with disabilities. Each state and local area, of course, also has its own programs. Many of these programs at all levels include individuals on the basis of mental health problems. Even more are available to persons with mental health problems who also have some other disabling condition. Some programs are only available to those who became disabled while working in a particular industry, such as coal mining, railroads, or longshore and harbor work. A large number of programs provide benefits to veterans of the armed forces, particularly those who have a service-connected disability (which could include mental health problems). These programs are run or coordinated by the Veterans Administration, which is a federal agency. If one's client is a veteran of the military, the counselor should direct that client to the local Veterans Administration office to explore possible benefits to which that client is entitled.

Finally, it should be noted that there are a number of health insurance plans, both private and government-sponsored, which provide coverage for mental health services. These include the Civilian Health and Medical Program of the Uniformed Services (CHAMPUS) which covers the civilian dependents of military personnel, Blue Cross/Blue Shield, and many commercial plans. These programs all tend to change both their benefits (proportion of costs paid) and lists of services covered (specific treatment and type of professional who may provide it) frequently. Therefore, the mental health counselor should advise the client to check with his/her insurer, or if not yet insured, to check with a number of insurers about the coverage they provide before obtaining coverage from any one of them.

Health Resources

Health resources that the mental health counselor should utilize, as appropriate, to meet clients' physical and mental health needs include hospitals and clinics, hospices, community service programs, self-help groups, and hotlines.

Hospitals may be publicly (municipal, state, United States Public Health Service, Veterans Administration) or privately (religious groups, for-profit or not-for-profit corporations, etc.) supported. Community clinics are generally state supported and cover the population living within a certain defined area of the state. The state, in turn, may get part of its funding for these clinics from federal block grants. Many hospitals and some clinics provide facilities for persons experiencing severe emotional distress. Indeed, hospitals and clinics range from those that provide services only for problems of physical illness to those that deal only with mental health problems to those that offer service to both sorts of clientele. On occasion, a client may become so distressed as to require or to benefit from the environmental controls that many of these facilities can provide. Generally, admission to these facilities requires a physician's signature confirming the appropriateness of inpatient treatment. Mental health clients may, of course, also require hospitalization for physical conditions that may or may not be connected with their mental health problems. If one's client requires hospitalization, the mental health counselor should work out with the institution's professional staff a plan to continue or to coordinate treatment for the problems being worked on in counseling. Some institutions allow the counselor to visit the client and continue counseling while the client is an inpatient; other institutions do not allow professionals not on their staff to treat their inpatients. If the client is entering one of the latter sort, the mental health counselor should make it clear to the client that the counselor is not abandoning him/her, but is prevented from pursuing the counseling process during the time that the client is in the institution.

The hospice movement is a relatively recent phenomenon, arising in good part from medical advances that have prolonged life and extended the dying process. Hospices aim to provide for the physical and emotional care of individuals who are terminally ill and, in some instances, for the social and emotional needs of members of their families. Some hospices offer residential facilities, whereas others provide supportive services for the home care of the terminally ill person. Some hospices concentrate on children with terminal illnesses, but most work primarily with adults or elderly persons. In cases in which a client or a member of the client's immediate family is facing terminal illness, a hospice can be an excellent resource in helping the client to cope with the attendant set of problems. Hospices generally provide some combination of medical, nursing, social work, religious, and counseling services. The counselor and/or client should determine which services each locally available hospice program offers and make the selection among them on that basis.

Community support programs are a very recent development, supported by the National Institute of Mental Health (NIMH) during the late 1970s under President Carter but not subsequently. Nonetheless, some of these programs remain. The NIMH defined a community support program as "a network of caring and responsible people committed to assisting a vulnerable population to meet their needs and develop their potentials without being unnecessarily isolated or excluded from the community" (Turner & TenHoor, 1978). The functions of a community support system are to provide:

1. Identification of the target population;
2. Assistance in applying for entitlements;
3. Crisis stabilization services;
4. Psychosocial rehabilitation services;
5. Supportive living and working arrangements;
6. Medical and mental health care;
7. Backup support to families, friends, and community members;
8. Involvement of community members in planning and providing housing and work opportunities;
9. Protection of client rights;
10. Case management to ensure continuous availability of appropriate forms of assistance.

Thus, community support programs seek to fulfill two basic thrusts. The first is to focus on providing mental health services in the community insofar as possible, rather than in isolated, segregated institutions. The second thrust is to provide coordination for these services. Historically, many clients have had to go from agency to agency for different services. Each of these agencies has different criteria for eligibility for services, and some services are not provided by any local agency, while other services are unnecessarily duplicated. Many clients have viewed this situation as an insurmountable barrier to help-seeking and have "dropped out of the wild goose chase" to obtain the help they need. By providing coordination, the community support programs were intended to help change this situation.

Even if no such program exists by name in the community in which the mental health counselor works, the counselor should seek to implement the principles of these programs (as outlined in this discussion) in his/her own community.

A major resource for mental health counselors is self-help groups. Paskert and Madara (1985) noted that there are over 100,000 different self-help groups throughout the United States, with over 3 million active members. These authors suggested that these groups may be broadly classified as: (a) those that assist clients/patients and their family members with almost any specific major physical illness or mental health problem; (b) those that offer behavior modification programs for a wide range of addictive behaviors (e.g., alcohol abuse, drug abuse, smoking, overeating, gambling); (c) social support groups for persons facing life transitions (e.g., parenthood, divorce, bereavement); and (d) advocacy groups for special population groups (e.g., elderly, gays, racial or ethnic groups). Self-help groups are valuable in that they not only allow a sense of community and of empowerment in coping with a problem, but they also give a client an opportunity to take an active role as a helper, thereby helping themselves as well.

The relationship between self-help groups and professionals has not been a smooth one. The self-help groups have accused professionals of acting out of self-interest, being unsympathetic or ineffective because they have not personally experienced the condition they are treating, and of treating their clients as experimental subjects rather than as suffering fellow human beings. Conversely, professionals have accused self-help groups of acting unprofessionally (not a surprising observation), of being too committed to their agenda to be willing to stop and see if they are really helping those in need, of distorting their success rates by avoiding applying scientific standards, and of helping themselves more than they help others with the same problem. Over time, however, these accusations on both sides have been attended to; and today, one is less likely to find the kind of mutual hostility that typified professional–self-help group relations in the past. Professionals recognize the unique effectiveness of certain self-help groups, such as Alcoholics Anonymous. If anything, professionals may be able to learn what makes certain self-help groups effective, so that they may assist other self-help groups to apply or to adopt those principles to make themselves more effective. Also, as mutual distrust and competitiveness decrease, professionals and self-help groups are becoming more willing to learn from each other ways of benefiting those individuals they both seek to serve. Gartner (1982) emphasized both the sense of independence and empowerment and the cost-effectiveness of self-help groups, in that they can turn problems into resources for coping with those problems.

In the area of mental health, there are a number of self-help groups, including Recovery, Incorporated, founded in 1937 by a physician (Lewis & Lewis, 1983). The organization is now administered completely by individuals who have encountered serious problems of living. Local groups meet weekly to study mental health literature and to hear members discuss how they have come to deal more effectively with their problems. Members also speak to community groups, to promote public awareness of mental health needs. Another group is the National Alliance for the Mentally Ill. This organization, through its state and local affiliated groups, offers advocacy, public education, and community support services for persons with severe problems of living and for their families. Biegel, McCardle, and Mendelson (1985) cited over 300 references to studies concerned with mental health self-help groups. Groups have been studied that deal with most major categories of psychiatric diagnosis (schizophrenia, manic–depressive psychosis, depression, behavior disorders, phobias, compulsions) as well as addictive behaviors (alcohol, drugs, gambling, overeating) and other problems of living (women's issues, men's issues, new parenthood, child abuse, divorce and separation, and bereavement and widowhood). Self-help groups have been oriented toward prevention, self-treatment, rehabilitation and/or advocacy. Chamberlin (1978), a former patient, has written a compelling book that documents the benefits and limitations of self-controlled care for those experiencing problems of living.

Hatfield (1981) surveyed members of self-help groups for families of persons with mental health problems on the following characteristics of their groups: (a) relationship of leaders to members, (b) ability of leaders to keep members informed, (c) liveliness of membership meetings, (d) involvement of members in activities, (e) rotation of leadership, (f) extent of contact with clients, and (g) degree of autonomy. She found significant differences among groups as to the perceived strengths and weaknesses along these dimensions.

Mental health counselors must familiarize themselves with the range of self-help groups and refer clients to them when it is appropriate to do so, given the type of problem involved and the compatibility of the client and the particular group.

Finally, hotlines are telephone services maintained by either volunteer or professional organizations to provide immediate, crisis response to a particular problem (e.g., spouse abuse, potential suicide, runaway children, poisoning, infectious diseases, consumer problems). Given the specific knowledge required of persons who work on many of these hotlines, they may provide excellent resources for clients facing specific problems toward which these hotlines are addressed.

CONCLUSION

In this chapter, a number of the major categories of resources that mental health counselors may bring to bear to assist their clients to cope with specific problems of living have been reviewed. Where these resources exist in the counselor's community, the counselor should know of them and how to access them. When a needed resource does not exist, the mental health counselor should use her/his skills to involve the community in establishing that resource, as discussed in chapter 10.

As has been pointed out throughout this book, the counselor and the client do not function in isolation but rather function in an environmental context. Resources are a major element of that context that can be used in coping with all sorts of problems of living. Involving the appropriate resources in the solution of problems is an essential part of any treatment plan, and the knowledge of how to do so is a basic professional skill that every counselor must possess.

REFERENCES

Aiken, L., & Mechanic, D. (1985, December 18). Communities must care for the homeless mentally ill. *Washington Post*, Health Section, p. 6.

Bachrach, L. L. (1980). Is the least restrictive environment always the best? Sociological and semantic implications. *Hospital and Community Psychiatry, 13*, 97–103.

Backer, T. E., & Trotter, M. W. (1986). Networks in the rehabilitation field: Local to international. *American Rehabilitation, 12*(1), 28–31.

Basler, B. (1985, December 8). Mentally ill rise in city hospitals. *The New York Times*, p. 89.

Berkowitz, E. D. (1979). The American disability system in historical perspective. In E. D. Berkowitz (Ed.), *Disability policies and government programs*. New York: Praeger.

Biegel, D. E., McCardle, E., & Mendelson, S. (1985). *Social networks and mental health: An annotated bibliography*. Beverly Hills, CA: Sage.

Chamberlin, J. (1978). *On our own: Patient-controlled alternatives to the mental health system*. New York: Hawthorn Books.

Erlanger, H. S., & Roth, W. (1985). Disability policy: The parts and the whole. *American Behavioral Scientist, 28*, 319–345.

Frieden, L. (1980). Independent living models. *Rehabilitation Literature, 41*, 169–173.

Gartner, A. (1982). Self-help/self-care: A cost effective health strategy. *Social Policy, 12*(4), 64.

Harold, M. (1985, September 5). Many of nation's homeless beset with mental disorders. *American Association for Counseling and Development Guidepost, 28*(3), 1, 12.

Hatfield, A. B. (1981). Self-help groups for families of the mentally ill. *Social Work, 26*, 408–413.

Krauthammer, C. (1985, December 2). When liberty really means neglect. *Time*, pp. 103–104.

Lesser, P. J. (1967). The legal viewpoint. In A. A. McLean (Ed.), *To work is human: Mental health and the business community* (pp. 103–122). New York: Macmillan.

Lewis, J. A., & Lewis, M. D. (1983). *Community counseling: A human services approach* (2nd ed.). New York: Wiley.

McLean, A. (Ed.). (1970). *Mental health and work organizations*. Chicago: Rand McNally.

National Council on the Handicapped. (1986, February). *Toward independence: An assessment of federal laws and programs affecting persons with disabilities—with legislative recommendations*. Washington, DC: Author.

Neff, W. S. (1977). *Work and human behavior* (2nd ed.). Chicago: Aldine.

Paskert, C. J., & Madara, E. J. (1985). Introducing and tapping self-help mutual aid resources. *Health Education, 16*, 25–29.

Schwartz, B. (1986). Decide to network: A path to personal and professional empowerment. *AMHCA Journal, 8*, 12–17.

Simmons, O. G. (1965). *Work and mental illness: Eight case studies*. New York: Wiley.

Slocum, W. L. (1974). *Occupational careers: A sociological perspective* (2nd ed.). Chicago: Aldine.

Tilgher, A. (1930). *Work: What it has meant to men through the ages* (D. C. Fisher, Trans.). New York: Harcourt, Brace.

Turner, J. C., & TenHoor, W. J. (1978). The NIMH community support program: Pilot approach to a needed social reform. *Schizophrenia Bulletin, 4*, 319–344.

Webster, B., & Perry, R. L. (1983). *The complete Social Security handbook*. New York: Dodd, Mead.

VI EPILOGUE

16 The Future of Mental Health Counseling

This chapter will examine the directions in which the field of mental health counseling is likely to move in the foreseeable future. We will begin by reviewing several surveys that have sought the predictions of mental health counselors or of mental health professionals in general as to the future of their profession. We shall then examine some of the emerging trends and issues in society and in the profession that will affect the future development of the field of mental health counseling.

FUTURE FORECASTS BY MENTAL HEALTH COUNSELORS

Anderson and Parenté (1980) used the survey technique of Delphic polling to obtain the forecasts of mental health counselors as to the future of their field. The authors specifically sought predictions of the eventual level and quality of training, employment prospects, third-party payment, and credentialing patterns for mental health counselors. Items on which most of the respondents (all respondents were members of the American Mental Health Counselors Association [AMHCA]) agreed included the predictions that it was very likely in the near-to-medium future that: (a) program accreditation will increase in importance, (b) certification will become mandatory for master's level mental health specialists, (c) mental health specialists will be included in a national health insurance plan, and (d) master's level graduate training will become highly specialized. The respondents thought it very unlikely that: (a) master's degree programs will be virtually eliminated; (b) chemotherapy will replace the traditional therapies; (c) the quality of doctoral education will decline significantly; (d) master's degree mental health workers will occupy all the jobs, making it difficult for doctorate-holding counselors to find work; and (e) the mental health professions will decline in popularity.

In their report of a Delphic polling of a broader sample of mental health professionals—including psychiatrists, psychologists, psychiatric social workers, psychiatric nurses, and mental health administrators as well as mental health counselors—on the same issues (Anderson, Parenté, Gordon, 1981), the respondents (summed across all professions) predicted essentially the same scenarios, with the additional point that it was very unlikely that third-party payment would cease to provide a funding base.

Finally, Randolph, Lassiter, and Newell (1986) reported a survey of 287 human service agencies representing 49 states and the District of Columbia as to their projected staffing patterns for the mid- and late 1980s. The results indicated that these agencies project about three times as many master's degree level positions both for replacements and for expansion, compared to doctoral degree level positions. Master's degree level positions were projected to expand at the rate of 12% annually, in addition to an annual replacement rate of 23% for turnover and promotions of current staff.

Thus, those now in the profession appear to feel that the mental health professions, including mental health counseling, have a secure future. They also appear to predict that master's degree level practitioners will increase in numbers and in professionalization (certification, program accreditation, specialization). Both of these trends are comforting, if they prove to be true, because they will benefit both mental health counselors and their clients.

EMERGING TRENDS AND ISSUES

We may turn now to an examination of the trends and issues that are already in evidence and that will unquestionably have an impact on the field of mental health counseling in the near future. These include:

1. Societal trends that will affect the profession, that is, changes in client populations and in settings for practice, de-institutionalization, consumerism, the growth of technology, and the economics of mental health care.
2. Trends and issues within mental health counseling that will affect the theory and practice of this profession, that is, the shift from emphasis on removing pathology to emphasis on promoting assets and coping; the increased emphasis on environment–behavior interaction; the shift from theory-based to skill-based practice; the movement from an exclusively direct treatment-oriented mission to one involving a full range of interventions; and a focus on evaluation and research.
3. Issues and trends related to the professionalization of mental health counseling, including models of practice and reimbursement, credentialing, professional education, and international expansion of the field.

Although it is not possible to predict with absolute certainty exactly what changes will result from these trends and issues, we can be sure that they will have an effect on the directions the field of mental health counseling will take over the rest of this century.

Societal Trends

Changes in Clientele and Settings

The first societal trend we shall examine is the shift in clientele and in settings. As the birthrate has declined and longevity has increased, there will be proportionately less call for counselors for school-age children, but markedly increased need for gerontological counselors. The decline in the number of children being born will be somewhat offset by the fact that proportionately more children are being raised in one-parent families. Such children may well require more services from mental health counselors. The absolute increase in the number of older individuals is indisputable. Because of shifts in the ethnic and racial composition of American society through immigration and differential birth rates, mental health counselors will be working more with populations that have been underrepresented in the provision of services in the past, such as cultural minorities. Mental health counselors, through their professional organization, are currently involved in educating legislators, insurance providers, and society as a whole about their ability to provide effective, more economical services to clientele from which they have been excluded by older, larger, more politically active mental health professions. This, too, will place mental health counselors in contact with clients who differ socially and culturally from those served in the past, particularly those clients who are covered by third party insurers such as Medicare, Medicaid, Civilian Health and Medical Program of the Uniformed Services (CHAMPUS), Blue Cross/Blue Shield, and other private insurance plans.

As the value of counseling has become recognized in the workplace and as the structure of work has been changing to accommodate a broader range of lifestyles, new settings in business and industry — such as employee assistance programs and human resources development offices — will be hiring proportionately more mental health counselors. Moreover, mental health counselors continue to find increased acceptance of their professional role in hospitals, clinics, community mental health centers, family service agencies, and health maintenance organizations (Forrest & Affemann, 1986). With the increase in the proportion of older persons in the society, we may expect an expanded role for mental health counselors in nursing homes, senior citizens' centers, and hospices, as well.

De-institutionalization

A second major societal trend is the continuing movement toward de-institutionalization of mental health services. This includes the development of self-help groups and of the private practice of counseling, as well as the major societal thrust toward placing clients in the least restrictive environment. This trend significantly changes the roles and responsibilities of the mental health counselor. Advocacy and environmental intervention become essential skills for the mental health counselor. Consultation, coordination, linking, and referral skills are necessary for working with self-help groups and other community resources. Although de-institutionalization has, on balance, been a positive trend, it has had at least one major unintended negative consequence, the increase in the number of homeless persons who formerly received shelter within institutions. Mental health professionals have not paid sufficient attention to the needs of these homeless persons, many of whom could benefit from the approach advocated by mental health counseling (i.e., mobilization of client assets and skills and environmental manipulation).

Consumerism

A third societal trend is the growth of consumerism. This has had its effects on counseling in the development of self-help groups as an alternative to seeking help from professionals, in the demand for freedom of choice of services and service providers, and in the dramatic increase in the number of malpractice suits against mental health professionals and institutions. Clients are demanding the right to be informed about the cost and effectiveness of services and to hold professionals, including mental health counselors, liable for misrepresentations and inept practices. Despite its hazards for the individual counselor, this trend has significant potential to benefit the profession as a whole. Insofar as mental health counseling can demonstrate superior cost-effectiveness as compared to other mental health service providers, it stands to gain wider acceptance and recognition throughout a society that embraces this value.

New Technology

The fourth societal trend affecting the future development of mental health counseling is the growth of and value placed on technology. This trend has both general effects on the emotional well-being of those living within the society and specific effects on the practice of mental health counseling. We live in a time and culture in which technology is valued because of its contribution to our material comfort and despite its potential for mass destruction. It is incumbent on the mental health counselor to assist people to live with both the benefits and the threats of technology. It is also necessary for the counselor to learn to use technologies for the betterment of society.

Living with the constant threat of nuclear war certainly has had its impact on mental health, and advances in other technological fields will unquestionably also have implications for mental health counseling. Genetic engineering may change the types and incidence of emotional problems in future generations. The emotional effects of living with a transplanted organ have yet to be evaluated. What will be the emotional effects of the relative isolation, disorientation, and weightlessness experienced in space travel? Nearer at hand, mental health counseling must become prepared to assist people to deal with the emotional effects of job obsolescence resulting from advances in computer technology and in robotics. The latter may represent a particularly severe problem, because the majority of those displaced by robotics will have the lowest level of compensatory skills and, often, the fewest developed resources to cope with their displacement.

The other aspect of this trend is the development of a technology for use in mental health counseling. This technology involves the areas of electronics (audio and video recording), data processing (interactive systems, information storage and retrieval), psychoactive drugs, and behavior modification (biofeedback, relaxation programs, etc.). These devices will increasingly affect the counselor's role, functions, practices, and effectiveness. Electronic recording technology has changed the nature of counseling supervision and also allows replay to clients as part of the counseling process. The gathering and providing of information can now be done on a computer, thereby freeing the counselor's time to work with the client on solving problems. These technologies do, however, raise issues concerning client confidentiality, such as limiting access to electronically stored records. Also, counselors must take care that the use of this technology does not interpose a barrier between the counselor and the client, depersonalizing the counseling process. Psychoactive medication administered by physicians allows counselors to work with clients formerly too withdrawn, agitated, or confused to benefit from counseling. The negative side of this development, of course, is the criminal misuse of psychoactive drugs by addicts and thrill-seekers, presenting a major problem for counselors and other mental health professionals to address. Behavioral technology is already well established within mental health counseling practice and will certainly be even more broadly applied in the future. Relaxation techniques can be used to help eliminate phobias, reduce physical complaints, and otherwise contribute to positive health. Similarly, biofeedback may be used to treat physical (blood pressure, headaches, etc.) and emotional (anxiety) symptoms. The potential benefits of behavioral technology are great; but in the past, these techniques have too often been applied by overzealous advocates to populations who had no choice in their use—school children, prisoners, persons in mental institutions, and mentally retarded individuals. Thus, all of the technological developments applicable in mental health counseling present both potential benefits and potential risks, and the counselor must be aware of both aspects in determining their appropriate use.

Economic Considerations

The final societal trend to be considered is the effect of economic considerations on the development of mental health counseling. Inevitably, economic factors are used to justify the political decisions to support or to cut back on publicly funded mental health services at the local, state, and national levels

(Fein, 1958; Rubin, 1978). In the views of many policy analysts (e.g., Boulding, 1967), economic considerations outweigh the social ones in political decision making, even on social issues such as mental health. Therefore, it is important for the mental health professional in general, and the mental health counselor in particular, to be aware of trends in the economics of mental health and of mental health service delivery. This involves such issues as: (a) the cost of providing mental health services, (b) the cost of not providing those services, (c) the cost-benefit ratio that is acceptable to society, (d) the relative costs of different service delivery alternatives, and (e) who pays for the services that are rendered. In purely economic terms, divorced of any social or moral considerations (although economists do take these factors into account), the question becomes: What is the least society needs to pay in order to attain a level of mental health that it finds acceptable? This question, of course, can never lead to a single, permanent answer, because poorer societies are forced to accept lower levels than richer ones, and richer ones are forced to accept lower levels in periods of recession than in periods of prosperity.

Figuring the costs of mental health problems and services is an extremely complex process, requiring that one make certain assumptions that can significantly affect the final figure. Rubin (1978) cited certain categories of direct costs, including: (a) direct care (e.g., public and private mental hospitals; community mental health facilities; general medical services, nursing homes, and rehabilitation facilities for those with mental health problems; private practice by mental health professionals; children's programs; and psychoactive medication); (b) research on mental health problems; (c) training of mental health workers; (d) construction and development of mental health facilities; and (e) management of mental health. The indirect costs of mental health problems include the loss to society of the productive capacity of those with mental health problems, including those in long-term institutions, those who experience short-term work absences, and those who work at less than their full potential as a result of their problems. One can, if one chooses, add complexities such as how to figure in the cost of disability payments to persons with mental health problems, whether to figure in the cost of food for those in institutions, and whether to figure the differences in productive output by those now engaged in providing mental health services as compared with their output if available for employment elsewhere in the economy. As one can see, by including or by excluding certain considerations, one can raise or lower the stated costs of mental health problems and the costs of services to treat them (Fein, 1958). In general, political liberals try to maximize the stated costs of illness and minimize the stated costs of services, in order to justify providing more services. Conservatives, on the other hand, seek to minimize the stated cost of the problem and maximize the cost of services as a justification for cutting back on services.

Figure 16.1, compiled by the National Institute of Mental Health (Taube & Barrett, 1985) shows the total expenditures for salaries, operating expenses, and capital outlay for mental health services and program administration between 1969 and 1981. Figures are given in both constant (1969) dollars and in current dollars (not corrected for inflation). Over this period of little more than a decade, the increase in constant dollars was by a factor of 50% (from $2.8 billion to $4.2 billion), while the uncorrected dollar total more than tripled. Naturally, this runaway rate of cost increases for mental health services caused the federal and state legislatures to recoil. It is noteworthy that the only costs that were reduced since 1975 are those for psychiatric hospitals, which reflects the policy of deinstitutionalization discussed earlier. This apparent saving, however, may well have caused some of the increases in costs in other categories.

Another economic consideration is who is to pay for these services—the federal government, the state, the local community, the person's employer, or the individual? Again, the pendulum has swung back and forth among these levels, depending on the contemporary social and legal views of what responsibilities should be assigned to what level. One factor that frequently enters into the consideration of this matter is who can best insure against the loss. As such, the insurance companies have, through profit motive or social pressure, moved into providing third-party payment for mental health services. As the costs of health care have risen at a much more rapid rate than is accounted for

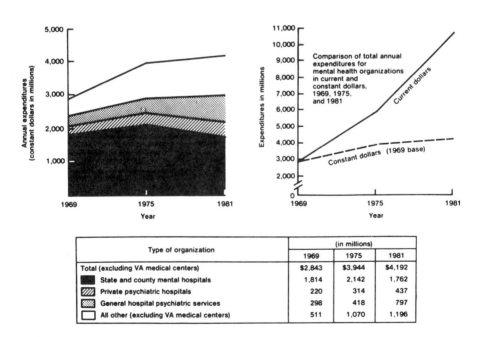

FIGURE 16.1. Estimated annual expenditures (constant dollars), selected mental health organizations (excluding VA medical centers): United States, 1969, 1975, and 1981. (Source: From *Mental Health, United States, 1985* edited by C. A. Taube and S. A. Barrett, National Institute of Mental Health, 1985. Washington, DC: U.S. Government Printing Office.)

by general inflation, providing coverage for mental health services has no longer proved profitable; and insurers have sought to limit or to stop coverage for these services. This, in turn, has become a major political issue, in part reflecting differences of political opinion as to the responsibilities and rights of insurance companies.

Finally, no matter who pays, that party will have the same economic concern: Am I getting the most effective use of my money? Could I receive equal (or better) services for less cost? This becomes a marketplace issue among the providers of mental health services, each trying to convince the public (both the ones who pay and the ones who legislate as to who can provide services) that their service is better or cheaper than that offered by the other mental health fields. Much of the problem with the contest, however, is that it only focuses on providing services to clients who can pay (or can get a third party to pay) for them. No professional groups are seeking exclusive rights to treat the destitute client. On the other hand, none of the "in-groups" that now receive third-party payment (psychiatry, clinical psychology, psychiatric social work, or psychiatric nursing) can afford to allow an "out-group" to treat these clients; for once an "out-group" does so, it has established the principle that it is competent to provide treatment and can therefore compete for paying clients. Thus, ironically, the competition for the paying client most hurts the person who cannot pay. If mental health counseling does make it into the in-group of "core providers" (those mental health professions paid by insurance companies or by the government, in the case of the elderly, the poor, the disabled, or dependents of persons in the military), it is to be hoped that the field will not lose sight of this phenomenon but will remain sensitive to the needs of those who cannot offer payment for the mental health services they require.

Trends and Issues Affecting Theory and Practice

Five trends and issues within mental health counseling that will affect future theory and practice in the field will be examined in the following paragraphs. These include the emphasis on mobilizing client assets and skills; on environment–behavior interaction; on skill-based practice; on primary and tertiary, as well as secondary, prevention; and on evaluation and research.

Assets and Skills

The principal unique contribution of counseling to the mental health field is counseling's focus on mobilizing client assets and skills as the essential strategy for promoting growth and coping. This strategy avoids the long-standing, unresolved debate as to whether mental health problems are biological, learned, psychodynamic, or socially imposed in origin. Clients cannot wait for the resolution of this issue (if it will ever be resolved) to get on with the tasks of life. Even in the unlikely chance that eventually all mental health problems are found to be biochemical in etiology and curable by psychoactive drugs, all persons will still encounter problems of living that will require them to use their assets and skills in order to cope. It is, therefore, safe to say that mental health counseling is well advised to pursue this approach and to develop further its methods for identifying and mobilizing client assets and skills. For mental health counselors, this requires the development of two sets of skills: (a) the skills needed for living and coping with life situations, and (b) the skills needed to help clients to recognize, develop, and apply these life skills. Recent outstanding examples of progress toward these goals is represented by the work of Carkhuff, Pierce, and Cannon (1980); Goldstein (1981); and Janis (1983).

Environment–Behavior Interaction

The second trend affecting the theory and practice of mental health counseling is an increased focus on environment–behavior interaction. As early as 1936, Kurt Lewin defined the principle that behavior is a function of the person and that person's environment; that is, that one can only understand a person's behavior when considering it within its environmental context. A few of Lewin's students, such as Barker (1968), attempted to follow up on this doctrine by studying "behavior settings," namely, environments that elicit or are associated with particular behaviors. In time, other scholars, such as Moos (1977), undertook the study of "social ecology," examining the relationship between behaviors and characteristics of their environmental settings. This principle, however, is only beginning to find its way systematically into the doctrine of the longer established mental health fields, even though it is doubtful that one could find a mental health professional who would dispute its validity or its relevance to practice. As the newest of the mental health professions, and hence the one with the least rigid set of premises, mental health counseling can most easily incorporate this unquestionably valid principle into its basic working principles.

Thus, for mental health counseling, behavior is viewed contextually, rather than in isolation. This has fostered an emphasis on community-oriented preventive measures and has promoted an advocacy role for counselors. Changing client behavior is now generally recognized as an ineffective goal unless the new behavior is adaptive to and supported by the setting in which it will be practiced. The importance of behavior–environment interaction is also an underlying principle in the development of cross-cultural counseling, with its recognition that behavior that might be appropriate in one cultural context may be viewed as grossly inappropriate in another. For example, one of the authors recalls seeing an unemployed Puerto Rican client fly into a murderous rage when asked at an intake interview whether he helped his working wife with the housework. Within this client's cultural context, that apparently innocent question was seen by the client as an aspersion on his masculinity, which is a central value for men within his culture.

Skill-based Practice

A third trend affecting theory and practice is the shift from theory-based to skill-based counseling practice. The defining of specific counselor competencies and the demonstration of these as determinants of fitness to practice is a major change in the field. Rigidly following the techniques dictated by a single theoretical model, regardless of the nature of the client or the problem, is no longer professionally acceptable. Counselors now not only must possess a range of skills derived from a variety of theoretical approaches, but also must know when to apply each of them and how to combine them into a multimodal approach. This shift moves the counselor from being a technician to being a true professional. Among the best articulated skill-based approaches to date are those of Goldstein (1981), mentioned earlier, and of Anthony (1979).

Full Range of Interventions

The fourth trend affecting mental health counseling theory and practice is the shift from an exclusive emphasis on individual treatment for specific problems of living to a recognition that the aims of the field can only be accomplished if the full range of services, including preventive and rehabilitative services, are brought to bear in promoting mental health. This change reflects the shift from the medical, treatment of individual illness model to the public health, promotion of community health model. This is consistent with mental health counseling's posture as a profession that seeks to promote health, rather than to cure illness. Medicine has long had the task of treating persons who are ill, which is unquestionably a much needed, full-time job. The allied field of public health has defined its role as preventing illness, rather than curing it after it has occurred. Consequently, public health has defined three types of prevention: primary prevention, or preventing a disease from occurring; secondary prevention, or preventing the disease from further damaging the patient, once it has occurred (that is, the traditional medical treatment role); and tertiary prevention, or preventing the effects of the disease, once they have been contained, from further incapacitating the patient (that is, the traditional rehabilitative role). Thus, a complete health-oriented approach requires all three types of activities: preventive efforts, direct service treatment, and rehabilitation for those treated (i.e., primary, secondary, and tertiary prevention, respectively). Mental health counseling, as a health-oriented discipline, has adopted this model in defining its role.

We have, throughout this book, looked at mental health counseling's efforts in prevention (community counseling, education, consultation, etc.), treatment, and rehabilitation (e.g., Anthony, 1979). Unquestionably, mental health counseling will continue to develop and improve its methods in all three areas, but a special comment is warranted concerning preventive services. Certainly, there is much truth to the old adage that an ounce of prevention is worth a pound of cure. It is part of the doctrine of the mental health field that this adage is applicable to its domain. For example, Albee (1985) has pointed out that we will never have enough mental health professionals to treat all those in need of such services, so that we had better devote efforts to preventing mental health problems rather than to the hopeless task of producing enough professionals to help people deal with these problems. To date, however, no really adequate technology of preventive services has been developed in the area of mental health. This has not been a result of overlooking this issue (for example, Buckner, Trickett, & Corse, 1985), but rather reflects the pressure society has put on these fields to deal with the huge numbers of those in immediate need of services. Moreover, it is frequently difficult to demonstrate effective prevention, because it requires proving that something did not occur as a direct consequence of a particular intervention. Most funding bodies are more ready to support a campaign to fight an existing dramatic crisis than to support efforts to prevent a potential crisis that may not come into being. Finally, there must be agreement on the cause of a phenomenon if one is to figure out a way to prevent it, and no such agreement exists in the mental health field. Nonetheless, given the prevalence of mental health problems, there is good reason to devote greater attention to efforts at prevention, and one may expect proportionately more emphasis on prevention in the future.

Evaluation and Research

The final trend affecting theory and practice to be mentioned here is the increased emphasis on evaluation and research in counseling. The quality of counseling is now measured by its effectiveness and economy, rather than by its artistry or conformity to a theoretical model. This trend moves counseling into the category of scientifically based endeavors, which both increases its validity and justifies its existence according to the values prevalent in our society. Through evaluation of its techniques, processes, and outcomes, the parameters of the field can be carefully defined and the necessary competencies for practice can be determined.

The line between evaluation and research is, at best, blurred. Research essentially addresses basic, theoretical issues, whereas evaluation assesses the efficacy and cost-efficiency of applied techniques and programs. To remain viable, mental health counseling must pursue both these processes. The ultimate question for counseling is: What *techniques*, applied by what *counselors* working with what *clients* facing what *problems of living* under what *environmental conditions*, produce what *outcomes*? Obviously, it is impossible at the present stage of development of the field to answer all of that question at once. We assume, however, that by answering parts of the question we will eventually be able to build a full answer. Thus, we may now test whether reflection works better with dependent or independent clients in increasing feelings of self-worth, or whether hearing-impaired clients resolve conflicts more rapidly working with counselors who use sign language or by using an interpreter with non-signing counselors. Until thousands of such bits of information are accumulated, we cannot put them together to answer the general question. We can, however, use research to determine the validity of some basic theoretical issues, such as whether repression exists as a phenomenon, and if so, under what conditions it leads to hostility, passivity, or other behaviors. If, for example, we were to find that repression does not exist, there is no need to develop or evaluate techniques to deal with it.

Issues and Trends Related to Professionalization

In addition to the issues of theory and practice, mental health counseling faces issues related to its existence as a profession. In this section four such issues shall be explored: models of practice and reimbursement, professional credentialing, professional education, and the worldwide scope and potential for this field.

Models of Practice and Reimbursement

Traditionally, mental health counselors have been employed as staff members in agencies and clinics. Recently, however, a rapidly increasing proportion of practitioners have sought to establish independent practices. This has brought the field into contact with the issue of third-party (that is, government or private insurance company) payment for services to clients. Originally, third-party coverage was only available to psychiatrists, because they possessed medical degrees and so were covered under medical insurance policies. Psychologists and social workers attacked this practice, on the grounds that their "talking therapies" were essentially indistinguishable from those practiced by psychiatrists and that clients were entitled to "freedom of choice" in selecting a mental health service provider. Using these arguments, psychology and social work gained insurance coverage despite the opposition of psychiatry. When, however, mental health counseling began to seek coverage under exactly the same rationale, psychology and, to a lesser extent, social work sought to oppose it. The basis for opposition (psychiatry against psychology's and social work's claims; these latter two against mental health counseling's similar claims) has clearly been on economic grounds. The fewer the number of practitioners entitled to reimbursement, the more the law of supply and demand works in their favor. This alone can explain why those who advocated "freedom of choice" for their own profession have sought to deny "freedom of choice" to other, later arriving claimants. The field of mental health counseling is just beginning to assert its claims to third-party reimbursement with success. Covin (1985) reported a recent survey of licensed counselors in Alabama, in which 84% of those who submitted requests for third-party payment were paid. This figure shows an improvement over an earlier survey in Virginia, in which only 45% of counselors' claims were paid (Seligman & Whitley, 1983). Although mental health counseling's demands for coverage will require active pursuit against the self-serving, protectionist interests of those professional groups now covered, there is every reason to expect that mental health counseling will eventually gain inclusion in government and private insurance plans by demonstrating its greater cost-effectiveness, as compared with its older sibling professions that are now covered.

Credentialing

Another trend, related to the issues of consumerism, evaluation, and third-party payment discussed earlier in this chapter, is that of professional credentialing. Counselor licensing and certification and the accreditation of counselor education programs are, in good measure, responses to consumer demands for an indication of competence. Counselor certification is also a possible basis for determining who will qualify to receive third-party payment. To be credible, these processes must be functionally related to the trend toward evaluation; otherwise, the credentials will merely appear to be self-serving. That is, the credentials must be based on the counselor's demonstrating skills that have been shown through research to be effective in working with clients like the one to whom the services are being rendered. Moreover, credentials must be used to attest to competence rather than to limit competition among mental health service providers. As discussed in chapter 3, two types of certification exist: general certification as a counselor through the National Board for Certified Counselors (designation: national certified counselor, abbreviated as NCC following the counselor's name and academic degrees) and specific certification as a certified clinical mental health counselor (CCMHC) through the National Academy of Certified Clinical Mental Health Counselors. The National Board for Certified Counselors is associated with the American Association for Counseling and Development, the national professional organization of the field of counseling. Mental health counselors make up one division (the American Mental Health Counselors Association) within this organization, along with other divisions for school counselors, rehabilitation counselors, and so on. The National Academy of Certified Clinical Mental Health Counselors is similarly associated with the American Mental Health Counselors Association. To date, these two certification processes have not been sufficiently integrated with each other, and it is to be hoped that this will occur in the near future.

In addition to professional certification, a number of states now license counselors, based on their professional education, experience, and ability to pass a licensing examination.

As is the case with most professions, counselors must participate in continuing education in their field, in order to maintain their certification and/or license. This helps counselors keep up to date with advances in their field.

As has been suggested, certification and licensure are intended to protect the public from unqualified individuals offering services. To the extent that these processes are used for this purpose, they are valid and should be enthusiastically supported. They should not, however, be allowed to become mechanisms for excluding competent practitioners in order to control the marketplace for services.

Education of Mental Health Counselors

The third issue is that of professional education. No profession can exist without established patterns of training for its practitioners. As indicated in chapter 3, entry level education for mental health counselors, as defined by the professional organizations in the field (National Board for Certified Counselors; American Mental Health Counselors Association; Council for Accreditation of Counseling and Related Educational Programs), consists of 2 years of full-time graduate study that include courses in counseling theory, human development, social and cultural aspects of behavior, counseling and consultation techniques, appraisal of clients, group processes, career and lifestyle development, professional ethics and practices, research and evaluation methods, and some specifics of mental health counseling practice. Supervised practicum and internship experiences are also included in the educational requirements. This is a demanding and wide-ranging set of knowledge and skills, but is it sufficient to produce effective mental health counselors? What about preventive, educational, or administrative skills? What about knowledge of the effects of drugs or of exercise? As professionals, counselors can never stop learning. Obviously, no member of any professional is fully educated at the time of graduation from professional school. When a physician graduates from medical school, that physician is not immediately qualified as a neurosurgeon. Further specialized learning and experience are required. Similarly, no counselor fresh out of a graduate program is an expert advocate, consultant, or counselor. Lengthening the period of formal training might resolve this problem; but then the cost of fully trained personnel might become prohibitive, and even more persons in need of services would remain unattended. Therefore, part of the solution is in continuing education for counselors educated up to a reasonable entry level in programs of minimal feasible length. Over the years, that minimum length has increased from 1 to 2 full academic years. Perhaps, as the knowledge base of the field expands, the length of academic programs may have to be increased to 3 years; but any lengthier preservice educational programs for mental health counselors will need to be thoroughly justified relative to the cost of longer time in school before professional entry.

Another issue confronting mental health counselor education is that different professional roles require different mixes of knowledge and skills. Thus, a line counselor (i.e., a direct service provider) must be more proficient at individual client appraisal than an agency administrator, whereas the administrator must be more proficient at management techniques. Most agency administrators, however, start out their careers as line counselors. Should the education of line counselors therefore place weight on the learning of management techniques when that means that less time can be devoted to teaching basic counseling skills? Perhaps a better model is the shortest feasible education required to become competent to provide direct client services (2 years), followed later in one's career by further education (1 additional year) in supervisory or management techniques, as one's career path dictates.

International Aspects

The final issue of professionalization to be touched upon is the international potential of this field. For many historical, economic, and social reasons, mental health counseling has been primarily an American phenomenon. Foremost among these reasons are the prior existence of counseling as a recognized occupation within American society, sufficient affluence in the society to support this occupational role, and America's awareness of and concern with its mental health needs. Nonetheless, problems of living are not confined to people who live in the United States. Indeed, the environmental causes of many such problems — starvation, unemployment, disease, the threat of attack — are infinitely more severe in most other countries.

Although the model of the mental health counselor — the effective professional educated in the essential knowledge and skills in the minimum necessary period of time — is highly appropriate to meet the needs and resources of these countries, we must be careful that the content of professional education is appropriate to the local culture. An American model, based on an assumption of freedom of choice and self-determination of one's destiny, does not fit the prevailing ethos in many places on earth. Therefore, much of the field's knowledge base and skills training must be adapted to local conditions. Nonetheless, the ultimate aim of assisting people to use their assets and skills to cope with the problems of living that confront them appears valid across cultures.

Many countries, particularly those that are relatively better off economically (e.g., Belgium, Britain, Denmark, France, Japan, Sweden), already have settings in which mental health counselors could function, such as clinics and community agencies (Jansen, 1986). In other cultures, perhaps different modes of service delivery would prove more effective. Thus, Third World countries might utilize native healers, supervised by mental health counseling professionals, to assist their citizens to mobilize their personal assets and to develop ways to cope with rapid cultural change. That a similar arrangement could work effectively was demonstrated by a pilot project in social psychiatry in Columbia, South America (Argandoña & Kiev, 1972). Only by careful attention to the consideration of cultural relevance can mental health counseling become the worldwide accepted approach it has the potential to be.

CONCLUSION

In this book, an attempt has been made to present an overview of the newest of the recognized mental health professions, mental health counseling. By the very fact of its recency, mental health counseling has been able to benefit from the contributions and limitations of the longer-established mental health professions, incorporating their effective elements while discarding those ideas and techniques that have proved to be outmoded or ineffective. Additionally, arising from a different basic discipline, mental health counseling has contributed its own unique elements to the process of helping clients to cope with problems of living. Foremost among these are the emphases on coping skills, on environmental influences on behavior, and on growth promotion (rather than on the removal of intrapsychic pathology).

It is the belief of the authors that the mental health counseling approach represents "the wave of the future" and offers the greatest potential for helping clients—be they individuals, families, groups, organizations, or communities—to attain optimal mental health, both in the United States and across other cultures.

As a field dedicated to the principles of human growth, development, and potential for change, mental health counseling will remain open to change and development within itself in the future. Therefore, this book has presented a still photograph of a moving object; but the only real constants that can characterize mental health counseling are continual growth, increasing professionalism, and improving service to its clients.

REFERENCES

Albee, G. W. (1985). The answer is prevention. *Psychology Today, 19*(2), 60–64.

Anderson, J. A., & Parenté, F. J. (1980). AMHCA members forecast the future of the mental health profession. *AMHCA Journal, 2*, 4–12.

Anderson, J. A., Parenté, F. J., & Gordon, C. (1981). A forecast of the future for the mental health profession. *American Psychologist, 36*, 848–855.

Anthony, W. A. (1979). *The principles of psychiatric rehabilitation.* Amherst, MA: Human Resources Development Press.

Argandoña, M., & Kiev, A. (1972). *Mental health in the developing world: A case study in Latin America.* New York: Free Press.

Barker, R. G. (1968). *Ecological psychology.* Stanford, CA: Stanford University Press.

Boulding, K. E. (1967). The boundaries of social policy. *Social Work, 12*, 3–11.

Buckner, J. C., Trickett, E. J., & Corse, S. J. (1985). *Primary prevention in mental health: An annotated bibliography.* Rockville, MD: National Institute of Mental Health.

Carkhuff, R. R., Pierce, R. M., & Cannon, J. R. (1980). *The art of helping IV*. Amherst, MA: Human Science Press.

Covin, T. M. (1985). Trends in third-party reimbursement among licensed professional counselors in Alabama. *AMHCA Journal, 7*, 156–161.

Fein, R. (1958). *Economics of mental illness*. New York: Basic Books.

Forrest, D. V., & Affemann, M. (1986). The future of mental health counselors in health maintenance organizations. *AMHCA Journal, 8*, 65–72.

Goldstein, A. P. (1981). *Psychological skill training: The structured learning technique*. Elmsford, NY: Pergamon.

Janis, I. L. (1983). *Short-term counseling: Guidelines based on recent research*. New Haven, CT: Yale University Press.

Jansen, M. A. (1986). *European mental health policies and practices: Rehabilitation of the chronically mentally ill* (Final Report: International Exchange of Experts and Information in Rehabilitation). New York: World Rehabilitation Fund.

Lewin, K. (1936). *Principles of topological psychology*. New York: McGraw-Hill.

Moos, R. H. (1977). *Coping with physical illness*. New York: Plenum.

Randolph, D. L., Lassiter, P. S., & Newell, K. G. (1986). Agency staffing needs for the mid- and late-1980's. *AMHCA Journal, 8*, 27–34.

Rubin, J. (1978). *Economics, mental health, and the law*. Lexington, MA: D. C. Heath.

Seligman, L., & Whitley, N. (1983). AMHCA and VMHCA members in private practice in Virginia. *AMHCA Journal, 5*, 179–183.

Taube, C. A., & Barrett, S. A. (Eds.). National Institute of Mental Health. (1985). *Mental health, United States, 1985* (DHHS Pub. No. [ADM] 85-1378). Washington, DC: U.S. Government Printing Office.

Author Index

Subject Index

About the Authors

David B. Hershenson is a National Certified Counselor and is listed in the National Register of Health Service Providers in Psychology. He holds a PhD in counseling psychology from Boston University and has been involved in counselor education for the past 20 years. He has authored over 40 book chapters and journal articles in the field of counseling, as well as being co-editor of *The Psychology of Vocational Development: Reading in Theory and Practice*. He has served on the editorial boards of *The Journal of Counseling Psychology, The Journal of Vocational Behavior*, and *The Rehabilitation Counseling Bulletin*. He has been Chairman of the Department of Psychology at the Illinois Institute of Technology and Dean of Sargent College of Allied Health Professions at Boston University. He is currently Chairperson of the Department of Counseling and Personnel Services at the University of Maryland, College Park. His professional interests are counselor education, career development, and mental health rehabilitation. He is a fellow of the American Psychological Association, and a member of the American Association for Counseling and Development, the American Mental Health Counselors Association, and Sigma Xi. He is a member of the Maryland State Board of Examiners of Professional Counselors.

Paul W. Power is a Certified Rehabilitation Counselor and a National Certified Counselor. He holds an ScD in rehabilitation counseling from Boston University. He has been in counselor education for 10 years and is currently Director of the Rehabilitation Counselor Education Program in the Department of Counseling and Personnel Services at the University of Maryland, College Park. His professional practice has focused on such family issues as the role of the family with disability and family violence, and he is the co-author of *The Role of the Family in Rehabilitation of the Physically Disabled*. His professional involvements have included conducting workshops for mental health professionals in the areas of the family and program evaluation. He is also the author of *A Guide to Vocational Assessment*, and has been a member of such professional organizations as the American Association for Counseling and Development, the American Mental Health Counselors Association, The American Congress of Physical Medicine, and the National Rehabilitation Association.

Marita McKenna Danek, PhD, is an Associate Professor in the Department of Counseling, Gallaudet Univerity, Washington, D.C. She has been a counselor, consultant, and counselor educator for over 20 years and has contributed monographs, articles, and book chapters in the field.

Michael Waldo, PhD, is an Assistant Professor in the Department of Counseling and Personnel Services, University of Maryland, College Park. He is a member of the American Mental Health Counselors Association and is listed in the National Register of Health Service Providers in Psychology. He has extensive experience offering group counseling on such issues as substance abuse, family violence, depression, career decisions, and interpersonal skill development. He is a member of the editorial board of the *Journal of Specialists in Group Work*.